THE RISE OF THE ATLANTIC ECONOMIES

WORLD ECONOMIC HISTORY
GENERAL EDITOR CHARLES WILSON

THE RISE OF THE ATLANTIC ECONOMIES
Ralph Davis

THE EARLY GROWTH OF THE
EUROPEAN ECONOMY
Georges Duby

ECONOMICS AND EMPIRE 1830-1914
D. K. Fieldhouse

INTRODUCTION TO THE SOURCES OF EUROPEAN
ECONOMIC HISTORY, 1500-1800
Charles Wilson and Geoffrey Parker, editors

The Rise of the
Atlantic Economies

RALPH DAVIS

CORNELL PAPERBACKS
CORNELL UNIVERSITY PRESS
ITHACA, NEW YORK

First published 1973 by Cornell University Press
First printing, Cornell Paperbacks, 1973
Fourth printing, 1984

International Standard Book Number 0-8014-9143-6
Library of Congress Catalog Card Number 73-77683
Printed in the United States of America

Contents

Foreword ix

Preface xi

1. The Portuguese in the Atlantic 1
2. Western Europe: 1460–1560 15
3. Spain in America: The Sixteenth Century 37
4. Sixteenth-century Spain 56
5. Western Europe and the Atlantic 73
6. The Sixteenth and Seventeenth Centuries:
   Population, Prices and Incomes 88
7. Agriculture in the Sixteenth and Seventeenth Centuries 108
8. The Peopling of America 125
9. Spain in Decline 143
10. Latin America: The Seventeenth and Eighteenth Centuries 157
11. The Rise of the Dutch Commercial Empire 176
12. England: The Untroubled Island 194
13. France: The Unsteady Giant 212
14. Capital, Credit and Financial Institutions 231
15. The Tropical Colonies in America 250
16. The British Mainland Colonies 264
17. France and England in the Eighteenth Century 288

vi

18. France and England:
Industrial Growth and Industrial Revolution   301

Maps   318
Select Bibliography   323
Index   341

Maps

Between pages 317 and 322

1. The Portuguese Atlantic
2. Spanish and Portuguese America
3. Western Europe in 1500
4. Western Europe in 1700
5. North America and the Caribbean

Foreword

The specialized study of economic and social history is a comparatively recent development. The nineteenth-century founders of the modern techniques of historical research, in Germany, France, the Low Countries, Britain and the United States, took at most only a passing interest in these aspects of history. Their business was with one or another facet of political history. Not until the early 1880s was it clear that a new historical movement was under way.

In England it may conveniently be dated from Arnold Toynbee's Oxford lectures of 1880-1, published three years later as his famous study of the Industrial Revolution. At Cambridge, William Cunningham published the first edition of his *Growth of English Industry and Commerce* in 1882. Cunningham especially was strongly influenced by the work of the 'historical economists' in Germany – especially that of Gustav Schmoller – on the impact of state policy on economic development. In France, perhaps because the pace of industrialization there was slower, the new inquiries tended to be more concerned with socio-economic problems, especially the conditions of labour. Levasseur's great *Histoire des Classes Ouvrières en France* was begun in 1859 but the work continued on more modern periods down to the twentieth century.

Industrialization, technology, state policy, the history of prices and wages – each national school gave its new history a different emphasis. But everywhere the subject was taken up by scholars who shared similar feelings: that economic theory as it then stood was too abstract and generalized to help to explain the growing complexity of the industrial society that was springing up around them.

Economic history arose therefore as a study of actualities, a revolt against abstract economic dogma. Its strength lay in its concern with real institutions, not imaginary ones, and in spite of a growing realization that historians cannot do without some theoretical guidance, this sense of realism remains one of the solid assets of economic and social history.

Since the 1880s schools of socio-economic history have developed in all the advanced countries of the world and a large volume of original and highly sophisticated research has been produced. Views have been continually challenged and modified, not least in hundreds of articles in specialized journals. This continuing output creates an equal need for a continuing effort to synthesize and interpret the work of the specialists.

This series is conceived in the belief that its volumes, each by a scholar of acknowledged mastery in his area and period, will help to fulfil that need. Secondly, that synthesis is far from being merely scissors-and-paste work: on the contrary it calls for the constant exercise of the creative imagination. For each minor adjustment in knowledge must be seen as modifying in some degree its totality. Historical synthesis is much more than the sum of its parts. Third, that each study should be written and presented in terms which will make it intelligible not only to students and scholars with specialized training in economic history but also to the wider body of readers who want to know how, where and why economic history impinges on other kinds of history.

Authors have not been asked to provide a 'complete coverage of facts'. Even if that were possible it would not be desirable for our purposes. We have rather worked together to present views that are at once individual, personal, even occasionally idiosyncratic, yet based upon a wide and deep professional experience of the themes of economic history, ancient and modern.

In this way we hope that these volumes will not only help to focus and recapitulate but continue and extend the debate that began nearly a century ago.

C. W.

Preface

T his book is about the economic history of the countries on the western fringe of Europe – Portugal, Spain, France, England and the Netherlands – and the colonies they established or had dealings with in North and South America, from the beginning of Portuguese discovery in the fifteenth century to the revolution that transformed the English colonies into the independent United States of America. It is not specifically about the relationship between Europe and colonies; indeed, I have tried to show that the main influences on European economic development arose within the countries of Europe themselves, though Europe was powerfully affected both by Spanish America in the sixteenth century and English America in the eighteenth. I do not attempt to indicate that this group of European countries had a special unity in its course of development. On the contrary, this book shows that the common economic forces that pervaded western Europe, and the influences arising from its participation in transatlantic enterprise, were so modified by each country's particular natural resources and political and social structure that the final outcome was a diversity of courses of development. This is to state the obvious; the economic history of western Europe in the seventeenth and eighteenth centuries embraces both the rapid rise of the English and the catastrophic decline of the Spanish economy.

Nor have I supposed that events of economic importance are necessarily to be explained primarily by economic causes; rather, that economic forces were hampered and profoundly modified in their effects by the rigidity of resource capacities and political and social structures, so that a vital feature of the economic history of the time – as of all times – was the extent to which the capacity of these structures to resist change was broken down in different countries. Moreover, forces which from the economic point of view were accidental had powerful effects on economic affairs. Important among them were wars; if economic causation entered into Dutch-English and to some extent into French-English wars of the seventeenth and eighteenth centuries, it had little part in those of earlier times, which were dynastic and above all religious. Their economic effects were nevertheless profound. The changing climate, apparent in the slow worsening and the slow improvement, over many decades, of the 'average' weather conditions around which each year's weather fluctuated, was a factor of the utmost economic importance which is only now beginning to be cautiously approached by historians. The conditions of growth and decline of the major epidemic diseases, influenced partly by patterns of human life but also by quite different factors that favoured or destroyed particular types of virus and bacillus, may well have been more important in their effects on society and economy than anything else written of here. We have always to be conscious, in dealing with these early times, of the relatively small role played in human affairs by the things that we know and can write about extensively; we must remember the still overwhelming pressures of the forces of nature. Finally, a single person occasionally had great influence on the course of affairs, shaping the *particular* way in which a developing process finally came to its fruition. All fifteenth-century history, for example, points towards a discovery of America being made by the Portuguese; but Columbus discovered it for Spain in 1492. If he had not done so, there would certainly have been a Portuguese discovery within the next decade; America would initially have been a wholly Portuguese sphere, and European history could not have been the same.

So far, I have been explaining what I have not done and what are not my attitudes to the subject of this book. Its clear theme, as of all economic history, is the working out of economic causes; tracing their effects as these were modified by non-economic factors of many kinds and observing the interaction with this process of the economic impact of events arising from many other, non-economic causes. Beginning with an event, the discovery of the New World, whose economic results were slow to make themselves felt, I have ended with the onset of a process whose effects were immediate and shattering, the English Industrial Revolution. But I have been at some pains to show that this was by no means an inevitable outcome of the long history that had left Spain, Portugal and the Netherlands so far behind England and France in the movement towards the economic hegemony of Europe. The multiple causes of the Industrial Revolution were deeply embedded in previous centuries of development, but its proximate causes arose in a more immediate past and were related to a narrow area of economic activity.

Finally, the economic development of the Americas under Spanish, Portuguese, English and French rule took their widely different courses chiefly because different populations, climates and resources were found in the various parts of the New World. The particular economic and political characteristics of the home countries had some importance to the forms of development of their colonies. But Mexico and Peru were ripe for dominance by a conquering race, and their growth was further shaped by the discovery of great silver deposits. Temperate North America, with its scanty native population, could be developed from overseas only by the settlement of working people. The resources of the tropical Caribbean and Brazil, so different in every way from Europe, could have been developed in more than one form, but to a ruling race with experience of African slaves the natural one appeared to be a society and economy of master and slaves. All these colonies were bound to Europe economically, to a greater or less degree. There was an Atlantic economy; but it was subsidiary to, a modification and enhancement of, the economies of the individual countries of the Atlantic seaboard that took part in it.

After much consideration I decided to include few tables and no graphs in this book. Nevertheless, like nearly all economic history, it is grounded in statistics; for it is usually concerned with the behaviour of very large numbers of people, who cannot be treated as individuals except by way of illustration, but only as statistical aggregates. The movements of population, prices, national incomes, industrial and agricultural production and productivity, or the volume of trade, are all essentially statistical concepts, if we have to go outside statistics to explain their origins and the character of their effects in society as a whole. Even dubious statistics can point towards important questions that need solution, and sometimes suggest the directions in which answers may be sought. Nevertheless, I have thought it undesirable to impede the argument of a book of this character with large quantities of raw statistical data; and while there are a few attractive long series, their use would concentrate attention in misleading ways. The good long-term price series are for various kinds of corn; important though they are as reminders of the enhancement of the value of land as population grew, they are misleading as indicators of the general price rise, in any country or as between countries. The long-term wage series are of building workers' wages, which cannot safely be taken as representing anything but themselves. The Sound Tables offer a useful index of Baltic trade, but it is peripheral to this study; the long-term Spanish American trade statistics are about tonnage of ships employed, whose exact significance is by no means clear, and the important bullion statistics, whose validity becomes doubtful just as they become interesting. I have used all these extensively in writing this book, and refer to them, I hope with due caution, in appropriate places. The interested reader can find references to them and to a mass of other statistical material in the bibiliography.

I am indebted to colleagues too numerous to name for their comments and discussion on particular problems. I must, however, express special thanks to Miss Judith Watts who typed the many drafts and to Mr D. M. Williams who read the proofs; to Dr M. A. Havinden and Dr R. B. Outhwaite who read and commented in detail on the most difficult sections; and above all to Professor A. G. Dickens and Professor F. J. Fisher and to my wife, whose astringent commentaries on the whole of the text helped me to effect great improvements in it. I did not always follow the suggestions made to me, and the faults that remain are entirely my own.

Ralph Davis
May 1972

1 *The Portuguese in the Atlantic*

The westward expansion of Europe after 1492 rested on the foundation of eighty years of Portuguese enterprise in the Atlantic. Portugal was the Atlantic pioneer, colonizing Atlantic islands and exploring and trading down the west coast of Africa. It was in Portugal that a body of experience of ocean sailing and navigation was built up during the fifteenth century, and it was almost accidental that at the climax of Portuguese pioneering enterprise the most crucial of all the discoveries was made by a Genoese in the service of Spain.

The seamen of Portugal and western Spain had long been acquainted with nearby Atlantic waters, trading in the harbours of Morocco, fishing off its Atlantic coast, and making occasional voyages to the Canaries in search of dyewoods and slaves. But to the southward the beginning of the Sahara desert marked the limit of their regular voyaging; beyond it stretched a thousand miles of desolate and uninhabited coast. It was well known in southern Europe that the Sahara did not mark the end of the inhabited world, for into every town on the Mediterranean and Atlantic coast of north Africa, from Tunis round to Safi, Moorish traders brought the produce of an overland traffic across the desert. At the far southern end of these desert routes, jealously guarded from Christian access, was a land of dark men, and the island of Palola where they were reputed to dig the gold that supplied most of medieval Europe's needs, and the mysterious trading city of Timbuktu. Yet the sea route was untravelled. No Moorish opposition troubled it, but the ships and navigation of the time were not adequate to meet the problems entailed in long voyages down such a coast. As far back as 1291 and 1348 unsuccessful attempts had been made by Italians and Catalans to sail farther south. The Canary Islands were discovered, and some of them were settled from Spain soon after 1400. But the exploration of the Sahara coastline was abandoned, and when it was taken up again in the years round 1415 it was not by Mediterranean traders but by adventurers and seamen of a poor nation on the fringe of Europe; by the Portuguese, and for Portuguese ends.

Why was the exploration of the Atlantic coast of Africa renewed at this time, by the Portuguese alone, and accompanied by the colonization of Atlantic islands? Answers given in the past in political or technical terms are not adequate. It is true that four-teenth-century Europe had ample reason to be alarmed at the ad-vance of the Turks, who overran most of Balkan Europe between 1345 and 1396 and threatened Constantinople. The years in which Portuguese exploration began, however, saw the Turks in disarray, shattered by the blows dealt them in 1402 by the Mongol invader Tamerlane, from which they took two generations to recover. Moreover, alarming though Turkish advance might be to far-seeing princes and cardinals, and dangerous to the interests of Italian trading cities with business in the Levant, there is no sign that it influenced the Portuguese. The wars against the Moors of north Africa upon which Portugal embarked in 1415, though given dignity by the title of crusades, were fought for perfectly clear Portuguese aims. The chronology of maritime innovation, again, will not support the view that exploration began because the means to carry it out had ripened. On the contrary, technical innovation was called forth by the urgent needs of oceanic exploration after it had taken the decisive strides southward. Exploration began with quite primitive means; with no navigational instruments beyond compass and log, and with ships which, though strongly built to face Atlantic weather, were so rigged as to be very limited in their operation in the prevailing wind systems of the African coast. The Portuguese explorers set off in square-rigged, one- or two-masted vessels of between twenty and forty tons, flat-bottomed, with shallow draught and few upperworks, carrying large crews be-cause they had to rely on oars in adverse wind conditions. The ships and navigational methods were decisively improved around the middle of the century, when the Portuguese had already ventured south beyond the Sahara coast; these improvements enabled exploration to penetrate farther but had no part in its commencement.

So neither ideological crusading nor technical changes can account for that sudden fifteenth-century achievement in exploration by a hitherto insignificant nation. The real causes were both more fundamental, emerging from the complex interaction of economic stresses and internal politics, and at the same time more personal and accidental. Portugal, a country fully recovered from the Moors only in 1253, was small and poor, much of it mountainous and uncultivable. A coast of fishing villages, trading towns and seaports was backed by a hinterland of poor peasants and big estates; there was little traffic across the land frontier with Castile. Portugal's climate made it northern Europe's nearest supplier of Mediterranean types of produce, and its cultivation was directed increasingly to the support of this trade. A great area was kept under forests of cork-oak; vineyards, olive-groves and orchards were spreading rapidly, and cornland declined, so that from the middle of the fourteenth century Portugal had regularly to import corn from Morocco. Much of the land was parcelled out in the vast estates of magnates and ecclesiastical houses and the peasantry was impoverished by the burden of seigneurial dues and taxation. Even after the Black Death of 1348–9 had reduced the rural population heavily, the condition of peasants and rural labourers was not alleviated. They continued to move into the towns, where there was growing demand for men to serve trade, shipping and the fisheries. The extent of the export trade in oil, cork, fruit, wax and honey, and the need for imported corn, fostered the growth of the Portuguese shipping industry. The economical craft which it used found favour with the merchants of the great Mediterranean trading cities – Genoa, Barcelona, Florence – and were widely employed in their carrying trade. Portuguese fisheries were well developed and extended far beyond native waters, to the north African and Irish coasts, while whalers of the Algarve sought their quarry far out in the Atlantic. Enterprise in Portugal was directed towards the sea and adequate resources existed not only for exploration but also for the vigorous exploitation of new discoveries, whether on the African coast or Atlantic islands.

So strong were the urban trading and shipping interests of medieval Portugal that in 1385 they even achieved some measure of political influence, by lending decisive support to the revolution

B

which put the Aviz dynasty on the throne in opposition to a great part of the nobility. In the revolutionary war the old nobility was almost destroyed, and links were forged between the royal family and the bourgeoisie that lasted for some generations. Early fifteenth-century Portugal therefore had a large and vigorous trading and shipping interest, and a weakened nobility whose perennial financial problems evoked little sympathy from the crown. Both were prepared to look beyond Portugal, the merchants to find fresh employment for their resources in new branches of trade, the nobility – old and new – in search of traditional ways' to wealth and honour through the conquest and overlordship of new lands.

Down to 1437 conquest and settlement predominated in Portuguese expansion. The invasion of Morocco, begun by a royal army in 1415, should have provided glory for noble warriors and lands for them to rule over; but the conquest of Moroccan towns was economically fruitless and the campaigns were halted when, in 1437, the Portuguese army suffered a shattering defeat at Tangier. The story was different in the islands. The first Portuguese colonists landed on Madeira in 1420; an attempt at a Canaries settlement in 1425–7 was driven off by the natives; the Azores, rediscovered in 1425, began to be settled soon after 1430. At first the only produce of the island settlements was timber and small quantities of dye-stuffs, but the settlers soon cleared large areas, and corn from Madeira, and later the Azores, replaced Moroccan supplies. Noble settlers were awarded 'captaincies' by the crown – feudal rights of tribute and jurisdiction over land in the islands – the profitability of which would depend on their success in attracting settlers to cultivate them. But the islands presented few attractions to the Portuguese peasant and colonists had to be found from other sources. There was a considerable Flemish migration to the Azores and slaves were soon introduced by means of slave raids in the Canaries and later on the west coast of Africa.

At the beginning of the fifteenth century, therefore, mixed motives of glory and gain carried the Portuguese to Morocco and the islands. It is less clear that social forces were sufficient in themselves to carry African exploration through to success. Economic motivation – the search for new trade and for gold – was certainly present but its weakness is indicated by the unpopularity of the early expeditions in Portugal. For thirty years they were supported only by a small circle, who were criticized for wasting the country's resources on nothing more useful than the revelation of fresh stretches of Saharan coast. The task of carrying on exploration to the point at which it showed results might have defeated the desultory efforts of merchants and mariners, as it had done in the previous century. After 1415, however, it had firm and persistent backing from a single Portuguese of great influence and wealth, a younger son of the King of Portugal, who has been christened by English writers 'Prince Henry the Navigator'. Wealthy himself, he also had at his disposal the great resources of the Order of Christ, a knightly order of which he was master. He was at one and the same time a religious fanatic, dedicated to anti-Muslim struggle, and a genuine seeker after knowledge. For over forty years he steadily gave his support to exploration; he encouraged his men to persevere in the early years when obstacles seemed overwhelming, and in mid-century, when most of them were tempted to stay and take their profit in trade with lands already discovered, he persuaded a few to persist in venturing farther still.

Despite Prince Henry's support and urging, coastal voyaging was slow to produce results. The coast was barren and discouraging and the tools of exploration were poor. The square-rigged ship of that day could not sail with a contrary wind; to make progress it must have a wind abaft its beam, and consequently seamen had for centuries regarded Cape Bojador, in 26 degrees north, as the limit of southward voyages. A ship that followed the ever more southerly trend of the coast beyond Cape Bojador moved far into the belt of the north-east trade winds, in which it could not shape a course more nearly homeward than WNW. This involved an immense detour out into the Atlantic (this may be why Madeira and the Azores were discovered in this period), slowly working northwards to pick up the westerlies that would bring it safely home, and the farther south the explorer ventured the longer this detour had to be – and the greater the risk that provisions and water would fail to last out the homeward voyage. But more than this, Cape Bojador was a psychological obstacle, long seen as the last point before the unknown, which seemed more terrifying with each voyage that hesitated to penetrate farther.

For nearly thirty years Portuguese exploration was carried on by small square-rigged vessels. Each year after 1415 one or two *barcas* were sent down the coast, always turning back before Cape Bojador, but gaining experience and building up a knowledge of the wind systems and currents. It was in such a ship that Gil Eannes, after much pressure and coaxing by Prince Henry, mustered courage in 1434 to push many leagues beyond the Cape, and returned safely to Portugal. This was the decisive step; once it was achieved, other voyagers sailed hundreds of miles farther along the coast during the next few years, passing beyond the completely empty desert to reach 'lands without habitations, but with imprints of the feet of men and camels'.

It was only after the pioneers had left the old limits of the known world far behind that the decisive change was made in the Portuguese vessels. The lateen-rigged caravel, familiar to historians as the perfect instrument for voyages of exploration, was evolved after 1440 because of the urgent need to assure seamen's safe return from voyages taking them ever farther southward. The example was ready to hand in the lateen sails of Moorish craft that plied round the north-west coast of Africa, for these, though less useful in a following wind than square sails, and dangerous to handle in severe weather conditions, gave a capacity to sail much closer to the wind. Either permanently lateen-rigged, or changing its spars and sails to lateen rig at the commencement of the homeward voyage, the new caravel that could tack into the teeth of the trade winds was the ship that enabled the Portuguese to penetrate, eventually, to the farthest tip of Africa and beyond into the Indian Ocean.

With the barrier of Cape Bojador overcome, Portuguese seamen were ready to push forward rapidly to the inhabited lands beyond the Sahara. The phase of unrequited exploration ended in 1443 when Nuno Tristão brought back the first substantial cargo of slaves from Arguim (just south of Cape Branco) and disposed of them profitably in Portugal. Exploration had paid off at last, and a rush to join in the slave trade began. Lancarote, a royal official in Lagos, sent six caravels slaving in 1444, and the following year no less than twenty-six vessels went down the African coast, in the service of a variety of traders and shipowners. To these Portuguese licensed by Prince Henry was soon added a contingent of Castilian vessels from the small ports adjoining the Portuguese frontier, who had also sniffed the prospects of gain. In 1448 the Portuguese found it necessary to build a fort on the island of Arguim to control the slave trade, and this was the centre of their activity for a few years. Further exploration took them to the mouth of the Senegal river, marking the end of the desert, and on to Sierra Leone in 1448. At this point exploration virtually ceased for two decades, while they settled down to exploit the well-populated region they had reached.

There was an extensive market for slaves in Portugal and as early as the mid-1450s a thousand slaves a year were being brought back from Africa. The far south of Portugal had never been fully developed since its conquest from the Moors because of shortage of labour; its exploitation in big estates now became possible, with slave labour working in fields and sugar plantations. The islands, too, needed more labour for their full development and large numbers of slaves were sent to them, to turn Madeira from corn to sugar production. Negro servants became common in well-to-do Portuguese households, and indeed the whole economy was permeated by slave labour to an extent unknown elsewhere in Europe. The local traders in the coastal region, who were accustomed to buying Mediterranean wares that had been brought across the desert at great cost, bartered slaves with the new traders from the sea on terms which were at first very favourable to the Portuguese. Inevitably, as the trade became better organized and the number of competing Portuguese increased, the terms shifted against them.

From the middle of the fifteenth century, therefore, the African trade brought wealth to African traders, to the crown and to some members of the nobility. It called for an expansion of the Portuguese shipping industry and improvement in the ships, and it diffused among Portuguese seamen a knowledge of Atlantic wind systems and currents, and of the detailed geography of the islands in the Atlantic. Yet they had stopped a little short of far more valuable discoveries. A new wave of exploration in 1469–74, again requiring the initiative of the royal family to get it started, took the Portuguese right round the bulge of Africa to the Bight of Biafra, opening up the section of the west African coast that has remained into the present century the richest for European traders. Here they found a native slave trade far larger and better organized than they had yet seen; a land that produced malaguette pepper – a tolerable substitute for the true pepper of the Indies; ivory in great quantities; and above all gold. At last they had come close to the source of the precious metal that had for so long drawn them southward. Full development of the discoveries was delayed by war with Castile, 1475–9, but when it was over Portugal began a systematic organization of African resources, signalized by the building of a fort at Elmina on the Gold Coast, to control operations in the richest centre of the gold trade. Foreign traders were rigorously excluded, Castile having acknowledged in the peace treaty of 1479 that West Africa was an entirely Portuguese sphere. Portuguese traders were allowed in only under royal licence, and the gold trade was reserved entirely to the crown.

The pattern of Portuguese trade on the West African coast in the last years of the century is set out in Pacheco's *Esmeralda de Situ Orbis*, written at the time. From Arguim southward to Sierra Leone there was little to be had but slaves. This, the original Portuguese trading interest, continued to be important, sending 3,500 slaves a year to supply Portugal, the islands, and its customers in other parts of Europe. The crude raiding expeditions of the earlier days had ended; slaving was now a real trade, carried on at a number of points on the coast by bartering with the coastal natives, who bought slaves in the markets of the interior. Beyond Sierra Leone was the hundred miles of the Grain Coast, where there was a barter trade in malaguette pepper. Then came the Gold Coast, where Portuguese trading posts were few but vitally important as the centres to which gold was brought from several places in the interior. A large quantity was bartered every year at the fort of St Anthony at Axem; but São Jorge de Mina, or Elmina, was the chief centre of Portuguese commerce in west Africa, where thirteen to fourteen thousand ounces of gold were brought every year. The first economic objective of Portuguese exploration at last came to full realization in the trade at Elmina. They had set out to reach the trans-Saharan lands from which Moors had brought gold across the desert. Now the Portuguese had reached those lands, and the destructive effect their presence had on the old trans-Sahara traffic is illuminated by one fact; the chief demand of the native traders bringing gold into Elmina was for 'lanbens' – striped shawls made in Tunis and Oran! But, like the slave traders farther north, they also bought European goods – red and blue cloth, brassware, bracelets, handkerchiefs and trinkets – as well as slaves. The profit on this barter for gold, says Pacheco, was five for one, or more. Along the coast to the east, Benin and a few other places supplied slaves to be bartered for gold at Elmina, as well as a little ivory and pepper. Beyond the estuary of the Bonny river almost all trade ceased; the south-trending coast was traced in the 1480s along its whole heart-breaking length not by traders with Africa but by explorers seeking the route to India.

All this made up a rich trading realm for Portugal, and alongside it the islands – Madeira, the Azores, the Cape Verde Islands (discovered in 1455) and Fernando Po and São Thomé in the Bight of Biafra (discovered in 1471) were being settled and made productive under the Portuguese crown. There was no foreign encroachment on it for half a century after the Castilians retired in 1479, and Portuguese wealth, and its maritime and administrative experience, grew undisturbed in exploiting it. In the process, however, Portugal was brought under the eye of Europe, ceasing to be a small, poor, remote country of little account. Gold, pepper, ivory and slaves introduced the Portuguese to European markets that had not previously known them and drew the attention of wealthy outsiders to new opportunities that were opening beyond the bounds of Europe.

While the Portuguese pursued their petty voyaging down the coast of Africa, European history was dominated by tremendous events taking place at the farther end of the Mediterranean. Turkish pressure on the Balkans was resumed in 1448 after an interval of half a century; Mohammed II took Constantinople in 1453, extinguishing the relic of the Byzantine Empire that had upheld eastern Christendom for a thousand years. The shock made all Europe tremble, for it appeared to bring closer the day when contact with the world beyond the Muslims would be severed – a world that might contain Christian allies. Portugal's immediate response to the Pope's appeal for help following the fall of Constantinople was an old-fashioned military one; the opening of a crusading war in Morocco in 1458, marked by the minting, from African gold, of a new coin which was named the *cruzado*. But the Turkish advance did have a more direct influence on Portugal and its possessions, for Genoese traders and financiers whose eastern interests were overthrown intensified their business activities in the west.

The Turks did not suddenly block the routes of oriental trade in 1453; the route that Constantinople dominated, through the Black Sea ports and central Asia, had been closed far back in the fourteenth century by the collapse of the Mongol Empire, and the Turks did not establish themselves across the route through the Red Sea and Egypt until 1517. Before 1400, however, Genoa and Venice had made a division of the Levant trade between themselves, the Genoese concentrating on the lands round the Black Sea, the Aegean Sea and the ports of Anatolia; the Venetians on Egypt, including the lucrative oriental trade through Cairo. It was the

Genoese, therefore, whose business was damaged by the Turkish advance of the mid-fifteenth century. Genoa attempted to maintain good relations with the Turks, even after the fall of Constantinople; but its Black Sea trade was constricted, its client cities of Caffa and Trebizond did not long survive the fall of Constantinople, and its Anatolian interests were soon threatened. As one after another of these succumbed to Turkish rule, the Genoese turned their attention towards the western Mediterranean. To add to Genoa's troubles, Portuguese diversion of Guinea gold from 1471 onward was seriously damaging Italian trade with the Moorish states of north Africa.

The Genoese looked westward, in the first place, to find alternative means of supplying foods and raw materials they had got from the east. Alum, vital to the west European woollen industry, had come from Phocaea near Smyrna; when the Turks secured control there in 1455 they imposed an unsupportable burden of taxes, and a crisis of alum supply was only resolved by the discovery in 1462 – surely no accident – of alum deposits at Tolfa, near Rome. Their concessionaires for several decades were Genoese. Silk production was started in Calabria and Mediterranean Spain to supplement near eastern supplies that had become precarious. Most important of all was sugar production, organized by Genoese in Andalusia and the Algarve, in north Africa, and then in the Atlantic islands. Both Madeira and the Canaries had produced a little sugar from the early days of settlement, but after 1460 Genoese capital poured in for the establishment of new plantations and by 1468 Madeira sugar was sold as far afield as England and Flanders. Madeira, first valued as a supplier of corn to Portugal, quickly turned over almost entirely to sugar; it ceased to export corn in the 1460s and by 1480 was importing some of its own requirements from the Azores and Morocco. The tropical islands of Fernando Po and São Thomé were developed very rapidly as sugar producers after 1475, and the latter became the largest supplier until it was overtaken by Brazil in the following century. By the end of the fifteenth century, therefore, the Portuguese islands were supplying most of Europe's sugar, though the trade in it was handled by Genoese and Florentines. Genoese capital was similarly directed, between 1455 and 1470, to expanding sugar plantations in Spain's Atlantic islands, the Canaries, and a new campaign to conquer the remaining islands, begun in 1479, extended sugar production to them all by the end of the century. The big labour supply needed for sugar cultivation could not be obtained from Europe and the planters used great numbers of African slaves. Thus the Genoese came into African affairs too, taking a part in financing the slave trade and promoting the sale of malaguette pepper in competition with the Asian pepper the Venetians brought into Europe.

The crowning achievement of Portuguese exploration in this period, however, owed nothing to the Genoese. This was the opening of the sea route to India, which Prince Henry had seen, in the last years before his death in 1460, as a possible outcome of continued exploration of the west African coast. Portuguese mercantile interests and the Genoese capitalists associated with them were fully occupied in exploiting the resources already discovered, and the interest of the royal family was again needed to initiate a new phase of exploration whose rewards, though potentially dazzling, were distant and speculative. In 1482 King John II organized a new effort to find the southern limit of Africa, and he sustained it through a succession of disappointing voyages down the long south-trending African coast, until at last, in 1487, Bartholomew Diaz turned the Cape of Good Hope. Meanwhile Pedro de Covilha, who had travelled through the Levant to India, was sending back to Portugal detailed reports on the commerce and navigation of the Indian Ocean. The exploitation of Diaz's success was delayed for some years by political troubles in Portugal, but in 1497 Vasco da Gama was despatched, and he reached India in the following year, returning with a cargo whose richness met all the expectations of those who had fostered the search for a sea route to the Indies. Vasco da Gama's voyage to India was followed by that of Cabral, which touched the coast of Brazil on the way out. Portugal had reached the New World too – but eight years after Columbus.

The opening of the sea route to the Indies presented great economic opportunities, for the Indian Ocean contained no ships that could face Portuguese guns, and they were able to disrupt Arab trade routes at will and force trading concessions from the rulers of coastal and island states. For many decades, therefore, the attention of maritime Portugal was directed to the African and Indian trades, which strained the resources of this small nation in shipbuilding, and in seamen, soldiers and administrators. The Indies voyage was itself a much more formidable undertaking than the Atlantic crossing. Indeed, the Portuguese now touched the western shores of the Atlantic almost casually, their Indies ships often calling at

Brazil and their fishermen hastening to the Newfoundland cod fisheries when these became generally known after 1497. But Portuguese interest in seeking a western Atlantic route to the Indies ceased when Diaz broke open the eastern route in 1487. America fell to Spain, not Portugal.

Yet the discovery of America, by a Genoese in the service of Spain, owed everything to Portuguese methods and experience. The caravel, as it had been developed by the Portuguese, was the necessary vessel for Columbus's voyage; the *Santa Maria*, his square-rigged Spanish flagship, was an unsuitable vessel for exploration, and was wrecked in the Caribbean. If Andalusian seamen shared with those of Portugal an understanding both of Mediterranean navigation using chart and compass, and of northern navigation with its greater reliance on log and leadline, the refinements necessary for long-distance ocean voyaging were brought from the astronomer's study to the ship's deck only by fifteenth-century Portuguese, or Italians in their service. The great innovation was the use on shipboard (first recorded in 1456) of the simple quadrant to measure star altitude for the determination of latitude. It was with this aid that the latitudes of new discoveries on the African coast were accurately mapped; and a standard practice of ocean navigation – finding and running down the latitude of the ship's destination – began to emerge. Columbus learned these methods and used them on his voyages. He could dispense with the more sophisticated ways of determining latitude by solar observations and tables, which the Portuguese developed in the 1480s to assist them in long runs down the coast of Africa when the Pole Star had disappeared beyond the northern horizon. Experience and confidence in ocean voyaging were essential ingredients of success, that had been built up by the Portuguese in more than half a century of Atlantic exploration and trading. Columbus himself owed almost all his useful background to Portugal, where he first arrived through the accident of shipwreck. He lived for some years in Portugal – for a time on Porto Santo in the Madeira group; he sailed in Portuguese ships to Guinea and to the northward; he mixed with Portuguese seamen and mapmakers amongst whom knowledge, tradition and mythology of western and south-western voyaging were strong and not always distinguishable from one another. He looked naturally to the crown of Portugal, the champion of oceanic discovery, for help in his enterprise; and Portugal turned him down.

Columbus failed to get Portuguese support because the king could muster advisers with a sound knowledge of world geography. The plans of Columbus were based on nonsensical geographical notions that grossly understated the distance westward from Europe to Japan, which was his intended destination, and the Portuguese experts exposed them. Invited to Lisbon to present his scheme a second time, in 1488, he was in time only to see Bartholomew Diaz come into the Tagus with the news that the road to India by the Cape was open. The King of Portugal, grasping this certain prize, dismissed Columbus to seek support for his speculative project elsewhere. England and France were too remote from Atlantic voyaging to take much interest. But south-western Spain had an Atlantic coast with a strong maritime tradition; its ports had long engaged in Atlantic fisheries, in trade on Atlantic coasts and out to the Canaries; its seamen had some of the skill of the Portuguese in ocean navigation. Castile, a kingdom far larger and richer than Portugal, its rulers flushed with their final success, in 1492, in defeating the Moors of Granada and so bringing the whole Iberian peninsula under Christian rule after eight hundred years; Castile showed Columbus favour, granted him money, ships and the promise of titles and rewards if he succeeded in finding – what? A western route to the Indies, clear of the Portuguese, or new lands, islands in the ocean sea?

Seville and all its outports, including Cadiz, were choked with activity in the summer of 1492, arranging the exodus of all those Moors of the old kingdom of Granada who wished to migrate across the straits to Morocco. Columbus was therefore bidden to find his ships and crews in Palos, a small harbour close to the Portuguese frontier. Such places were full of tiny craft, including many caravels of the type the Portuguese favoured; until the signing of the Treaty of Alcacovas only thirteen years before these ships had been busy in trade with west Africa; they still carried on a Moroccan and Canaries trade, and very likely they sometimes took the risk of pushing farther south. Here on a tiny scale, and without the backing from government which their Portuguese neighbours secured, were centres of Spanish Atlantic enterprise, and it was not difficult for Columbus to pick up a couple of caravels, supplementing them with a larger Basque vessel for a storeship, and to find crews familiar with the Atlantic and ready, up to a point, to take risks in its further exploration.

So it was from Palos, this little harbour at the extreme south-west corner of Spain, that Columbus sailed in August 1492; and it was at the feet of Ferdinand and Isabella, sovereigns of Aragon and Castile, that he placed his discoveries when he returned the following spring. Trivial though his results may then have seemed by comparison with the vistas that had opened before the Portuguese, he had led Spain to the threshold of a far greater empire.

2 Western Europe: 1460–1560

*T*hough Columbus's voyage of 1492 was one of the great landmarks of world history, it had only a limited significance within the framework of its own time. It was one more move in the European extension of its oceanic frontier that had been in progress for over seventy years; its ultimate consequences were momentous not because it was evoked by greater necessity than earlier discoveries but because it led into a continent that had hitherto been entirely unknown, and opened it to European exploitation. The discovery of America was made when Europe, after a long spell of hibernation, was already bustling with a spiritual and material awakening. The growth in European production and wealth that had been going on since the middle of the fifteenth century had been generated within Europe, and it continued with little assistance from beyond the oceans for more than half a century after Columbus. Western Europe's expansive phase ran from about 1460 to 1620 – even more precise dates can be allocated to individual countries. The first century of this expansion – that is to say, the period before the American impact began to be important around 1560 – forms the subject of this chapter.

Why was Europe's economic activity increasing? Was Europe becoming more prosperous? At bottom, the answer is that more people were producing more goods and services – here and there in more efficient ways – but that the growth of production lagged behind that of population because so much of it depended on the resources of the land, which were limited. Average income per head of population, in real terms, was probably falling; so in one important sense, which accords with the economist's view of economic growth, prosperity was declining. But such a modern concept of prosperity – framed to illuminate the relation between rising population and rising productivity – cannot be applied automatically to the upheavals of a more primitive age, one in which the most powerful upward regulator of income per head was a calamitous drop in population. The economy of modern Europe would never have come into existence on the basis of population decline; the pressure of growing demands, which challenged producers while offering opportunities for division of labour and specialization, stimulated advances in the organization and methods of production in industry and trade. The growth of population in a society almost wholly dependent on the land caused a sharp worsening in the condition of the mass of the people during the sixteenth century, concentrating a larger share of income in the hands of the well-to-do: the landowners, officials, merchants, lawyers and financiers. It was their demand, for good quality woollen and linen cloth, furs, silks, wine, armour, ornaments, and other luxuries, that promoted some concentration in industry and in specialized agriculture, expanded the international market economy, and gave opportunities to economic enterprise, outlets for accumulating capital, and scope for experimenting with new economic institutions.

The advances made in this century were on the whole (with an important exception in Low Countries agriculture) in organization rather than in techniques. While Renaissance humanism was beginning to encourage originality in thought and to teach a little scepticism of derived authority; while new thinking was being stimulated by the rediscovery of Greek classical texts, and its results disseminated by the widening use of the printing press after Gutenberg's beginnings in the 1440s, most of the everyday processes of production were carried on much as they had been for centuries before. The general character of economic change was shaped by the conjunction of prolonged population growth with a limited supply of land and a technology that showed little advance in the main sectors of production. The Black Death of 1348–9 had reduced the population of western Europe by at least a third. More than a century passed with little recovery in numbers, but between 1450 and 1480 population began to grow in most parts of Europe and this movement continued with only temporary interruptions until the early seventeenth century. Between 1460 and 1620 the population of Europe may have doubled, and around

1560 it passed the highest levels attained during the fourteenth century.

Population decline in the fourteenth century had made it possible to feed the reduced numbers without resort to cultivating the worst and most poorly situated lands. Recovery is most simply explained in terms of response to this relaxation of pressure upon real resources, but it is hard to see why it was delayed for so long and came when it did. There are no records of births or mortality from which we can get direct evidence of the reasons for the new upturn. Though epidemics continued to occur throughout the fifteenth century, it is possible that they were more intense during its earliest part. In the second half of the century there was some abatement in wars' devastation: the Hundred Years War, which time and again had ruined large tracts of the French countryside and had destroyed numberless towns, ended in 1453; Italy enjoyed an unusual period of tranquillity from 1453 until a new phase of war and invasion began in 1494; and the series of civil wars in Spain ended with the succession of Isabella to the throne of Castile in 1474. Yet the influence of these relatively peaceful conditions must not be overestimated, for population growth appears to have continued through the destructive wars which broke out in the second quarter of the sixteenth century. We can only say that the demographic balance was a delicate one, with a death rate that could be only marginally influenced by deliberate human effort; and that somehow the rough equilibrium which had been maintained down to the middle of the fifteenth century was disturbed in the following decades so that the losses which were still incurred in years of disease, famine or war came to be outweighed in the periods of growth. Despite the great variety of European experience, this cannot be ascribed to purely local causes, for it was Europe-wide; there is clear evidence of fast-growing population in England and Flanders, France and Spain, Italy and the Ottoman Empire, Germany and the Scandinavian lands.

As population recovered towards its old levels, the old difficulties reappeared of providing more people, from an almost unchanging land, with the corn to make their bread. Abandoned fields were cultivated again; remote and empty heaths again grazed flocks; in the Netherlands reclamation of land from the sea was accelerated after 1540. Nevertheless it became more difficult each decade to keep up with rural demand for food and to send surpluses to the towns. Landlords no longer had to relax dues and lower

rents to get tenants, and employers, encountering the new phenomenon of a labour surplus, were able to resist demands for rising
wages. Income was beginning to be redistributed away from
peasant and wage-earner towards landlord and employer; from the
poor to the well-to-do. The demand for luxury foodstuffs – fruit,
dairy produce, wine – was expanded, and industry called for more
raw materials from the land – wool, flax, dyestuffs. For a time,
therefore, land was being pulled away from the cultivation of rye
and wheat that provided the basic food of the masses, and corn
prices moved upwards, erratically but continuously, from the low
levels to which they had drifted during the fifteenth century. They
were rising rapidly in Spain immediately after 1500 and everywhere
in the west at some time before 1530.

Agricultural improvement was not widespread. Real advances
were evident only in the Netherlands, where the pressure of town
demands had encouraged innovation in husbandry during the
fourteenth and fifteenth century. The introduction of convertible
husbandry and the insertion of fodder crops into the crop rotation
were practices making it possible to keep larger flocks and herds,
but they reacted in providing more manure and so led into a cycle
of increasing corn yields. They were eventually to transform much
of European agriculture but were little known outside the Netherlands before the latter part of the sixteenth century.

Growing population ended many regional corn surpluses. In
Spain the surpluses in Old Castile became less regular and the
heavily populated coastlines of the Basque country and Andalusia,
which had relied on them, had to look farther afield. Portugal,
which had solved its food problem by the development of Atlantic
island granaries, was left in deficit as these were turned to sugar
production. In the Low Countries, despite improved methods and
supplies from their thinly populated eastern regions and the north
of France, there was not enough corn to feed the towns. Western
Europe as a whole was drifting into food deficit in the middle
decades of the sixteenth century, from which it was only partially
rescued by the development of a new source of supply in the
lands east of the Baltic. The landlords of eastern Europe, faced
like others in the fifteenth century with a shortage of tenants that
threatened their income, had been ruthless in finding means to
maintain it. The exceptional weakness of their rulers enabled these
landowners to act virtually without political restraint and they
used local power to seize peasant land, expand their demesnes to

create large economic units of production and force the peasants back to labour services on these demesnes. The low-cost corn was sent down to Danzig or Konigsberg for export to Netherlands markets, and as western population expanded and corn prices rose, the Baltic lords responded by further encroachments on their peasants' land and liberty to increase the exportable surplus. In the first half of the sixteenth century Baltic corn – mostly rye – met nearly a quarter of the needs of the Low Countries, was beginning to go to Spain and Portugal, and occasionally helped out an English deficiency. The amount involved – a hundred thousand tons a year in mid-century – was small in relation to total consumption, but it relieved pressure at vital points, notably where Low Countries industry and Andalusian viniculture were producing for European markets on a scale that could only be maintained by importing food for their own people.

Corn – principally rye, but also wheat, oats and barley – was the basic foodstuff on which most of Europe's population depended. Despite this, land was still being turned from corn growing to other uses until far into the sixteenth century. In some parts of the west it was becoming rather easier than it had been for an enterprising person, whether landlord or tenant, to change traditional uses of land in order to enlarge his own income. Monarchs were powerful and some regard had to be paid to law, so the sweeping harshness with which east European landlords treated their peasantry could hardly be imitated. Nevertheless, landlords everywhere were rich and influential while peasants were poor and individually weak, with their economic bargaining power lessened by the rising number of aspirants to land holdings in each generation. Thus in France, where the peasants' rights to the soil were very firmly grounded in law which the royal courts would uphold, landlords found it difficult directly to increase dues and rents. The old nobility suffered loss of income, disposed of much of their land and ultimately turned to dependence on royal charity or offices in the service of the crown. Yet many old-established landowners, and perhaps even more of the merchants and officials who bought estates, were sufficiently enterprising or unscrupulous to search out defects in land titles, ambiguities of tenures, accumulations of small dues forgotten and unpaid in the chaos of the fifteenth century, and use these to harry peasants, seize back pieces of land and accumulate demesnes to grow cash crops for profit, or to create farms to lease at rack rents for short terms. In England down to about 1520, and again for a few years in the 1540s, land-lords took advantage of a rural jurisdiction which was largely under their own control to seize common lands and occasionally arable holdings – defying villagers to summon them before the royal courts – and so to extend sheep and cattle ranges which they managed or let out to capitalist graziers paying high rents. As early as 1489 this activity provoked the crown to attempt prohibition of encroachments on arable land, but it ceased only when rising corn prices ended its profitability. In Castile the weight of royal authority was exerted in the opposite direction, to prevent small cultivators from interfering with the great tracts reserved for migratory sheep farming, until the demand for wool fell away in the 1560s. In southern Spain the peasant was generally a short-term tenant, and merchants from the towns who had capital to spare bought up estates and found little difficulty in forcing out these tenants and turning land into olive groves, orchards and vineyards, cultivated by day labourers.

Until the second quarter of the sixteenth century – and in some places even later – such changes were generally away from corn, towards dairy produce, meat, wool, fruit, vines, flax, woad, madder, linseed and olives. The net result was to expand the value of agri-cultural production, to bring a much bigger return to some pro-ducers and landlords, a more varied diet for the well-to-do, bigger industrial crops, and a wider trade in agricultural produce. But it accentuated the rise in corn prices, and in the second half of the sixteenth century this became so steep that it checked the conversion of land away from arable except in the most favoured situations, and even brought some land back again to corn production.

In industry as in agriculture, technical advance was modest. Im-provements in the spinning wheel, and the spreading use of the gig-mill for cloth finishing, had some significance for the woollen industry. The growing needs of the Dutch polder system for mechanical pumps, of mines for ventilation and drainage, and of furnaces for powerful bellows, were met by improvements in wind- and water-mills and extension of their use. Cannon-founding, pumping machinery, printing, the blast furnace – all emerging during the latter part of the fifteenth century – were of great im-portance in the long run but they were in industries still very small.

The productiveness of industry was increased more by changes in its organization, particularly as much of it came to be directed by merchant-capitalists who saw advantages in controlling production of the goods they sold. This is most clearly seen in the development of the 'domestic' or 'putting-out' system. Far back in the Middle Ages the geographical expansion of the markets of some local industries had made the merchant a key figure. Craftsmen came to rely on him to sell their products far afield and to finance the credit operations that distant trade demanded, and so gradually lost their independence, becoming effectively, if not formally, his employees. Town authorities resisted this process nearly everywhere, and in the Netherlands cities where society polarized between a prosperous bourgeoisie and a proletarianized artisan class there were savage social conflicts. The employers sought to escape these troubles by organizing new sources of labour among peasants and labourers in agriculture, looking only for by-employment, who were cheaper, more amenable and less able to combine. From the later Middle Ages to the general adoption of the factory system in the nineteenth century this 'putting-out' system was spreading through one branch of industry after another, merchant capitalists handing out material to be worked on by wage-earners in their own homes, usually in the villages. By the late fifteenth century the system had embraced much of the good-quality textile industry of western Europe, though the poor still bought the coarse products of the independent craftsmen of villages and small towns. In Flanders, Holland, England and western France woollen spinning and weaving had come largely to be the occupations of families scattered through the countryside, often the possessors of land holdings, who worked on spinning wheels and looms in their own homes. The linen industry was similarly organized in Picardy and Normandy (where it was replacing woollen manufacture), in Maine and in the Courtrai region of Flanders. Only in Spain was the woollen industry still mainly urban, though there were important woollen manufacturing towns in Holland and northern France. Free from the regulation imposed by the towns, employing the women-folk of rural families and men who were seasonally underemployed on the land to perform easily learned operations, these industries were able to expand low-cost production of fairly standardized good qualities. The more skilled processes – dyeing and finishing – remained in the hands of town craftsmen (Antwerp finishers, for example, handled most of the English cloth going to European markets), whilst in the long run the expansion of settled rural industry caused numbers of weavers to take to it as their full-time occupation, abandoning agriculture.

But from the entrepreneur's point of view this organization remained highly flexible, his capital being employed in debts and advances and stockholding that were easily run down in periods of slack trade, rather than locked up in fixed plant whose idleness was costly to him. Merchant control brought greater responsiveness to the precise demands of particular markets, and some degree of standardization and economy of producers' time, and it built up concentrations of capital in the hands of a quite small number of individuals.

The textile industries were much the largest, and the domestic system spread most rapidly in the districts where they manufactured for international markets. Outside them, two other general forms of industry may be distinguished. One was a group of industries that required fairly large capital for fixed equipment, engaged on the whole in the production, refining and early treatment of minerals – iron, coal, lead, copper and zinc. The costs of permanent shafts, pumping, drainage, furnace equipment, haulage, etc., were rising as the scale of operations increased, and these industries were the seats of some of the most striking technical improvements of the period. Improved systems of pumping and ventilation enabled the coal industry to dig deep pits and attain an altogether fresh scale of operation in England, where the annual production of some 150 thousand tons, in the mid-sixteenth century, far surpassed the fifty thousand tons of the Liège area or the forty thousand that came from the Scottish pits. The big advance in iron smelting was the blast furnace, coming into general use in the Liège area and eastern France at the beginning of the sixteenth century and in England after 1540. The English coal industry, with its pits employing twenty or thirty workers apiece after costly shaft-sinking and drainage operations, and the Liège furnaces and forges with their teams of a dozen or more workers, typified industries moving decisively away from the craftsman stage towards capitalism with a wage-earning labour force. In iron-making, indeed, the organizational unit rapidly became larger than the technical one, as traders in iron brought in capital and acquired the ownership of groups of furnaces and forges.

At the other extreme was the continuance of small-scale industry of independent craftsmen. In every village some spinning women, a weaver or two, a shoemaker, supplied their neighbours with goods of the cheapest quality, chiefly made from local materials; these were ousted only very slowly, over centuries, by the products of specialized industries. Besides these, the village had its essential agricultural and building crafts, among which the blacksmith's was most universal. Towns provided for other needs of their rural neighbours, with saddlers, wheelwrights, iron-workers, as well as such food processors for their own inhabitants and for market visitors as bakers, brewers and butchers. In the largest towns, and above all in the capital cities, craftsmen of a quite different order of skill made luxury products – fine leatherware, clothing, gold and silver plate – usually dealing directly over the counter with wealthy customers but sometimes, like the silkware makers of Tours and Lyon, sending goods out to European markets.

Many of the crafts carried on in towns required considerable skill, and insisted on long apprenticeship for prospective entrants. In England, and to a much lesser extent in France and Castile, the craftsmen in the corporate towns had drawn together in gilds and companies of each craft, protecting craft interests against outsiders and upholding their own members in the affairs of the town. From the end of the fifteenth century the governments of France and Spain began to recognize the potential usefulness of gilds as instruments for controlling industry and encouraged their proliferation in the larger towns. Gilds were given privileges – which created interests in restricting the numbers of real beneficiaries of the privileges. Particularly in industries using costly materials, divisions appeared within the gilds between genuine masters who sold directly to customers – and who sometimes abandoned the making of goods to become simply traders – on the one hand, and workmen on the other who were effectively in the employment of these trading masters. Sometimes the workmen remained permanent journeymen, who had served apprenticeship to the gild but were unable to fulfil the costly conditions for taking up full membership; in other crafts they were members of separate gilds of inferior status. Here again changing organization was working to create a more efficient division of functions between traders and producers. But the achievement of it through the manipulation of these rigid and increasingly conservative organizations had an economic as well as a social price. It encouraged the setting of increasingly rigid controls over types and qualities of production and limitation on innovation in design and methods, and was in general a drag on change within these town industries. The Castilian government quickly enmeshed industry in regulation – the ordinances of Seville in 1511, for example, contained 120 rules on cloth weaving – and the kings of France were taking the same path late in the century. Most of these crafts were too small to escape regulation by burying themselves in the countryside, and they sold their products not at the fairs but over the counters of their workshops, which had to be readily accessible to their customers in the towns.

In short, while only a few branches of industry reveal useful progress in techniques, organization on capitalist lines was steadily making headway. The division of labour within industrial communities, within and between nations, was being changed, and one result was the growth of international trade to embrace a larger – though still tiny – proportion of western Europe's production and consumption.

Long-distance trade makes a large figure in the writing of economic history, for it always had a literature, it was commonly the object of government concern, and it was taxed so that records of its extent have been left behind in most countries. But beneath the well-documented trades that crossed international frontiers was a vast network of trading operations that we know very little about. There was the small-scale division of labour between the little market town and the dozen or two villages within a day's walking distance, where peasants sold their eggs, butter, cheese and livestock in the weekly market, buying in return the simple products of the town crafts and a tiny range of essentials from outside (notably salt and iron wares); and where at the right seasons they earned cash to pay their rents by selling bigger quantities of corn, wool, hides and flax, for which their market town served as a point of transit on the way to a larger regional market centre. These towns were connected with a wider market through the bigger towns, and in particular through the fairs, where the regional surpluses, gathered together, became the subjects of large-scale operations by wealthy professional dealers in them; where the mercers and ironmongers and grocers of the market towns came to buy their stocks, and the monastic bailiffs and baronial stewards to buy cloth, jewellery and bulk supplies of provisions. Fairs and capital cities attracted the foreign-trading merchants who unified the economy of Europe. History has not yet looked at the workings of this internal trade or attempted to assess its size and development, but has almost confined itself to examining the formalities of its regulation by municipalities and gilds.

There are good reasons, however, for giving special attention to long-distance trade. The importance of trade does not lie entirely in values; a farmer's sale of a hundredweight of butter on the market of a town five miles away created few problems, and required none of the specialized services that were recruited in selling a hundredweight of Portuguese salt in Danzig or half a dozen yards of Italian silk in York. In the first place, as we have seen, a decisive change in economic relationships took place when producer was separated from final consumer; when the whole trade in an article no longer came down to a face-to-face meeting between two individuals over a counter or a market stall. The complications of dealing over the counter, though they involved haggling and sometimes the granting of credit, were trivial by comparison with those of organizing the sale of goods to distant, unknown customers, delivering them and getting payment in return. Long-distance trade enhanced the importance of the specialist intermediary, the merchant, and it created entirely different needs for transport and financial services which called in their turn for further specialists.

The merchant was the specialist in trading, just as the craftsmen and peasants were specialists in producing. These middlemen themselves, in fact, became differentiated by a variety of functions; there was the merchant of the manufacturing area, buying from the producer; the travelling merchant, dealing at the fair with customers from far off; the exporting merchant, who sent goods to agents abroad to be sold; the merchant in the consuming area, selling to small-town merchants and also to some final customers. Once the producing craftsman came to depend on an ultimate market that he never saw, he was in danger of subordination to these trading specialists. The merchant who dealt directly with the producer was likely to be badgered by him for payment before the final customer had paid for the goods sold; by paying the producer to keep him going, the merchant developed a debt relationship which often grew permanent and in time made the producer virtually an employee of the merchant. The merchant then ceased to handle goods for producers who were not in this dependent relation and the whole industry became merchant-dominated. The craftsmen often declined into mere wage-earners, and the capital (except so far as this was embodied in the craftsmen's tools) and the profits belonged to the merchants; merchants made the crucial decisions about styles, markets and the volume of production, and employed or turned off the craftsmen at will. This was the line of development in all the great textile industries of western Europe, observable as early as the twelfth century but still extending five hundred years later. In the great new worsted industry growing up in southern Flanders around 1500 there was a further refinement: the small merchant employing a few score workers himself sank into financial dependence or became simply an agent for great men in Bruges or Antwerp. The same condition can be seen in much of the English woollen industry around the end of the seventeenth century, where local merchant-capitalists were completely in thrall to a small group of London dealers.

Long-distance trade, therefore – whether national or international – transformed the structure of large sections of European industry, and these were on the whole expanding ones. It also required special facilities for the transfer of money, and it employed transport on a scale and of kinds that were unknown to local trade. Much the greatest part of the total money value of European trade was made up by goods of high unit value, especially textile manufactures, dyestuffs and spices. They did not need to employ very great transport resources, but complicated arrangements for accounting and paper transfers had to be made to settle money balances between individual merchants and between trading regions, if the physical transfer of large amounts of gold and silver coin over long distances was to be avoided. On the other hand, the greatest part of European trade as measured by volume was made up by goods of low unit value, such as corn, salt and timber. These too, of course, called for means of payment over distances, but their chief special requirement was transport facilities on a large scale, generally by river or sea. In geographical terms, the high-value trades often involved the ultimate transfer of money to Italy, the centre of luxury industries and the source of imports from Asia; while the low-value trades required the carriage of corn and salt to the centres of the most dense industrial populations, northern Italy and the Netherlands, though they also had to handle English and Spanish wool, French and Spanish wine, and Baltic forest products.

For two millennia the economic centre of Europe – so far as it had one – had been the Mediterranean. Even in 1500 the influence of the Italian cities was still strong in the west. Because the manufactures and spices the Italians handled were demanded in every court and city of Europe, and they sought out acceptable local specialisms in return, Italian traders had penetrated to nearly all parts of western Europe during the thirteenth and fourteenth centuries. In every considerable trading city south of the Baltic coastlands,

Italian trading settlements had been established – and there were no corresponding northern settlements in Italy. The rise of Iberian shipping in the fourteenth and fifteenth centuries that had completed the amalgamation of northern and southern sailing-ship types was largely due to its employment by Italian merchants in the corn and salt trades of the Mediterranean. Improvements in navigational methods and cartography, on which the Portuguese explorers built, arose from the work of Italian cartographers or their Catalan rivals. Though the tide of Italian mercantile power was receding throughout Europe during the fifteenth century, though the colonies of Italian merchants in London and Rouen diminished, and German and Flemish merchants and financiers began to usurp their places in Antwerp and Seville, the deposit of methods, forms and instruction which the Italians left behind was a permanent one. From the thirteenth century onward they had been developing very elaborate commercial techniques; of credit trading; of money transfer (through bills of exchange and letters of credit) and banking; of commercial partnership and agency; of foreign exchange dealing over distance and time; of marine insurance; of book-keeping and general documentation. Castilian merchants and bankers had mastered these methods by the early sixteenth century, and in the course of that century French and English merchants learned them too. The advance of shipping techniques had come mainly from the west; in commercial and financial methods the credit for innovation must be almost wholly Italian.

Long after Italians had ceased to dominate European trade they retained a powerful hold over its finance. At Lyon, the most important financial centre in the west, 143 out of 169 banking houses in the mid-sixteenth century were Italian. Though Spaniards took a leading place in financial operations at the fairs of Medina del Campo, the finance of overseas trade at Seville was almost entirely in Italian hands. At Bruges – still an important trading city, though in decline before 1500 – Italian financiers played a dominant role. In Liège, the centre of heavy industry, Italians handled large-scale finance until very late in the sixteenth century. Italians were less important, by mid-century, in England and the French Atlantic ports, but these included no financial centre of the first rank. At Antwerp the dominant Italians were thrust out of first place by German bankers during the first two decades of the sixteenth century, but they remained important. Some Italian financial activity lingered in western Europe until the second quarter of the seventeenth century, long after Italian traders had almost disappeared; and it left behind it a legacy of business methods that have survived into the present century.

Finally, long-distance trade employed transport facilities. The trade of late fifteenth-century Europe was being diverted away from the sea routes, in an interval between the overcoming of the extreme insecurity of land travel and the great seventeenth-century expansion of bulk trades that had to take to the sea. As central Europe became wealthy, pulling in supplies from north and south, tying firm connections with Antwerp through Cologne and Frankfurt, and with Genoa and Venice across the Alpine passes, interest revived in carrying goods overland between north-western Europe and Italy. Since the late thirteenth century this overland carriage had been largely replaced by the Italian ships which had crept round the Atlantic coasts of Europe. Well before 1500, however, the Florentine and Genoese galleys and argosies ceased to make the voyage to Bruges and London, and though Venetian traffic continued a good deal longer their vessels were rare visitors after 1509. The Rhone valley route between the Mediterranean and the north, through Marseilles and Lyon, also came back into heavy use after peace returned to France in 1453. The arrival of Ottoman sea power in the western Mediterranean in the second quarter of the sixteenth century tipped the balance even more decisively against the use of sea routes from southern Europe.

Nevertheless, only the more valuable goods, mostly manufactures, could easily bear the cost of long journeys by land. The sea-borne trades of the west European ports were expanding fast. Corn, as we have seen, was being despatched from the Baltic not only to Dutch ports but also farther south to Spain and Portugal; by 1570 it was going into the Mediterranean. French salt from Biscay went north to all the Atlantic and North Sea coasts and into the Baltic, and before 1500 it was being supplemented by Portuguese salt from Setubal and Aveiro, taken home by Hanseatic grain carriers. Wine from Bordeaux, Rochelle and Nantes was carried to England, the Netherlands and the Baltic, and the Dutch shipped great quantities of herring north and south. These, along with timber, were the great bulk trades that kept big ships moving outside the Mediterranean; and one bulky product, Roman alum, came from the Mediterranean for the cloth industries of Flanders and England. These trades employed ships that were large for their day; indeed, no bigger ships were successfully used in commerce for three more centuries than the thousand-ton hulks of northern Europe and the carracks of the Mediterranean and the Portuguese India trade. These, as well as the rather smaller Dutch and Hanseatic cogs, and the Iberian nefs and nãos, were slow and clumsy vessels, but cheap to run, for they had small crews and little defence.

Few ports could accommodate vessels of this size, and few branches of trade were big enough to offer them secure employment. Salt, wine, corn, timber, herrings and the rest were distributed to the minor ports of the Atlantic coasts in smaller ships, which served a host of other seaborne trades as well. Sugar from the western Mediterranean and the Atlantic isles, fruit and woad of southern France, fish out of a multitude of small harbours, cloth and coal from England to the nearby continent; these employed numbers of vessels of a quite different order of size – twenty, fifty, eighty tons – belonging to the ports of northern Spain, Portugal, Brittany, Normandy, the Dutch Zuider Zee, and southern and eastern England. The evolution of ship types over two centuries had produced some uniformity in rig; the lateen sail of the Mediterranean and the square rig of the northern vessel had been married in the fourteenth and fifteenth centuries, chiefly through the intermediary of Basque and Portuguese seamen whose ships had served all the coasts of Europe from Bruges to Venice in the later Middle Ages. In hull construction there was greater variation; this was the period in which the old shell construction was being abandoned for the smaller ships, and the great hulks were perhaps the last examples of it. Sailing ships were now being built to face the ocean and to be manœuvrable enough to make progress against contrary winds.

All these developments in the basic elements of economic organization, which affected in turn agriculture, industry, commerce, finance and transport, can be seen coming to a focus in the dazzling pre-eminence of early sixteenth-century Antwerp. To see why they focused on that particular corner of western Europe rather than on any other, it is necessary to glance beyond the seaboard states to Germany, where in the later decades of the fifteenth century a vigorous new impulse to growth arose from factors quite independent of those we have been considering. A greatly enlarged exploitation of silver, copper, lead and zinc deposits in the mountainous borderlands of south Germany, Poland and Hungary created employment and wealth that not only helped to build up a variety of industries in south Germany itself but also pulled in goods from the Mediterranean lands and western Europe. Italian manufactures – especially fine woollen and silk goods – and eastern spices, dyestuffs and cotton were carried across the Alps; while from the other side Flemish and English woollen goods and French linens were brought up the Rhine valley from Bruges and, to an increasing extent, from Antwerp. This central European activity had a very strong impact on the cities of the Low Countries; and through them it noticeably accelerated the belated and stumbling return of western Europe to the path of economic growth and oceanic expansion.

The most densely populated and economically advanced area of western Europe was the western fringe of the collection of duchies and counties that, after 1477, comprised the Habsburg possessions in the Netherlands. Though the medieval fine-cloth industry of Flanders had gone down before English and Dutch competition, it had been replaced there by production of thinner and cheaper woollen cloths of the type called 'says'. This industry, carried on in villages round Lille, Arras, Tournai, Valenciennes and Armentières, using wool imported from Scotland, Friesland, Germany and above all Spain, was reaching maturity in the first years of the sixteenth century. Farther north, Leyden and Delft had captured a big market for their fine heavy woollens. Antwerp itself was the centre of many small branches of luxury industry, such as jewellery, paper-making and printing and sugar-refining, and it dyed and finished immense quantities of English cloth that were sold in the city for European markets. In Flanders the linen and tapestry industries were growing fast; and Holland and Zealand were by 1500 the centres of the greatest shipbuilding industry of Europe.

Netherlands manufactures went to every part of Europe, and the highly concentrated industrial population needed large supplies of imported raw materials as well as imported foodstuffs. Moreover, the situation of the Netherlands ports, where the mouths of the Rhine and Scheldt, opening up the long river ways into the heart of Europe, debouched on the seaway that connected northern and southern Europe and the short sea crossing to England, gave these ports an international role. They not only served the Netherlands themselves but were also trans-shipment ports, from river to sea-going craft and from sea to river. They offered the warehousing facilities necessary in an age of prolonged voyages, when all seas were dangerous in winter and the Baltic impassable; and consequently they were markets for goods which had been produced and would find their final sale in far-off and widely separated places. This international trade had two parts, one centred on the Dutch ports and the other on the single Brabant port of Antwerp on the Scheldt. The Dutch handled a trade in corn, timber and other bulky goods coming from the Baltic coasts and Norway to western and southern Europe, and a northbound traffic in salt and wine cargoes, filling out the ships with smaller ladings of Netherlands manufactures and Dutch-caught herrings. These were on the whole cheap and bulky goods that naturally travelled by sea, often bought and sold in foreign ports by the shipmasters themselves, their cost heavily weighted down by freight charges. The Dutch ports of the Zuider Zee – notably Enkhuizen, Hoorn and the rapidly rising Amsterdam – which were most actively engaged in these trades, provided warehousing and marketing facilities for the goods as well as the ships that carried them. In the late fifteenth century all this business was expanding very rapidly and the Dutch had become the greatest shipowners of Europe; yet Amsterdam and the others were still minor places among Europe's trading cities, their richest merchants and shipowners not approaching levels of wealth that were common in Antwerp, Lübeck or Seville. But the foundation was being laid for the future role of the Dutch, and of Amsterdam in particular, in extra-European expansion during the seventeenth century.

The other trade of the Netherlands cities was in the manufactures of the Netherlands, England and Germany. In the Middle Ages Bruges had grown rich as the port of export for Flemish cloth, and of the corresponding import to Flanders of wool, dyestuffs and corn. As far back as the thirteenth century Bruges had attracted the Italian galleys, coming first to lade Flemish textiles but later English wool, and had been the magnet that drew Hanseatic merchants from Hamburg and the Baltic ports to buy cloth. During the fifteenth century, as the Flemish manufacturing towns were weakened by internal social difficulties and by Italian, Dutch and English industrial competition, the trade of Bruges declined considerably. Antwerp rose in its place, but developed far beyond it in the sixteenth century in the scale and variety of its commercial and financial operations.

Bruges had been too closely identified with the particular industrial interests of Flanders to adapt itself fully to the more independent role of an international port; it repeatedly erected barriers against growing branches of trade that competed with the interests of its own hinterland. Dordrecht, the market centre of the lower Rhine and Moselle basin, and Middelberg, close to Antwerp at the exit from the Scheldt, both restricted the activity of foreign traders in order to maintain the business of their own merchants. Antwerp by contrast was less restrictive, once its rulers had understood what its major trading function was to be. This was to act as the link between Cologne and the German lands beyond it, on the one side, and London and the English cloth-producing area on the other. Cologne was a member town of the Hanseatic League, but its interests did not altogether coincide with those of the seaport members, which remained faithful to their Bruges connection throughout the fifteenth century. Its main western outlets had long been down the Rhine to Dordrecht, or northward through Kampen and the Zuider Zee. Cologne merchants did have a modest trade with Antwerp, however, buying skins and hides in exchange for metalwares and wine, and when new municipal regulations hampered their trade at Dordrecht they transferred much of it to Antwerp. There they encountered English cloth merchants, who had been excluded from the trade of Bruges – and several towns of Zeeland and Brabant – because they competed with local industry or local traders. Indeed, their position in Antwerp itself had been threatened in the first decades of the fifteenth century because of the devastating impact of English competition on the Antwerp fine-cloth industry. But the profitable business in finishing English cloth before it was sent on to the final consumers turned the scales in their favour, and despite some recurrences of hostility the English firmly settled on Antwerp as their staple market from the 1440s. The Cologne merchants found they could sell high quality English cloth in the interior of Europe; they sent it on to the greater mart towns of Frankfurt and Nuremberg, and it was distributed beyond to south-west Germany, Venice and the Levant and eastward into the Habsburg lands and Poland, where it became well known at the Lemberg and Cracow fairs, and northward through Kampen into the Baltic. In return for English and Netherlands cloth the Cologne merchants brought silver and copper, German metalwares and fustians, and presently Italian silverwares and silks and oriental spices.

The distribution of Flemish and English in exchange for German and Italian manufactures was the basis of Antwerp's prosperity. So great was the trade thus invoked, so ample the financial facilities created to serve them, that many other branches of trade were attracted to Antwerp. The Portuguese, who had first used Bruges as their northern outlet for African pepper and Madeira sugar, switched to Antwerp in 1488; it was the natural place to settle their factors for the sale of Asian produce after 1504; and there they sold brazilwood, the one early import from their Brazilian possession. At Antwerp the Portuguese were able to buy the German copper and copperwares demanded in the African trade, and the silver needed after 1498 for their ships going to the Indian Ocean. Hanseatic merchants were abandoning Bruges, despite the privileges given to them there, in the first years of the sixteenth century, and bringing to Antwerp those Baltic products whose trade they had retained – flax and hemp, copper, furs, wax and potash. They sent back English cloth, arms and armour from Liège, silks and spices – valuable goods which generally went overland to Lubeck for further distribution. Venetian traders had used Antwerp as well as Bruges since the middle of the fifteenth century, and in succeeding decades the Genoese and Florentines followed them. The Italians did not merely trade with their own cities but joined many different kinds of enterprise in Antwerp, often in partnership with local merchants, providing capital and above all the business sophistication with which they were uniquely equipped, and so spreading it among other merchant communities in the city. Even Spanish merchants settled at Antwerp, though they were still rapidly expanding their wool export to Bruges, and Spain had a more direct connection with central Europe through Barcelona and Genoa. They sold fruit and oil, and presently American cochineal and indigo, at Antwerp, and took home Flemish and German manufactures. English and French merchants bought German and Baltic wares in exchange for woollen and linen fabrics, while England's direct trade with the Mediterranean and the Baltic faded away because the Antwerp market could handle all the goods involved.

Thus Antwerp became an entrepôt, attracting produce away from the direct routes between producing and consuming areas. All these nations settled colonies of merchants in the city, and most trade was carried on between them rather than by the native citizens. At its zenith around 1560 the total population reached over a hundred thousand, when it was only surpassed in the west by Paris and perhaps equalled by London and Seville. Its four fairs had almost merged in trading all the year round – though the fair times remained important for the settlement of financial transactions – and the most advanced commercial methods of the Italians were in general use. Moreover, though Antwerp's shipping was small – it took no part in the bulk trades beyond meeting local needs – Antwerp merchants played a large part in financing the great international trade in corn, salt and wine carried on through the Dutch ports, and the ships that carried it. The final advance of the Dutch from being simply shipowners and carriers of other people's goods was largely accomplished after 1500 with the support of Antwerp capital, and brought much profit back to Antwerp.

Antwerp's old rivals were buoyed up by the general prosperity of the region centring on Antwerp but they ceased to be serious competitors with it. Bruges became merely the port for the area of Flanders just behind it, retaining an important connection with Spain for which it still provided the principal wool market; but much of the money Spanish traders earned in Bruges was spent in Antwerp. Dordrecht fell to merely local importance; Middelberg and Bergen-op-Zoom, once fierce rivals for the English trade, became outports of Antwerp. Only the Dutch ports, with their wholly different type of trade, were advancing fast, handling immense tonnages of goods, but inconsiderable either in the value of their trades or the wealth of their merchants by comparison with Antwerp. In 1543–4, 80 per cent of the Netherlands export tax was paid in Antwerp, 3¼ per cent in Amsterdam.

Antwerp's pre-eminence was to be destroyed by war and the division of the Netherlands between 1572 and 1585, never to return. But in any case the concentration of north-western Europe's trade upon this city was so extreme that it could hardly have lasted, and the tide was already beginning to turn before 1560. One factor was the diversion of Portuguese-German exchanges. The seizure of the eastern spice trade by the Portuguese after 1497 was not permanent, because they were too weak to dominate the Indian Ocean so completely as their successors, the Dutch and English, were to do. By 1530 the old route through the Red Sea and Cairo, leading to Venice, had recovered much ground and was offering Antwerp severe competition in supplying central Europe. At the same time the appearance of large Spanish-American silver supplies at Cadiz made it an alternative source for the Portuguese Indies trade. After 1549 spices were being sold in large quantities in Lisbon itself rather than in Antwerp. Even the copper trade was changing its route; by mid-century the great German metal traders had established agents at Lisbon and were carrying copper there through Venice and the Mediterranean rather than by Antwerp.

As markets became larger and better organized, the interest of many of the richest merchants in Antwerp turned from commodity trading towards finance. The Antwerp financiers in the fifteenth century had mostly been Italian, and Florentines continued to dominate exchange business in Antwerp and Bruges until at least 1520. But already the great German mining magnates were settling agents in the city and despatching funds there for investment; Antwerp became the base for their financial operations because it was the principal market for their silver. After 1510 these financial resources were being increasingly used in loans to governments rather than for the support of trade. The Emperor Charles V borrowed on the security of silver; the kings of Portugal on the security of spices coming through the Indian Ocean; the rulers of England and France against the guarantees of their merchant colonies settled in Antwerp. In the great wars of the mid-century they went bankrupt one after another – Spain and France in 1557, Portugal in 1560, the Habsburgs of central Europe more frequently though less thoroughly; their creditors found short-term loans arbitrarily transformed into long-term ones at lowered interest rates. Only England always paid up in full, if sometimes late. A considerable number of local bankruptcies in the 1550s was the consequence, as the great lenders called in debts from commercial customers and Flemish municipalities, which could not repudiate their liabilities so easily as the crowned heads. The increasing diversion of resources into finance – and above all into risky government finance towards mid-century – imposed periodical stresses on the Antwerp money market, and the withdrawal of some of the great finance houses because of state bankruptcies damaged Antwerp's international trading position a generation before war destroyed its trade.

Finally, the prosperity of central Europe, the pillar on which Antwerp's position had been erected, was weakening in the second quarter of the century. The Peasant Wars of 1525, the disturbances of the Reformation and the religious and dynastic wars of the mid-century years, all caused disruption of the textile and metal industries that had been built up in south Germany, and interfered with trade to the west. The silver mines were becoming unprofitable in the face of American supply and the falling value of silver, and their output was in decline before 1540. South German expansion

C

had done much to build up the industries and the commercial and financial institutions of western Europe, largely through the intermediary of Antwerp. The yeast was working in Holland, England and the western parts of France. But before their day came, the dramatic consequences of the new influence on European development, the expansion of Spain's American empire, had to be worked out.

3 Spain in America: The Sixteenth Century

W hen Christopher Columbus sailed westward into the Atlantic in the summer of 1492, expecting to make his landfall among the outlying islands of Japan, he encountered instead an entirely new continent. In the half century of extraordinarily rapid discovery and conquest that followed his voyage, Spain reached out and conquered nearly all of America that was ever to be Spanish. Castile and Portugal determined their spheres in this New World by the Treaty of Tordesillas in 1494, and for over a century no other nation could achieve more in America than petty incursions on these established positions.

In the first two decades, settlement was almost confined to the islands of the Caribbean. For some years the only important Spanish settlements were on Espanola, and then they occupied Puerto Rico, Cuba and Jamaica in 1509-13. There was little settlement on the mainland until Hernan Cortes's landing on the Mexican coast in 1519 opened two years of campaigning in which he overthrew the Aztec Empire and transformed the character of Spanish America. While central Mexico was being consolidated, exploration pushed north and south from it, and expeditions from the feeble colony on the Panama isthmus prepared the way for the overthrow of the Peruvian Empire of the Incas by Francisco Pizarro in 1532-3. Spain concentrated attention, from this time onward, in the two thickly populated regions of Peru and central Mexico.

There was a wide variety of Indian peoples and cultures within the tropical and near-tropical areas of America that Spain conquered.

All were close to stone age level, but the range of their cultures extended from the most primitive hunting and gathering tribes of the Orinoco basin to the sophisticated agricultural empires of Peru and Mexico that were already smelting copper for ornaments and making a form of bronze. The true savages, however, lived beyond the limits of effective Spanish penetration, in the tropical jungles east of the Andes, the plains of temperate America and the rain-drenched highlands of southern Chile. The Spaniards settled in those lands where long-established agricultural communities regularly cultivated food crops – cassava in the islands, maize on the Mexican plateau, maize and potatoes in the upland valleys of Peru.

In many of the Caribbean islands, and in the central American isthmus, population was scattered thinly, living on a very primitive agriculture supported by hunting and fishing. There were differences between rich and poor in the villages but no privileged military or religious superstructure stood above them. Three regions, however, had evolved different forms of society: those of the Maya in the Yucatan peninsula (which was already decaying when the Spaniards came), the Aztecs on the central plateau of Mexico, and the Incas in the moister plateau and valley regions of western South America. Over half the population of America, at the time of the conquest, lived in these three small patches of its vast land area. There were important similarities between the Inca and Aztec societies, although they were separated by thousands of miles. They had both developed in mountainous regions, where altitude tempered the climate but where the cultivable land was limited to areas of valley and plateau wedged among the mountain masses. In these climatically favoured but confined regions the population had thrived and grown dense, to the point at which land was scarce, carefully tilled, and fought for. A settled class of cultivators, their methods carefully adapted to their soil and crops, became habituated to peace and order, and therefore vulnerable to attack and conquest by the nomad tribes of the desert fringes who had retained warlike ways. In Mexico the Aztec ruling group was descended from nomads who had come down from the north in the mid-thirteenth century and gradually extended their overlordship all round the central valley during the succeeding two hundred years. In Peru the Incas began to extend their rule beyond the Cuzco region in the thirteenth century and were still making fresh conquests up to the time the Spaniards arrived.

In these societies, therefore, the mass of the people were peasants holding hereditary and inalienable allotments of land, who were bound to cultivate it, and also to pay tribute and cultivate public lands devoted to the upkeep of the nobility and priesthood that had been imposed on them. The privileges of Aztec and Inca nobility were based not only on military overlordship but also on close association with the religious structures that had been created alongside their rising power. Tribute and labour, extracted from many millions of peasants, were enough to support the great cities of Cuzco in Peru and Tenochtitlan in Mexico, which were centres of government and trade, as well as many lesser towns. In these cities, nobility and religion decked themselves in splendour, served by great numbers of skilled artisans who worked on metal, jade and turquoise ornamentation, fine cotton fabrics, stone carving and a host of other crafts. A substantial merchant class organized the gathering of materials for the craftsmen, the disposal of crops harvested on noble lands, and the feeding of cities and palaces. Yet despite the sophisticated social organization, the advanced methods in textiles, pottery and jewellery, and the enormous and elaborate buildings, these American civilizations did not know iron, used other metals chiefly for ornament, and had not discovered the wheel. The social structure, with its small close-knit nobility resting on the exploitation of a peasant mass, was precarious and vulnerable to attack from without, in the same way as Anglo-Saxon England in 1066, or Mogul India in the eighteenth century. Inter-tribal division and resentments were exploited by Cortes and Pizarro to overthrow the central authorities, and once this was accomplished Spaniards could step readily into the places of the former overlords.

The crown's part in the colonization of the New World did not extend far beyond giving its formal sanction to exploration and settlement projects, covering them with the mantle of Castilian authority and setting up a framework of government within which orderly development could proceed. Resources for conquest and settlement came, for the most part, from private individuals, who had to attract and supply sufficient numbers of men to explore, fight, settle and finally organize the society and economy across the ocean. The motives of the supporters of American enterprise were not always predominantly materialistic. Isabella of Castile was an unusually pious woman in a pious age, and the conversion of an

Indian population to Christianity was gratifying to her. Many of the fighting men sought glory and honour for themselves and for Castile, while others were simply turning their backs on troubles at home – debt, crime, women or enemies. But few can have been indifferent to the prospect of gain, and for some the repairing or making of a fortune was the only objective. We came here, said Cortes, to serve God and to grow rich. Consequently, if America was to attract a continuing flow of resources in men, and the money to send them there, after it had become apparent that it was no staging-post on the way to the Indies, it had to demonstrate its material attractions. The powerful attraction it offered was gold. The barter and seizure of the Indians' gold ornaments and treasures, and the hope of finding the deposits from which the gold had first come, were the chief influences that maintained Spanish interest in the Caribbean and the mainland, from the day on San Salvador when Columbus first encountered Indians wearing tiny gold nose-plugs until, a decade after the seizure of Peru, the far greater wealth of the silver mines was revealed.

The crown and its officials had met some of the small cost of Columbus's first voyage, but merchants and nobles flocked to lend support to his much larger second expedition of 1493, and they provided the funds for all later ventures. Partnerships of merchants, nobles and soldiers competed for royal licences to explore and to organize new settlements, guaranteeing shares of their gains to the crown. Capital to provide the ships and their stores, and the colonists' armament, was raised in Spain itself for the early expeditions, but by 1506 a few of the colonists had accumulated sufficient fortunes from the gold of Espanola to mount the conquests of Cuba, Jamaica and Puerto Rico. Similarly, while the first attempts to settle the mainland coast were organized from Spain, the series of expeditions after 1516 which culminated in Cortes's conquest of Mexico were backed by Cuban resources; and the wealth of Mexico paid for the northward and southward extension of exploration and gave some backing to the colonization of the Panama isthmus and, a decade later, to the conquest of Peru. The net investment of Spanish resources in the New World itself, therefore, was significant only in the first fifteen years after Columbus's arrival. The profits of island gold production, when they reached their peak, not only permitted some handsome remittances to Spain but also financed the next wave of conquests. The American Empire was developed by Spaniards using largely American resources, and while a large and continuing Spanish investment was needed to support the building up of European trade with the New World, and to provide ships for trading and defence, even this was met to some extent out of the flow of royal dues and private remittances of profits from America. Indeed, by the 1570s the investment movement had been reversed and returning colonists were investing capital accumulated in America in entirely Spanish financial and industrial enterprises.

Fighting men and early settlers sought gain for themselves. The experience of the early years showed how apt the first colonists were to conquest and how unsuited most were to settlement. Their main body was made up of seamen, soldiers from the wars in Granada and Italy, rustics who had drifted into Seville in search of a living and were now scooped up by the New World adventure, criminals and debtors escaping from their troubles. The leadership was drawn from a minor nobility that regarded rank and social distinction as attributes dependent on the possession of land and wealth, which were themselves, ideally, the fruits of valour in successful battle; and their restless and fortune-seeking attitudes were absorbed by their followers. Even artisans and agriculturists who had been carefully selected to go and exercise their skills in America succumbed to the prevailing ethos. The fantasy of gold for the taking lured them all, and they followed this will-o'-the-wisp from island to island and to far corners of continental America.

The problems of empire-building that faced the monarchs of Castile were to turn a frontier of plunder into a frontier of settlement; to reward the conquerors to whom empire was owed yet to replace them by stolid and governable settlers; and to check the concentration of political power in the hands of the Columbuses, the Cortes, the Pizarros and their like and place it firmly in the hands of paid servants whose loyalty was to the Castilian crown rather than to the Indies. None of this could be done easily, especially as the first conquerors appropriated most of the real economic resources upon which local political power could be based. The degree of success and obedience that the crown achieved is a tribute to the respect in which it was held and to the ability and energy of early generations of royal officials in America.

Many of the early conquerors shared in gold finds, from the small ones in the islands to the hoard in the treasure house of Atahualpa that astounded Pizarro's followers in 1533. Yet these hoards were quickly distributed and when the king's share and the leaders' big portions had been taken out few rank-and-file soldiers secured enough to take them home to the longed-for life of luxurious idleness in Castile. Later arrivals who had been attracted by the news of loot found it already distributed, though some managed to trade or gamble a part into their own hands. The followers and hangers-on of the conquerors, restless, unreliable material for permanent colonial settlements, were therefore constantly on the move to seek fresh opportunities of fortune. The opening of Cuba rapidly drained Espanola of most of its Spanish population after 1513; news of the entry to the mainland accelerated this exodus after 1517 and it turned into a stampede from all the island settlements when Cortes secured a firm grip on the Aztec Empire in 1521. But the palace and temple hoards of Tenochtitlan were not adequate to satisfy the cravings of all the Spaniards who followed Cortes. Large numbers of them pushed on, under other leaders; into the jungles that separated Mexico from the little colony on the Panama isthmus, over vast desert plateaus towards California, south to Colombia where gold mines were found by Quesada in 1537, and above all, after 1532, to the new bonanza in Peru. Every township established by the Spaniards in Mexico, with the exception of Mexico City and perhaps Vera Cruz, lost most of its Spanish population within a few years of its foundation. Two things brought this outward movement to an end. The royal promulgation of new laws governing Spanish-Indian relations made it evident that, whatever their effect on situations already existing, the exploitation of any newly discovered Indian populations would be severely controlled. Then the discoveries of great deposits of silver in Peru and Mexico in 1545–6 opened new places of attraction to fortune-seekers, and the crown encouraged concentrated development of these new silver mines – which were soon yielding a large revenue – rather than dissipation of resources in the uncertainties of further exploration. After mid-century, therefore, effort was directed to consolidation of the Spanish Empire in the most-favoured areas of Mexico and Peru and the coastlands and islands were left to weak and neglected settlements.

Whether Spanish incomes were to be based on agriculture or on mining, they would be secured only by some form of exploiting of the labour of the Indian population. Here economic and social necessity clashed with justice and religion, at first triumphed over them completely, but eventually had to give some ground. The Pope had given his blessing to Castile's claim to the New

World, in 1493, in consideration of Ferdinand and Isabella undertaking the conversion of the Indians to Christianity. From the
point of view of Church and society it was necessary to bring the
Indians into subjection in order to convert them. They were inno-
cents, not Muslim enemies of Christianity whom anyone might
enslave; they were new vassals of the crown of Castile, which had
a duty to protect them unless they deliberately rejected the blessings
of Christianity when these were tendered, or rebelled against
rulers set over them by the crown. The royal obligation to convert
and protect the Indians, and to rule them and Spaniards with an
impartial hand, was in direct opposition not only to the obligation
to reward the Spaniards who had pioneered these lands for the
crown and raised the cross in the Indies, but also to the pressing
need to encourage Spaniards to settle down there and the desirability of securing for the crown itself some revenue from America.
Nevertheless the crown and its officials turned their faces sharply
against Indian slavery, so that outright slaughter and enslavement
began to be checked after 1503, while agitation by priests to put
more stringent limits on the extremities of exploitation quickly
made itself heard in Spain. On the other hand, royal authority did
for some decades support the colonists in keeping Indians in servitude, for without countenancing slavery, the crown authorized
forced labour. The royal instructions given to the new Governor
of Espanola, Ovando, in 1503, declared:

Because of the excessive liberty the Indians have been permitted, they
flee from Christians and do not work. Therefore they are to be compelled
to work, so that the kingdom and the Spaniards be enriched, and the
Indians Christianized. They are to be paid a daily wage, and well treated
as free persons for such they are, and not slaves.

A model for Spaniards' relations with a subject race was offered
by the practice of *encomienda* (commendation) which had been introduced into the Canary Islands after their recent conquest. The
theory was that if Indians were to be converted into Christians
and to be made civilized, each of their villages should be put under
the protection of an individual Spaniard, who would accept responsibility for undertaking these tasks. In return, the Spaniard would
be entitled to the performance of some services for him by his
village Indians and to receive tribute in gold or other goods. The
way in which this system actually worked was bound to be determined by the character and the attitudes to Indians of the Spaniards

(*encomenderos*) to whom the grants were made, by the opportunities they had for the profitable use of labour, and by the extent to which royal officials or the Church were able to influence their behaviour. In the islands in the first quarter of the century the system was even worse than slavery, for a slave-owner who had paid for his slaves did have an interest in keeping them alive. The Indians of Espanola were driven to work far beyond their strength in gold placer mining, in building and porterage, and were compelled to dig deep into their limited resources of food to maintain Spanish households. Pressing the Indians without mercy or reason, the Spaniards destroyed them; in a few decades the Indian population of Espanola fell from some hundreds of thousands to a few hundred. The Puerto Rican and Cuban populations suffered similar fates, and the Bahamas and some of the Leeward Islands which the Spaniards never settled were raided and stripped of their populations to work the mines of Puerto Rico. The wiser colonists, as well as the crown's advisers, recognized the futility as well as the immorality of this holocaust. Cortes was pursued to Mexico in 1519 by letters from Charles v positively forbidding him to introduce *encomienda* there; and indeed Cortes himself, who had spent twenty years in the islands, was fully convinced of the evils and dangers of the system. But neither Cortes nor his master the emperor could ignore the need to make conquered lands attractive to settlers, and against his instructions and his own inclinations he proceeded rapidly to allocate the Indian villages of Mexico in *encomienda*. It proved far less shattering in Mexico than in the islands. The settled peasantry of Mexico, accustomed to hard work in their own fields and on the lands of nobles and priesthood, were producers of a surplus that was simply transferred to new rulers. Moreover, the mainland gold deposits were trifling, so there was not the same temptation in Mexico as in the islands to drive Indians to work far from their homes. Their numbers were so great that even their humdrum tillage of land could provide substantial incomes for the most-favoured Spaniards and enable these to support bands of Spanish retainers.

In Mexico, and soon afterwards in Peru, the leaders of the Spaniards – Cortes, Avila, the Pizarros and a handful of others – received many thousands of Indian families in *encomienda*, and a considerable number of Spaniards received grants enough to secure them good incomes. The *encomenderos* therefore formed a powerful and wealthy class, with large numbers of Spanish dependants, who had the strongest possible interest in the continuance of the system. The political overtones were alarming to the Spanish crown, conscious always of the way feudal privileges in its European territories hampered its own freedom of action. It had no wish to see such semi-independent powers growing in America and endeavoured to lessen the danger by a long series of modifications in the legal forms of lordship. Though these had a good deal of success, the foundations were nevertheless being firmly laid from which developed the Latin-American society of great landed proprietors and poor peasants that has survived into the present century.

By 1540 the New World was nearly conquered, so far as Spain was ever to conquer it, and the Spanish dominions seemed to be settling down to a mainly agrarian economy after their different and more dramatic beginnings. After the first stage of simple trade in, or seizure of, accumulated gold, and the working of gold deposits, the means to sustained income was coming to be through Spanish overlordship of agrarian society in the most populous areas of the mainland. The island economies changed and went into decline. Their gold production reached its peak in 1511–15, and when it fell away the shipment of bullion to Spain did not again reach such a high level until the Inca treasure hoards of Peru were looted in 1533. Nothing replaced the attractiveness of gold in the islands. The eight thousand Spaniards in Espanola in 1509 had dwindled to a few hundred only ten years later. Merchants bought their rights over land, and a feeble new island economy struggled upward. Sugar plantations were started after 1515 on the lands round the town of Santo Domingo with the aid of skilled workmen brought from the Canaries, and by 1520 export of sugar had begun. These plantations were worked not by Indians, who had been almost wiped out, but by African slaves; the slave trade made its first landings in America as early as 1503, but large shipments began after 1518 when the sugar plantations were being established. The herds of pigs and cattle which had bred from the first Spanish importations increased and roamed wild over the islands as the Indian population disappeared, and many poor Spaniards found congenial employment in rounding up and slaughtering them to provision ships, feed settlements and above all make up cargoes of hides and tallow for Europe. In 1574 there were some 1,500 Spaniards in the islands (mostly in Espanola) and some thousands of Negro slaves.

Mexico changed much less rapidly and completely than the islands, because its agriculture was the Spaniards' most certain source of profit. Though the number of Indians declined very rapidly, Indians still made up much the greatest part of the total population. Under the Spaniards, as under the Aztecs, the principal peasant crops were maize, beans and squashes. New products were introduced by the Spaniards to supply some of their own needs locally and to provide export crops. Wheat cultivation, though it met difficulties in a strange soil and climate, was on a large enough scale to meet local needs by 1560. Cortes introduced silkworm rearing in 1523 as a means of turning some of his huge force of Indian dependants to producing an exportable crop, and it flourished and expanded. Many varieties of European fruits were cultivated successfully but efforts to promote the vine and olive in Mexico fared less well. It was in Peru that, in the latter part of the century, their cultivation was so successful as to supply Spanish needs there and leave some surplus for Mexico. On the lower lands round the fringes of the plateau, sugar planting with African slaves was begun, and supplied the local Spaniards' needs. But despite all the efforts to encourage products that had been familiar in Europe, the most successful export crop was the native cochineal, the best of all red dyestuffs, which found a ready market in Europe from the time of its first shipment in 1526 and remained for three centuries second only to silver in Spanish exports from America.

But the Spanish innovation that transformed American rural life was the introduction of domesticated animals. The Indians had none but the dog; the Spaniards brought numbers of horses, cattle, sheep and pigs, which bred even more rapidly on the wide empty hill spaces of the mainland than they had done in the islands. The gentlemanly life in Spain was associated with pastoral economy, and for the man with a horse and no fortune cattle herding was a good deal less distasteful than other forms of work in the New World. As the Indian population declined precipitously in the course of the century, moreover, herds and flocks tended by a couple of men could be grazed over abandoned lands once tilled by hundreds of peasants. Long before this – indeed as early as the 1540s – animals overstocked the hill country of central Mexico and were encroaching on the cultivated land of villages. The government defended the cultivators, imposing restrictions on the number of animals that might be kept on each land grant, requiring the fencing-off of crops; and it encouraged the opening of ranching beyond the areas of cultivation, in the lands of the nomad Indians to the north. In the meantime, cattle and sheep were changing the ways of life and work beyond the ranches. The Indians added meat to their diet, adopted woollen clothing, and saw draught animals – especially mules – coming in gradually to replace human porterage. The new flocks of sheep made it possible to establish a woollen cloth industry on Mexican soil. Aztec Mexico had a big production of cotton fabrics, and large numbers of skilled craftsmen could be turned over to producing warm woollens which Indians as well as Spaniards were glad to adopt to meet the cold winters of the plateau. Woollen manufacture was begun in Spanish-owned workshops in many towns and villages, and some of the worst features of Indian exploitation appeared in these; but the woollen blanket became a characteristic article of Indian culture. Cattle provided large quantities of tallow and hides for export, earning money in Spain for American ranchers and filling the holds of homeward-bound ships. And finally, as we shall see, it was the extension of ranching into the north that led to the discovery and working of silver mines there, carrying the Mexican economy into a new phase of development in the second half of the century.

Peru was developed more slowly, because the Indian wars and the civil wars of the conquerors were not concluded until 1548, and the country did not settle firmly in the grip of royal government until the 1560s. By that time the silver deposits of Potosí were being exploited and the Spaniards in Peru never had to depend on agriculture to provide for trade with the world outside. Apart from the mines, it remained largely a country of subsistence agriculture, but it widened its range of products with vines, olives and cattle and was gradually able to draw away from its partial dependence on Mexico.

The Spanish population of the New World was no more than a few tens of thousands in the middle of the sixteenth century, and within this the number remaining of the original conquerors was small. A few hundred of these, together with those of the later arrivals who possessed influence at the court of king or viceroy, had substantial *encomiendas* that enabled them to live comfortably, with their families brought from Spain, amid circles of dependent Spanish retainers. Most of them had their residences in Mexico City, the one place with a big concentrated Spanish population. Here were Spanish merchants, a growing body of artisans, great numbers of priests (for the work of converting the Indians was taken very seriously) and an underworld of poor Spaniards who made the best living they could. Mexico City – and Lima in Peru – were great administrative centres, residences of the viceroys and their councils and of a host of officials responsible ultimately to Spain.

With the gradual passing away of the original conquerors, the crown set to work to break down the structure of *encomienda* in which it had at first reluctantly acquiesced. The morality of these grants had long been fiercely questioned by the Church, and the crown was anxious to curb the independence of *encomenderos* and prevent them forming a hereditary aristocracy. The establishment in 1535 of the Viceroyalty of New Spain (that is, central and southern Mexico) was intended to begin the eradication of any tendency towards the devolution of power in Mexico, and the 'New Laws' that Charles v promulgated in 1542 aimed at destroying the foundation on which hereditary wealth and power were being created. These laws declared that Indians should not be compelled to work against their will; they abolished certain types of *encomienda*, ordered that the original ones should escheat to the crown on the death of their holders, and totally prohibited the creation of new ones. The New Laws were too drastic to be enforceable at once; the first Viceroy of Peru, Blasco Nuñez, provoked a violent Spanish rebellion when he arrived in 1544 and proposed to enforce them rigidly, and there were dangerous stirrings in Mexico. Nevertheless the heyday of *encomienda* had passed. The laws rapidly made the working of the system more innocuous; the right to demand the services of Indians, which was dangerously akin to slavery, was abolished after 1549, and the remaining right to tribute was gradually assumed in the following decades by the state, which paid over what was due to the *encomenderos* as a kind of state pension. Control over the Indians passed into the hands of royal officials acting through the village headmen, and jealously watched by priests who regarded themselves as guardians of the Indians; forced labour, now known as *repartimiento*, became a prerogative of royal service alone, though officials could hire out Indians to private service or the mines. Thus the personal authority of the *encomenderos* was undermined (though, as we shall see, they recovered much of it in other forms), the threat of a new feudal structure in the Indies was weakened, and the remarkable ascendancy of royal officials was established throughout the Indies. The pressure on

Indians relaxed a little, and its operation became less arbitrary in the hands of royal officials.

Grants of *encomienda* were rights over people, rights to services and tribute. They were not grants of land, and most of the good land of the valleys and plateaus remained in the hands of the Indian peasants. The colonial government was diligent to preserve Indians' land in heavily cultivated areas, to the extent of making it impossible for Indian communities to transfer their lands to Spaniards. Interspersed with the peasant lands in Mexico were big tracts that had supported the Aztec nobility or its religious establishment, and much of this was initially appropriated after the conquest by these nobles or by village headmen. Nevertheless, after mid-century there was an accelerating transfer of cultivable land to Spaniards. A good deal of noble land was sold, and Indians of all kinds willed land to the Church; from 1536 the authorities began to make land grants in regular form, and if at first this was in less well-populated areas, after 1550 much land that became vacant in the Puebla district south of Mexico City was granted to Spaniards for wheat cultivation. Grants were more readily made of the poorer hill country which was suitable only for rough grazing, and cattle and sheep multiplied fast in these empty lands. Land grants – generally known as *estancia* – were easily obtained by anyone who had a claim on or influence with an official; and naturally many of them went in fact to the same powerful and wealthy individuals who had grants of *encomienda*, though they disguised multiple ownership in the names of relations and dependants. Moreover, many of the smaller men who first obtained grants of this kind were ruined by the fall in the price of meat at the end of the 1530s and had to sell out, so that before mid-century a great part of Mexican grazing had come into the hands of a few rich men who owned enormous flocks and herds.

The herds of central Mexico grew quickly to the limit the land could support, and a further big expansion of ranching could take place only by breaking out to the north, across the frontier of settlement into the lands of the nomadic Indians. From the 1540s cattle herds began to be driven farther north. Land grants of immense size were readily made by the government if they were outside the area already under Spanish control, and the richest and most powerful ranchers were encouraged to create new settlements, maintain ways of communication with them and bring some sort of order and government into the areas so handed over. The movement was first into the north-west (New Galicia) where the Indians were least dangerous; the drive due north into the heart of the territory of the hostile Chichimecs (New Biscay) became vigorous only when silver mines were discovered there. To the north-east, a handful of graziers, each with flocks of scores of thousands of sheep, took over the relatively empty lands of New Leon towards the end of the century. By 1565–70 the number of animals in central and southern Mexico had ceased to expand but growth in ranching continued in the north until the end of the century.

The colonization of the north for cattle and sheep ranching was a great pioneering achievement, creating new sources of wealth and power for a few individuals; but it took effect in the second half of the sixteenth century, when it was completely overshadowed by the results of the discoveries of great silver deposits.

Gold hoards and gold workings were big enough to maintain Spanish interest in the New World for half a century after 1492, but the total amount they provided made only a modest addition to Europe's existing supplies. Until after 1533 its annual value never exceeded that of the gold the Portuguese brought from the west coast of Africa. Silver came in quantities that were not large, though they ate into the profitability of European mining. The hoards of Mexico and Peru kept alive the hope of new finds – of Eldorado and the Seven Cities of Cibola – but what actually remained to be discovered was not a treasury of accumulated wealth, but gold and silver mines to be worked. The first great discovery of workable deposits was the gold of the Magdalena river valley in Colombia in 1537; but it was the spectacular silver discoveries of the following decade that transformed the whole economic situation of the Spanish Empire.

The silver deposits of Potosí in Peru were discovered in 1545; those of Zacatecas in northern Mexico in 1546. A wave of prospecting followed the end of the civil wars of the conquerors in Peru, and it was inevitable that the 'mountain of silver' at Potosí, near old Inca silver mines and probably well known to the Indians, should have been discovered quickly. The Mexican discoveries, however, were associated with the new northward drive of the cattle ranchers. Exploration to the north was made possible by the suppression of a large-scale Indian rebellion, the so-called Mixton War of 1540–2; the Zacatecas silver deposits were discovered in 1546, and within four years they were the site of a big mining camp with stamp mills and ore refineries, fifty mine owners, slaves, Indian workers and a few traders. This carried the frontier far north of the slowly advancing line of firmly settled ranches and missions, and a road with supporting settlements was developed to bring supplies of foodstuffs, lead and mercury for refining from the south. From Zacatecas a series of new mine discoveries was made between 1548 and 1574 and settlements were established on them, stretching northward to Santa Barbara and Charcas. Development took place under great difficulties, for the hostility of the Chichimecs was inflamed by attempts to enslave them to work in the mines. A long war of sporadic raids and punitive expeditions brought soldiers to the region in large numbers, and fortified settlements were set up. Permanent ranching, and patches of cultivation, developed round these as well as the mines. Indian war prevented further northward advance until serious efforts at pacification were made after 1585. Thereafter the mining frontier moved on, to San Luis Potosí in 1598, Ramos in 1608 and the last big finds at Parral in 1631–3.

The early discoveries were easily worked from the surface, but by 1570 networks of shafts and tunnels going deep into the hills were essential. Large-scale silver mining could only be continued with the introduction of new techniques. The Basques, who were often the prospectors, had little experience of silver mining and ore reduction, and this was organized on modern lines largely by Germans, who came to Mexico first in the 1530s and 1540s, and then in a new wave in the 1570s as the technical problems were changing. They introduced the mercury amalgamation process, which could handle ores of poor quality, to Mexico in 1556 and Peru in 1573. Spain possessed the two major deposits of mercury, at Almadén in Spain which served the early Mexican industry, and at Huancavelica in Peru, where the mine found in 1563 served Mexican and Peruvian needs until the Peruvian demand absorbed it all. About the same time, water-powered crushing machinery was introduced to Mexico and Peru. Mining rapidly became a capital-intensive operation, for the costs of tunnelling, stamp mills and pumping machinery were heavy. Some of the early miners had already made fortunes sufficiently large to finance this new-style industry, but most of the later comers were financed by advances from merchants or religious institutions and saw little of the profit of mining operations themselves. Labour costs rose rapidly, for the local Indians in Mexico died if they were enslaved for the mines and the government would allow only small numbers of forced labourers to be sent up from the south. Some Negro slaves were brought in but in the long run the mines had to attract free Indians by the offer of relatively high wages.

The silver mines were new centres of demand, towards which the Spanish owners of lands and herds in Mexico could send their produce. In the early years the mines were fed and supplied entirely from the south, and even when the greater proprietors built up ranches round their properties these supplied little more than meat, tallow and hides. Wheat and all other foods had to be carried northward, along with the local and imported manufactures that the mines needed. So silver flowed into the pockets of Spanish proprietors living in the towns of central Mexico, and from them to town merchants, artisans and professional men. This enormously increased the economic activity of the towns, and in the last decades of the century the Mexican economy came to revolve around the mines. Moreover, most of this silver, along with the royal fifth from the mines collected by officials, and remittances made for their own purposes by mine owners and financiers, eventually went on to Spain. From the beginning of the 1550s Mexico's trading relations with Spain were transformed, with remittances of silver rising in each decade to the end of the century, and the problem of paying for goods imported from Europe disappeared. On the contrary, Mexico was able to buy ever-increasing quantities of luxuries from Europe.

The transformation in Peru was even more striking, for the single site at Potosí produced, in the last quarter of the sixteenth century, far more silver than all Mexico. The high plateau from which the 'silver mountain' rose was barren, and the whole supply for the mining complex and the city of Potosí had to be brought up from the coast and the valleys. Within four years of the discovery there was a substantial town at the mine and by 1570 the concentration of miners, porters, traders, craftsmen and officials reached a total of 120,000 people, making Potosí the largest town in either Old or New Spain. The labour was Indian, at first hired from local *caciques*, but this source soon became inadequate to meet the demand. It was supplemented from 1559 by the labour of Indians who had been condemned to death or exile, and then in 1573, faced with a worsening shortage in a rapidly declining population, the viceroy prescribed that forced labour might be drawn from Indians working out the payment of their tribal tribute to the crown (*mita*) in a defined group of villages in the neighbourhood of Potosí.

The silver was shipped out through the ports of Arica and Arequipa, but the centre of trade and the finance of mining was the capital, Lima. There, all silver was supposed to be assayed and registered by royal officials, and the king's fifth was extracted at this point. But it was not difficult to evade this regulation, for Potosí was on the east side of the main ranges of the Andes, close to the upper reaches of the Pilcomayo river that led down a course of fifteen hundred miles to the river Plate, with its hovering Portuguese traders. The Spanish port of Buenos Ayres was established in 1580 to keep the Portuguese away, but itself became a smuggling base.

In Peru, as in Mexico, the scale of silver exploitation helped to sustain an urban civilization with a trading and professional middle class between the few rich *encomenderos* and the Indian labourers, and to develop local markets for the produce of the land. The merchants of Lima became financiers of the mines and drew most of the profits into their own hands, and the concentration of people at the mines made work for traders and carriers. As in Mexico these demands, providing outlets for the produce of great estates, made it less necessary for the owners to develop export crops. Peru remained a country producing for its own needs, gradually extending its range to vines, olives and animals as well as cereals, drawing away from dependence on Mexico, remitting silver to Spain in such quantities and for so little return that towards the end of the century the name *perulisto* was coined for homecoming colonists who were investing in Spain itself.

For over half a century – from 1550 to 1610 – the economies of Peru and (to a somewhat lesser extent) Mexico centred on the mines, the needs of the mining communities and the trading opportunities they presented. Indians and some Negro slaves worked the mines; Spanish miners directed them and took some share of the gains; merchants and religious foundations financed mines and smelters and profited from them; farmers in north-central Mexico and in Peru directed their production to the mines; the king took his fifth and his American officials what they could. But though the economy was dominated by the mines, serving Europe's apparently insatiable demand for silver, society remained primarily agricultural, most people working on the land, and the basic agrarian institutions survived and adapted as the mines began to decline.

Agriculture was profoundly modified by the demands of the mining townships. Even more, in the long run, its form was determined by the continuing spread of Spanish habits because of the steady if small influx of Spaniards, and the increase of mixed breeds and their adaptation to Spanish culture. The most powerful influence, however, was the continuing fall in Indian population, which by 1600 made it impossible to maintain cultivation on the old scale. If the prosperous economies which emerged both from the stumblings and difficulties of mid-century Mexico, and from the chaos of mid-century Peru, depended too much on mineral exploitation, this gave them a breathing space in which a more diversified and reasonably self-sufficient economy grew up, adapted to a reduced population. Half a century after Columbus the economic results of Spain's American conquests were still limited and their future conjectural; even the appearance of syphilis in Europe around 1500 is no longer confidently blamed on Columbus' seamen.

The Spanish impact on the New World, on the other hand, was from the beginning of a kind and a magnitude which the mind can hardly compass. The island Indians were wiped out quickly; the more advanced peoples were reduced more slowly but in the long run nearly as drastically. The population of the Americas in 1500 may have equalled that of Europe, and was certainly not vastly different; in 1600 it is unlikely that it was a tenth of Europe's. In the lands of peasant cultivation in central Mexico some small part of the population was driven to death by excessive labour in the mines and elsewhere, but an immense toll of the native peasantry was taken by diseases of Europe which the conquerors unwittingly brought with them. Throughout the sixteenth century smallpox, measles and typhus struck in waves of a ferocity Europe had not known since the Black Death. The Espanola smallpox epidemic of 1518–19 spread into central Mexico immediately ahead of Cortes's conquest. By 1540 the population was no more than half its pre-conquest level of twenty-five million; and the violent epidemics of 1545–6 and 1576–8 were big waves in a continuing process that brought numbers down to a little more than a million by the end of the century.

Little is known about Peru's original population, though it was almost certainly smaller than Mexico's. Much reduced in the 1520s by European diseases spreading from the north some years before the Spaniards themselves arrived, it was down to one and a half million in 1561 and continued to decline all through the seventeenth century. Despite the great savagery of early Spanish rule in Peru, it is certain that there too the principal reason for the continuing fall in population – which is well attested by literary evidence – was European disease. Indians were not replaced by Spaniards; even the contemporary estimate of 160,000 Spaniards living in America in 1574 is probably excessive.

Nearly all migrants from Europe were men; in consequence the pure-blooded Spaniards came to be outnumbered quite soon by the *mestizos* (of Spanish and Indian blood) and the *mulattos* (Spanish and African). These were the groups whose numbers were eventually to become dominant in Latin America. By 1650 there were half a million 'considered to be white' – including a great number of people of mixed race who were sufficiently Spanish in appearance and culture to pass; nearly as many Negroes, mostly in the islands and the Caribbean coast; a similar number of acknowledged mixed blood; and perhaps two million pure Indians in Mexico and the central Andean regions of Peru and Bolivia. Allowing for unacknowledged mixtures, there were few pure Spaniards and probably no more than half the population was pure Indian. Spain built a new society in America, based on a European model albeit much distorted by the legacy of its Indian background; but Spain's principal gift to America was the destruction of its people.

4 *Sixteenth-century Spain*

*S*pain is a land of great geographical diversity. The north is a narrow wet coastal belt backed by high mountains that cut it off from the arid interior plateau interspersed with mountain ranges which slope down to warmer Mediterranean coastlands to the east, and to the wetter coast and river valleys of Andalusia and Granada in the south. Each of these regions had its natural centre – Bilbao, Valladolid, Barcelona, Seville – and Spain's Habsburg rulers, Charles v (1516–56) and Philip ii (1556–98) struggled to overcome the tendencies that pulled the regions apart, and symbolized their considerable success by making Madrid, in the dry heart of Spain, a new capital which became a genuine centre for its kingdom. For although the Spanish crowns had been united by the marriage of Ferdinand of Aragon and Isabella of Castile and their joint accession to the thrones of the two kingdoms in 1479, and their descendants remained rulers of both, this was simply a dynastic union. Aragon and Castile remained constitutionally separate, in much the same way as England and Scotland between 1603 and 1707, with separate laws and institutions, with customs barriers and jealously preserved local privileges; it was only the activity of the crown that joined them.

Most of Mediterranean Spain was embraced within the dominions of the kingdom of Aragon – Aragon, Catalonia and Valencia. The kingdom of Aragon had flourished in the Middle Ages, developing a large woollen industry in its Catalonian cities and a trading and financial centre at Barcelona that rivalled Genoa. It was a Mediterranean power that added much of southern Italy to its territory in the early fifteenth century, and this came eventually, along with

Aragon, to the Habsburgs. Yet already the growth of the Italian woollen industry had encroached on Catalonia's Mediterranean markets, and the extension of Genoa's commercial influence on the western Mediterranean undermined the prosperity of Barcelona. The mercantile leaders gradually abandoned industry and commerce for moneylending, and between 1462 and 1472 civil war struck blows at public confidence that seriously damaged the financial community. Though Aragon made some recovery during the sixteenth century, it failed to keep up with the progress of Castile, and was prevented by Castilian jealousy and Genoese influence from securing closer economic ties with Castile or any direct part in the exploitation of Castile's American Empire.

The kingdom of Castile embraced most of the area of Spain, and at the end of the fifteenth century more than five-sixths of its population. So far as it looked outward, it was to the Atlantic through Bilbao and Cadiz rather than to the Mediterranean. Castile itself was sharply divided into regions. The thickly populated Cantabrian coastlands and mountain valleys of the north, a land of fishermen and small farmers, contained the ports that carried on much of Spain's trade with north-western Europe, as well as shipbuilding and iron-making; the central plateaus of Old and New Castile were largely given over to pastoral activity but had substantial areas of peasant cultivation and a scattering of important towns that were centres of industry or of wool trading; and the fertile and well-watered lands of Andalusia and Granada in the south, still thinly populated in the fifteenth century, grew corn, wine and olives on peasant lands and great estates, supplying the cities of Seville and Cadiz that linked the trade of the Mediterranean and the Atlantic.

Castile as a whole was a land of very great estates, the property of crown, nobles and Church, that were cultivated by a depressed peasantry, interspersed in the south with large holdings worked by day labourers. Most of Castile had been recovered from Moorish rule only during the previous three centuries, and extreme inequality and the slender rights of the peasantry derived from the distribution of Moorish lands among knightly conquerors, and the subjection of a race of cultivators who were largely descendants of the conquered. The nobles to whom the crown had surrendered local jurisdiction were able to use the economic and social influence this gave them, and the threat of allegations of uncompleted conversion to Christianity, to override the strict rights of the peasantry and to dispossess tenants where they saw economic advantage in doing so. If this made possible some advance towards rational use of land resources, its social consequences in maintaining most of the population in deep poverty were in the long run disastrous.

The most notable example of specialized rural production was the long-established sheep rearing of Old and New Castile, which provided wool for Aragonese, Italian and Netherlands woollen industries. Most of the interior of Castile was dry and infertile, with a rainfall that was light, largely concentrated in the winter months and, worst of all, erratic, so that moderate average rainfall conceals years of abundant rain intermingled with too frequent droughts. Nevertheless, Old Castile was quite thickly populated, and until late in the sixteenth century its cultivators were able to produce a corn surplus that supplied the needs of the towns of much of Spain. It was the growth of population in Old Castile, swallowing up this surplus in the third quarter of the century, that drove Spain into regular corn import. Above all, however, Castile was the domain of the *Mesta*, the gild of sheep rearers whose flocks were driven seasonally between the north and south of Spain to graze its thin pastures. Here more than anywhere else in western Europe the interest of grazier and cultivator clashed, and the desires of the peasants, trying to raise grain crops, to prevent the encroachment of animals and to extend their fields were made to give way to the pastoralists' claims for free grazing, which were violently enforced by migrant shepherds conscious of the power of the noble owners of the flocks they were tending. From the time of Ferdinand and Isabella the rulers of Castile consistently backed the wool-producing interests, which were sources both of taxes that were easily assessed and of export earnings. The crown confirmed the extensive grazing privileges of the *Mesta* in 1501, and time after time – in 1480, 1489, 1525 and 1552 – decreed that lands which had been turned to arable should be reconverted to pasture. Royal financial needs, it is true, dictated the imposition of heavy customs duties on wool exports in 1558, but even then the woollen interests were relatively well treated.

A strong Castilian merchant class grew up to handle the trade in wool. Burgos had been nurtured as a mercantile centre by Genoese and Florentine capital, but at the height of the wool trade in the first half of the sixteenth century it was dominated by Spaniards. The wool fairs of Villalon, Medina de Rio Seco and above all Medina del Campo had a European importance, and the last-named continued to be a centre of European financial and banking operations for some decades after the wool trade went into decline. For, in the middle of the sixteenth century, the general malaise coming over central Europe spread its influence to the hills of Old Castile; the demand for Flemish textiles slackened and was reflected in declining export of Spanish wool. The collapse of the woollen industry of the southern Netherlands during the wars of the 1570s brought an end to the long prosperity of the Spanish sheep graziers. The Castilian fairs were badly hit by the decline of the trade, but the cause of their final ruin was the collapse of royal finances, sapping the confidence necessary to centres of foreign exchange business. The state bankruptcy of 1575 marked the beginning of the end, though Medina del Campo survived in a weakened state until the end of the century.

The agricultural economy of the far south was a different one, but becoming equally export-oriented. Here, in the Guadalquivir valley and along the southern coastlands, all kinds of fruit and olives could be grown. Their cultivation was steadily extended as European prosperity brought an increasing demand, augmented presently from the American colonies. The landowner found that direct production of these things on his own land or through substantial lessees, using hired day-labour, brought a greater return than he could get from the rents of peasant corn producers – particularly as corn could readily be imported by sea into this area. Andalusia had always taken some corn from northern Spain, and during the fifteenth century was importing it in years of bad harvests from Sicily, France and later the Baltic. The natural increase of population was augmented by migration from Old Castile into the towns and to work in the vineyards and olive groves; so corn prices were rising even before 1500 and after 1535 the rise was severe. Even so, the south still found it worth while to expand its production of fruits and wine, setting low labour costs against the rising value of land under corn, and in the latter part of the century was regularly importing much of its corn supply. When, late in the sixteenth century, the price of corn was again rising steeply despite the government's efforts to check it, cultivation was extended to lands in northern Castile made available by the decline in the demand for wool, rather than at the expense of orchard and vineyard cultivation in the south.

Agricultural wealth was concentrated in the hands of those great landowners who controlled sheep grazings, or big estates in the south. Though there was a scattering of modestly prosperous farmers everywhere, the majority of peasants in the Cantabrian valleys and on the Castilian plateau lived in great poverty. The gains from rising prices, from which producers should have benefited, seem generally to have gone to the landlords, except in the mid-century decades of very rapid price rise and good harvests. Although, as elsewhere in Europe, ancient feudal dues were not easily altered and lost much of their real value in a period of rising prices, Spanish landlords did not have great difficulty in getting rid of old customary tenures and imposing new terms with high and rising rents, or taking over land to work themselves with day labourers. Around Seville much land was bought or leased by town merchants, and their investment was responsible for much of the development of vineyards and orchards. The increasingly labour-intensive cultivation of Andalusia attracted a large migration from Old and New Castile, but it offered a hard and ill-rewarded life on the land, and many northern peasants preferred to seek a new fortune in the cities, or to press farther on, across the ocean to America.

The ending of nearly twenty years of civil war in Castile and Aragon in 1480, and the consolidation under Ferdinand and Isabella that followed, opened a phase of continuing economic expansion in Castile that was hardly checked before 1560 and was not decisively turned back until almost the end of the sixteenth century.

The growth of population that was experienced throughout Europe in the late fifteenth century was slowed in Castile by a number of special factors. The civil wars of the 1460s were very destructive, and the wars in Italy in the first years of the next century, which forged a Spanish infantry that was to command European battlefields for more than a century, took the lives of great numbers of them. There was migration from the Pyrenean region into France during the years round 1500, and a modest emigration to America after 1493. Above all, the religious campaign whipped up in Isabella's reign against converted Jews (*conversos*) and the introduction of the Inquisition to smell out doubtful Christians in 1480, caused many thousands of them to emigrate. This campaign was capped in 1492 by a decision to deport all Jews who would not renounce their faith, and in that year some 150,000 were forced to go – to Portugal, Africa, Turkey and Flanders – largely from the south of Spain, where they had made up a considerable part of the artisan and trading population. Adding to this the Moorish exodus from Granada after it was conquered in 1492, a total of some half a million people left Spain, voluntarily or under pressure, during the half century after 1480. When the heaviest emigration had ceased and the last of the civil wars of Castile was over, in 1521, the growth of population was very rapid for some decades, slowing in the last quarter of the century because of losses in new dynastic and religious wars and the beginnings of food shortages – in the bad harvests after 1580 – that began to sap the resistance of the poor to disease. In the course of the sixteenth century the total population of Spain grew from less than six million to a peak of over eight million in the 1580s, from which it was to fall suddenly in the very last years of the century.

Population growth was spread very unevenly. It was heaviest in the central region, Old Castile, which was the recipient of a continual flow of migrants from the always overpopulated mountainous region to the north, not fully balanced by the onward movement of migrants to Andalusia. There was a strongly-marked movement from the countryside into the towns, many of them doubling their population between 1530 and 1590. Seville's population passed a hundred thousand, and such towns as Bilbao, the Cantabrian port and shipbuilding centre, the industrial towns of Cordoba, Toledo, Segovia and Cuenca, and above all the new administrative capital Madrid, grew very fast. On the other hand, a few of the towns of Old Castile began to lose population with the decline of the wool trade in the 1570s. There was a net movement, too, into southern agriculture. This migration was beneficial both to Castile and to the south, where rural and urban demand was heavy. The persistent labour needs of the south attracted the Portuguese slave dealers and by 1600 there were a hundred thousand African slaves in Spain.

Rising population, the growing rents and profits of sheep rearing, vineyards, olive groves and orchards, and in mid-century of corn growing, joined the profits of merchants and the expenditures of the crown to expand the market for products of industry. In the sixteenth century, American colonial demands were added to those of the home market. Though the mass of the poor bought their few industrial needs from local artisans, the well-to-do were customers for a number of specialized industries situated in the towns. Castilian industry expanded vigorously through the first half of the sixteenth century and maintained itself in the face of growing difficulties into the 1580s. The woollen cloth of the town producers was of a middling quality that sold well in competition with imports from Aragon and Italy and found overseas markets in Portugal and Italy as well as in Castile's American possessions. The silks of Malaga, Granada and Murcia had good markets at home and in Italy, and though the industry was severely set back by the expulsion and flight of the *conversos* at the end of the fifteenth century, it slowly recovered and from the 1530s achieved a rapid new expansion based on the import of cheap raw silk from Mexico. Leather working was another high quality industry, centred on Cordoba and selling its produce throughout southern Europe, and it benefited after the 1530s from the supplies of cheap hides and skins shipped from America. And in the north, the Biscay iron industry went through a technical revolution at the beginning of the sixteenth century, going over rapidly to using the blast furnace and water power, so that it was well situated to cope with rising shipbuilding, armament and export demands.

Yet industry laboured under many difficulties. Some branches of it were damaged by the flight of the *conversos*; the speed of recovery from this blow testifies to the strength of demand in Spain in this period. Nearly all industry was in the towns, and industrial expansion coincided with the beginning of vigorous promotion by the government of Ferdinand and Isabella of gilds of urban craftsmen. Although in the beginning these gilds gave encouragement to the development of particular industrial groups, assuring them of some stability in their markets, they inevitably introduced elements of rigidity and conservatism. The woollen industry, favoured by growing supplies of wool of the kind suited to making light cloths – which were most demanded in Spain – did not attempt competition with the heavy woollen cloths that England made. But it soon began to encounter, in the Spanish market, Flemish and Dutch light cloths that were being brought into large-scale production at this time, and were made of Spanish wool whose export the state encouraged. Finally the industrial policy of the crown tended to favour consumers. The crown put few obstacles in the way of imports; under the pressure of rising prices it actually banned the export of Spanish woollens to America for a few years after 1552; between 1552 and 1558 it encouraged merchants exporting wool to bring back some of the proceeds of their sales in the form of woollen cloth.

American colonization had only a limited effect on economic activity until the great flow of mined silver began in the 1550s. From the beginning it had rapidly increased the commercial activity of the city of Seville. The monarchs determined that all trade with America should be centralized and kept under strict surveillance, and to this end they established the *Casa de Contración* (which may be interpreted as Department of Trade) at Seville in 1504, through which all shipping bound to the Indies had to be cleared and all goods and bullion in American trade registered. Though Seville was situated eighty miles up a winding river, it was sufficiently accessible to the ships used in the early Atlantic traffic, and was thoroughly secure. Seville was already the centre of Andalusian commerce, a large and rich city and the long-established place of business of the richest merchants and financiers in southern Spain. Through Seville, therefore, flowed the gold of the Caribbean islands and the treasures of Mexico and Peru, and presently a more humdrum trade in Mexican dyestuffs and hides. Seville, Cadiz and the surrounding region gained through the provisioning and arming of the trade. Wine and oil, and Spanish manufactures of all kinds, found a substantial demand in America, and despite the early attractiveness of the trade to Flemish and English merchants who sent their goods through Seville, their competition did not prevent Spanish industry securing a useful new market. The ships used in the Atlantic trade were built on the Basque coast, requiring a huge expansion in the scale of shipbuilding to provide for the forty thousand tons of shipping going to America each year in the 1540s, rising to a peak of four times that level at the end of the century. Ocean-going ships of 200–300 tons, which were large for their time, were required in numbers altogether unknown before.

Beyond this, if we bear in mind that until after 1530 colonization hardly repaid the Spanish outlay on it, and that colonists would have been consumers in Spain itself – albeit on a smaller scale – if the New World had not been discovered, the influence of America on Spanish economic development was not very large before the middle of the sixteenth century. Moreover, an important part of the profit of trade itself went to the Genoese, who had long dominated the overseas trade of the south and who provided the richer part of the merchant class of Seville. The Castilians who had driven the Moors from southern Spain during the thirteenth century were nobles, who had neither the wealth nor the experience to exploit the commercial opportunities opened by their advance. Italians had at once moved in to carry the trade in Andalusian produce, and using Cadiz as an intermediate stopping place in long-distance trade they sent galleys from Pisa, Genoa and Venice to voyage regularly to Bruges and London. Cadiz developed into an important port, sending out oil, wine, dyestuffs and mercury as well as Moroccan and Canary sugar. Seville became the centre from which Italians organized the trade, a great city gathering together the products of southern Spain, not merely for export but also for the Andalusian nobility who made it their capital, and for the industries that served their needs. Seville and Cadiz did not shake off Italian influence as Burgos had done, and at the time of Columbus's voyage the large-scale and particularly the overseas trade of Seville was mainly in Genoese hands, though at lower levels Spanish merchants were active. Genoese business houses, through their branches in Seville, had already taken an important part in Spanish enterprise in the Atlantic, financing the development of sugar production in the Canaries and controlling its trade; they went on to share in the financing of the new American trades and acquired some footholds in the New World itself. Their influence was even further enhanced when, in 1528, a political turnabout brought Genoa into permanent political alliance with Spain, and the Genoese began to take over the financial business of the Spanish crown which had briefly come into the hands of Charles v's Flemish and German bankers.

During most of the sixteenth century Spain was flourishing economically. The bounding energy of the late fifteenth century could survive all the mass emigrations of the persecuted; the extraordinary pace of American conquest and settlement was parallelled only by the rapidity with which the central government asserted control over its empire four thousand miles away; industrial and agricultural expansion, though most marked in the south, was apparent in Old Castile as well; Spanish merchants were becoming more active and wide-ranging, more sophisticated in their methods, establishing their own factors abroad in Bruges, Rouen and Antwerp, and enormously expanding their shipping. Around the middle of the century all the indicators suggested that Spain had entered on a long pathway of rapid growth. If food supply was becoming precarious in Spain itself, American silver and cochineal would readily buy it; if labour was scarce in the prospering areas of the south, migration from the north or slaves from Africa would fill the gap. The most obvious sign of stress, rising prices, was the local aspect of a phenomenon of more than European dimensions, observed in America and at least in the Turkish corner of Asia, and it looked for a time as though the worst phase had already passed in the 1530s and 1540s. The brief faltering of some indicators of economic activity in the early 1550s marked a European crisis, not one that was felt in Spain alone.

Yet some writers have claimed that Spain was already in economic decline by 1560, and few would deny that there were serious strains on the economy during the later sixteenth century that made it less able to meet the catastrophes that struck from 1595 onward. Three particularly powerful and closely connected influences can be identified, weakening the forward drive of the Spanish economy: the excessive demands of the state, the rapid rise of prices, and the worsening conditions of the poorer independent producers in agriculture and industry.

At the heart of Spain's troubles was the dynasty that involved it in the affairs of all Europe. Too powerful among the states of Europe, so that it attempted to don the mantle of supreme protector of Catholic Christianity against the dual attack of European Christian heresies and of the old Muslim enemy in Asia and Africa; too powerful at home once it had crushed the revolt of the *Comuneros* which had in 1521 attempted to assert the liberties of Castile against its king, the Habsburg dynasty was able to drain the resources of Spain – or rather of Castile – in causes Castile had little concern in. After 1521 there was no effective check to the dynasty using Castile to support its own ambitions. No serious invader touched Spanish soil but its own kings ravaged it.

Charles v split up the Habsburg Empire in 1555 and his successor, Philip II, inherited Spain and America, the Netherlands and parts of Italy, but not the central European lands of the Habsburgs. Philip II inherited, too, the traditional convictions of the Habsburgs of their right and indeed duty to take the chief place in the politics of western Europe, and the responsibility for defending Catholic lands from Muslims and heretics alike and recovering those that had been lost. At first sight these ambitions do not seem hopelessly outside the compass of the ruler whose empire in Europe alone embraced some thirteen to fourteen million people, including two of Europe's richest states (the Netherlands and the Duchy of Milan), and that was profiting from the new riches of the American continent. Yet this was a mistaken view of an empire that was now based on Spain. The advance into America was in the main line of Spanish development: a step by Castilian conquerors to military conquest and rule of lands held by non-Christians, following on from the reconquest of Spain from the Moors which had extended over many centuries and was only completed in 1492. But the Habsburg consciousness of their European role, which led them into endless continental wars, derived from the territories and status of their dynasty in central Europe. The Spaniards who were compelled to sustain the costs and military burdens of Philip II's European ambitions had little interest in – or indeed knowledge of – what went on outside Spain. Moreover, the resources of Flanders and Italy, that had given some support to the dynastic and religious aims of Charles V, ceased soon after Philip II's accession to make any much contribution. His policies had to be furthered by the resources of Spain alone, and within Spain by the kingdom of Castile – together with its American dependency. In Castile alone the king ruled subject only to weak constitutional restraints. In the first decades of the sixteenth century the crown had reduced the pretensions of the Castilian nobility and towns, so that the representative body, the Cortes, could obstruct but not in the last resort prevent royal tax-raising and the mobilization of troops (though even within Castile the Basque and Asturian provinces retained special privileges). Charles V's energies had soon to turn from continuing domestic political reforms in Spain (in the contemporary terms of establishing a more absolute government) to his European wars. In the remainder of his dominions, therefore, which Philip II inherited in 1556 – in Aragon, Catalonia, Valencia and Navarre, in Milan, Naples and the Netherlands – the ruler's authority continued to be closely limited by the entrenched privileges of individuals, corporations and cities, which Philip II had sworn at his accession to maintain. Solemn and binding constitutional promises made by himself and his predecessors required him to secure the express consent of the local form of representative assembly to any new taxation, any raising of troops. Again and again attempts to override these privileges led to revolt. The Netherlands revolt, which in the long run ruined Philip II, found its first leaders in nobles who resented encroachment on their privileges; in the next century his bankrupt successors, still seeking to recover the Netherlands, attempted to break through the taxation privileges of Catalonia and Portugal, bringing about their revolts in 1640 and the loss of Portugal; the Naples revolt of 1647 was sparked off by new taxation. Portugal and half the Netherlands were lost; eastern Spain and the Italian possessions were retained, but their essentially medieval institutions remained almost unchanged for two more centuries. To secure Italy and the parts of the Netherlands that remained Spanish, military expenditures even in peacetime in the seventeenth century exceeded the local revenues; these places were still burdens on Castile, rather than supports of the King of Spain's empire.

So the costs of empire fell mainly on Castile; on the people of the densely populated and impoverished Cantabrian mountain valleys, of the arid plains of Old and New Castile, of the wetter valleys and coastlands of Andalusia; at their peak in the late-sixteenth century less than seven million largely rural people with little of the wealth of the Italian and Netherland dominions of the Habsburgs. Their produce had, of course, an important supplement in the silver and gold that flowed from America. In Castile the king could tax – not without protest, nor in extremity entirely without limit – but very largely according to his own will, so long as he confined serious additions to taxation to the non-noble classes, that is to the producers and traders. The nobility was generally exempt, until urgent need compelled the overriding of some of their rights in the 1620s. The burdens of campaigns that brought glory or disaster to generals far afield, at Nordlingen or Corbie or Rocroi, and at sea off Lepanto or Gravelines, were supported mainly by the tribute of the peasants and artisans, the burghers of the towns, the wage-earners and servants of Castile. This too was the principal recruiting ground; there were many volunteers, but compulsion could be exercised, and large numbers of the men of Castile died on far-distant battlefields of land or sea. Vigorous and expanding though it was, and supported by the growing torrent of American silver, by the 1570s the Castilian economy was already groaning under its financial burdens.

Much of the cost of Charles v's wars had been met from his rich Netherlands possessions, and though Spanish taxation was more than trebled during his reign this increase was not vastly in excess of the growth of national income (in the rising prices of the time) in one of the most progressive periods of its history. The revolt of the Netherlands in 1572 simultaneously deprived Philip II of most of his revenues there, and involved him abruptly in the costliest of all his wars, which dragged on in thirty years of increasingly hopeless struggle against Dutch, English and French. This war had to be financed in the main from Castile though there was a useful and growing contribution from America. The total revenues

D

of the crown were raised fivefold during Philip ɪɪ's reign; expenditure, with the help of loans at home and abroad, a great deal more.

The Castilian revenues of Philip ɪɪ, at their peak in the 1590s when they were ten times as great·as those of the English crown, were drawn from a limited base. The Church bore quite heavy taxes; but the nobility, the main landowning and official class, had as its central privilege complete exemption from direct taxation. Moreover, the main direct tax on laymen, the *servicio*, could only be increased with the consent of Castile's representative institution, the Cortes, and sixteenth-century rulers who were anxious to avoid difficult negotiation and to build up absolute power preferred to increase other branches of taxation. The *servicio*, therefore, provided only a small part of royal income at the end of the century. The wars of Spain were financed to some extent by customs duties, and even more by raising the level of the *alcabala*, a sales tax which was pushed to the maximum feasible level in 1575, and by supplementing it with a separate tax on certain categories of goods, the *millones* in 1590. These provided nearly two-thirds of the crown revenue at the end of Philip ɪɪ's reign; most of the remainder came, in equal proportions, from Church taxation and from America. By the last quarter of the century the tax burdens were very heavy, cutting into the already limited purchasing power of the peasant, wage-earner and craftsman (though many foodstuffs were exempt until the *millones* were applied to them), and into the profits of traders. Much of the income so transferred to the crown was laid out in ships and armaments provided in Spain but a great deal was used for the pay and provisioning of Spanish troops overseas and a growing share to meet interest payments on royal borrowings abroad.

For these huge crown revenues fell far short of expenditure. Charles v had early resorted to the issue of *juros* – interest-bearing bonds secured on particular revenues, and *asientos*, which were contracts with German, Flemish and Italian bankers for loans of money, usually secured on the king's share of arrivals in the treasure fleets. These debts mounted rapidly, and towards the end of Philip ɪɪ's reign interest payments swallowed two-thirds of his revenue. Twice, in 1575 and 1596, he had to declare himself unable to pay his debts, on each occasion turning short-term into long-term obligations. The first occasion left his troops in the Netherlands unpaid, and provoked the sack of Antwerp by them in 1576; the second finally discredited the fair of Medina del

Campo, already shaken by the bankruptcy of 1575. Through all the latter part of Philip II's reign, foreign payments drew out of the country most of the silver that came in, paving the way for resort to a debased currency of copper immediately after his death. In this sense American silver was as essential as Spanish taxation for the execution of the king's European policies, for it gave him the means to convert Spanish taxes into soldiers' pay in Flanders and the purchase of supplies in central Europe, and to subsidize his friends in France. The burden on Spaniards, however, was the taxation they bore.

American silver made it possible for Spanish taxes to pay for wars on foreign soil, which otherwise they could hardly have done. What of its direct influence on Spanish society and economy? Many writers, from the seventeenth century to the present day, have regarded it as a principal cause of Spanish economic decline. The argument is that Spain, into which American silver first came, experienced a monetary inflation that pushed its prices ahead of those in the rest of Europe; and that high prices in Spain encouraged an inflow of foreign manufactures that began the ruin of Spanish industry. The bullion outflow that paid for some of these goods, and that financed crown expenditures abroad, spread Spanish silver through Europe, and rising prices along with it. This argument has an attractive simplicity; but although the inflationary pressures of American silver supply were dangerous, they cannot wholly explain Spain's economic decline.

It must be borne in mind that the inflationary factor was not the gross arrival of bullion in Spain but the net addition to coinage in circulation in Spain. Spanish prices were rising much faster in the second quarter of the century, when the inflow of bullion was quite small, than they were in the third and fourth quarters when the inflow was immensely greater. In this earlier period, royal payments outside Spain were quite modest, and there was a serious effort to meet them without shipping silver abroad. In Charles V's reign – and to some extent right down to the state bankruptcy of 1575 – foreign creditors of the crown commonly realized their debts by accepting payment in Spain and using the proceeds to buy Spanish goods for export. This reinforced the inflationary effects of crown expenditure. In the latter part of the century, however, silver went out very fast in official shipments through Barcelona and a growing contraband. The annual addition to silver supplies in Spain was small and may even have ceased in the fourth quarter of the century because payments overseas as well as American silver shipments were at their height. The turn to a copper currency, indicative of a desperate shortage of silver in Spain, was initiated in 1599.

A number of influences were at work on Spanish prices. There as elsewhere rising population was a very powerful one; the periods when prices rose most steeply were, as in the rest of western Europe, those of clusters of bad harvests – the 1530s and the 1590s. Crown demands partly met by borrowing, and the colonists' purchasing power expressed in silver and gold, must have given further impetus to the upward movement of prices. But American demands were modest in the first half of the century, and largely met by foreign manufactures in the second half. As we shall see later, the growing European economy needed an expanded money supply; if the expansion was greater than necessary it would be inflationary; and if on balance this inflationary influence was more vigorous in Spain than in other countries this would harm the sectors of that country's economy that were vulnerable to foreign competition. The corrective exercised by a worsening balance of payments was ineffective, because Spain's large inflow of American silver enabled it to postpone the effect of such a balance of payment deficit for a very long time.

Positive decline, as distinct from cessation of growth, is not clearly apparent in Spain before the 1590s; the prolonged economic decline that followed took place amidst a reversal of direction of the major sixteenth-century influences. Population was falling in a series of steps and the net inflow of bullion probably ceased; and in these new circumstances the real expenditure of the crown could not continue to rise. Too much has been made, in fact, of decline in Spain before the seventeenth century, and reports of it are too all-embracing. How heavily, in fact, did the *alcabala* fall on a peasantry primarily concerned with producing corn for its own subsistence? Even the nobility, according to Spanish writers, largely avoided the *millones* because they lived to so large an extent on the produce of their own estates. Some part of the landed community should have gained at a time when agricultural prices were rising faster than others; if peasants suffered from landowners' oppression, and the condition of the labourer worsened, should not landlords have prospered? Yet the land incomes of the upper nobility, at least, failed disastrously to keep up with the general price rise; who were the middle groups that took the gains there must have been? In other countries, historians explain how industrialists gained from rising prices; but in Spain, that their hardships and difficulties drove them out of business, into bankruptcy, or to become landlords or rentiers, investors in state bonds – the most disastrous of all occupations to take up in a period of inflation. Did no considerable body of merchants flourish on a corn trade whose prices were rising to their peak, or by handling the flourishing fruit, wine and oil production of Andalusia?

Rising prices cause changes in income distribution; these changes must bring gains to some sections as they do losses to others; some sections of the Spanish economy must have been prospering, if only at the expense of others whose struggles have engaged the attention of historians. It is not enough to say that taxation was crushing, that there was a flight into unproductive occupations, that gains all went to foreigners. Heavy though the burdens of taxation were, cutting into the margin of incomes – above all of labourers who had to buy most of their needs – on no plausible estimate can it have reached a tenth of national income at any time before the imposition of the *millones* in 1590. To the extent that the *alcabala* was borne by the seller, it did not oppress the consumer; to the extent that it was passed on to the consumer it did not cut into the seller's profits, except as far as it restricted sales.

In the seventeenth century there was probably an overall decline in production, associated with the population fall. But population was maintained until 1595 and the effect of flight from productive occupations was very limited. The long wars took their toll of men in every generation, removing some of the most vigorous; but in the economic sense this is hardly more than a restatement of the fact that the crown took money in taxes and used it to employ men unproductively. The same applies to the movement into officialdom. If noble incomes were lagging, how was it possible for them to increase the number of unproductive people by employing more retainers and hangers-on? If they were doing so by getting into debt, who were the people making fortunes that they were able to lend, and how did they make them? The Church, it is true, accumulating through bequests in generation after generation, was able to support more monks and nuns; the commonly discussed flight into the Church was a reality, though one of very modest net effect on production. But the economic history of Spain is full of questions which still await plausible and consistent answers.

Decline was in the spirit rather than in material things. There was a growing consciousness of burdens borne, it seemed endlessly, for the wars; it was evidenced by constant grumbling in the Cortes, which actually forced a reduction in the *alcabala* after 1575. More demoralizing in the end was the growing realization, after 1588, that the sacrifices had been in vain; yet Castile had still not only to pay for continued war, but also to meet the interest payments that had resulted from mortgaging the future. Perhaps the productive and enterprising classes felt the burdens more heavily, or the waste more bitterly. The turn came at the end of the century. One new feature, that must not be underestimated, was the succession of incompetent government after the death of Philip II; but England experienced this after Elizabeth I's death without major economic disaster. Spain, emerging from long and costly wars, was struck by the demographic catastrophe resulting from famine and plague in 1595-1602, which cost hundreds of thousands of lives. Spain seems never to have solved the problem of feeding the masses of its people in bad years as well as in good, though it is not clear whether the deficiency was in agricultural production or in a social structure that left the bottom layers of the population with too small a share of income to survive. The effects of this, felt increasingly from the 1580s, struck a hammer-blow at economy and society at the end of the century. This was the real end of Spain's century of triumph. The establishment of American Empire that was the supreme manifestation of this triumph, and the long costly European failures of the Habsburg dynasty, both depended on the Castilian base. The empire was founded sufficiently firmly to stand when Castile failed; but in Europe the Spanish Habsburgs began to lose their place among the great powers.

5 Western Europe and the Atlantic

*W*hen Portugal discovered the sea route to the Indies, it wrenched an important section of Europe's trade away from the Mediterranean, where it had been dominated by Venice, to the Atlantic in which Lisbon took the lead. The early economic effects of Spain's American discovery were by comparison inconsiderable. The search for the western passage to India, which had led to the American landfall, was continued by Spanish, Portuguese, French and English voyagers for more than a decade after Columbus, but the solidity and length of the American land barrier soon became apparent. Though the Spanish and Portuguese claim to monopolize all rights in the New World was nowhere explicitly accepted – and was indeed openly denied by the French king – there was little intervention by other powers. Until after 1530 the only foreign presence in America was that of the occasional French trader or plunderer on the Brazilian coast, venturing into the Caribbean during war between France and Spain, and the French, English or Flemish cod fisher working in Newfoundland waters very remote from Spanish settlement.

The prosperity of Europe during the first half of the sixteenth century grew out of the development of its internal resources. Until Cortes's conquest of Mexico in 1519–21 it seemed doubtful whether the New World justified the Spanish effort in economic terms. The loot of Mexico and Peru resolved this doubt, and the hope of discovering other rich weak empires was long sustained. Yet until mid-century revealed the silver mines it seemed that America's long-term future would be the slow growth of an agricultural economy supplementing that of Spain. If Zacatecas and Potosí revived hopes that even the most desolate parts of America might justify their exploration for minerals, the first way that foreigners saw to gain from the silver mines was by plunder on the routes that brought Spanish silver to Europe. During the decades after 1560 plundering expeditions, real or planned, occupied foreign resources that might have been turned to colonization.

All relations with the New World – colonization, privateering, piracy, the plunder of towns or illicit trade – were bounded by considerations of European politics. There were encroachments on Portuguese Brazil almost from the time of its discovery, for Portugal carried little weight in European affairs. If she could not defend her extra-European possessions from foreign interlopers, no European power would do much to restrain them. The route to the Indies was safe enough, for it was the longest and most difficult of sea voyages, far outside the reach of the resources and experience of petty plunderers. Foreign interference in the Indian Ocean had to await the gradual dissemination of Portuguese knowledge of it, and the emergence of powerful merchant backing in England and the Netherlands. But Brazil could be reached without much difficulty; French traders appeared on its coast in 1504 and by the 1530s were establishing small settled posts, and Englishmen traded there from 1530. Spain, on the other hand, was a great power, which had to be courted or opposed for reasons of European politics or trade; alongside such considerations the prospects of petty gain at her expense beyond the Atlantic had no substance. Since France was Spain's chief political antagonist in western Europe, almost constantly at war between 1494 and 1559, the French Government rarely attempted to check the activities of its privateers or pirates against Spain; and from the 1520s – almost as soon as the treasures of Mexico began to reach Europe – the French moved on from Brazil into the Caribbean, where their enterprise took the simple form of seizing Spanish ships and looting Spanish settlements. This growing French attack compelled Spain to begin, after 1530, the costly measures to protect the homeward-bound treasure fleets that grew into an elaborate convoy system by the latter part of the century.

England, on the other hand, had strong political and economic reasons for maintaining good relations with Spain, for France was normally the enemy of England as well as of Spain, and the King of

Spain ruled over the Netherlands where most English overseas trade was concentrated. Until after the Reformation there was no anti-Spanish feeling in England of the kind that added moral indignation to the greed of French privateers. Moreover, Englishmen could legally carry on trade with Spanish America, so long as they conducted it (as Spaniards themselves were bound to do) through the city of Seville and under the regulations imposed by the *Casa de Contratación*. The Treaty of Medina del Campo in 1489 had given Englishmen rights of trade to all parts of the Spanish dominions, and there were substantial English merchant settlements in Seville and San Lucar. Government, merchants and seamen in England had no reason to support piratical exploits against Spain either in European or in American waters. Nevertheless, England did not accept the claim of an exclusive Spanish title to North America. An English interest in the Atlantic had grown up during the second half of the fifteenth century, with ships from Bristol visiting the Canaries, the Azores and Madeira. It is possible that they touched new land across the Atlantic at some time after 1480, but the discovery of Newfoundland is usually attributed to John Cabot, who added sophisticated Italian notions of a western route to Asia to the practical experience of Bristol seamen, and made his first successful trans-Atlantic voyage in 1497. The prolific cod fishery south of Newfoundland then began to attract large Portuguese, French and Spanish fishing fleets, but the English, who were fully occupied in working the Iceland fishery, took little part. Cabot's voyage was followed during the next few years by others directed to the discovery of a western passage to Asia, but when they proved fruitless the connection with America was abandoned to the fishermen.

Englishmen soon pushed southward in the wake of the Portuguese. William Hawkins and others began to trade on the coast of Brazil in 1530, bringing home valuable dyewoods, and the trade was carried on from Plymouth and Southampton for more than a decade without interruption. After 1548 Englishmen were trading for sugar on the Moroccan coast, and in 1553 they were on the Guinea coast, the heart of Portugal's African interests. These English enterprises – north-western exploration and fishery, the Brazil, Morocco and West African trades, and brief forays against Spanish shipping during a period of cool relations in the 1540s – were organized and financed, with one or two exceptions, from Bristol, Plymouth or Southampton, ports that had been losing ground as England's expanding European trade concentrated on the London connection with Antwerp.

The scale of English activity in the Atlantic completely changed in the second half of the century, when national and London interests were drawn into it. Yet this change was essentially a minor repercussion of the rise of Protestantism in France, the Low Countries and England. The new religion took a firm grip in France, particularly among the merchants and the seafaring population of the western ports, adding religious passion to the older hostility to Spain. In the 1560s, Huguenots operating from a number of ports of the Biscay and channel coasts were carrying on a privateering campaign that made the English Channel a dangerous place for Spanish and Flemish ships and goods. In the Netherlands, the same religious wave allied with growing nationalist feeling led to defiance of Spanish authority and in 1567 to rebellion; many Dutch vessels joined the Huguenot privateers of Rochelle, and in 1568 Alva's vigorous repression caused the Dutch to throw most of their effort into a sea campaign against Spain. At this point Englishmen joined them. Privateering as an accompaniment of Anglo-French war was a well-understood occupation of many seamen, merchants and small gentry, particularly in the west of England; now it was turned against Spain. The persecution of English Protestants under Queen Mary (1553–8), who was supposed to be under the influence of her husband, Philip II of Spain, united fanatical Protestantism in England with French Huguenot feeling. Her death coincided with the ending of war with France, and many of the legitimate privateers of the French war reconciled a desire to carry on their occupation with anti-Spanish feelings, by taking privateering commissions from the Huguenot authorities across the channel and joining the offensive against Spanish shipping.

The situation of English merchants in Spain and the Indies first became difficult when Henry VIII broke with the Catholic Church in 1532. Though relations were patched up, the merchants were never again safe from intermittent harassment. The strains on old ties of legal trade with the Indies through Seville, and the spread of anti-Spanish popular sentiment in England, provided the background for the first serious attempt to penetrate directly into Spanish-American trade in 1562. Though organized by a Plymouth man, John Hawkins, it was not merely a provincial venture; Hawkins secured moral and financial backing from connections in court circles and among London merchants. A series of quite successful trading voyages was made under his command, in defiance of Spanish authority, until in 1568 the Spaniards attacked and nearly destroyed his little fleet at San Juan de Ulua on the Mexican coast. When he limped home in 1569 with the news of this setback, it set ablaze the anti-Spanish fury of the west country seamen.

The year 1568, when Hawkins was struggling to get home, was one of crisis for Protestant Europe. The Netherlands rebels were being put down by Alva; there was Catholic plotting in England that led to a rising in 1569; the French Huguenots were heavily pressed in renewed civil war. English public opinion hardened against Spain as the champion of Catholicism in Europe. When a flotilla of small ships laden with silver to pay Alva's troops took shelter from privateers in Falmouth harbour, the treasure was landed and seized by the English Government. This precipitated a major crisis in Anglo-Spanish relations, with trade embargoes and seizures of goods, that was not patched up until 1572, and then precariously. In these four years, 1568–72, English privateering raged uninterrupted, and Spanish booty poured into Falmouth and Plymouth. In the same years English interest in America was revived, and English seamen joined with French in operations in the Caribbean. When peaceful relations at government level were restored in Europe, freebooting expeditions to America were hardly affected, for they were now supported by powerful interests at the English court.

Step by step, royal antagonism to enterprises that might provoke Spain was being eroded; Spain gradually replaced France as the principal European enemy, as civil war reduced France to impotence and Spanish power mounted. Alongside this evolution of government attitudes, an interest in Atlantic affairs was spreading spontaneously from adventurous young men in provincial seaports to fire the enthusiasm of rich landowners, sober London merchants, and thoughtful strategists at court. This was the development that distinguished English experience from French or Dutch. French privateering always depended on the resources of Huguenots in the western ports, which were weakened rather than reinforced when the religious struggle reached its crisis; and the Dutch, when they had the energy to spare from the direct struggle against Spain, threw their oceanic effort into the more obviously profitable trade with Asia rather than into America.

Why did so many influential and wealthy Englishmen begin to interest themselves in Atlantic ventures? Ordinary people, other than seamen, were not yet called on to play much part; the time for mass colonization had not come. Support had to be found in the landowning families from which the ruling group in England was recruited, and among merchants, financiers and officials. To an important extent motives were non-economic. Militant Protestant gentry found outlets for their zeal in financing privateers. Their enterprises brought them less profit than glory. Few family fortunes were built upon them, for the gentry were the least successful among the participants in privateering, and exploration and early colonizing projects brought nothing but loss. But they developed, in the most articulate and influential section of the community, an interest in oceanic affairs and in colonization that was the indispensable foundation for the efforts of the next century. In 1540, France was the place for a gentleman to win honour; in 1590, the Atlantic. The fact that landed fortunes were unstable in this period, and that younger sons were especially plentiful for a couple of generations, gave added strength to the movement.

Similarly, London merchants who joined wholeheartedly in the privateering drive after 1585 followed this up, two decades later, by becoming backers of sustained colonization. The support of their capital and experience was essential to both. Their interest dates back to the weakening of Antwerp's trading pre-eminence after mid-century and the signs of saturation in England's old continental markets, which led them to look farther afield for trading opportunities. English trade through Antwerp, after a last burst of rapid growth in the early 1550s, dropped back to a lower level from which no effort seemed able to raise it up again. In the two following decades, interference with Spanish interests produced the damaging counter-blows to England's Antwerp trade that crown and merchants had long feared. In 1562–3 English piracy in the channel was a pretext for an embargo on English trade with the Netherlands, and in 1568–72 the Spanish response to the seizure of Alva's treasure ships was a fresh embargo in the Netherlands and Spain. Finally, the spread of war through the Netherlands during the 1570s shattered Antwerp's position as a centre of international trade; the sack of the city by mutinous Spanish troops in 1576, and the closing of the river Scheldt by the Dutch in 1585, brought its international role to an end. Thereafter it was impossible for London merchants to maintain their European trade through Antwerp. Continental markets still wanted English cloth, but the old route to them had finally closed after thirty years of increasing difficulty. The earliest English reaction was to seek a similar trading centre near by that would offer a way into Europe. Most London merchants supplemented their efforts to find a nearby entrepôt by following provincial traders into other markets, where the latter had already made small penetrations. They threw their weight behind York and Hull initiatives in dealing directly with the German Baltic ports – a task made easier by the fact that the Dutch who had dominated this trade were involved in a war for their national life. They followed Bristol and Exeter merchants in pushing a direct trade with Spain and Portugal, when political relations allowed. No later than 1570 they opened trade by sea with Italy, rapidly building up an English merchant colony at Leghorn; after 1580 they were to be seen in Venice and Turkish ports. In the Baltic and Mediterranean they were reopening channels their grandfathers had used, which a century of concentration on Antwerp and the overland routes had nearly dried up; but they were now doing so with resources built up during the long peaceful expansion of English trade that were altogether larger than their predecessors could muster. Once they were obliged to lift their eyes beyond Antwerp, it was not long before some began to look beyond Europe altogether, to the opening of a direct trade with Asia; the first theme of Richard Hakluyt's propagandist work in 1578 was how to bring in the riches of the east without intermediaries, as the Portuguese had done.

These traders were not simply seeking markets for English goods; that was the interest of the makers, who were much in the background. Profitable trade had also to involve the buying of goods that would sell in England; the essential raw materials of the Baltic, hemp, flax and mast timber; and even more the exotic produce that the wealthy demanded, fruit, oil and dyestuffs from the Mediterranean, dyes and sugar from the Atlantic coasts and islands, silks, spices and precious stones from Asia. In the years between 1551 and 1585 when the southern trades were being opened, they were buying these not only in Antwerp but also in Morocco, Leghorn, Lisbon and Venice. In taking up the carriage of valuable cargoes in the dangerous, corsair-infested Mediterranean, London merchants had to build larger, more manœuvrable and better-armed ships than they had used for North Sea and channel trading. There was a striking increase, from 1570 onward, in the number of English ships large and powerful enough to defend themselves. When war with Spain came into the open in

1588 and made it difficult to carry on legitimate southern trade, many of these London-owned ships were diverted into privateering, and their prizes introduced more of the products of southern Europe and America to English taste, or provided quantities much greater than trade had ever brought in. At the same time the extension of privateering to the Caribbean made the Atlantic as familiar as the English Channel to large numbers of seamen.

The French were the first outsiders to establish colonies in America in defiance of the Portuguese and Spanish claims. French settlements in the St Lawrence region in 1541 and Brazil in 1555–8 broke down from their own weakness; the Florida colony of 1562–5 was attacked and destroyed by the Spaniards, who saw it as a privateering base close to their shipping route out of the Caribbean. The Brazil and Florida undertakings were both Protestant colonies, and French colonizing activity was crippled because from 1567 onward it came to be regarded as part of the Protestant offensive against Catholicism rather than a French national enterprise against Spain. When the Catholic cause reasserted itself strongly in France in 1572 and began to lean on Spain for support, French privateering became ever more plainly the action of one party to the religious wars. In the same period the Dutch entered into their life-and-death struggle against Spain for independent nationhood. For a time trans-Atlantic enterprise against Spain was almost entirely English; and it was the English who took up afresh the project of colonization in North America.

Yet America was far away, whilst English colonization had already begun just across the Irish Sea. Ireland was not an almost empty land like North America, but its population was Catholic and of doubtful loyalty to the crown, which was anxious to consolidate its hold. In the 1560s and 1570s the crown began to establish settlements, largely of ex-soldiers, on the fringe of the Dublin Pale and in Ulster. The motive was political, but in 1582 this colonizing work was put into the hands of private projectors seeking to make profit from it, and its scale greatly expanded. Whole cross-sections of English population were settled in Munster and Ulster – landowners, farmers, craftsmen – to create communities resembling the ones they had come from. Wave followed wave of Irish colonization projects for half a century, and drew attention away from America to more attractive prospects in Ireland, where gentry might hope to collect rent from their lands, and tenants could expect holdings of land under familiar conditions. But Ireland had a positive influence on American colonization as well. It provided experience of some of the problems of new settlement, and if this was sometimes misleading when applied to American conditions, it gave confidence in men's capacity to meet them. Humphrey Gilbert, Walter Raleigh and George Peckham, early in the field of Irish settlement, were also the leaders in American colonization. The seed of the idea of true colonization by self-supporting settlements was fertilized in Irish soil and flowered prematurely in Gilbert's last unsuccessful American expedition of 1583; and though the colony that Raleigh, as successor to his rights, set down in Virginia in 1584–7 was intended first as a privateer and trading base, Raleigh was already contemplating agricultural settlements. The fruition of these ideas was delayed for twenty years by war with Spain that left no resources free for the establishment of colonies, though during the war Englishmen's activities on the American coasts brought them more knowledge that would prove valuable.

The England that emerged from war with Spain in 1604 was very different from the country to whose throne Elizabeth 1 had succeeded in 1558. War at sea, privateering, and greatly widened spheres of trade had opened many eyes to wider ambitions. A wide range of gentry and merchant interests was now ready to give financial and sometimes personal support to colonization. The projects themselves were firmly in the hands of London merchants and their court connections, who had acquired the rights granted by Elizabeth to Gilbert and Raleigh.

By the beginning of the seventeenth century there was little danger of Spanish reaction to settlement on the North American coast. In the 1560s Spain had destroyed the French settlement in Florida; in the 1570s it established posts as far north as Chesapeake Bay; in 1586 it sent ships to search for and destroy Raleigh's colony. After 1598 Spain, under a new monarch and exhausted by war, concentrated on holding on to its rights in the area its colonists had settled and did not attempt to assert its claims beyond the Florida coastline. This was the situation in which English colonization took its first successful steps in 1606–7. But the situation changed still further. When the Dutch resumed war with Spain in 1621, after twelve years of peace, they at once exhibited their power in American waters, where they had determined on seizing the valuable part of Brazil (Portugal and its possessions had come under the crown of Spain in 1580) and, as a subsidiary to this operation, dominating the Caribbean and capturing Spanish treasure fleets. Throughout the 1620s Spain was on the defensive in the Caribbean, and English, French and Dutch were able to occupy unsettled islands there, close to the heart of Spanish power. By mid-century Spain had dropped out of the ranks of the great powers, and could not challenge the positions taken up by others in the Caribbean; indeed in 1655 England seized Jamaica, an island long occupied by Spaniards, and a few years later the French began to settle in deserted parts of Columbus's original conquest, Espanola. The colonial struggle from that time was between England and France; the Dutch, who had momentarily seemed poised to take the commercial pickings of all these colonies, were excluded from them by protectionist legislation, passed in 1651 and 1660 in England, and in 1664 and 1673 in France.

At the southern end of the North American continent Spain's effective occupation put a limit to other settlement. At the northern end, colonial development and the delimitation of French and English territory took shape from the way they operated in the Newfoundland fishery. From the early sixteenth century the fishery was worked by vessels that crossed the Atlantic each summer from all the western maritime countries of Europe, caught fish as fast as they could, and took their cargo back preserved in salt. In the wars of the 1580s the Spaniards and Portuguese were driven away, and as the Dutch were occupied in Europe only French and English fishermen remained active in large numbers in the last years of the century. French and English fishery methods, and their markets in Europe, were quite different. The French salted the fish heavily in their ships and rushed it home to their metropolitan market. The English, less lavish with salt in the absence of a good home supply, dry-cured their fish and sold much of it in southern Europe; indeed after 1604 Spain was their main market. Dry-curing had to be carried out on land, when the fish were still fresh, and English fishermen set up stages ashore for this purpose, generally on the Avalon peninsula of eastern Newfoundland. Their fishery consequently located itself in the coastal waters and on the Grand Bank immediately to the south. The French fished over a wider area, presently came to avoid the area of English concentration since there were other good fishing grounds, and occupied themselves off west and north Newfoundland and the Cape Breton coastline

and in the Gulf of St Lawrence. As early as 1530 they had established contacts with Indians along the St Lawrence and begun a
sporadic trade in furs, and this fur trade was expanding rapidly
after mid-century.

Both in England and France this activity across the Atlantic
attracted the attention of hangers-on of the court, who were not
slow to point out how insecure the fur trade and fisheries were
without a firm colonial base under the rule and protection of the
mother country. Between 1583 and 1626 a number of attempts
were made to settle permanent English colonies in Newfoundland,
all of them foundering on the fishermen's hostility to any interference with the beaches they dried their fish on. French court circles
showed more interest in the fur trade, and a series of companies
was chartered by the French crown, from 1598 onward, with
monopoly rights over trade in the St Lawrence. All were required,
in return for trade monopoly, to settle permanent colonists; one
after another they defaulted on this obligation and collapsed.
Nevertheless, fur trading stations spread up the St Lawrence during
the course of the seventeenth century, and among them Montreal
and Quebec eventually grew into little towns. None of this cold
region was attractive to farming settlement, and the big rewards of
trade were secured through the medium of tiny groups of fur
traders who relied on the Indians as trappers. French Canada could
never, therefore, attract a massive population; as future struggles
with the English were to show, it was an inadequate base for long-
term colonial expansion.

When Englishmen resumed their interest in colonization after
1604, the geographical bounds of their activity were therefore set
by the need to keep well clear of the Spanish limits in Florida, and
of tacitly accepted French territory in the St Lawrence area. Two
companies were chartered in 1604 – the Virginia Companies of
London and Plymouth – to occupy places on this stretch of American coast, between the 34th and 45th parallels of latitude, that was
regarded as open to the English. The northern part was known
from many casual landfalls of fishing vessels, fur traders and explorers, to be rocky and infertile, with climatic conditions not
markedly different from those of Britain. The lands from Virginia
southward, which had been visited by privateers and by Raleigh's
colonists, were warmer and might grow things the English climate
would not support. There was no mineral wealth that the seventeenth century was able to exploit, and though settlers in the

northern parts could expect to engage in fur trade and fishery, the real prospects of colonization lay in farming settlements on European lines. These possibilities always distinguished the English colonies from the thin scatter of trading stations in French Canada, and from the Spanish lands to the south where a vast indigenous population made it pointless and impossible to attract a mass immigration of working people from Europe.

Colonial enterprise required not only the willingness of men to venture themselves in strange places, but also capital resources which adventurers and colonists were rarely able to provide. There were several ways in which colonies were promoted and the resources secured for them. The first successful English colonizing enterprise was that of the London Virginia Company, a joint-stock company whose capital was provided largely by merchants, exploiting the rights in America originally granted by the crown to Humphrey Gilbert. The company provided ships and stores to establish the colony, and sent out colonists who were their employees. The expectation was that labourers working under the company's officials in Virginia would produce goods for export to Europe, and these would earn profit for the company. There were hopes, too, of a profitable trade with the Indians, and even that an easy route to the Pacific and Asia might lie close behind the Virginia coastline, or that precious metals would be found in the interior. Within little more than a decade it had been realized that wage labour would produce nothing of value in Virginia, and the company began to make grants of land to newcomers for themselves and for any other settlers they would transport. The company gradually ceased to bear the cost of expanding the colony.

The proprietary colony – of which Barbados and Maryland were successful examples – was the common form after the Virginia settlement. These colonies originated in grants of territory and some jurisdiction over it made by the crown to individual courtiers it wished to reward. But the settlement of these colonies was not financed to any important extent by the proprietors; they made grants of land to individuals who would finance the transport of other settlers. The role of the proprietor was to publicize his willingness to make land grants, and to provide some sort of government; and the return he expected was in cash payments for the grants or rent.

Finally there were religious promotions, among which the Massachusetts Bay Company was outstanding. This was established by men of some wealth seeking to make a safe refuge for persecuted sects across the ocean, using influence at court to get a grant of territory for the company. The capital was raised, on the whole, from people who intended to go to the new colony themselves; each stockholder was given by the company a land grant of two hundred acres, with an additional fifty acres for each person he transported to America; and anyone who paid for his own transportation also received fifty acres. In Massachusetts, therefore, as in Barbados and Maryland, capital for setting up the colonies came largely from people who wished to settle and cultivate their own land; the provision of capital was intended primarily to give a right to settle rather than a rentier income. In the long run, the possibility of becoming an independent cultivator with a secure freehold title to land was found to be the lasting attraction that would bring migrants to America.

The colonizing voyages of 1606–7 resulted in the foundation of Virginia. This settlement taught a number of fundamental lessons about colonization, from which later foundations benefited, but the original investors in the Virginia Company lost their money. The various hopes of the promoters were disappointed. The passage to Asia, if it existed, was remote from Virginia; local Indians had no gold or silver, or indeed anything of value except furs and skins, to trade; most local produce was not worth the cost of shipping it to England; and colonists would not work hard for the company's wages. The Indians were at first helpful, selling food and showing how crops could best be brought up in their land, but as settlement spread they became increasingly hostile. Early Virginia, in fact, was a drain on its promoters' resources and survived only because, through the years of failure, they were still ready to send out fresh fleets with provisions and tools and more settlers.

Two things transformed Virginia into a viable colony, offering real economic inducements to voluntary settlers. The first was the discovery that tobacco offered a cash crop for export. Tobacco had been brought to Europe from the West Indies and Florida as early as 1560, and though very expensive it became popular among the well-to-do. The propagandists of English settlement had included it among the many products they had recommended colonists to cultivate, but Virginia colonists were at first oppressed by the need to grow food to keep themselves alive. Moreover, the local tobacco was of poor quality, and did not sell easily in England.

However, when tobacco plants were brought to Virginia from Trinidad, their produce was well received in London. As their production began to increase between 1614 and 1617, Virginia settlers found the problem changing from one of lacking an export crop to finding means to keep pace with the growth of demand for their product. Tobacco prices in Europe gave the planters a good return while leaving a high profit for the merchant; this encouraged a huge expansion of cultivation and a revived inflow of settlers to undertake it. The whole price structure was changed; within ten years Virginia tobacco came down from several shillings to one or two pence a pound, while Spanish tobacco remained an expensive luxury. For several years the planters made great profits; and even at lowered prices they were able to survive, while cheap tobacco became an object of mass consumption in Europe.

Associated with tobacco production was a change in the land system. The company came to despair of getting useful production from wage labour, and from 1616 it was transferring land to the private ownership of settlers. After 1618 a grant of land was available to every new settler, although unless he had paid a subscription to the company he had to work out a term of years as an unpaid servant in America before he could take up his grant. From 1619 blocks of land were being granted to English syndicates that undertook to send out settlers to occupy them. Within a few years the typical form of English North American settlement had emerged: small farms owned by settlers who had usually earned their right to land by a few years of bonded servitude on the lands of others. From this time, and for a century to come, the English labourer or peasant was offered the opportunity to become proprietor of his own land in America.

The progress of the Virginia colony was almost unbroken after 1618, despite the vicissitudes in tobacco prices and the competition of the West Indies and New England in attracting settlers. For three-quarters of a century, ever-expanding demand for tobacco solved economic problems, and determined the economic history of the southern colonies; Maryland, founded in 1633, took up tobacco planting on the same scale as Virginia. With the first sign of success on the Chesapeake, the impulse to other settlements revived. Both the Pilgrim Fathers in 1620, and the Dutch settlers on the Hudson in 1624, sought places closer to Virginia, and only the accidents of sailing-ship navigation landed them farther to the north.

The northern colonies began, effectively, with the Pilgrim Fathers' settlement of 1620. This was not a settlement of adventurous men like the first Virginia colony, but a community of men, women and children, religious separatists seeking a place where they would not be molested. The problems of motivation to work for the success of the colony, which had held back Virginia, were much less serious here. The colonists suffered great hardships; but the colony needed only to survive, not to prosper greatly, to attract more settlers of the same kind. Other small Puritan settlements sprang up, and from one of these, sent by Dorchester merchants who presently became associated with much wealthier London interests, came the great Massachusetts Bay Company of 1629, which began a mass migration that set New England on its feet as a colony of corn- and stock-raising farmers.

Freedom from one form of religious persecution attracted a large group of colonists to New England; the expected profits of tobacco planting took the more economically motivated to Virginia. The latter was a more generally operating incentive, and it spread colonization southward far beyond Virginia. As early as 1600 tobacco had attracted handfuls of Englishmen to settle in Guiana – the stretch of South American coast that lay between the extreme outposts of Spanish and Portuguese settlement. But it was an unhealthy region, and always in danger from Spanish attack. After the Dutch established their naval power in the Caribbean, there was a wave of English and French settlement in West Indian islands. Between 1624 and 1636 a series of islands was settled, and the principal crop in most of them was tobacco. They were able to attract large numbers of settlers, who secured their own plots of land, found the struggle for early subsistence much less severe than in Virginia, and encountered little of the difficulty from hostile natives that had hindered the spread of Virginia settlement. By 1640 the English and French had plainly come to stay in the New World, and a rapid expansion in the number and size of settlements was under way.

6 The Sixteenth
and Seventeenth Centuries:
Population,
Prices and Incomes

Between the mid-sixteenth and mid-seventeenth centuries the structure of political relations within Europe was
wrenched violently into a new shape, the change formalized by two
peace treaties that mark the beginning and end of the period. In
1559 the Treaty of Cateau-Cambrésis had brought to a close, in
mutual bankruptcy and stalemate, a long struggle between the
Habsburg Empire that drew its main strength from Spain, and
the French Valois monarchy. These were the great powers, and the
Habsburg Netherlands and England were no more than useful
make-weights in the struggle. With the Treaty of Munster in 1648
the seven Dutch provinces of the Netherlands, triumphant after
eighty years, wrested final acknowledgement of their independence
from Spain. The power of Spain had collapsed; France was weakened by prolonged foreign wars and internal quarrels; the rising
powers were England and the Netherlands, competing with each
other for succession to Portugal's monopoly of the Indian Ocean,
and asserting claims to colonize in the New World.

The political strength of the powers of Europe was expressed in
their success in maintaining their supposed interests and in imposing their wills on others; it required the support of some genuine
economic strength, and of political institutions that enabled the

state to make drafts on the nation's economic resources and bring forward some skill and talent to the direction of affairs. The important thing was the ability to *mobilize* economic resources; to draw or direct men, capital, organizational skills, commercial connections, towards desired ends – whether for industrial or commercial expansion, for agricultural reconstruction or for war. A vast population was not sufficient by itself. Sixteenth-century Russia, with its endless communities of lord and serf, could mobilize almost nothing; in sixteenth-century Turkey, on the other hand, much of the surplus product of a large and variegated population was taken by the state rather than by a hierarchy of nobles, and the sultan could present an impressive military power even if the economy stagnated. The mobilizable economic strength of the western European states – all of them smaller than Russia or Turkey – lay in conditions that permitted the growth, on the foundation of initially unprogressive landlord and peasant economies, of industries, trading activities and services whose productivity was relatively high and which in favourable circumstances could originate innovations in technique or organization or effect regular capital accumulation. Even in western countries industry and trade were subject to restrictions that lessened their capacity to change and advance; they were least severe in the Dutch Republic and tightest in Spain and France. These developments eventually played a part in encouraging changes in agriculture, which increased incomes further. There was a tendency towards cumulative growth of wealth and income in western Europe, when they were not drained away by the costs or the devastation of war; and as income rose, mobilizable income rose still faster.

The Treaty of Munster in 1648, therefore, had as its background changes in the relative economic strength of Spain, France, the Netherlands and England. In a wider European context, a decisive shift in economic strength towards the countries of north-western Europe took place during the first half of the seventeenth century. It was a movement away from Italy, the centre of economic power for so many centuries; away from central Europe, which had recently flourished so vigorously; and away from Spain, which had dissipated its economic resources in war and was now too weak to preserve its monopoly of the gains of Atlantic discoveries. It was a movement towards Holland, to which much of the old commercial and financial activity of the Low Countries had gravitated in the last years of the sixteenth century; towards England, treading on the heels of the Dutch in every sphere; and towards France, temporarily weakened by war and held back by continuing social and political instability, but populous and endowed with varied economic resources. A new international division of labour was emerging, in which the lands of the Baltic and Mediterranean, and of the Spanish Atlantic, were suppliers of primary products for the increasingly industrialized societies of north-western Europe. In the seventeenth century the Baltic lands, which had long supplemented the granaries of the west, were called on to be suppliers of a wide range of materials for western industries – timber, iron, hemp, flax, pitch and tar; and the Mediterranean to contribute wine and fruit, oil, silk and dyestuffs rather than manufactured goods. Though the staple of Spanish Atlantic trade remained at Seville, its silver was drawn away to finance Dutch and English trading operations in the Baltic, the Levant and the Indian Ocean. The countries that bordered the Baltic and the Mediterranean were requited with woollen and linen goods from the Netherlands, France and England; with the services of ships owned and built in England, Holland and Hamburg; and with the facilities of commodity and capital markets of Amsterdam and London. The effects of these changes were long-lasting; an international economy that had been dominated for centuries by the cities of northern Italy and had then seen the brief scintillation of south Germany and Castile, was to be led for the next three hundred years by the economic powers of the west; by the Dutch briefly, and then, overtaking the Dutch in the course of the seventeenth century, by the English and French.

The western European countries all experienced rapid population growth until near the end of the sixteenth century; it was halted everywhere during the next three decades, and in many places reversed. The money supply of Europe was greatly expanded during the last decades of the sixteenth century, in consequence of the great inflow of newly mined silver from America, but after this flow declined from the highest levels reached in the years 1590–1620 different countries took divergent courses in their monetary conditions and policies. The growth of population, supported by more abundant money supply, was at the base of an economic expansion that was general during the sixteenth century. This expansion was decisively checked in Spain before 1600, and in France no later than 1630. In England, growth was slowed briefly, from the 1620s to the ending of the civil wars. It was in the early seventeenth century, however, that the Netherlands flourished anew; the southern (Habsburg) Netherlands had been so devastated by war that the peace of 1609 ushered in a prolonged recovery, while the new Dutch Republic to the north, gaining by the accretion of skill, labour, capital and commercial connections brought by immigrants from the south, bounded forward into a prosperity that was hardly interrupted before mid-century. This was the period in which the new pattern of European economic power was made plain.

Medieval population history had been one of a rapid growth that was checked early in the fourteenth century, with a steep fall resulting from the Black Death of 1348–9, followed by a hundred years of stagnation. The period covered by this book began on a new phase of generally rapid population growth to the early seventeenth century; then a halt and in many countries a decline was followed by a hundred years of near-stagnation or of fluctuation without any long-term progress. However uncertain the statistics, they all point this way unhesitatingly. French population rose from twelve or thirteen million soon after the mid-fifteenth century to some nineteen million around 1600, and fell off appreciably during the seventeenth century; Spanish population rose from well under five million to over eight million at its peak by 1590 and also fell in the seventeenth century; England, with well under three million people in 1500, had some four and a half million in 1620, after which population growth was markedly slowed and perhaps halted for a time; the Netherlands population rose to over three million at its early seventeenth-century peak and then checked.

The ebb and flow of population is the summing up of births, deaths and migrations. What caused the number of births and deaths to fluctuate, and how important were migratory flows in this period?

From the economic point of view the most important of all western European social habits is, perhaps, the late marriage of women; marriage deferred, that is, for several years after the age of puberty. Throughout western and central Europe men and women married at much later ages than they did in Asiatic or even eastern European societies; generally well into their twenties rather than in their teens, so that the child-bearing period of women's life (given a fairly high degree of pre-marital chastity) was reduced by nearly a third, and the most potentially fruitful third at that. How and when this specifically European marriage pattern emerged is still unknown; but it is certain that from the end of the Middle

Ages at least, average age at marriage fluctuated only narrowly over a stretch of time that comes nearly down to the twentieth century. When population was low, or when economic activity was vigorous, the good opportunities for young men to secure land-holdings or employment might have been expected to encourage early marriage. It is true that people married younger during the year or two following a major epidemic (so that a briefly higher birth rate repaired some of the ravages of the epidemic); but no firm evidence has been found – despite much searching for it – to show that marriage age was in fact very responsive to long periods of economic prosperity or depression. Fertility within marriage, and the probability of miscarriage, were affected by general levels of health and nutrition, and when the living standards of the poor in most European countries declined in the later sixteenth century the number of live births began to fall too, and probably for this reason. But despite all the work that has been done on the subject, the influence of economic factors on birth rates – beyond very short-term movements – remains conjectural. As to deliberate control of births within marriage, we know virtually nothing; there are scraps of evidence but it is impossible to judge the extent of birth-control practices.

On the other side, some of the ways in which economic conditions must have influenced death rates are easily seen. The under-nourished succumbed to deficiency diseases; their resistance to the ever-present danger of tuberculosis was weak; exceptionally bad harvests brought some deaths directly by starvation, and reduced resistance to all disease, including epidemic typhus, plague and smallpox. But the pattern of mortality that is repeated in numbers of local studies from various countries in the sixteenth, seven-teenth and eighteenth centuries is a peculiar one. It shows that each town or village or region had an underlying death rate, chang-ing little from year to year, and regularly lower than the birth rate. Every few years there was a wave of mortality that doubled, trebled or quadrupled the death rate in a single year. Sometimes this was due solely to an upsurge of epidemic disease – such a year was usually marked by a heavy late summer peak of deaths. It was very commonly, however, associated with an exceptionally bad harvest the previous year; deaths reached a spring and early summer peak as prices rose steeply so that buyers went short of food, the small peasant ate roots and grasses or rotten and diseased corn and the meat of diseased animals, and the desperate fled to the towns.

Diseases of malnutrition and food poisoning took their worst toll among children; but the weakening of adults, and migration in search of food, commonly resulted in the rise of a raging epidemic from one of the pools of plague, typhus or other fever that always lurked in the cities, and high mortality continued into late summer. The birth rate fell briefly, as fertility declined with privation. The excess of deaths over births, in this year – or occasionally two or three years – of catastrophe, was large enough to cancel out several years of normal growth of population. Long-term changes in the direction of population movement, from growth to either stagnation or decline, and vice versa, seem to have taken place much more frequently through the increasing or decreasing frequency and raised and lowered levels of these mortality peaks, than through gradual change in the 'normal' death rate of the good years. In England and the Netherlands, years of high mortality held back the growth of population; but in France and Spain their effect was sometimes much more dramatic. In these two countries years of exceptional death rates occasionally followed so closely on each other's heels that there was a great population fall which took some decades to be replaced. In France in 1628–31, 1648–52, 1692–4 and 1709–10, and in Spain in 1595–1602 and 1649–50 such catastrophes occurred, and go far to account for the seventeenth-century decline in population.

Earlier population history, and particularly the prolonged population growth from the late fifteenth century, is hard to explain, for almost all detailed studies of birth and death statistics relate to the seventeenth and eighteenth centuries. It is possible that, within the general growth of population running from the 1460s to the early seventeenth century, there were pauses and periods of temporary decline that have not yet been identified. We can only say, in the most general terms, that a Europe emptied of people by the Black Death eventually filled up, and that towards the end of the sixteenth century – commonly from the 1580s – food shortage appeared, with dearth and occasional famine. There was some fall in the living standards of wage-earners in the second quarter of the sixteenth century and in most countries they worsened much further in the 1590s. Many peasant families were made poorer by the need to maintain enlarged families on their holdings or by the division of holdings, while rising rents were an affliction for those who sold little of their produce on the market. The surprising phenomenon is not the slowing of population growth, but the lateness of this slow-down in England and the Netherlands, coming apparently a whole generation after the most rapid period of price rise had ended with prices very nearly at their peak level.

The risks of mortality were being increased, moreover, by an extraordinary expansion of the towns, going on at its maximum pace between 1550 and 1630. In 1550, Paris alone of the cities west of Italy had more than a hundred thousand inhabitants; soon after 1600 there were six cities of this size – Paris, London, Amsterdam, Seville, Lisbon and probably Antwerp. In most of western Europe – England was the exception – the number and size of towns of the second rank increased as well; Madrid and Valencia, Rouen, Lille and Lyon, Brussels, Ghent and Leyden are typical of a host of others. The widening of international trade accounted for the growth of many towns; four of the five greatest cities were sea-ports. Other cities, notably Paris and London and even more remarkably Madrid, expanded because they were centres of administration, seats of royal courts and of legal and military establishments, the focal points of competition for prestige and of the social life in which it was demonstrated. London and Lisbon, which were both seaports and capitals, concentrated their countries' urban population to an exceptional degree.

Yet towns were dangerous to life, and the larger the town the higher its death rate. The towns gave greater scope for the rapid spread of disease and for the neglect of small children than the country villages. They were above all killers of children; in seventeenth-century French towns one-third of the children born failed to survive the first year of life, and in places – London about 1700 was one of them – the infant death rate may have reached a half of all those born. The exposure of an increasing part of the population to such death rates must have operated as a check on population growth.

But it is impossible to ascribe all demographic change to economic or social factors. Leaving aside, as having no perceptible influence before the eighteenth century, developments in medical and surgical treatment, there is no reason to suppose that the incidence of disease ever depended entirely on human environment. The disease-carrying rat or louse, the insect parasite, the bacillus or virus borne by the insect, do not exist either to benefit or to plague the human race. They have their own life-cycles, optimum conditions for survival, causes of extinction, which must come under many influences besides the human ones. The huddling of people into dirty city slums in which lice and fleas can more easily travel from body to body evidently hastened the spread of disease; so did the more careful watch upon granaries in years of famine, driving rats into houses to look for food; but other influences must have been at work, unknown and probably unknowable. The historian is often reluctant to accept the fact that human history can be profoundly affected by influences from outside his system, but medical evidence of the nineteenth century and after reveals many extensions and withdrawals of particular diseases that cannot be attributed to any kind of human action. It may be that the rise of typhus in the later sixteenth century was largely due to growing urbanization, but its actual origin is uncertain; and the sudden turning of smallpox into a killing disease at the end of the seventeenth century is hard to account for. The disappearance of Europe's old scourge, bubonic plague, late in the seventeenth century, may be accounted for in part by tightened quarantine regulation, or by the arrival in Europe of the brown rat, driving out the black rat which was a more dangerous carrier of the disease to man. There had been pools of plague in Europe, which caused a few deaths every year, and stood ready to burst from time to time into fierce epidemic; somehow these emptied themselves before the middle of the eighteenth century. Population growth and decline were affected, to an extent we cannot know, by phenomena no less random from the human point of view than the falling of meteorites; it would be as rash to deny as to affirm that the major upswings and downswings of population in the sixteenth and seventeenth centuries were primarily due to such random influences.

Finally, there was migration, not all of it into the dangerous towns. Here and there severe local population pressures were relieved by rural migrations. The valleys of the Pyrenees and the Cantabrian mountains, which closely limited the number of people who could be supported in them, always sent streams of migrants north and south; during the sixteenth century to southern France, and in the early seventeenth century to Catalonia and Valencia. Southern and eastern Spain received migrants not only from Castile's bleak heartland but also from Italy. Trans-Atlantic migration from Spain and Portugal was made more attractive after the mid-sixteenth century by the silver discoveries in Mexico and Peru, and the opportunities in planting in Brazil. But the scale of trans-Atlantic migration was small, hundreds rather than thousands a year, and for Portugal the drain of keeping up its Asian outposts and communications with them was probably more important. America only began to take large numbers of European migrants when the English and French established agricultural settlements in the seventeenth century; the brief wave of heavy migration from England in the 1630s made a small but significant dent in England's population growth. All these movements helped to relieve population pressure in limited areas; they had little effect on the total population of Europe.

The spreading effects of population growth in a society that made increasing use of the market depended on an adequate supply of money as a means of exchange; and for two generations, from a little after 1550 until towards 1620, the supply of precious metals in Europe was ample for monetary needs.

Silver had always flowed out of Europe into Asia, where its purchasing power was much higher. It went through Venice and Genoa; after 1497 through Lisbon; from 1600 through Amsterdam and London; and always to some unknown extent across the land frontiers of Europe. It disappeared, too, into non-monetary uses, for religious and lay ornament; into hoards, sometimes maintained intact for very long periods or even lost completely; and in the ordinary wear of coin. Medieval production of silver failed to keep up with these uses, and a prolonged and serious shortage of coin was not relieved until the expansion of central European production late in the fifteenth century and the arrival of American silver in some quantity from the 1530s. Gold was not so scarce, and it became plentiful after the Portuguese reached the gold-bearing region of West Africa in the 1470s and American stocks were tapped after 1492; but it was not an adequate substitute for silver in an era of silver standards and low prices. The great age of silver, foreshadowed by the loot of the Incas that reached Europe after 1535, was fully realized when the first great cargoes from the new American mines arrived in 1552. From that year the import of American silver rapidly mounted to reach a peak of some seven million ounces a year in the last decade of the century, maintaining this level until the 1620s, after which there was a rapid fall. These figures may be compared with a central European production of half a million ounces a year at its peak in the 1630s.

The seventeenth-century decline of American production came at a time of rising exports of silver from Europe. Dutch and English companies, penetrating the Indian Ocean, traded there on a far larger scale than their Portuguese predecessors, and required to export correspondingly greater amounts of silver. Where the Italians and Portuguese had sent, at the most, a few hundred thousand ounces of silver to Asia in a year, the Dutch and English from the 1620s onward sent millions. By the middle of the century, moreover, western Europe was exporting large quantities of silver to Russia and Poland, to pay for its new raw material needs, and some of this went farther eastward into Asia. Between declining supply and rising export it is likely that the net influx of silver into Europe came to an end before 1650.

The age of monetary plenty, and indeed of excess, was the age of American silver. Silver brought into Seville was rapidly diffused abroad by government payments to the crown's foreign creditors and by clandestine commercial transactions. Vast amounts were sent to Antwerp after 1551 to pay for Charles v's wars; the attempts to suppress the Netherlands revolt after 1567 took a swelling torrent of money, mostly channelled through the crown's Genoese bankers, and this grew bigger in the last two decades of the century, as Spain added support for Catholic revolt in France to its unending war in the Netherlands. A continuous Spanish trade deficit with France was met, from the end of the 1550s, by great transfers of silver, and Portugal was by this time buying the silver requirements of its Asian fleets at Seville rather than from the Germans at Antwerp. The silver that in these ways reached Antwerp, Genoa and France was distributed to other parts of Europe in the course of trading operations, though we have no clear evidence of the size of these subsidiary flows.

Europe's money supply was increased not only by growth in the quantity of silver in Europe, but by reducing the silver content of units of national currency and so stretching out the use of silver as money. Currency debasement took place in Europe in every century, and the sixteenth was no exception despite its more plentiful money supply; for debasement offered a profit to monarchs seeking to adjust their revenues quickly to pay for increasingly complex administrative machines and extravagantly prolonged wars. When Henry viii's land campaigns of the 1540s reduced his ministers to financial desperation, their remedy was to throw the silver coin that came in payment of taxes into the mint, mix it with copper and stamp a great many more new shillings than had been put in. In England there were small debasements in 1526 and 1542, and a series of large ones between 1546 and 1551 whose effect was partially reversed at the end of 1551; the net result of all these was to reduce the silver content of the shilling by a third. In France a long series of small currency changes halved the silver content of the standard coin in the course of the century. While the Netherlands remained under Spanish rule, the silver content of Flemish and Brabant groats was reduced in stages by a total of 42 per cent in eighty years. Spain alone was for a long time exempted from this process, though the Cortes attempted in 1523 and 1534 to persuade Charles v to devalue. Spanish coin retained its full silver content, but after 1599 the substitution of copper for silver coin in general use carried the currency in a long series of downward steps that reduced it to chaos.

The European economy needed more money in circulation as the sixteenth century progressed; population nearly doubled between 1460 and 1620, urbanization and rural specialization brought an increasing part of production into market transactions; greater distances and more complicated trading organization made necessary a proliferation of middlemen between purchasers and ultimate consumers. The volume of money transactions increased enormously – possibly ten- or twenty-fold. A growing use of bills of exchange and other paper instruments in international trade economized the use of coin, but was only a palliative to the general money problem. The European economy urgently needed a large increase in the supply of silver, and to a lesser extent of gold. The real problem about money supply is whether its increase after mid-century, as a result of the American mining discoveries, was so great that it pushed the price level further upward than the growing pressure on demand for the products of the land made necessary; that is, whether money supply was neutral, or superimposed a monetary inflation on a real cost inflation.

For the sixteenth century saw an extraordinary phenomenon that has been labelled 'the Price Revolution'. Taking the century as a whole, prices rose very much more rapidly than they did over any long period before our own century; and this rise followed prolonged price stability in the greater part of the fifteenth century, and was succeeded by a hundred years of very stable prices from the mid-seventeenth century. Corn prices (in terms of the actual currencies of European countries) rose in a series of short bursts from their lowest level in 1460–80, the phase of rapid growth starting in the 1520s and running to the end of the century, then slowing down and coming to an end about 1650 in the Low

Countries, France and England, and after 1679 in Spain. Other prices rose over the same period, though less steeply than corn. Rapid price rises over short periods – as in the 1520s and early 1530s, the 1590s, and in particular countries after sudden currency devaluations – outraged popular feeling and provoked widespread outcry, and in every country the state acted to try to control food prices. As the general upward movement of prices continued over a long period, people had a vivid impression of going through an unprecedented experience, gradually accepting that a permanent age of dearness had succeeded the good old days. The price rise had an immense influence in redistributing income between individuals, between classes, and between countries; it was a phenomenon whose effects penetrated into every field of economic and social activity.

It is impossible to construct a satisfactory general index of prices, because price data for individual commodities other than corn are scanty, and corn prices rose in the long run faster than any others, and fluctuated in the short run more violently than most. The price of corn rose seven-, eight- or ten-fold in different regions in the course of the sixteenth century. Scattered information suggests a much slower – but still considerable – rise in other prices; the price of coarse Dutch woollens in Brabant trebled in the sixteenth century and the wages of Dutch builders' labourers quadrupled; in England builders' wages no more than doubled. The most comprehensive general survey (based on very poor data) suggests that the price of corn rose nearly twice as much as the average of other commodities.

Except in the case of corn, which is unrepresentative, it is not possible to establish how the rise in general price levels differed between the countries of Europe. Monetary theory would suggest that rising prices in countries that were the early recipients of money flows would cause outflows, and so the supply would be spread steadily throughout Europe. Something of this sort may well have happened; there is no evidence to the contrary. But there was sluggishness in the response to movements of relative prices, so that bullion did not travel so readily; and every country tried to prevent the export of bullion. Price levels therefore varied between countries on no very clear pattern; there was not a simple spreading out of higher prices through Europe from Spain.

Modern debate on the Price Revolution is concerned with the relative effects on prices of 'real' and 'monetary' factors. The most

E

important of the 'real' factors has been discussed above; rapid population growth that filled up the usable land of western Europe, exploiting it through agricultural techniques that were only slowly changing. But there were others, such as the dissipation of resources in war, and possibly some excessive investment in the support of overseas enterprise by early sixteenth-century Castile. The monetary factors were the changing supply of precious metals, and currency debasement. Though it is tempting to assert the role of monetary influences – there is an astonishing similarity between the curves of prices (in terms of silver) and of decennial bullion shipments from America – strong reasons exist for emphasizing the role of less strikingly attested real factors. One is the unevenness of the price rise between different categories of products, showing a consistent pattern, with corn leading the way and rapid increases in the prices of some other agricultural products, while the prices of industrial goods seem to have risen much more slowly. This is fairly well attested even in the limited price data that are available. It suggests that landed interests were gaining in income from the scarcity of land in relation to people. Associated with this is the apparent failure of wages – at least of building workers and agricultural labourers – to keep up with the prices of the basic foodstuffs on which they were largely spent; again suggesting that the value of labour was falling as its supply became more plentiful in relation to that of land. Finally, the highest temporary peaks of corn prices (apart from those due to steep currency devaluations) were in periods of known successions of bad harvests – around 1530, and in the mid-1590s.

Yet this cannot be the whole explanation; money supply was clearly pushing prices upward at some points. The very steep English price rise around 1550 was associated with, if not wholly caused by, major currency debasements, and the French price rise of the 1560s corresponds exactly with a massive increase in the flow of Spanish silver into France. The continuance of rising prices in Spain through the first three-quarters of the seventeenth century, despite falling population, shows the price-raising effect of a money supply being increased by issues of copper coin. There was no single cause of the Price Revolution or of its ending. The influence of land shortage could not have worked itself out in higher prices if money supply to handle more transactions in higher prices had not appeared. Possibly the rise of prices up to the mid-sixteenth century was due mainly to real factors, and here and there to currency debasements, and was even being held back towards the end of that period by monetary shortage; from the 1560s onward silver supply was growing more rapidly than monetary needs and contributed directly to pushing up prices; the surge of prices in the 1590s was propelled by the pressure of growing population in years of bad harvests; and thereafter western Europe, with the exception of Spain, settled into some degree of equilibrium between supply, demand and money.

Population grew, the area of cultivation was extended, peasant holdings were subdivided here, the employment of wage-labour on the land increased there. By the latter part of the sixteenth century in most of western Europe there was little good land still available to be brought into cultivation without heavy new investment. Landlords' interest and peasants' habit and prudence put limits – varying according to local inheritance laws and customs – on the subdivision of holdings. The number of landless men increased faster than the demand for their labour in the villages, so their living standards fell as labouring became more casual, and many of them drifted into the towns in search of employment. All over western Europe the problem of pauperism was afflicting society on a new scale by the third quarter of the sixteenth century, creating alarm where it turned to vagrancy or even banditry. As families became larger the peasant wanted to keep back more of his crop from the market to feed his own family, and the townsman or labourer cut down on his tiny extravagances to spend more of his income on the food whose price was soaring. The tendency for the market supply of corn to dwindle, and for the demand for it from expanding towns to grow, could only be reconciled by rising prices. Some producers and some landlords prospered and spent their extra income on luxury foodstuffs – pulling land away from basic foods – and on services and the work of town craftsmen. By providing new kinds of employment for some of the poor displaced from the land, they were creating more urban demand. As corn prices rose, even wages had to go up a little or a large part of the population would simply have starved; so the prices of all the goods in which labour was a large part of cost went up too. This is an enormously simplified picture of European change in the sixteenth century, with grain prices leading the upward movement, followed more slowly by meat, timber and butter. In the southern Netherlands, and perhaps in Spain, wages lost more ground relatively to food prices in the first period of steep inflation in the

1520s; in England and France they lagged more steadily behind prices, and in particular they altogether failed to meet the pace of inflation in the bad years of the 1590s. The prices of goods that embodied labour as a large part of their cost – craft products such as clothing, candles and metalwares – therefore rose less rapidly than those of foodstuffs. No doubt some real costs were being added to food prices, in the form of carriers' and middlemen's earnings, as big towns came to draw on more distant food supplies, making more complex marketing organization necessary. But beyond this, the price rise undoubtedly favoured agricultural incomes as a whole. The way in which these gains were distributed between different kinds of agricultural incomes varied from country to country, from estate to estate, from farm to farm. The strength of verifiable custom, the character of legal tenure, the social attitudes and relations on which the desire and ability to enforce custom and law depended, and the degrees of ignorance on one side or the other of the village community, all were held in the balance. Everywhere, moreover, higher money income from the land had to be shared among growing numbers of people who worked or lived on it.

The landlord saw that the price of goods produced on the land he owned was rising. If he had no home farm he had to pay more for this produce himself, and inevitably he had to buy some goods at rising prices. Not only the economic strength of his position but also reason and equity must have encouraged him to seek means of raising his rental income, and to overcome any institutional obstacles to doing so. The process is best known, and has been most argued about, in England. The old view that the late sixteenth-century peasant suffered from exaction of excessive rents if he was lucky enough not to be evicted in favour of a capitalist farmer, was succeeded by the argument that only the smaller landowners (often recent purchasers of land, seeing it only as investment) rack-rented their tenants and secured a share of the increased product of the land, and that the larger landowners, giving less personal attention to the profitability of their estates, or anxious for their political or social standing in the county, allowed the rising profits of agriculture to go to their tenants. Both these views of the gains and losses of whole classes are out of favour now, and rising and falling individual fortune is seen on both sides of class boundaries.

It is particularly difficult to see how English landlords were able to break through the legal and customary barriers of tenurial relationships to increase their rental incomes. Since most peasants

held their land on very long terms of years at fixed rents, it appears
they should have taken most of the benefits of rising prices. Many
did so; there is much evidence of peasant prosperity in late sixteenth-century England. The smaller peasant, to whom the land
was principally the source of food for his own family, and who sold
little corn on the market except in years of unusually bountiful
harvest, did not share the same degree of prosperity, and he suffered badly if his landlord was able to push up rents in line with corn
prices. The strength of law and custom was sufficient in many
places to delay the operation of the economic forces that operated
in the landlord's favour; the general level of rents lagged far
behind the rise of corn prices during much of the sixteenth century,
and particularly in its third quarter (though not necessarily behind
the level of prices of the goods landlords customarily bought).
From the 1580s to the 1620s, however, rents were rising steeply,
and many landlords more than recovered the lost ground. In France
a much smaller part of the land was subject to rents that could be
altered; there was a very distinct lag of rents behind prices during
the sixteenth century which may not have been generally recovered,
although a rise in rents, starting to move after 1600, continued in
places into the 1670s.

There were common weapons that landlords could use to improve rental positions that were apparently hopelessly blocked by
peasants' tenurial rights. In both France and England, the ruin of
a significant section of the older landowning class that was slow to
adapt to rising prices brought much land into the hands of more
enterprising or ruthless neighbours, and of officials, merchants,
lawyers and others of the newly rich. In their hands, efforts to
raise revenue were actively prosecuted. The determined lawyer
could usually find some lapsed rights in land to be revived or some
pieces of land whose title, though long unchallenged, was uncertain.
Nearly everywhere the legal situation of common pasture and
wasteland, on which peasants grazed flocks and herds, was dubious.
The landlord could turn this to advantage, unless tenants were
exceptionally tenacious in defending their claims, by demanding
services, entering on disputed lands, or enclosing part of a common and putting his own flocks on it or letting it on fresh terms.
The mere threat of such encroachments was a powerful inducement
to tenants to accept the rewriting of their tenures, not merely increasing rents but substituting short leases and *metayage* for long
leases and customary tenures. In France the landlord was often the

financial power behind village moneylending; the small peasant who borrowed in years of famine and came eventually to default on re-payment might be faced with demands that he surrender his land, whether to be returned to him on short lease or thrown with simi-lar holdings into a large farm to be let at an enhanced rent. This process cannot have been unknown in England. Everywhere the influence of landlords as members of the national governing class could be brought to bear, beyond the law, in their own interests; and most particularly in Spain and in England where much of the local administration of law was delegated to landowners. There were many avenues for landlord pressure, and by means of them a great many landlords managed to ensure that they did not for long suffer the burden of rising prices without augmenting their own incomes.

All over Europe, the wage-earner suffered from rising prices. There are good records of the wages of building trade workers, and these have been compared with the prices of consumer goods. They suggest that builders' wages generally fell severely behind the price rise during the second quarter of the sixteenth century; that in the Netherlands this loss was partly recovered and wage move-ments thereafter kept pace with prices; that in Spain the lost ground was not regained but the wage-earners did not slip back further; and that in England and France there was a continuing decline in real wages until well after 1600, and only a slow recovery from the depths. These results, unfortunately, cannot precisely reveal the situation of the industrial wage-earner. Building labour-ing was one of the easiest occupations to enter, and building crafts by no means the hardest; the impact of a growing labour surplus and an influx of rural unemployed to the towns would have been severely felt in building. Moreover, building is of all industries the one most completely insulated from foreign competition. The figures themselves are dubious; in Spain a wider range of wage data suggest that wages kept more closely in line with rising prices than builders' wage rates suggest. In many occupations, moreover – particularly in the countryside – the wage-earner was partly insu-lated from the effect of rising prices by having some payments in kind as well as money wages; a meal a day, or a small share of a crop, could be very valuable when prices were at their peak.

It is not surprising that real wages fell heavily as population grew in France and England. With no organizations to protect their interests, and without the legal and customary supports on which peasants might rely, they suffered in a period of labour surplus. Governments in both countries, with confused notions about the causation of price increases, attempted to hold prices down by legislation limiting wages, and had little impact except on the latter. In the Low Countries, however, the sharply rising prices in the years around 1530 corresponded with the extraordinary expansion of Antwerp's trade, and of the cloth industries of Flanders. These non-agricultural sectors were far more important in the economy of the southern Netherlands than in any other part of Europe, and although wages lagged behind the first uprush of prices in the 1520s, the strength of demand for labour brought about an exceptionally quick recovery in the 1530s and 1540s. In Spain the picture is less clear, but it is likely that a substantial part of the recovery of levels of real wages that had been lost during the sixteenth century was made during a period of some labour shortage between 1598 and 1611, under the influence of a heavy population fall followed by the expulsion of the Moriscos.

These general views on wage movements are all based on the wages of building craftsmen and their labourers. Industrial wages were usually on a piece-work basis, and it is extremely difficult to construct indices of them. To suppose that the average level of industrial wages is reflected by builders' wage rates is mere speculation. It is certain, however, that varying local customs, the influence of national and urban institutions, the relative prosperity of different branches of industry, their dependence on luxury or popular demand, on home or foreign markets, must have caused considerable changes in the relative levels of wages between different industries, regions and countries.

The impact of the Price Revolution on industry – that is, on industrial profits, the level of industrial employment, and capital accumulation – is hard to determine. It has been argued that profits rose because a gap widened between prices and wages; but the relevant prices for this purpose are those of industrial products. If it is true that industrial wages in England and France rose slowly, at much the same pace as builders' wages, so also did the prices of those few industrial goods for which there are some data. It is likely that the rise in money wages in Spanish industry was more rapid than in other countries; and this would go some way to explaining the relative decline of those branches of Spanish industry that were subject to foreign competition, and the rapid overrunning of Spain and its colonies by Dutch, French and English textiles in the seventeenth century. In rural industry, for which there are almost no data, the wage-lag was probably even more marked than elsewhere, since the workers were so often merely supplementing family agricultural incomes and less able to bring pressure for higher wages. If this is so, there would have been special gains for rural industrialists that we cannot directly observe, and advantages to the countries of developing rural industry, especially France and England.

There were shifts in industrial demand as rising prices transferred income from the poorest of the population to more well-to-do people, whether landlords, peasant or capitalist cultivators or pastoralists, keepers of orchards or vineyards, or town merchants and craftsmen. The very growth of population and the intensification of the market economy were themselves sharply increasing the numbers of people in middle-income occupations, such as the internal grain and other food traders, the carriers by land, river and sea, the scriveners, lawyers, warehouse-keepers and market officials. State taxation and borrowing on an expanding scale created considerable industrial demand for weapons, clothing, saddlery and vehicles. For all these reasons, demand for many kinds of industrial goods should have been rising; and there was a corresponding decline in demand from the poor, the latter bought most of their needs from local village industries rather than from national specializing ones. Yet the apparent slowness of industrial prices to rise (and even more significant, the failure of the prices of industrial raw materials drawn from agriculture, such as wool, flax and hides, to rise at anything like the pace of foodstuffs) should induce caution in estimating the extent to which the profitability of industry was improved by the lag of wages. Economies in costs, through improved organization as industry expanded, were more certain sources for the enterprising manufacturer to enlarge his gains.

Substantial changes in relative prices between countries influenced international trade, though custom and old connections caused the effects to be felt very slowly. The relative prices of industrial goods in different countries (in terms of silver, the common unit) changed gradually with movements of costs, and suddenly in consequence of currency debasements or upward valuations. The Low Countries textile industries were sharply hit by the upward revaluation of the currency in 1527, and began to recover lost ground when this was reversed in 1539. The English textile industry experienced an export boom after 1547 under the influence of debasement, and this collapsed when the value of the currency was partly restored in 1551. The general recession of Spanish industry towards the end of the sixteenth century and of Italian industry after 1620 may arise partly from the failure of real wages to decline as sharply as they had done in northern Europe. Early in the seventeenth century, when the war with Spain was over, English and Dutch industry reaped market gains from rising Italian prices; on the other hand, currency devaluations in east German states and Poland after 1620 severely damaged their exports to those parts. The influence of currency changes on international trade is very clear, though it needs further investigation; changes in real costs worked their effect more slowly.

The Price Revolution had its importance, therefore, because it did not operate on all prices alike, and so it changed the economic relationships between men. Differences in wealth, abilities or knowledge; lack of information; the drag of government, and of municipal and commercial institutions; above all the unchangeability of the land area of Europe; all these prevented men from moving to the occupations or the countries where price differences revealed shortages. So those who had nothing to offer but their labour suffered nearly everywhere, if in greatly differing degrees; those who owned land or had rights of user over it struggled with varying success to maintain or improve their situations; capital perhaps flourished most where it employed rural labour. The redistribution of wealth between countries probably owed more to factors yet to be discussed; but institutional rigidities certainly opened some countries' industries to destructive foreign competition. Changes of this general character would have resulted from the rise of population alone; their particular form was profoundly influenced by the accompanying increase in Europe's money supply.

7 *Agriculture in the Sixteenth and Seventeenth Centuries*

*D*uring the last two decades historians have drawn attention to the contrast between bounding economic growth in the sixteenth century, and the stagnation and even decline that appears characteristic of the seventeenth. Indeed, the term 'the General Crisis of the Seventeenth Century' was coined in the 1950s, explaining the social and political developments of the whole century as part cause, part consequence of economic malaise, and pointing to the risings and revolts in many countries in the 1640s and 1650s as symptomatic of this general crisis, for which it was desirable to formulate a general European explanation. The facts cannot, however, support the labelling of this long period of western Europe's economic history with the term 'general crisis'. There was a mid-century crisis affecting nearly all Europe for a few years, probably associated with the imposition, on top of the culminating pressures of the long population growth that had preceded it, of the fresh strains of government demands, losses and devastations in the collection of wars labelled 'the Thirty Years War' centred on the years 1618–48. This was the one universal experience, and even so the intensity of the mid-century crisis varied enormously from country to country. Much more striking than general economic decline was the way in which lines of development came to diverge; the general advance of the sixteenth century was followed by a period in which the great differences between the experience of the various countries led to a redistribution of power among them. The sharp commercial expansion of Holland, which only slackened its pace after 1660; the first hesitant but later accelerating rise of the English trading and industrial economy; the rise of Sweden, insecurely based and coming to its limit by the end of the century, but impressive while it lasted; the new wealth of the Habsburg Netherlands once the most intense struggles on their territory were over; and the rising prospertiy of Portugal under the stimulus of trade with its fast-developing Brazilian Empire; these are no part of a general crisis. Contrasted with these is the experience of the two greatest states of western Europe. France, unable completely to solve its agricultural problems so as to feed its population, its recovery therefore collapsing after 1630 and again in the 1680s as a few decades of population expansion made demands that the land could not meet; France that had already been held back by the religious wars of the late sixteenth century, made little net progress between 1630 and 1730, and its experience provides much of the basis for generalizations about the 'general crisis'. And finally Spain went through a century of population decline darkened by a series of catastrophes, but without the intermediate periods of expansion that France could show; its native industries going down before foreign competition and its currency collapsing. Spain's decline had begun before 1600 and the worst was hardly over before 1680; then after a brief interval, foreign and civil wars ravaged Spanish soil into the first years of the eighteenth century.

Down to the last decades of the sixteenth century population was still growing, but its growth had been slowed, at least in France and Spain, as early as the 1580s. There was still plenty of land to be brought under the plough in the sixteenth century, and rising corn prices caused land to be turned from other uses. But in one country after another population growth halted, and was generally succeeded by some decline. The productive methods of the Middle Ages, hardly changed beyond the Netherlands, yielding three, four or five bushels of rye to the acre, could not support further growth of population. The corn prices that attracted fresh land into cultivation became so high that the poorer people starved under them; and the attempt to maintain larger numbers in peasant families once the limit of cultivation was reached caused starvation among those families too. In France and Spain the problem temporarily receded because of huge losses of population; in the Netherlands and England rising production was able to overtake population growth as the latter slowed. Nowhere was the old rate of population growth resumed until the middle of the eighteenth century; more than a century of falling or stagnant population intervened.

The degree of success with which different countries handled the problem of subsistence for the mass of their people goes far to explaining their differing overall progress during the seventeenth century. The preceding chapter discussed the effects of population growth on two assumptions. The first – valid for the sixteenth century outside the Netherlands – was that little progress was made in the techniques of agriculture; the second, that climate, the average behaviour of weather, was a constant. This chapter has to consider how the situation was modified by agricultural improvement that did take place during the seventeenth century, and also to examine the history of climate.

It is true that France and Spain both suffered from being principals in wars that were immensely costly in men and treasure, and both were also ravaged by internal wars in mid-century. War struck at agricultural production in many parts of Europe, as marching armies destroyed crops, killed cattle and burned villages and implements; but recovery from their depredations was usually rapid. The most serious experiences for France and Spain, however, were the subsistence crises that struck each of them several times during the century, as they never did in England or the Netherlands. In particular, the dreadful years of the 1640s and early 1650s, when England as well as France and Spain was afflicted by civil war, saw a million dead in France and as many in Spain, while England had nothing worse than two years of unusual hardship. At the centre of these differences in experience was not merely or mainly the impact of war, but differing progress in the improvement of agricultural organization and technique.

Agriculture made some progress everywhere; above all in the Netherlands, but in a slow, cumulative fashion in England as well, at periods during the seventeenth century in France, and towards its end in the Catalan region of Spain. This progress was too late and too weak to support continuing rapid growth of population, but it brought down food prices in the long period of stable population that followed, reduced dependence on Baltic grain imports after mid-century, and prepared the way for a more general acceptance of the need for agricultural innovation that was essential to maintain renewed growth in the eighteenth century.

The central problem of agriculture in the more thickly populated parts of western Europe – in France north and east of the Loire, in much of the Netherlands, and in southern and eastern England – was the ancient inheritance of a peasant preoccupation with corn growing. The very reason for their heavy population was that soil and climate had made possible the maintenance for a thousand years of an economy and society centred on corn, in which the maximum number of mouths would be fed – at a low level – almost entirely on some form of bread. Associated with this concentration was what some writers have called a 'rage for corn' – an intense fixation of producers on the need, before every other use of their land, to provide from it enough corn to feed their families without resort to an uncertain market. Great tracts of land that were too damp or whose soil was too thin to be ideally suited to corn, were nevertheless kept under wheat or rye or oats. Because of this, too little land was devoted to providing winter food for animals, and they were generally scarce. There were many modest flocks of stunted sheep, and pigs foraged in the woodlands, but cows were rare and draught animals were kept in far from adequate numbers. The use of land was not entirely fixed, however; under the influence of changes in population and in the relative prices of different rural products there were slow tidal movements of variation in land use. But they flowed reluctantly, and when corn cultivation approached its maximum extent it could do little more to keep pace with still expanding needs.

Throughout the fifteenth century, which was still under the influence of the population collapse of the Black Death, adjustment was being made to a lessened need for corn. The peculiarity of demand for corn was that, while it was the basic foodstuff, people's demand for it was almost fixed. As soon as this demand was met, the consumer turned to other foods, and would buy little more corn or bread or flour at any price; conversely, even a modest shortfall in supply caused an intense pressure from consumers bidding up prices to secure their needs. Harvest fluctuations, due to weather and to pests, caused great differences in the supply from year to year, while demand was exceptionally stable. In consequence there were enormous year-to-year fluctuations in corn prices. Thus the price of rye at Aix-en-Provence was 228 sols in the autumn of 1587, and 133 sols twelve months later; 500 sols in 1593 (admittedly an extraordinary year) and 148 in 1594. At Cambridge in the spring of 1631 wheat reached 73 shillings a quarter; the following spring it was down to 39 shillings. There was, beyond this year-to-year fluctuation, a tendency for the long-run average of corn prices to change quite substantially if average supply over a decade or so lagged only a little behind or ran only a little ahead of the normal movements of demand. The frequency and violence of fluctuations in corn prices discouraged peasants from altering their sowings in response to the experience of a single year; downward adjustment to supply by turning cornland to other use was likely to be made only when a long-term fall in the price level had clearly asserted itself, while upward adjustment of production was ultimately limited by the capacity of usable land, unless ways were found to improve yields.

In most of western Europe there was little adjustment to changing conditions in the fifteenth century beyond simple change of land use. Some ploughland was allowed to revert to grass, while some of the poorest and most remote rough pasture was abandoned altogether. This was economical of labour; it met a growth in demand for wool in Spain and possibly in England, and it cheapened a variety of foods such as butter, cheese and above all meat, for which demand was more responsive to price. In the Netherlands, however, there were major agricultural innovations, within which the reduction of the area under corn carried an improvement in the yield of corn per acre. These innovations had been the subject of experiment quite soon after 1300, and were adopted into general use during the fifteenth and sixteenth centuries. The earliest was the extended planting of peas, beans, and lentils, or of turnips in the stubble of the corn harvest. These crops were intended for feeding animals, though they supplemented human diets in years of bad harvests; they provided more food, while positively improving the land for corn crops by adding nitrogen to the soil. The second was the group of practices embraced within the term 'convertible husbandry'; less clearly defined and so less firmly dated, but certainly coming into widespread use during the fifteenth century. These required the replacement of the old crop rotations, which consisted of one or two years of corn crop followed by a year when the land lay fallow to restore itself, by much more complicated rotations in which corn figured less prominently. Thus a corn crop might be grown for two years, followed by a year of peas or beans, and then by four or five years when the field was under grass for the animals to feed. Prolonged recovery from corn growing, with plenty of animal grazing in the interval, was the feature of the system, whatever the particular variation in rotations within it. It was, of course, a form of reversion to pasture; the area under crops, in any one year, would be much less than it had been under the old rotations. And it was devised, indeed, as one of the ways of replacing crops with animals in the period of receding demand for corn, rather than to improve the corn supply. But the improvement in corn yield that was achieved in the years when seed was sown was found to be quite unexpectedly large. The land, invigorated by long rests from corn, and well-manured by years of cattle or sheep grazing, was able to produce more corn, in the long run, than it had done under the old system, as well as far more animals and their products. Convertible husbandry was indeed in the Netherlands – and eventually elsewhere in Europe – the chief agency by which the productivity of the soil was raised. The third Netherlands innovation appeared much later to supplement it, spreading southward through the Dutch provinces during the seventeenth century, in the introduction of high-yielding artificial grasses to the pastures, making it possible to shorten the ley period between corn crops and yet keep still more animals, providing still more manure for improved crops. The old vicious circle that had dogged medieval agriculture on the great cornlands of north-western Europe was at last being broken. Few animals had provided little manure; little manure had meant low corn yields; with low corn yields per acre, every possible scrap of land had had to be ploughed for corn; so there was little winter feed for animals, and few animals . . . . The Netherlands farmers of the later Middle Ages, faced with a declining demand for corn and falling corn prices, turned to alternative products; they did so in a way that broke into this vicious circle with more pasture and more fodder crops, and in consequence not only achieved their immediate object but opened a way to huge increases in corn yields per acre of land and per bushel of seed.

Both in England and France there was some extension of field cultivation of beans and peas during the fifteenth century, and isolated examples of convertible husbandry are to be found in England soon after 1500. But the big response in England to the fall in population, from the mid-fifteenth century until about 1520, was a considerable reversion from 'permanent' cultivation to 'permanent' pasture, chiefly for sheep.

Agricultural innovation was transmitted slowly – more so before the days of the printed book – and before the new ideas being developed in the Netherlands could spread more than sporadically beyond the border, conditions of demand were again changing. As population grew through the sixteenth century, the movement of the price relationship between corn and other products of the land reversed its direction. In this century, where corn prices rose eight- and ten-fold, those of many agricultural products, including the most important, meat and wool, rose no more than four-fold, and others like butter and cheese only a little more. The temptation once again to plant corn in every corner where it would grow, almost at any cost, was very strong for those producers whose eyes were on the market or who could expect to provide surpluses for it.

Yet there was no period when the responsiveness of rural society to the pressures of the market was so uncertain as in the sixteenth and seventeenth centuries. To a degree that was unknown before the late Middle Ages, and that was being steadily eroded through out the seventeenth and eighteenth centuries, the decisions about rural production were those of peasants. In the thirteenth and fourteenth centuries most estates in England and northern France had been mixtures of peasant land and lord's demesne, the latter occupying as much as a quarter or a third of the cultivated land and carrying with it extensive rights over pasture and common. The great extension of cultivation in the thirteenth century had been largely achieved by the clearing of wastes to add to demesne ploughlands, enabling lords to sell more corn in expanding markets. Despite the falling away of demand, it had not been easy to turn this ploughed land back to other uses once it had been incorporated in village open field arrangements, and a very great part of it was leased out as ploughland to peasants during the fifteenth century, often on very long terms. By 1500 little demesne cultivation remained, and the old lordship which had carried with it some farming under the direction of the lord's bailiff had usually been converted into simple rent-receiving; seigneur was transformed into landlord. There were, of course, many exceptions to this, particularly among great pastoral producers; but it was the general direction of movement in the typical villages of the primarily corn-producing areas. Two hundred years later, in eighteenth-century England, large parts of the land were under the control of substantial farmers, who leased their land on short terms from landlords who were always anxious to find means of increasing their rent rolls; and some progress had been made in this direction in France. There was never a period, earlier or later, when nearly so large a part of the cultivated land and best pasture was under the control of the peasants, as between 1450 and 1650. No class of users of the land was less able to innovate; and great numbers of them were subsistence farmers who grew corn, not for the market except in years of unusually good harvest, but for their own families. Though peasants were by no means unwilling to innovate if the practical advantages were clear and the risks small, they had the least facilities for information, the least resources to bear the costs and risks of change, the least capacity to coerce their slow-moving fellows into the cooperative effort that was usually necessary for large-scale changes. It was not easy for landlords to compel the peasant community of a village to try new ways so long as most tenures gave the peasants security at more or less fixed rentals, and the key to extensive rural change had to be found eventually in the breaking down of old tenures so that peasants could be subjected to economic pressures, or alternatively forced out in favour of market-oriented farmers.

Nevertheless, the recovery of market demand for corn was a powerful stimulus to change for those who were in a position to make it. The response was very rarely improvement in methods; it was usually the 'permanent' reversion of land to corn, the ploughing up of 'permanent' pasture; and beyond this the costly reclamation of forest, heath and marsh. No doubt the first, less costly and drastic process, was the earlier one; there are widespread examples of it, intensified in each of the upward surges of corn prices and notably in the last decade of the sixteenth century. Here and there land was turned back to corn from other specialized uses, as were vineyards in parts of northern France. More dramatic were the large-scale reclamation works, in which the Netherlands again showed the way. The pace at which Dutch land was recovered from the sea by poldering was sharply accelerated in the mid-sixteenth century, and after being halted by war in the 1570s and 1580s was resumed and intensified to reach a peak between 1630 and 1660, after which it dropped sharply. In those same decades of the mid-seventeenth century there was extensive drainage of peat marshes in the northern Netherlands. The experience built up by Dutch engineers was applied by them to draining large areas of marshland in eastern England and south-western France during the first half of the seventeenth century; there too the scale of the works fell away dramatically with the falling of corn prices in the 1650s.

Ploughing up pasture and reclaiming marsh and heath for crops could not produce enough corn to meet demand. The import of corn from the Baltic was rapidly increased during the later sixteenth century, and was extended from supplying the Netherlands to taking a more regular part in the feeding of London, the wine-growing areas of southern France, and southern Spain and Portugal.

Rising prices encouraged some producers to try to use more land for growing corn; they did not bring about any widespread improvement in methods of growing it. The stimulus to change – except when the means of change are well-known and well-tried – is adversity; and the corn producer for the market was doing well in his old ways. The assumption that underlies the whole argument of the last chapter, that population pressure was exerted on a land whose use was only modestly changed, without being mitigated by any marked improvement in methods of production (outside the Netherlands), is therefore a correct one. The evidence of corn yields per acre, scattered and inconclusive though it is, appears to indicate that they were not generally rising during the sixteenth century, and not doing so at all widely until very far into the seventeenth. There is, indeed, some evidence that they were actually falling in parts of France during the seventeenth century.

Moreover, one powerful influence was at work to pull land away from corn production. While malnutrition and its consequent diseases attacked the masses of the poor and eventually imposed a demographic check, courtiers and lawyers, along with merchants, prosperous craftsmen and many farmers, were able to widen and satisfy their tastes as incomes rose. The extraordinarily rapid growth of the great cities during the sixteenth and early seventeenth centuries, and the concentration of spending of the biggest incomes in them, made it profitable to turn much of the best land close to the cities to other produce. Despite the exceptionally rapid rise in corn prices, good cornland might still be used more profitably, at a time when wages lagged, in highly labour-intensive culture meeting luxury demands in an adjacent market. So the urban upsurge in Holland from the 1580s was accompanied by a great extension of dairy farming, and of market gardening fertilized by the ordure of the cities. Market gardens and orchards spread round London and Paris in the last years of the sixteenth century. The same influence operated more weakly, but not without effect, in other regions suited to orchards and viniculture though far from the cities.

Everywhere governments were alarmed by the steep rise in corn prices, and attempted to set limits on it; but if they were successful – which is doubtful – the effect would have been to slow the necessary turning of land towards corn growing. In Castile price fixing for corn was made permanent in 1539, and was fairly strictly enforced against smaller producers coming to the market; in England old restrictions on corn export were revived, licensing of corn dealers introduced in 1552, price control through the Assize of Bread reinvigorated in 1562; in France royal decrees began to impose maximum prices for corn in 1576.

It was not, as modern analogies have led some historians to suppose, the pressure of demand for corn in the period of rising population that led to the improvement of corn yields in western Europe. The reverse was the case: Netherlands agriculture was reorganized in the fifteenth century in response to falling, not rising prices; the first country to follow whole-heartedly was England under the influence of declining corn prices after 1650; and in France advance came during the low prices of the second quarter of the eighteenth century. It was the easing of the relentless pressure to a corn monoculture that, paradoxically, disseminated the discovery that mixed farming would dramatically increase arable yields.

Corn shortage came to an end around the middle of the seventeenth century because population fell in some countries and agricultural improvement made its mark in others. The steep rise in corn prices had ended with the famine years of the 1590s, but prices remained on a high plateau, with a slightly rising trend, until just before 1650 in England, France and the Netherlands, and continued to rise in Spain in terms of a currency whose value was being destroyed by debasements. In France and Spain the heavy fall in population, culminating in both countries in the great mortality of a few years round 1650, relieved the pressure. In the Netherlands, too, there was a small decline in population. In England, the level of population may have been maintained, except in the immediate aftermath of severe plague outbreaks, but for some decades growth probably ceased. Beyond this, an enlarged corn supply came not merely from an extension of land under cultivation that reached its peak around 1650 – or as late as 1680 in southern France – but also from the beginnings, in the seventeenth century, of improvement in methods beyond the Netherlands. Already in the early years of the century, alongside the conversion of land to corn there was a further quite widespread introduction of peas and beans to feed cattle on land otherwise left fallow, the improvement of land by marling, the spread of the practice of seed selection, and in England the flooding of upland meadows to produce more abundant hay. When population growth halted, this slow improvement overtook it, momentarily in France, finally and decisively in England. The Amsterdam corn market, which handled a great part of the Baltic trade, ceased to grow after the 1640s, and from 1680 its trade was declining rapidly. In the first half of the eighteenth century, Dutch corn shipments from the Baltic were only half those of a century before; corn shipments from the White Sea, which had become large, virtually ceased after 1650. England, whose intermittent corn imports had been growing in size and regularity during the first half of the seventeenth century, ceased to import at some time before 1650 and became an occasional exporter; after 1700 its exports were regular and, between 1730 and 1750, they were greater than those coming out of the Baltic. France, which had been importing corn in the early part of the seventeenth century, was able to dispense with imports again between 1660 and 1690. Spain and Portugal remained large importers, but in the early eighteenth century much of their supply came from England. By that time, in fact, western Europe was more nearly self-sufficient in corn than it had been for nearly two hundred years.

Agricultural innovation began to make its mark in both England and France before 1630, but after that date their experiences diverged. English agriculture went on into a long period of experiment and change, while in France the interruptions of mid-century were not followed by any real resumption of progress. After mid-century French population crept up again unaccompanied by substantial improvement; it outgrew corn supplies in the 1680s and suffered a violent new subsistence crisis in the next decade. In England the fall in prices was slower and shallower, but although there were wide year-to-year fluctuations there was no long-term recovery in corn prices until late in the eighteenth century. The indications are of continuous and accelerating agricultural improvement in England from the 1660s, while in France no movement on the same scale got under way before 1730.

English farmers, encountering low prices from the 1660s, followed the course of Low Countries farmers three centuries earlier by turning with much-increased determination towards animal husbandry, and in this period less for sheep – since wool prices were also low – than for cattle to produce meat, butter and cheese. They were given some aid by the Government, which during the

1660s banned the import of competing produce from Ireland. There was much deliberate imitation of Netherlands procedures during this period, for the prosperity of Holland was the subject of admiration and envy. Agriculture learned much from the translation of Dutch treatises into English, and from the writing of Englishmen who had studied Dutch methods and the introduction of Dutch practices by Englishmen who had lived in their country as exiles after the Civil War. The central feature of the changes introduced was animal husbandry reinforced by the variety of new crops available for fitting into the rotation, and of artificial grasses –lucerne, clover, sainfoin–to make pasture luxurious so that enlarged herds of cattle and sheep could be supported. Animal fattening areas were extended over the midland plain and the Essex coastland, where cattle reared in the Scottish and Welsh uplands were made ready for London and other city markets. There was a great expansion of cheese and butter production in the north and east midlands, and of fruit growing in the London area and the west. Yet alongside this, almost as a byproduct of animal husbandry, production of corn was pushed upward by larger yields per acre, turning England into a country of embarrassingly large surpluses by the 1720s, which were only partly relieved by the export of barley to Holland and of wheat to Spain and Portugal.

Meanwhile France tumbled again into shortage in the 1680s, and went through severe food crises in 1693–4 and 1709–10. There had undoubtedly been some advance in French agriculture; an increase in farms of medium size that could be well stocked with cattle and sheep; some development of large wheat farms in the Paris region and of stock farms in Normandy; the introduction of maize as a fodder crop in the south late in the seventeenth century. But the open field system remained little changed over all those lands north and east of the Loire where it had so long been dominant; indeed, when attempts to modify it were seriously begun in the 1760s, they caused great peasant discontent. Evidence on French corn yields is very scattered and has been variously interpreted, but it is probable that there was a little advance in places at least as early as the 1660s, and general improvement in the middle of the eighteenth century.

The reasons for the contrasting experience of the two countries that were assuming the economic leadership of Europe lie ultimately in the nature of land holdings and of peasant incomes. Ancient peasant freeholds were scarce enough to be of no great significance; over most land there were lords' rights and cultivators' rights. Old rights over land – the cultivator's right to the usufruct, the seigneur's right to an income or to services that were precisely defined – inherited in a variety of forms from the Middle Ages, had been crystallizing during the sixteenth and seventeenth centuries into land ownership, which was a concept the Middle Ages had not known. Land ownership gave all the rights to one party, rather than sharing them between cultivator and lord. In England this settlement had gone, on the whole, against the peasants, for while the traditional peasant tenure of copyhold was being transformed by a series of legal decisions between 1540 and 1620 into effectively full ownership, a large part of the peasantry was at the same time being persuaded or coerced into converting its copyholds into leaseholds. In leasehold tenure, old lord was new landowner, and the tenants had rights only within the period of their leases (which were commonly for short terms) and no rights at all beyond them. Thus peasant security of tenure was broken down, and a means of pressure to greater flexibility in land use created. It was only a potential, but it opened the way for centuries of enclosure of open fields, enlargement and consolidation of farms, and rack renting based on the possible earnings of the most efficiently managed holdings. There was a slow replacement of peasant farming that was largely for subsistence by tenant farming for the market with some employment of wage labour. The most rapid phase of this change only began in the eighteenth century but it had been on the move since before 1600 and it carried technical change in its wake.

In France the struggle over land rights went the other way. Peasant right to the produce came to be transformed, generally, into peasant landowning subject to some small fixed seigneurial dues. The peasant's position was not so strong as this would make it appear. A large part of the land – perhaps nearly half – was not old peasant holdings but old demesne, to which the peasant had no more claim than a lease could offer him, and since peasants often needed these demesne pieces to round off convenient holdings, the rents charged for them were squeezed upward. Common rights were uncertain, and lords were able to take parts of commons into their private ownership; and there were dues of a variable kind – for the use of the lord's mill, for baking in his ovens, etc. – that could be increased. Moreover, the confirmation of peasant ownership made the peasant an object for loans secured on his land; and as in all such peasant societies, the borrowing of money on mortgage to help out in difficult times was commonly followed by eventual default and the turning of peasant landowner into lease-holder. With all these reservations, however, the average peasant was much more legally independent, by the early seventeenth century, than his English counterpart; in most French villages a great central mass of holdings remained firmly in the absolute ownership of peasants, and their use of it was little susceptible to pressure from wealthy neighbours or territorial lords. The strength of village custom, the control by village elders of the time and place of the agricultural operations of the village, the capacity to resist enclosure and the consolidation of large holdings, were far greater and more widespread than in England.

While the French peasant was less susceptible than his English counterpart to pressures from outside, he was not economically better off and able to innovate on his own account. The English peasant, stripped of his quasi-ownership, came to be subjected to rack-renting, and if he could not pay either by tightening his belt or by adapting his production to the best markets, he was evicted and replaced by another tenant who could. Great numbers of French peasants, however, emerged from the religious wars into the seventeenth century as landowners only lightly burdened with dues and modest taxes even if they paid rising rents for some leased land, and the wave of agricultural improvement between 1600 and 1630 owes something to this situation. Then the state stepped into the gap, making itself the beneficiary of the peasant surpluses that had slipped from the hands of the seigneurs. Richelieu's tax reforms of 1620–40 trebled the total collection of taxes, and laid the main burden of them on the peasants. From this time, the French peasant paid very heavy personal taxes, of which the principal one was the *taille*, and a number of taxes on commodities, of which the *gabelle* or salt tax was the most onerous. The English peasant, in contrast, normally paid no personal taxes, and indeed no tax on anything of consequence until the malt tax was introduced in 1649 and the salt tax was made a serious one in 1698.

Thus in France the poor peasant producing his main crop for the subsistence of his own family remained the typical occupier of the soil, not easily removed from his land unless he got into debt, yet overburdened by a collection of charges among which national taxation might be the heaviest. He was not able to accumulate capital in order to change his practices, and could not be forced to make the attempt. In England, by contrast, the peasant was being converted into, or driven out in favour of, the commercially oriented farmer.

The whole situation was different in the high hills and dryer lands nearer the Mediterranean – in southern France and most of Spain – where the concentration on corn crops was far less intense. The difference of terrain, the more uncertain rainfall, and the long dry summers that were normal if not invariable, made corn yields poor and erratic; there was more dependence on animals, while the climate favoured the production of other crops on the better land. There were some important advances in food production during the seventeenth century; the introduction of buckwheat in southern and central France, and of maize in Portugal and parts of Spain, produced crops on land that had been unfit to bear the older cereals. In general, adaptation to changing demands was easier in these lands where animal husbandry had a larger place – if only the keeping of stunted goats and sheep – and where it was normal to reserve some of the best land for vines, olives and fruit trees. The tremendous effort of agricultural adjustment needed in the north was not seen here; but this was a counterpart of the existence of great areas of land fit for very little, so the south was poor.

The land area of Europe was almost fixed; its use could be varied only with some difficulty; techniques were slow to change. There is another factor that has commonly been taken as a constant one: the European climate. Year-to-year fluctuations in weather and consequently in the yield of the harvest were the most fundamental influences on the prosperity of society, affecting economic life far beyond agriculture. But they were random and their effects should normally have cancelled out, though occasionally the disaster of two or three exceptionally bad harvests in a row (and a tendency for them to cluster existed because of the temptation to eat the seed-corn in a bad year) brought about, in both France and Spain, hundreds of thousands of deaths and so affected the future for some time to come. The climatic question, however, is a different one: did the weather fluctuate annually around an unchanging average, or were there long-term movements of change in average weather itself, that is in climate? Was climatic change a major influence on the long-term movement of the European economy?

There is no doubt that climate has varied, in historical times, to an extent that was very important to European agriculture; it is much less certain whether its changes have had much significance for western Europe over such a short period as a century or two. The whole period of this book is embraced within the decline from a peak of warmness in the late Middle Ages to a cold trough that was deepest during the years 1550–1700, and the following slow swing back to a warmth that has probably passed its maximum in our own generation. The river Thames, which had not been frozen over once during the century before 1540, froze quite commonly in the winters of the next two centuries. In central England, average January temperatures in the late eighteenth century were more than two degrees Centigrade lower than they are today. A regime of cooler, dryer winters and springs was coming to its culmination in the seventeenth century, with summers that were stormier and had heavier rainfall. That is, the climate was becoming a little more continental, more extreme, with a slightly wider range of temperature between winter and summer, and a small shift from winter towards summer rain. It was quite sufficient to drive out crops from some land that had been in cultivation in the Middle Ages, to shift the limits of the vine and olive farther south, and generally to reduce the length of the growing season by as much as two weeks from its one-time maximum. But it is hard to identify important effects of so limited a movement outside lands that were already very marginal agricultural producers, such as Iceland and Finland, and it is dangerous to identify changes between the sixteenth and seventeenth centuries. French writers have, indeed, discussed smaller movements within this swing, and suggested a 'short' climatic cycle of some thirty-five to forty years, but this is still speculative. Some of them see the 'crisis of the seventeenth century' as one whose agricultural basis was to an important extent the consequence of worsening climate; and any adverse climatic influence, in the conditions of overpopulation that were emerging by the end of the sixteenth century, would have given another push towards famine conditions. But it is still uncertain how far the shorter movements are genuine trend movements with basic climatic causes, or the quite accidental clusterings of rather more years in which the weather veers towards good in this half-century, rather more bad years in that.

Whatever the reasons for them, the periods in which there were particular clusterings of bad years in western Europe are quite readily identifiable; in the north-west 1592–7, 1628–30, 1639–43, 1646–50, 1687–1704, 1709–17. These were periods in which wet summers predominated, and they embrace the years of extreme hardship, starvation and spread of disease. The longer uninterrupted intervals, 1597–1628 and 1650–87, roughly coincide with the more prosperous periods of the century, and the three nearby clusters of bad years between 1628 and 1650 cover the portion of the century when crisis was most general and most serious. The impact of weather at that particular point is undoubted, and it may be that the worsening of the 'Little Ice Age' was a real factor in the subsistence problem of seventeenth-century Europe; that agricultural improvement in England and the Netherlands was enabling them to escape from this problem as well as from population pressure, while France succumbed to it.

Spain provides a separate climatic puzzle, perhaps because its climatic history is even less well documented than that of England or France. The west European climatic regime that was reaching its most intense phase in the period 1550–1700 was cool, with a rainfall that was tending to become appreciably lower in winter and spring but to attain a higher summer peak. Excess summer cloud and rain underlay the tendency of weather during the seventeenth and very early eighteenth century to press round a trend unfavourable to crops in France and England. In north-western Europe the margin of cereal culture was one of excessive wetness and coolness, and yields suffered in years when there was serious divergence towards these from the average. Southern Europe, on the other hand, was much more dangerously close to the margins of excessive dryness and heat for cereal production. The view has been expressed, indeed, that the whole decline of the Mediterranean economy, which included Spain apart from its northern and southwestern coasts, was connected with a long-term worsening of aridity – that is, to a tendency for rainfall and summer cloud to decline. It is not easy to see why the northern and southern parts of Europe should have been suffering from such opposite effects, although the climatic regions are, of course, very different. Possibly the critical factor was the growing deficiency of spring rainfall in poorly favoured regions of Castile and Aragon in the rain shadow of the mountains, a serious matter for their precariously based agriculture, while the Cantabrian coastlands, always stormy and rain-swept, experienced colder winters and wetter summers along with the rest of western Europe. Climatic history is a young subject full of unsolved problems, and what it will finally reveal is uncertain; but it is too important to be ignored by the economic historian.

8 The Peopling of America

Some six and a half million people migrated to the New World in the three centuries between its discovery by Columbus and the American Revolution of 1776; a million of them white, the remainder Africans, who came unwillingly to slavery. The peopling of the Spanish colonies, which accounted for nearly all sixteenth-century migration, has already been discussed; here we shall look at the movement, white and black, into English, French and Portuguese America. In the seventeenth century English and French settlers went to the West Indies and the American mainland; after 1700 free migration was nearly all into the English colonies of North America, though most of the migrants were Scots, Irish, Germans or Swiss rather than Englishmen. Spain and Portugal continued to replenish officialdom, commerce and the Church in Spanish America and Brazil, and there was a small movement of French and Dutch. But much the greatest part of migration north of Mexico was to English colonies; in the south it was nearly all of Negro slaves.

English settlers, unlike the Spaniards a century earlier, came into nearly empty lands, either in the Caribbean islands that the Spaniards had denuded of native population long before to provide mining labour on a few favoured sites, or in the wooded eastern coastlands of North America, where the Indians were sufficiently few and barbarous to be treated as enemies and obliterated. The English (and the French in the West Indies) did not face the temptation of the Spanish conquerors to live idly on the exploitable labour force of a subject race; they had to work themselves or perish. The English and French West Indian colonies had been firmly established for some decades before their social character was changed by bringing in slave labour to work sugar plantations; and this change was so opposed to the interest of most colonists that it caused a mass exodus from the islands to mainland colonies where they could hope to labour on their own lands again. Only in the far north, in the St Lawrence basin, did a different pattern of colonization, based on the fur trade, preserve the Indian population for a time.

Table 1

Population of English and French Colonies in America
(thousands: slave population in brackets)

	1640	1700 (including slaves)	1775 (including slaves)
New England	20	130	676 (25)
New York, New Jersey, Pennsylvania, Delaware	—	65	623 (50)
Virginia, Maryland	8	87	759 (230)
Carolinas, Georgia	—	12	449 (140)
Barbados	—	54 (42)	86 (68)
Jamaica	—	53 (45)	210 (197)
Other British West Indies	20	43 (31)	113 (97)
Guadeloupe, Martinique, St Kitts	—	—	155 (23)
St Domingue	—	—	210 (193)

The earliest populations bear little relation to the number of migrants, for disease and starvation struck very hard at the pioneers in Virginia and New England, and in Barbados and St Kitts. Year after year from the first landings in 1607 newcomers poured into Virginia, but its population remained very small; two hundred in 1608, four hundred in 1618, 1,232 in 1625 – by which date some eight thousand others had died there. Unfamiliar climate, unknown foods, serious food shortages, and quarrels with the Indians caused a high death rate. There were few births, for colonists were unwilling to expose their womenfolk to the dangers and hardships of pioneering. Even Massachusetts had no more than two thousand people in 1632, although nearly twice that number, including some women, had been landed there in the previous three years. But the pioneers learned what crops to grow and how to grow them in American conditions; they acquired local hunting lore; they abandoned the most unhealthy sites and mastered the Indians; and by mid-century a native-born generation was appearing, acclimatized and growing up adapted to its surroundings. Then the favourable aspect of colonial life began to make itself felt. Nowhere in the colonies did men and women face the hazards of urban life that caused huge death rates among the poor huddled in London and Paris and only moderately smaller ones in the lesser towns of Europe. In the West Indies disease still took a heavy toll, and everywhere men suffered the accidents of frontier life and newcomers succumbed to difficulties of adjustment, but the dangers from these were much smaller than those of urban life in the home countries. Once Virginia, Massachusetts, Barbados and St Kitts were securely founded in the 1630s, they were able to attract some women and families as well as single men from Europe, and many reports attest the high fertility of women in the colonies, though because of the still predominantly male migration the crude birth rate remained low. In a first phase of population lasting no more than two decades, constant immigration was needed to maintain numbers. By 1640, however, with a high and rising number of births, and death rates at rural rather than urban levels, natural increase had begun to supplement immigration. By the second decade of the eighteenth century immigration from Europe had everywhere become secondary to natural increase in expanding the population, though migrations within America were still important. The colonies achieved a close balance between men and women, with a proportion of children even higher than in England; the striking contrast with early days is shown in Table 2.

Everywhere on the mainland, the expanding settlements

Table 2

	Population of Virginia 1624–5	Population of Maryland 1755
Men	873	29,141
Women	222	25,731
Children	107	52,337

displaced the Indian. Though these eastern Indians were hunters, they also had substantial patches of tillage. The early settlers learned from the Indians about such local crops as maize and tobacco and the way to cultivate them, but the eventual growth in English numbers demanded repeated clearances of forest for cultivation, and the taking over of Indian plots within it. Time after time the local boundary of settlement was agreed with the Indians by the colonial authorities, but as individual settlers began to push across the boundary again there were inevitable quarrels, and it was impossible for the authorities to support Indian rights for long in the face of their own public opinion. A few killings and burnings on each side, and the Indians moved on again or were annihilated, while another tract of forest resounded to the settlers' axes. After the first years in Virginia and New England the Indians were not strong enough to endanger the settlements seriously until after 1675, when some tribes came into alliance with the French at points where the English and French frontiers were in contact. In a complementary role to settlers as trappers of fur-bearing animals, or as rivals for lands that were coveted for settlements, the Indians were peripheral to colonial needs, and though at times they were treated with consideration, their interests were pushed aside without qualms when they conflicted with those of the colonists. European diseases, too, took a heavy toll, spreading among the hunting Indians and thinning them out before the colonists had pushed far into the interior.

Since these lands did not provide a docile native labour force, the problem from the very first years was to secure working colonists. The earliest expeditions were adventures; they attracted the adventurous and desperate – 'lascivious sonnes, masters of bad servants, and wives of ill husbands'. Whilst these had their uses, they were not the men to toil solidly at clearing woods and raising crops – though some of them were well suited to the dangerous subtleties of Indian trading. In any case, many of them had been drawn in by the expectation that the Virginia Company would discover rich mines, or the way through America to the South Seas, and they were soon disillusioned. The paupers and the criminals reprieved from the gallows who were scraped together to fill later ships were not better material. With such men it was difficult to get past the early phase of trading and hopelessly searching for gold to the laborious construction of settlements for tillage. To the man who was ready to leave home and work hard to better himself, the land grants offered in Ulster during this period seemed altogether more promising, and between 1610 and 1640 Ulster attracted some forty thousand English and Scots migrants of just the kind the American colonies needed. The Virginia Company survived this difficult stage by continually sending new settlers and imposing a military discipline to get some work done, until a sufficient body of real workers had been painfully accumulated to bring the settlement to a size compatible with civilized life, and then, on the basis of individual proprietorship of plots for tobacco planting, to make it positively attractive. In New England, after some years of small-scale precarious settlement, stable conditions were created at one stroke in 1629, when the Massachusetts Bay Company planted a body of settlers large enough to begin functioning almost at once as a fairly self-sufficient colony. The company and its colonists, moreover, were religiously motivated, and the colony was supported for more than a decade by large-scale religious migration, backed by a pressure of would-be refugees so strong that the organizers were freely able to reject unsuitable applicants. Future colonies built on these two centres of strength; the West Indies learning from Virginia to encourage small holdings growing a staple crop for export, and northern colonies, spreading out gradually from the firm base of Massachusetts Bay, following its example of corn and cattle farming supplemented by fur trading and fishing.

After the earliest pioneering phase, the requirements and attractions of the northern and southern colonies diverged completely. Though the farming communities of the north could expect to benefit from a general growth of the colony which would make some specialization possible, they had no great need to attract hired labour to work on the land. Indeed, in Massachusetts there was real fear that bringing in people of the wrong sort would pollute the religious atmosphere. After the great wave of migration between 1629 and 1640, which was under the impulse of fears for religious autonomy in England, little attempt was made to attract further settlers to New England. Thereafter, its population grew mainly by natural increase, which was so rapid that by 1660 the colony was reaching its natural frontier at some points, and there was a beginning of migration beyond it. The cultivable area of New England was in fact very limited, and in the latter part of the seventeenth century even religious migrants usually went to the Hudson valley or Quaker Pennsylvania.

The plantation colonies, however, continued to offer economic incentives to immigrants. The knowledge that land was freely available for men to take up the small-scale cultivation of saleable cash crops (even if the collapse of tobacco prices during the 1630s greatly reduced their profitability) was a strong attractive force. They seemed to offer far more to migrants than the stony soil, hard climate and religious bigotry of New England. The established colonists, moreover, quickly came into possession of larger holdings than they could work with their own hands, and were anxious to find a means of attracting workers. For twenty years after 1640 the tobacco colonies in the mainland and the West Indian colonies had little rivalry in attracting settlers, and their population soared as newcomers poured into them.

The difficulty was that few Englishmen who were willing to work with their hands had the resources to migrate across the Atlantic and maintain themselves while setting up as small-scale cultivators. The answer was found in linking their need to be supported during the process of uprooting themselves with the desire of settlers already established to bring more pairs of hands to work on their land. It was the system of indentured servitude – in practical terms, of strictly temporary slavery. This was introduced in 1617–18 in Virginia, and was so popular that by 1625 over a third of the colonists were indentured servants. It was adopted into newly founded Maryland in the 1630s, and almost from the beginning in the West Indies. With its introduction in both English and French colonies, the task of financing migration to the New World was largely taken over by the colonies.

Merchants and shipmasters in London and Bristol, Nantes and Rochelle, let it be known (by notices, leaflets, and agents travelling to surrounding towns) that they were ready to take single young men (or occasionally women) to a plantation colony. A restless, discontented, hard-up or ambitious young man would contract that in return for a free passage he would serve a master without pay, merely for his keep, for four years after his arrival in America. The shipmaster would deliver his cargo of servants to his colonial principal, or if he were venturing on his own account would sell the servants on the quayside to the highest bidders. After serving his time with the master so acquired, the servant became an entirely free citizen of the colony, and custom – soon hardening into law in most colonies – required him to be given a free grant of land by the colony, and some equipment by his former master. In Virginia, for example, he could expect to receive fifteen bushels of corn and two complete new suits of clothes; in Maryland tools, clothes and a year's supply of corn. He could reasonably hope to build up the modest subsistence of a small planter, and in time bring in indentured servants himself, get further grants of land, and become modestly rich. In French Guadeloupe and Martinique the system was generally similar, but the normal term of service was three years. Thus the master got three or four years' labour very cheaply, and in addition a further free grant of land from the government for bringing in migrants; and the servant, after a few years of very hard labour, the prospect of an independence which in England or France he might never have been able to secure. The whole arrangement depended, of course, on the continuing availability of supplies of good unappropriated land, and broke down wherever this condition could not be met.

Thus the peopling of the colonies took two general forms. On the one hand, small steady streams of employees in early projects, of indentured servants and other volunteers who had been given inducements to go, of throwouts of the state and the unfortunate victims of kidnapping; all these made a regular movement of a few hundred, perhaps in some years a thousand or two thousand people. They were nearly all single men, with some small admixture of single women; when the men were well settled they sometimes sent home for their womenfolk. On the other hand was an occasional wave of migration of an essentially non-economic character. The decisive Puritan wave of 1629–42 sent some twenty thousand people to New England, and many of the forty-five thousand migrants to Virginia or the West Indies were also Puritan refugees. There was a series of smaller movements; that of the royalists and others dissatisfied with the new government in a few years around 1650, mainly into the West Indies; the Quaker migration that established Pennsylvania in the years after 1681; the Huguenot migration to South Carolina in the 1680s; the deliberate despatch of refugees from the Rhine Palatinate to New York in 1708–9. These occasional mass movements carried over not just single men but whole families, often with servants (though men made up the majority even in these emigrant parties) and with big individual resources. No mass migration was caused chiefly by economic factors.

Two connected influences began to check English and French migration to the West Indies, after little more than two decades of development, and presently brought about the transition to slave labour. The first was the rapidity with which the tiny land areas of

F

the original French and English islands filled up with settlers. As early as 1647 there was no more land available in Barbados to allot to servants who had completed the term of their indentures; space was found for them for a decade or so, in the Leeward Islands, but these too were rapidly occupied. The second was the introduction of sugar planting in the 1640s. Sugar, unlike tobacco, cotton or even indigo was not suited to production on small plantations. The turn to sugar production was generally instituted by colonists who had already become wealthy or by rich settlers from England – notably some of the royalist refugees of 1648–52 – who recognized in sugar planting a colonial investment that would not require them to soil their hands. Buying up and extending plantations, these wealthy settlers made smallholdings scarcer and hard to obtain, first in Barbados, and then much more slowly in the Leeward Islands. The consequence was a rapid falling off in the migration of indentured servants to the islands. In Barbados this was evident by 1650; in the other islands, English and French, by 1670. When the Council for Foreign Plantations declared in 1664, 'People are increasing principally by sending of servants' this was already ceasing to be true. It was in the 1670s and 1680s that more or less voluntary migration to the islands was briefly overshadowed by 'spiriting' – the kidnapping of unwary young people in the western ports to be shipped out and sold as servants. In this period, too, Ireland for the first time helped to make up the numbers; a quarter of the indentured servants in Nevis were Irish in 1678. These expedients were not very effectual, and they were necessarily transitional, for the sugar plantations were highly labour-intensive, requiring not merely the maintenance but a very big expansion of the labour force.

The sugar planters of Barbados and Guadeloupe solved their labour problem by following the example of Brazilian plantations. These had been set up by European colonists who never intended to undertake manual labour and who, when indigenous labour failed to meet their demands, resorted naturally to the African slave who was already familiar to Portuguese through a century of slave trading. Slaves, at first provided for the English and French planters by Dutch traders, were no cheaper to buy than white servants (though of course they were permanent chattels); they seem to have been no worse treated – white servants were worked to get full value from them during their four years of servitude – and there is no strong reason to suppose they were more fitted by nature to long hours of work on tropical plantations. Slavery was adopted not because it was necessarily the cheapest or most efficient method of operating sugar plantations, but because it was the only one available when white servants could no longer be attracted.

The sugar planters' anxiety to extend their slave-worked plantations lowered the prestige of manual labour; on the other hand it enabled smallholders who were disappointed with the profits of tobacco, indigo or cotton to sell out. They, as well as indentured servants disappointed of holdings, rapidly abandoned the islands. The development of sugar was earlier and much more rapid in Barbados than in any other island. Thirty thousand white settlers left Barbados between 1650 and 1680, going first to other islands; to Antigua, Monserrat, and Nevis, which sugar was slower to overrun; or to Surinam, reviving the defunct English settlement there; or to Jamaica after its capture in 1655. By the 1670s, however, with sugar spreading in all the islands, the mainland had become the small man's refuge. From the beginning of the 1660s Barbados colonists and officials were showing interest in the uncolonized coast south of Virginia, and they played a part in the founding of Carolina in 1670, opening up a territory into which great numbers of islanders migrated. The white population of the islands other than Jamaica, which had reached a peak of some fifty thousand in the 1650s, fell to no more than twenty thousand by the end of the century, and the problem of the safety of this small white population among more than seventy thousand slaves constantly occupied colonial legislatures. Even Jamaica, which retained a more varied economy with substantial cotton planting, could not keep small planters for very long; by 1700 it had become an island of slave labour, with less than eight thousand white colonists among forty-five thousand slaves. The French islands faced the same experience. As early as the 1670s the flow of indentured servants to Guadeloupe, Martinique and St Kitts had slackened as sugar drove out the smallholders; but large numbers were beginning to go to St Domingue (modern Haiti), where they hoped to clear some of the great empty lands for tobacco or indigo holdings when their servitude was over. But in the 1680s sugar appeared in St Domingue too, spreading particularly rapidly after French rights to the colony had been formalized in 1697, and driving indigo planting from the most accessible lands. Increasingly the servants arriving there found that only impossibly remote tracts of land were available for them at the end of their term. Some migrated to small islands such as Dominica and St Vincent, that were now being occupied for the first time. When peace came in 1713 the hoped-for resumption of the flow of servants from France did not take place.

Such labour difficulties did not reach Virginia and Maryland until much later. Nevertheless, by the 1690s so much of the land had been granted to new settlers, and those who had financed their migration, that little land was left to distribute, though much good land lay idle in the hands of big landowners. It was held by its owners as speculation for rising value, so that far from the new-comer getting a free grant – unless he went into the back country – he was likely to be asked a high price for land. For this very reason the Maryland proprietors had abolished headright (the right to receive a grant of land for bringing in a new settler) in 1693, but they were too late to stop the concentration of lands in the hands of the wealthy. As grants to freed servants came to be remote from navigable water and less attractive for tobacco planting, these colonies suffered from the competition for settlers of the lands farther north. During the eighteenth century Pennsylvania, New Jersey and the Hudson valley above New York pulled in most of the indentured servants. The rapid continuing expansion in the demand for tobacco after the peace of 1713 could no longer be met with a labour supply of the old kind, and the larger plantations turned over to slave economy during the next two decades. The Carolina rice plantations were slave-worked almost from their beginnings in the 1690s. The use of slave labour, of course, still further lessened the possibility of bringing white indentured servants into the area.

Slaves, therefore, came to provide the characteristic labour force of the West Indies – French as well as English – before the end of the seventeenth century, and of the southern mainland colonies as far north as Maryland during the first half of the next century. The forced immigration of Africans as slaves into Brazil and Spanish America was already large: the addition of West Indian and North American demand caused it to swell from the latter part of the seventeenth century, into a flood that reached its peak around 1780, and despite the spread of anti-slavery legislation continued on a large scale for another eighty years. The great majority of immi-grants to America up to the end of the eighteenth century, there-fore, were not Europeans – whether free men, indentured servants or transported criminals – they were slaves. Men, women and children from Africa came in, to the number of a million or so before 1700 and over six million more during the eighteenth century. Up to 1781 their distribution was as given in Table 3:

Table 3

Imports of Slaves (thousands)

	before 1600	1600–1700	1700–81	Total
British North America	–	–	256	256
Spanish America	75	293	393	761
Brazil	50	560	1,285	1,895
Caribbean: British	–	261	961	1,222
French	–	157	990	1,147
Dutch and Danish		44	401	445
Total	125	1,315	4,286	5,726

The inseparable connection between the slave trade and the plantation economies of the tropics is apparent from these figures. There were domestic slaves and mining slaves in Mexico, and rather more of them in western South America; but the majority of slaves for Spanish America went into the plantations of the Venezuela, Colombia and Ecuador coastlands, and to the sugar plantations of Cuba after the 1760s. In northern America, too, there was a sprinkling of domestic slaves in all the colonies, but slavery was important only in the service of the rice plantations of Carolina and the tobacco plantations of Virginia and Maryland. Four slaves out of every five went to the tropical plantations of Brazil and the Caribbean, and the great majority of these were to work in sugar plantations.

Most of the slaves died early and left no descendants behind them. Colonial white populations far exceeded those of Africans in America, despite the much larger migration of the latter. Figures of European migration are very hard to determine, but they are unlikely to have exceeded a million down to 1781. Net European migration into the non-Spanish Caribbean was numbered only in tens of thousands, for a great many of the early migrants to the islands moved on to the North American continent, and later migrants were commonly transients with no intention of spending a lifetime in any colony. Yet the French and English island population of European descent numbered nearly a hundred thousand in

1774, while the migration of nearly three million Africans as slaves had left a population of no more than seven hundred thousand. As a general rule, plantation slavery killed its subjects prematurely. To the shock of translation into a new world with new diseases – which imposed severe losses on European settlers as well – was added the cultural shock of changed role within a totally different type of society; and to this the very heavy and at some seasons prolonged labour, generally in sugar plantations and on a diet that was rarely adequate. Much has been written on the planter's need to conserve the slaves who represented a heavy capital investment for him; but the facts say that he worked them to an early death. Towards the end of the colonial era, in a very old-established slave society like Barbados, something like a balance was appearing between slave births and deaths; but in most colonies the slave population was in natural decline, and was only maintained and increased by large new importations. In mainland North America, away from the sugar plantations, the situation was different. The slave populations in Carolina and Virginia were reproducing themselves quite early in the eighteenth century, and by the end of the century their rate of natural increase was approaching that of the white populations. Whatever the hardships of life as a tobacco plantation slave, it did not compare with the tropical slavery, and above all the sugar slavery, that swallowed up and destroyed Africans. It is true that births in slavery were uncommonly low in the West Indies, whether because of the unbalance in numbers between men and women, or deliberate checks imposed by the organization of slave life or by the women themselves. Nevertheless, censuses show that the number of slave children was by no means negligible.

Almost the whole length of the west African coast was drawn on, at one time or another, to provide slaves. The trade of this coast was under undisputed Portuguese control until 1530, and they dominated it for almost another century despite foreign interloping. Its main function was to supply Brazil, but the Portuguese also made contracts to send slaves to Spanish America. The earliest slave trade to supply Portugal itself and the Atlantic Islands was on the Senegal and Gambia coasts, but by 1500 slaves were being bought in the Bight of Benin, and in the mid-sixteenth century the Congo met the great new needs of the sugar plantations of Sao Thomé. Only in the 1590s, as Sao Thomé began to flag in the face of Brazilian sugar's competition, did Congo and Angola slaves, as well as those from farther north, begin to go to America in large numbers. The Portuguese monopoly was broken by the Dutch offensive against Spanish and Portuguese interests after 1621. The Dutch drove away Portuguese shipping, and between 1637 and 1642, at the height of the war over Brazil, seized the Portuguese bases north of the Congo. Thereafter nearly all slaves for Brazil and Spanish America came from the Congo or, increasingly, from Angola. The 'old' west African coast did not remain a Dutch monopoly, for in mid-century the English were pressing in to satisfy the new need for slaves in Barbados, and their interest came to predominate in the slave trade before the end of the century. Despite the organization of the French Senegal trade, much of the supply of slaves to the French Caribbean islands remained in English and Dutch hands far into the eighteenth century, and Spanish American needs were met in the same way.

The importance of the slave trade to Europe and America lay not in usual profitability – which was probably mythical – but in its indispensable support for the tropical economy of the Caribbean. Without slaves, the Caribbean must have remained largely undeveloped. The Caribbean economy, as we shall see, came to be a main support of the North American colonies, which found markets there for surpluses they could not otherwise dispose of; and the whole colonial complex had some importance to European – and especially English – economic development in the eighteenth century. It is far from true to say that the Industrial Revolution in Europe was built on the necks of millions of African slaves; but their contribution to its preconditions was not a negligible one.

Looking forward into the eighteenth century, therefore, white migration went to those of the English mainland colonies where slavery made little contribution to the labour force; and among these largely into the middle group – New York, New Jersey, Pennsylvania and Delaware. In New England, the land was becoming filled up and Indian war repeatedly threatened the farms between 1675 and 1713, causing the frontier of settlement to retreat towards the coast.

Migration was checked by a long period of war, but was resumed after 1713, and was then largely directed into the middle colonies. But English migrants were not easily secured. The violence faded out of English political and religious quarrels after 1715; there was little that either impelled Englishmen to leave their country, or that attracted them in adequate numbers to America. Eighteenth-century migration was by less-favoured peoples, to whom even the back-lands of the farming colonies offered great hopes of improvement. There was a continuing migration of Scots, after the colonies became fully open to them by the Union of 1707. A heavy migration of Scots-Irish from Ulster began with the ending of war in 1713, and rose to a high level after the famine years of 1728 and 1741, the first going into Massachusetts and New Hampshire, but the great majority to Pennsylvania. Above all there was a wave of foreign migration in the years of peace between 1713 and 1739.

Foreigners had been excluded from holding land in some of the early colonies by the original charters, but the middle colonies abandoned most restrictions and set out to discover pools of possible immigrants and to attract them. In Germany the wars of 1689–1718 repeatedly devastated parts of the west, and particularly the Rhine Palatinate, while a variety of radical religious sects suffered under state enforcement of conformity. The Swiss valleys had always produced a surplus of young men who had to go and seek their livelihood elsewhere; traditionally they had served as mercenaries in the armies of Europe. The colonial proprietors therefore fostered propaganda campaigns in German states with awkward religious minorities, in the Rhineland, the Swiss cantons and Austria. Agents known as 'newlanders' were employed to travel through these states recruiting migrants. Some migrants were indentured servants, but the majority were the rather different 'redemptioners' who paid as much as they could of the cost of their transport to America, and were then indentured, if at all, only for a time depending on the unpaid balance. They included a good proportion of artisans, who introduced many crafts to America, even if their original practitioners intended to push farther on to landholdings on the frontier after a brief spell of settlement in the towns. It was a migration, moreover, of whole families bringing some property with them, rather than of indentured servants, and entirely national communities were set up at various places in Pennsylvania and New York. This flood of central European migration was checked by the outbreak of war in 1739 and not resumed on any scale until the end of the Seven Years War in 1763. Then with the political settlement of North America apparently completed, the floodgates of migration were opened, pouring in Scots and Irish and some foreign settlers during the last decade of colonial rule.

White migration always depended mainly on the real or supposed attractions of America itself, first in the warm southern colonies of export staples, and when these were monopolized by great land-owners, in those of the farming colonies where soil and climate were most fruitful. Because northern America as a whole offered so much land that was virtually free, there was only a limited scope for rural landowners of the type that had dominated European society or for the creation of the peasant or labouring dependence from which most migrants had come. Indeed, industry was held back by the ever-present call of available land, for even in the substantial towns of mid-eighteenth century America, it kept wages at so high a level that few manufacturing industries could compete in price with imported goods from Europe.

Only in exceptional circumstances of religious and political up-heaval did any large numbers of people desire to emigrate, and of course most migration for reasons of this kind simply carried people from one country of Europe to another. The Puritan wave of 1629–40 was all-important to the establishment of farming America, the base from which the distinctive English type of colonization ultimately spread, but no other refugee movement had so profound an effect. Persecution sent Protestant Walloons, Huguenots, Catholic and Protestant Germans, and Jews, in great waves across Europe; few of them looked beyond it. In the sixteenth century numbers of Portuguese Jews fled to Brazil; there was a trickle of Huguenot migration to French colonies, though the government discouraged it. England had no comparable persecution, though fear of it drove many people across the seas in the 1630s; and when Scotland briefly experienced a savage putting-down of dissenters in Charles II's reign, Scots refugees found their main place of escape in Ulster. The main regular flows of migration to the New World were fostered, both in the seventeenth century when the survival of colonies depended on migration and in the eighteenth when the proprietors of particular colonies wanted to augment their income, by the deliberate measures of established communities or colonial proprietors to popularize it and to make the way easy.

But propaganda for colonies was also needed to secure the acquiescence of governments in the migration of their people overseas. Until colonies had shown that they did have some value to the mother country – in supplying gold or silver, or commodities that could not be produced at home – it was not easy to show why governments should allow large numbers of men to go to them.

The literate, vocal section of public opinion had to be convinced that it was good for the country – the country they regarded as theirs – that colonization should proceed. This was a quite different task from persuading the labourer in Somerset or the dissenter in Suffolk that he would be personally better off or would be able to practise his religion more freely, in America.

This is the practical significance of the discussions on over-population and the desirability of alleviating it by the plantation of colonies that was going on in England in the decades around 1600. The view that America was a kind of safety-valve for an overpopu-lated Europe is entirely derived from this propaganda. The European population problem was of a magnitude hardly to be affected by the emigration to America; and when it had solved itself to some extent in Malthusian ways, through disease and famine sharply reducing Europe's population, emigration nevertheless continued. Demographic pressures on the small numbers of fami-lies of the landowning classes deserve more attention, for these provided many of the most vigorous enterprising spirits, most of the major and minor leaders overseas, and a great number of sup-porters of colonial ventures. In the mass of the growing popula-tion of sixteenth-century England, each extra mouth had a pair of hands to work with, and if work was becoming harder to obtain, it was taken for granted that hands could somehow produce a living. Among gentlefolk, each new mouth needed, ideally, an estate worked by other people from which to draw an income from its maintenance; and in a society of primogeniture this was available to only one of the sons in each family. The population surge of the late sixteenth century has been studied only in the most general way, but for the highest strata of the population it is well attested from good evidence. Studies of the English nobility show that births into each noble family in England were at a very much higher level between 1580 and 1630 than they were in the decades around 1700, and it is very probable that they were also much larger than they had been around 1500. What applies to the nobility must apply quite closely to the whole of the landed gentry. There really were two or three generations, in this period when colonizing propa-ganda reached its height and when actual colonization was added to war and privateering as a gentleman's occupation, when the number of younger, landless sons in families dependent on the land, was for some reason exceptionally large. When Hakluyt wrote of an England 'swarming at this day with valiant youths rusting and hurtful by lack of employment', he was describing a situation in which his generation and the one that followed were unusual. Though in England such young gentry could go more readily into the professions or overseas trade than in continental countries, they were brought up to exalt the military and governing virtues, and for many the opportunities presented in colonizing projects must have seemed more attractive than the humdrum means of earning that were open at home.

The fear of overpopulation, ready to catch a hold on public opinion because of the growing number of vagrants and paupers at one end of the social scale and of landless younger sons at the other, was fed by propaganda, and became one of the influences that caused literate people to think of sending their fellow-countrymen over-seas. Because it touched the families of nobility and gentry, it secured acceptance in court circles whose positive agreement to overseas colonization was essential. Nevertheless, general propa-ganda for colonization preceded the real colonizing phase; it reached its peak in the 1580s, was checked by experiences at the end of the century and by the tasks of building English and Scots settlements in Ireland, and was already fading before a substantial movement of people began in the 1620s. Its part was played in keeping favourable attitudes to colonization open until the self-interest of government, or the new propaganda of merchants who saw and wished to expand the profits of colonial trade, made themselves felt.

Little was asked of governments beyond acquiescence in colon-ization, carrying with it a readiness to defend colonies overseas against other powers. Governments did not have consistent long-term policies on migration, because it was not a sufficiently impor-tant matter to them. Details were regulated, for in principle every subject required his monarch's permission to leave his country. The Spanish colonies were freely open to Castilians, though only after 1717 to other Spaniards, and after the earliest years they were closed to foreigners. Brazil, tolerant towards foreigners in general, discouraged non-Catholics; the French colonies, first dreamed of as Protestant refuges, were presently barred to would-be Huguenot emigration, if not very effectively. The English Government im-posed no such restrictions, though some colonies that were well provided with people imposed their own religious and social tests on prospective migrants. Though by the end of the seven-teenth century pamphleteering argument had turned to discussing the danger of colonies draining the mother country of necessary labour rather than relieving it of a labour excess, little government action followed from this. Emigration from England was always completely open for those who could meet the cost. Government intervention confined itself to attempting to prevent the abuses of 'spiriting' and to ensure some fairness in the treatment of servants in the colonies. Slavery, which was completely unknown to English or French law, was left entirely to colonial regulation; the slave did not even receive the limited protection that in Spanish America and Brazil was afforded by a legal system that carried memories of European slavery.

Yet the fact that the English stance on migration was rather more open than that of France or Spain had only a modest influence on development. The essential thing was that the economy of the English North American territories required much labour, unlike French Canada; and had neither a native labour supply (as in Mexico and Peru) nor an overwhelmingly strong incentive to use slaves as in the Caribbean. The economic strength of the colonies of small settlers far surpassed that of all others in the end because they created balanced societies whose numbers multiplied rapidly and incessantly, to a degree that even before the middle of the eighteenth century had reduced immigration to being a minor factor in their growth.

9   Spain in Decline

The economic history of Spain has been less studied than that of the other countries of western Europe, and though considerable fresh work has been done in the last decade the real depth of its seventeenth-century decline is still by no means clear, and the explanations for it are unsatisfactory. It is a phenomenon above all of Castile in the ninety years after 1590, for in the kingdom of Aragon, Catalonia flourished modestly during part of this period, while the downfall of the Valencian economy can be attributed largely to the expulsion in 1609–11 of the Moriscos, the artisans and the practitioners of advanced agriculture in eastern Spain. The causes of Castilian decline were much discussed by early seventeenth-century writers, the *arbitristas*, and a good deal of modern writing rests on their diagnoses, and because of this has dated the decline too early. The reality of economic decline is unquestionable, but it may be doubted whether it was either so uninterrupted or so all-embracing as many accounts suggest. It is especially hard to determine whether the great fall in population was in part a result as well as a cause of the weakness of the economy. The tremendous loss of population in 1595–1602 was in part recovered during the next twenty years, and the expulsion of the Moriscos had only a modest effect on Castile, but famines and new epidemic waves struck Spain repeatedly through the seventeenth century – with a particularly heavy catastrophe in 1647–52 – and population in 1690 was a fifth smaller than it had been a century before. Several of the larger towns lost half or more of their population; industry after industry succumbed to foreign competition; and the handling of overseas trade passed largely into the hands of Portuguese and later of Dutch and English merchants settled in Spanish ports. But the net effects of changes in agriculture – the support of the great majority of people in Spain – are still obscure, and it is impossible to judge whether the real national income of Spain fell as fast as population.

Most of western Europe went through economic difficulties that were more or less serious, between the 1620s and the 1650s, but Spain's difficulties began much earlier. Everywhere the series of bad harvests of 1594–7 caused hardship, and in many regions they were associated with famine and pestilence; but nowhere had these struck so savagely as in Spain. There was no real recovery from the troubles of the 1590s; the disasters of the mid-seventeenth century fell on an economy that was already shattered, and at the end of the period the first steps towards returning prosperity after 1680 were presently to be halted by the war over succession to the throne of the Habsburgs. Spanish experience, unlike that of England, the Netherlands or even France, was not so much one of periods of recovery interspersed with setbacks as of continual depression that from time to time worsened into disaster.

There is no completely acceptable explanation of Castilian decline, but its timing and long continuance suggest an approach through the central fact of Castile's state experience; it was at war somewhere, and usually on a very large scale, for over eighty of the hundred years before 1659. An earlier chapter has shown that it was Castile that bore the main burden of financing the dynastic ambitions and the religious crusades that involved the Habsburgs in war throughout central and southern Europe, in the North Sea and the Mediterranean and the Atlantic. The effective limits of taxation on the Castilian population were reached in the 1590s, and this fact, together with the growing difficulty of borrowing on the security of taxes already mortgaged for years ahead, contributed to the temporary abandonment of a war that seemed unlikely to attain its objectives. Peace was made with France in 1598, with England in 1604 and with the Dutch in 1609. The economic situation then was by no means hopeless, but little advantage was taken of the interval of peace to economize or to overhaul the financial administration. Then in 1621 came a fresh plunge into war in pursuit of the old aims, and it continued uninterruptedly, with one power or another or with several, until 1659. In the last twenty years of this period economic collapse could not be staved off and the Spanish economy reached its nadir.

The most visible effect of the financing of this long series of wars, continuing from 1568 to 1659 with only two brief interruptions, was inflation in Spain. This continued to be severe until 1680, long after it had ceased elsewhere in Europe; and it was interspersed with sharp periods of deflation when the crown attempted to retrieve the state of its currency. During much of the sixteenth century, pressure on real resources had been largely responsible for pushing Spanish prices upward, and the influence of rapidly growing money supply had added little to it. The seventeenth-century inflation, however, arose from crown financial needs for its wars, and from the exhaustion of silver coinage through its export from Spain. There is no direct evidence in the balance between import and export of bullion, but it is clear that payments to creditors outside Spain, principally by the crown to meet military costs but supplemented by individuals' transfers to meet trading debts, grew continuously. Whereas in the sixteenth century they had kept pace fairly closely with the rising import of silver, they continued to grow after the early 1590s when silver imports were levelling out, were maintained at a high level during the twelve years' interval of peace, and rose to a new flood after the renewal of war in 1621 just as the bullion import began to fall away rapidly. Spain was already becoming short of silver in the 1590s as war expenditures reached their peak. The crown's response was the currency debasement of 1599 which, while it maintained the standard of the silver currency, poured out copper coins in replacement of a large part of the silver circulation. Thus Spain at last followed the rest of Europe into a debasement of its circulating currency which the mines of America had long enabled it to resist.

The copper coinage produced a revenue for the crown, as coins were issued with a face value far above that of the metal in them. It was, therefore, too useful a source of revenue not to be resorted to again in time of financial stringency. There was a fresh copper issue in 1602–3, another in 1617; and it was resumed in 1621 and continued for six years on an increased scale, bringing a profit equivalent to one and a half years of the crown's normal expenditure. But the volume of the copper issues were now so great that they raised prices, cutting into the profitability of the process to the crown, particularly as part of the proceeds of taxes paid in copper coin had to be transformed into silver to pay foreign creditors. In 1628 the crown reformed its ways, reducing the face value of copper coins by half – a savagely deflationary measure – and promising that there would be no more such issues. This good intention could not, however, be adhered to when the war with France reached its climax in the 1630s; there was a further big issue of copper coins in 1636–41 that brought renewed inflation and the same cycle of diminishing profit to the crown. In 1642 the value of the copper coins was again called down by a quarter, creating another sudden deflationary crisis. But once more copper issues had to be resumed on a large scale in 1651, and the next thirty years saw a worsening monetary chaos, with soaring inflation interrupted briefly and disastrously by the calling down of the value of the copper currency in 1652 and 1664. In 1679, payments in silver commanded a premium of 275 per cent over payments in copper coin. The following year the currency was brought under control, copper coin strictly limited, and there was no return to the worst situations of the greater part of the seventeenth century.

In the sixteenth century, prices had risen in surges, interspersed with periods of price stability. In the seventeenth century, too, there were waves of inflation, steepest in 1620–8, 1636–42 and 1664–80, as government met urgent needs by making big issues of copper currency; and in each case they were ended by precipitous price falls when coins were revalued downwards. So to the normal difficulties of an inflationary period were added those of extreme and unpredictable price fluctuations in *both* directions. Though these had less effect on transactions in moneys of account than on those in which coin changed hands, they made it difficult to carry on trading or industrial activity with any confidence. Moreover, they were coupled with other activities of the state – discussed below – to drive the business community to a despairing realization that its interests were always to be sacrificed to the needs of the government. The external effects are hard to judge, because the inflation was an internal one related to the valuation of copper coins, and the silver equivalent of Spanish internal prices did not take the same course. In terms of silver, Spanish prices had ceased to rise significantly even before 1600, much earlier than the price rise halted elsewhere in Europe. Foreign manufactures nevertheless continued to invade the Spanish and American markets at an increasing pace, ruining much of Spanish industry, but in the seventeenth century this penetration cannot be accounted for simply by monetary factors.

War imposed burdens on the economy through taxation, some of which was used to transfer resources out of Spain to pay and equip armies abroad. In a peculiar but important sense there had been a gain from this in the sixteenth century, for these transfers were anti-inflationary, going far to counter-balance the inflationary effect of the silver inflow. But the other aspect of taxation had been a weakening of consumer purchasing power and a dampening of some kinds of enterprise, and this became more serious as the inflow of silver slackened after 1622. Taxation, as we have seen, was greatly augmented during Philip II's reign, and because he left enormous debts to be serviced and repaid out of taxation – absorbing nearly two-thirds of his regular income just before the suspension of payments in 1596 – there was little remission of tax pressure when peace came. After 1621 war thrust the Treasury's needs upwards again but its receipts from taxes did not rise very much. The burden borne by the taxpayers did increase modestly, but corruption in tax collection and administration was leaving an increased part of revenue in the hands of the collectors. The crown met its excess expenditures during the next half century by the profits of currency issues, by the sale of offices and honours, and by further borrowing on the security of revenues in a receding future. There was little fresh taxation on the old taxable classes to account for the worsening economic situation of the mid-century decades; if they found taxes more burdensome it was because the economy had become weaker and productive incomes had declined. War added to uncertainties in other ways. The seizure by the crown of the silver and goods of merchants in the American trade, in 1637 and 1639, encouraged the scuttle into clandestine trading; the Genoese who had financed much of Spanish trade were ruined by the royal suspension of payments in 1627, and their Portuguese successors by the royal bankruptcy of 1647; the silver fleets on which the annual cycle of payments depended were twice lost, to the Dutch in 1628 and the English in 1657. All these were blows of the kind that in other countries in the seventeenth century caused short-lived commercial or financial crises; in Spain they fell so frequently as to discourage enterprise, destroy faith in the goodwill of government, and cause those who could to seek more secure incomes in land or office, if only until quieter days returned.

The drain of manpower losses was a great and continuing one; but Castile had borne similar losses during its expansive period, in the Italian wars of the early sixteenth century and the French wars under Charles V, through the Netherlands campaigns, the struggles against the Turks and the naval war with England. For many decades population had risen steadily though thousands of Castilian soldiers died in foreign lands or on the seas; continuing war in the seventeenth century aggravated a population fall whose main causation lay elsewhere. The Castilian economy had been able to bear enormous burdens of war through most of the sixteenth century; it faltered under them in the 1590s so that peace had to be sought, and collapsed under them after 1621 although the wars of the seventeenth century were on a scale no greater than their predecessors. This progression points either to the emergence of new fundamental weaknesses in Spain or to an accumulation of stresses during the first period of war that so fatally weakened the economy that it could not support the second.

Other possible influences on Spanish decline must be sought, beyond the effects of war. It was in the fact of positive economic decline that Spain was differentiated, during the first three-quarters of the seventeenth century, from England and both the Habsburg and the independent Netherlands, and in some degree from France. Yet it did not decline alone, for there is a sharp contrast, as yet unexplained, between the seventeenth-century experience of the Mediterranean lands – Italy and north Africa as well as Spain – and that of north-western Europe. Italy too went down economically from the 1620s, and began its economic recovery in the same tentative way as Spain in the last quarter of the century. This process of the relative decline of the Mediterranean lands was a cumulative one; once the north-west forged ahead the gap widened continuously. But the beginnings of it are not very obviously connected, except in quite minor ways, with the reasons for north-western advance.

The most striking difference between Spanish experience and that of all the other nations of the Atlantic periphery was the extent of its population fall, concentrated heavily on Castile. Two great catastrophes, in 1598–1602 and 1647–52, account for a great part of it. The Mediterranean kingdoms of Spain showed a smaller decline than Castile, and it is notable that in Catalonia, for which good statistics by districts are available, population actually grew in the coastal lands whilst it fell in the inland districts adjoining Castile. Within Castile, the population of Andalusia suffered less than that of the inland provinces, Old and New Castile and Estremadura. The Castilian plateau, whose population and wealth had been the original basis of its monarchs' power, was weakening rapidly in relation to the coastlands. Northern and central Spain had been thickly peopled, in relation to their soil and climate, and even the southward migration from the plateau only began to lessen this density in small patches from the 1560s, while most of the towns of Old Castile were still growing. After 1580, harvests repeatedly fell short of needs and total population ceased to rise; famine followed by pestilence struck hard in 1595–1602 and reduced numbers steeply. If population recovered after this disaster, it was reduced again and again by the return of famine and plague; in 1629–31, most savagely in 1647–52 and 1676–9, and again in 1683–5. Many of the cities of the north were almost emptied, and Seville lost half its population in the mid-century epidemics and did not fully recover. Yet still the reduced population was not adequately fed; there was some continuing failure in agriculture or in income distribution that historians have not identified, and famines recurred.

There are some particular reasons for Spain's population decline: the expulsion of the Moriscos in 1609–11, military losses, the considerable expansion of the numbers of men and women in the Church and therefore, presumably, celibate. But the causes that made famine, and in its wake plague, hit Spain with such severity are far more important. Possibly these causes lie wholly or partly outside economic explanation, in subtle climatic changes upsetting the barely viable economy of the Castilian plateau, or in special reasons for severity of the plague connected with climatic conditions or living habits. Such questions can only be raised here, not answered. But was Spain further afflicted by the peculiarities of its social structure? Most writers of the time answered in these terms, but the arguments they produced seem confused, conflicting and at times implausible. Castile lost a tenth of its population at the end of the sixteenth century, leaving large tracts of its countryside deserted. This is the classical situation in which, time after time in western Europe, the restoration of conditions of labour shortage has given labour – the producing peasant and the wage-earner – the bargaining power that has enabled it to improve its conditions, whether of land tenures or wages. It has in fact been argued that the population losses of the years 1598–1611 were responsible for a sudden upsurge of industrial wages that worsened the international competitive position of Spanish industry. Yet the condition of those who remained on the land as peasant cultivators or wage workers was apparently unrelieved. This paradox has been explained by the power of the great landlords, as it has elsewhere; but in other countries and at other times the economic pressures of labour shortage broke through landlord defences, seigneurial authority, and raised peasants' and wage-earners' incomes. If it is true that consumers and producers alike suffered from high food prices, while simultaneously merchants withdrew from trade that had become unprofitable and landowners found their incomes falling, then there was an extraordinary situation of universal disadvantage. Such a situation could be accounted for only by an actual decline in productivity, for which an explanation might be found in a worsening of climate causing a fall in the yield of land, or alternatively in withdrawal into unproductive activity or changes in attitudes to work, causing a fall in the yield of labour. But it is far from certain that it is true.

It has been suggested that the aversion to manual labour was stronger in Spain than elsewhere in western Europe. It is impossible to evaluate the relative strength of such feelings among people now dead, and their influence in different countries. In every country, independently, historians have rightly pointed to the existence of notions of 'gentility' which ascribe to all manual occupations a taint of degradation, and even to trade a social status below the highest level. It has been shown that in most countries – the Netherlands and the Italian trading cities have at times provided exceptions – the urge to acquire gentility has drawn talent and wealth out of productive enterprise into the land-owning and rentier classes. Nevertheless, reasons can be adduced to support the view that these attitudes were particularly strong in Spain. A military society that had been built up in four centuries of struggle against the Moors in Spain itself, in the piecemeal conquest of territory that was finally recovered from them as late as 1492, was revived when on the point of becoming obsolete by a long phase of American conquest and of the success and high prestige of Spanish arms in Europe. The military image was hardly dimmed until Philip II's efforts ran into disasters after 1588, and the attitudes it engendered still had potency when the collapse of their true basis was made patent in the dismal campaigns of the seventeenth century. If Spain's military strength at its height actually rested on the humble and unregarded infantryman, success in arms could still burnish the image of the horse soldier. The reconquest of Spain from the Moors had left, as a legacy from the past, an exceptionally large class of people with accepted claims to minor nobility – hidalgos – constituting perhaps a tenth of the population of all Castile, and a much higher proportion in the northern provinces. In France no more than 2 per cent of the population had this noble status; in England, where formally it hardly existed, no more than

3 per cent had the kind of claim to gentle blood that most nearly corresponded to it. Only a handful of this section of Spanish society was well-to-do. There was a small group of very rich nobles associated with the court, and a number of moderately prosperous *caballeros*; but most *hidalgos* had nothing but consciousness of their noble blood, and a deep fear of losing their status as they would do if they worked with their hands or even in small-scale trade. These were the descendants of conquerors; the peasant population and townspeople were descended from generations that, whatever their racial origin, had lived under a Moorish society. The gap was not only one of blood but of religion; the long campaigns of the Inquisition, the persecutions and deportations of Jews, crypto-Jews and Moriscos, were reflections of a fear that within a once-subject population Christianity had only shallow roots. Moreover, noble status was still something that newcomers could aspire to; there was no serfdom in Spain to taint men's blood, and the acquisition of a little unearned income from land or government loans would permit a man to buy his way into the ranks of the *hidalgos* – from which he or his family might progress into the military orders of knighthood and the higher nobility. That is, the lower ranks of the nobility contained far more people, and offered wider opportunities for entry, than the small knightly orders of England or France; and once entered they closed the door to participation in industry or trade much more firmly. Admission was a certificate of freedom from Jewish or Moorish blood – a valuable asset in the heyday of the Inquisition; it was a necessary step towards obtaining any public office that provided a good income; and the *hidalgo* was by custom free from nearly all direct taxation, from conscription and from degrading punishment. Men who had acquired land or *juros* on a scale sufficient for them to abandon their original occupations found such privileges worth buying, and the withdrawal from earning, by men who had achieved modest worldly success, may have been more common than in England or France. The sheer size of the *hidalgo* class was, however, probably of greater importance, a class withdrawn from labour by pride in status, even if this was status in a military hierarchy that offered no function corresponding with its pretensions. Many went off to America, where in early days they provided the backbone of the conquering expeditions, and to the incessant European wars; but the numbers of *hidalgos* were maintained by fresh recruits from the useful sections of society.

It has also been suggested that enterprise was affected, in a rather different way, by the nature of the investment opportunities offered by Castilian crown finances. In most countries interest-bearing loans could be made to the government from time to time; in Castile there was an almost continuous availability of short-term securities (*juros, censos*) secured on particular branches of the revenue and therefore apparently safe. Though most lending was undertaken by foreigners, Spanish participation was considerable in the latter part of the sixteenth century, and was growing. These government loans offered an alternative to investment in land. The risks of industry were so great – in the face of foreign competition, collapse of demand in famine years, violent and unpredictable inflations and deflations – that many might seek this way of escape from them. This argument, again, is not a wholly plausible one. A state that periodically declared itself bankrupt (in practice, postponing rather than repudiating payment of its debts, and unilaterally reducing its interest rates) and which laid taxes on incomes it had contracted not to tax, did not offer the security that investors in government loans normally seek. A period of long-term inflation was not a good one for lending at fixed interest even under circumstances of the greatest security. The interest rates paid to ordinary lenders were not high by European standards of the seventeenth century. The extent to which people engaged in lending seems less an indication of the attractiveness of government security (particularly after the two state bankruptcies of the sixteenth century) than of the gloomy prospects of commercial and industrial investment, which have to be accounted for in other ways. The same considerations apply to the purchase of offices from the crown, which was a form of permanent loan, though one that might provide a rising revenue. Most offices in Spain, as in France, came to be saleable and from the 1620s there was continuous creation of offices deliberately for the purpose of selling them; offices whose duties, if any, were performed by low-paid deputies whilst the salaries and fees came out of the pockets of the taxpayers. These were essentially investments, and the terms on which they were held were manipulated by the crown, in disregard of the original grants, in the same way as the terms of public loans.

The agrarian history of Spain has been little studied, and it may eventually be shown that the seventeenth century saw a renewed movement away from corn production into export crops, and little or no overall decline. There is no doubt, however, about the decline of some branches of industry. The case of shipbuilding is a very clear one. The needs of Atlantic shipping had grown so fast during the sixteenth century that the Basque shipbuilding industry was unable to keep pace with them, and colonial shipbuilding was begun, first in Havana in the 1570s and then in Cartagena and Maracaibo. By the 1640s a large part of Spanish shipping in trans-Atlantic trade – whose total was much reduced from its old peak – was colonial-built. But a more striking change was coming in the middle of the seventeenth century, with a positive decline in Basque shipbuilding and the abandonment of use of Spanish-built ships in long-distance trades of all kinds, and even for the use of the navy. The advances made by the English in building warships, and by the Dutch in building bulk carriers, were not paralleled by the Basque shipbuilders. At one time the technical leaders in European shipbuilding, they were now falling behind. Their success in creating the galleon for the Atlantic trade early in the sixteenth century, brilliantly meeting the needs of the time, resulted in a long refusal to look at possibilities of further improvement and of specialization.

The Basque and Asturian iron industry was unfortunate in encountering the competition of Swedish iron-making in the 1620s and 1630s, as this became technically advanced under Dutch and Flemish direction. This competition was felt by iron industries all over Europe; but the decline in the manufacture of iron goods, notably at Toledo, cannot be accounted for in this way.

The woollen industry provides the greatest example of industrial decline. Woollen making, in Spain as elsewhere, was a great and widely diffused industry. The poor everywhere bought local cloth of coarse quality. But the best-known parts of the industry were in towns where specialized production of medium and good qualities was centred: Segovia, Cuenca, Toledo. Their products had not only been sold to rich Spaniards but had entered international trade. During the seventeenth century the population of Segovia and Cuenca fell by half, and that of Toledo by two-thirds. The Spanish and Spanish-American markets were encroached on both by English and by Dutch cloth in the late sixteenth century, and when peace came in 1604 and 1609 both countries began to pour their manufactures into Spain. Yet Dutch industry was largely, and English industry was to some modest extent, making its fabrics with wool imported from Spain.

There were internal influences on the failure of the Spanish woollen industry in the face of competition. The gild system that was imposed on Spanish industries during the sixteenth century created rigidities in methods of production, and standardization of types, that may have put them at a disadvantage in competition with more flexible northern industries. There is some evidence that the demographic disaster of 1598–1602, followed by the expulsion of the Moriscos in 1609–11, created labour shortages in whose aftermath skilled workers were able to secure large increases in their wages, raising Spanish costs in relation to those of imported fabrics. It is dangerous to talk of technical backwardness in the textile industries, for there was little technical advance in England or the Netherlands, but the increasingly efficient organization of their rural industry may have been adding to their advantages. Whatever the reasons, the Spanish woollen industry was losing its vigour by 1580, and plainly went downhill in the seventeenth century. Very little was left of the specialized branches of the industry by 1660, and the American trade was then supplied almost entirely by foreign products. Decline was not the consequence of failure of demand; there were still large numbers of wealthy Spaniards, but they and the merchants trading to America found reasons for preferring to buy foreign cloth. English writers, for example, claimed a great market for their cloth in monks' and nuns' habits; from all we are told of the inordinate growth in the number of clerics in Spain this was an important and expanding market; in the seventeenth century it came to be supplied by foreigners.

Industries that had no strong foreign competition to face did not suffer so badly. This again suggests that there was no great collapse in the home market; the absence of export-oriented foreign industries enabled paper, pottery, leather wares and (for most of the seventeenth century) silks to continue in modest prosperity, and even to recover from the blow dealt by the expulsion of the Moriscos, who had included so many of the artisans.

Explanations of decline in terms of technical or organizational backwardness, or slowness to adapt, all lead back to the rather indefinite and unsatisfactory answer of lack of enterprise among Spaniards. The opening of a new frontier on the far shore of the Atlantic had created new opportunities, and a climate of thought that encouraged confidence in the success of enterprise. In the early decades of the sixteenth century, merchants and financiers, as well as noblemen and *hidalgos*, had flourished in this bracing climate. But

it had a long-term influence in encouraging backward-looking elements, the feudal Spain that had sustained itself for so long in the
crusade against the Moors. The windfall gains of military conquest,
the permanent profits of lordship over an entirely fresh multitude of
near-serfs, the openings for an enlarged bureaucracy, the call to a
vast missionary effort – these had more powerful influence on men's
minds than the opportunities that opened in America for trade. An
important part of the explanation of Spanish decline lies outside the
material plane, outside the failure of rewards in the new conditions
of the seventeenth century; it is derived from the prolongation of
the military-feudal dream, and the exaltation of extreme religious
attitudes sometimes at the expense of sanity. Failure in war – the
Armada disaster of 1588, the surrender to the Dutch in 1609 and
1648 and to the French in 1659 – shattered the dream; the momen-
tum of effort so long thrusting through these channels could not
easily be turned back in its old strength to humdrum productive
pursuits. Goals of achievement were changing. By the middle of the
seventeenth century Spain was a tired nation, and those who could
sought quiet lives as rentiers, sinecurists, landlords or monks.
Many of the best incomes that were still to be had by work now
went to foreigners, especially those controlling overseas trade.
There was too much parasitism, too many people whose ambition
was to be parasites.

Yet the timing of economic depression brings us back once more
to the economic and social influence of war; it reached its worst in
the war years 1621–59. In Spain as to some extent in France, the
addition of the strains of mid-century wars to basic inadequacies of
agriculture was one of the most decisive factors in weakening the
whole economy.

The century from 1680 saw recovery from the very lowest levels,
if no very considerable economic advance until near its end. Population recovered after the last great plague outbreaks of 1677–83.
The War of the Spanish Succession (1702–18) finally stripped the
Spanish crown of its Netherlands and Italian possessions – though
not of costly ambitions to recover the latter – and as a result of the
war the provinces of the crown of Aragon were reduced to a subjection to the royal will nearly as thorough and complete as Castile's.
The customs obstacles between the kingdoms of Spain were
lowered in 1714–17, free movement of people between the kingdoms was made possible, and the way was open for a greater economic integration. The chief gainer from this was Catalonia, which had

long been forced to look eastward to sell its produce. Its industry –
especially cotton manufacturing – was expanding fast in the 1730s,
and Catalans were making their way into the economic life of
Castile and bringing it a new vigour. The end of the Habsburg
dynasty and the arrival of a Bourbon king made possible some
improvement in the efficiency of government. The new French
interest in a Spain now closely allied to it brought economic benefits; there was some development of state enterprises on the French
model and French investment gave a stimulus to the Catalan cotton
industry. But Spain could not resume its old place in Europe, or
look any more to a relationship of superiority with its American
empire. There was no substantial growth of a native middle class
fostering industry and commerce until the last quarter of the eighteenth century; trade and shipping continued largely in foreign
hands; agriculture remained backward, the disregarded occupation
of peasants and day labourers. The main currents of economic
change passed Spain by; if its history was no longer, as in the mid-
seventeenth century, all tragedy, it had lost its interest.

10 *Latin America:*
The Seventeenth and
Eighteenth Centuries

If the economic history of Spanish America is judged by the volume of its dealings with Europe, a slackening of activity will be discerned there too, in the second quarter of the seventeenth century. Yet this would be a false view; the importance of external relations to the Spanish American economy, though still great, was declining. At the moment when population was beginning to fall in many parts of Europe, the decline of Indian numbers in Mexico was coming to an end and a slow rise in total population had begun. In Peru, numbers continued to fall during the seventeenth century, but no longer in a precipitous way. Throughout the central lands of the Spanish Empire, economic activity was diversifying, society was becoming more urban and more hispanicized. The recession in silver mining was real and had repercussions on many parts of the economy that had found important markets in the mining communities, and among town dwellers and officials whose incomes were derived ultimately from the mines; but the economic balance between mining and other activity that had grown up in the later sixteenth century was not the only balance possible for Mexico and Peru.

There is no doubt that silver production declined. The official record of silver shipments to Spain shows a steep climb from the 1540s until soon after 1590; shipments were then maintained with some vicissitudes until about 1630 and then fell away steeply. These figures of export to Spain through official channels, however, become increasingly unreliable as indicators of production in the seventeenth century. Much more silver was retained in the Indies as the economy grew, and shipments of silver across the Pacific to Manila – for the China trade – already large by 1580, were also growing rapidly. The export of silver to Europe through unofficial and therefore illegal channels became common: after 1580 there was a growing clandestine trade in Peruvian silver through Buenos Ayres; and the foreign trading bases set up in the Caribbean in the 1620s and 1630s attracted silver from the smaller Spanish ports in return for European goods and slaves. The illegal silver traffic was probably kept within fairly close bounds until 1621, but during the forty years of war that followed the motive to evade controls became much stronger. In the 1630s and 1640s the crown's desperate need for money caused it repeatedly to confiscate private silver that was being shipped to Spain through the official channels, and this drove many more owners of silver either to send silver to Spain in ways that escaped official notice or to find outlets for it beyond Spain. The records of shipments therefore exaggerate the decline in production.

There is ample descriptive evidence from the mining areas, however, making it clear that there was a real fall in production. Potosí, which had accounted for well over half the silver mined in America during the second half of the sixteenth century, was failing rapidly after 1640, and though there were fresh Peruvian discoveries – at Oruro in 1608 and Pasco in 1630 – they were on a smaller scale. In Mexico the overall situation is less clear, for big new mines were being opened between 1590 and 1633 and their production offset the decline of older ones. Within a few years of the last great strike at Parral in 1633, production was falling; but the fall may not have been very steep and it was protracted for no more than thirty years. After 1630, gold production was falling in Colombia as the Marquita and Buriticá deposits were worked out.

The dramatic decline in silver production at Potosí is most in need of explanation, but Peruvian mining has been much less studied than Mexican. The maximum output of Potosí was so much greater than that of all other producing sites that new Peruvian discoveries could not make up for its decline. It had surmounted very serious difficulties during the boom decades, making the advance around 1570 from the essentially handicraft-form mining of the best soft deposits close to the surface to a heavily capitalized industry engaged in deep mining with expensive shafting and tunnelling and mule-operated mills for crushing the hard ores, and using the new mercury amalgamation process for extracting silver from poor-quality ore. It was not labour shortage that struck Potosí; when Indian numbers declined the government widened the area from which forced labour for the mines could be drawn. Indeed in the mid-seventeenth century many Potosí mine operations were accepting Indian monetary tribute in place of the *mita* or forced labour they were entitled to, preferring this certain income to whatever profits mining might bring. Nor were difficulties in the supply of mercury decisive; when the production of the Huancavelica mine flagged at the beginning of the seventeenth century the crown diverted Spanish mercury from Mexico to Peru, and the crown-controlled price of mercury was actually reduced several times.

Mexican mining encountered rising labour costs, yet had continued to expand. Each of the early mines had made the transition to deep-working, expensive machinery, and the amalgamation process – at Zacatecas as early as 1560. There was little forced labour to be had in northern Mexico and well before 1600 the mines were commonly employing free Indians, attracted to the mines by high wages – four times as much as they were paid by the authorities for forced *repartimiento* labour. *Repartimiento* rapidly went out of use in the early decades of the seventeenth century, although after 1609 the government reserved it for mines and public works. Probably shortage of mercury, which held up treatment of ore for long periods and ruined some Mexican miners and drove others into debt to the merchants, accounted for the beginning of the fall in production more than any other influence on the side of supply.

On the whole, however, rising costs were accommodated. Silver mining was checked because of the declining value of silver in terms of the goods it could buy. The price of silver was determined by royal decree, and was absolutely fixed until 1732, and then only slightly increased. The silver peso – one ounce of silver – bought less and less of other goods in each decade of expanding mining developments; indeed, while Spanish prices (in terms of silver) stabilized about 1600, Mexican prices were rising until a little before 1630. The price of European goods in America was further increased after 1621 by the costs and risks of bringing them across an ocean dominated by Dutch maritime power. These processes must sooner or later have made the purchasing power of silver so low that it was not worth while continuing to produce it at constant or rising real costs. By the second quarter of the seventeenth century, when

European prices in terms of silver had risen at least three-fold since the discovery of Potosí, the marginal American producers with the deepest mines, the most floodable workings, were being squeezed out; it was becoming difficult for the miners either to accumulate for themselves or to attract from outsiders the fresh capital that was needed to push shafts to still greater depths and to construct adits and pumps to cope with ever-worsening flood problems. Many of the Potosí mines from which such enormous quantities of silver had been extracted could no longer be worked profitably; production began to fall about 1635 and continued downward for over a century. Mexican production was probably falling in total from the 1630s; but the decline ceased about 1660 and was soon followed by a rapid expansion, although the general price rise (that is, the decline in the value of silver) had been merely halted rather than reversed. It has been suggested that in Mexico the shortage of mercury (for the amalgamation process that produced silver from low-grade ore) caused fresh intensive searches in the neighbourhood of old deposits for high-grade ores that could be smelted (without mercury) and that sufficient of these were found to set a new silver boom going in the 1670s.

In the middle decades of the seventeenth century, therefore, mining contracted and silver exports fell; Mexico and Peru were able to buy less from Europe; Peru was able to buy less from Mexico; in America itself agricultural producers were able to sell less to the miners and to townsmen whose incomes ultimately depended on the mines. Thus the Mexican ranchers found that the rising price of beef stabilized about 1630 and then fell slowly; while the price of maize, which had doubled in half a century, ceased to rise in 1627 and fluctuated around a stable trend for over a hundred years. The end of the price rise had come in the New World as well as the Old.

The weakening of the old economic bond that had tied America and Spain – the flow of silver – had consequences of two kinds. On the one side, as the colonies were able to pay for lesser quantities of Spanish or European goods – wine and olives as well as manufactures – they were further stimulated to replace them by local production; on the other, the profitability of the existing forms of agriculture was checked because of the slackening of internal demand arising from the mines. The response could be a turn to new products to replace imports or provide exports to Europe, or alternatively the strengthening of internal self-sufficiency within great estates. There was a stimulus to more capitalist forms of enterprise – plantations, workshops, putting-out systems, commercial ranching – which had already grown up alongside an Indian peasant economy in the late sixteenth century but came to far greater importance during the next hundred years. Yet at the same time there was a regression into the self-sufficiency of some great estates – particularly in the north of Mexico – and the development of relations of a feudal kind.

During the seventeenth century the Spanish Empire found no adequate compensation for the declining role of silver in its trade with Europe. Cochineal and hides continued to provide substantial exports but apart from these the main export possibilities lay not in the products of the Mexican plateau or of remote Peru but in the lowlands and islands that grew tropical products. The full development of export crops was delayed until the end of the seventeenth century by insecurity and the difficulties of getting a sufficient slave labour supply. Mexico's principal economic response to the decline of its earnings from sales of silver was therefore the expansion of its own industrial production to replace some European goods. This seventeenth-century industrial history has been little studied, though the origins of much of Mexican industry are well known. Many crafts had been established in the towns during the sixteenth century – blacksmiths, potters and furniture makers, for example – and in Mexico City at least these were strictly organized in gilds for Spaniards only. Much native textile and jewellery-making had been preserved. But more important was the development of capitalist textile industries, employing Indian labour in large workshops, owned by Spaniards or Indian *caciques*. In the towns south of Mexico City – Puebla, Toluca, Texcoco – a large woollen industry grew up before 1600 and was expanding in the next century, although the best qualities were still imported from Europe. In the south the cotton-producing regions of Oaxaca, Michoacoan and parts of Campeche supported a manufacturing industry. The making of leather goods – saddlery, shoes and gloves – to Spanish styles was another natural occupation in a country where hides and skins were cheap, and replaced most imports from Spain. Only silk manufacture, which had flourished vigorously down to the 1580s, was driven into depression by the competition of imported Chinese silk fabrics, though it tried to sustain itself by turning from the use of Mexican to Chinese raw silk. On the whole, the goods that Mexico produced in quantity were the cheaper, low-quality ones, while the high-grade woollens, linens and metalwares continued to come from Europe. Shipbuilding, however, which had begun with small vessels for intercolonial trade before 1560, was providing Cartagena- and Havana-built galleons for the trans-Atlantic run early in the new century which acquired such a high reputation that in the following decades nearly half the shipping that crossed the Atlantic was colonial built.

The course of development in Peru was rather different, both in form and timing. Its dependence on external trade was diminishing in the seventeenth century, if partly as a result of government suppression of it. In the early part of the seventeenth century Peru bought most of its manufactures in Mexico, some of them Mexican products but a great and growing part of them the Chinese wares that were brought annually from Manila to the Mexican port of Acapulco. So heavily did this buying of Chinese goods trench on Peruvian silver shipments that a series of government measures was instituted from 1598 onwards to reduce the trade; and these culminated in the drastic step, in 1631, of forbidding all direct trade between Peru and Mexico. Peru's remoteness had compelled it from the beginning to attempt self-sufficiency in agricultural produce. Much of the land that had been dedicated to the Incas was handed over to Spaniards for wheat farming; there was much cattle ranching, though it did not come to dominate the rural economy so completely as in Mexico. By 1600 Peruvian production of wheat, sugar, fruit and wine was adequate for the needs of the Spanish population. The capital and chief commercial centre, Lima, which had some sixty thousand inhabitants in 1650, was supported by wheat- and maize-growing in the inland valleys to the northward, while the coastlands produced sugar and cotton. Vines, introduced in 1551, were so successfully naturalized that at the beginning of the seventeenth century wine export to Mexico was prohibited because it competed too severely with Spanish production. Olives also flourished and by 1600 the Lima district met all South America's requirement. Cultivation was extended far south into Chile in the seventeenth century and the Santiago area became an important source of wine and fruit, sending its produce not only northward but also across the Andes to the river Plate basin. The mining region of Potosí was supplied by farming on the lower part of the Bolivian plateau, and from the pampas east of the Andes in the Tucuman district. The links of Peru and Chile with the lands east of the Andes, and their outlet at Buenos Ayres, were being strengthened from the 1630s at the expense of the old connection with Europe through the Panama isthmus.

The decline of Indian population in Mexico halted very early in the seventeenth century, and total numbers began to rise, with a rapidly increasing component of mixed blood rather than Indian. After the great epidemics of 1576–81 there had been fewer than two million Indians left in central Mexico. The continuing fall in numbers for three more decades was due much less than in the past to epidemics, and more to the hardships of particular forms of forced labour in mines and textile factories, the disturbance of Indian peasant agriculture by the encroachment of Spanish livestock, and the continuing adjustment to the shock of break-up of Indian village culture. The most visible consequence of sixteenth-century decline had been the emptying of lands where peasant cultivation had been carried on most intensively, bringing a pastoral economy to land that had long been under the spade. The Spaniards in central Mexico were therefore affected at first less by a shrinkage of labour supply than by a decline of *encomienda* tribute, as Indian plots and villages from which it was drawn were abandoned. The towns of central Mexico, which in early days had been provisioned largely from Indian peasant surpluses, began to suffer shortages and food prices rose steeply from the 1570s. After 1580 labour scarcity was being felt in the free labour market on which some sectors of the economy depended, particularly on the wheat farms that were being expanded to replace imports and serve the needs of Spaniards in the cities and mining areas. Rising wages led to the introduction of some African slave labour in the towns – where they took over some crafts but were chiefly employed as household servants – and even to the mines, where they were not found very suitable. The extension of sugar plantations was checked for half a century after 1570, as much of the small inflow of African slaves was absorbed by other occupations. The Indian worker could not be dispensed with; but he now had to be attracted by wages as a free man.

Forms of social relationship were changing, although the reality of Spanish rule and Indian subjection remained the same. *Encomienda* – the right of Spaniards to the labour and tribute of Indians – lost much of its importance by the end of the sixteenth century, whereas land ownership by Spaniards, which had been exceptional, was extended rapidly after 1570 so that by the middle of the seventeenth century nearly all land in Mexico was owned by

G

Spaniards unless it was part of the great Church estate. The majority of Indians were no longer peasant cultivators bearing obligations of tribute and labour; they were freed from state-imposed obligations but divested of their land, and turned into wage-labourers, commonly burdened by debt. The typical unit of land ownership in Mexico – and a common one in Peru – came to be the *hacienda*, a great consolidated estate embracing many thousands of acres that employed not only herdsmen and labourers but crafts-men of many kinds. In its extreme form, found most commonly in northern Mexico, the *hacienda* was nearly self-sufficient, its dependent households producing most of the needs of the estate, so that its surpluses were entirely available for the expenditure of the proprietor who spent most of the year, with his immediate family, in Mexico City.

The *hacienda* emerged not out of the grants of rights over Indians – *encomienda* – but from the entirely separate grants of land, or originally of the right to graze animals over land, known under the title of *estancia*. A number of *estancias* survived far into the seventeenth century – more in Peru than in Mexico – growing wheat and maize and bringing their owners comfortable livings. They were the chief sufferers from labour shortages, turning very early to attracting free labour with high wages, and by the time forced labour was formally abolished they had long since ceased to use it. On the whole, however, land came into the hands of the great estate owners, securing grants from the crown, buying Spanish and Indian land as epidemic or economic depression brought it to the market. In the mining north, of course, the pioneers had been granted huge areas of Indian territory for ranching from the beginning, and during the seventeenth century they rounded off their *haciendas* by taking in some of the irrigated arable that smaller proprietors had developed, which had suffered particularly from the decline in mining activity. From 1591 onward the government was prepared to issue secure titles to landownership in place of the old defective or uncertain ones, on condition that their owners acknowledged they were subject to taxation. The negotiation of land titles and taxes over a vast area was a very protracted task; though well advanced by 1620 it was not completed until late in the seventeenth century. During this same period fresh land was being brought into *haciendas*, for though most of the land available for royal grant had been given away by 1610, by that time the purchase of Indian lands, which had once been prohibited, had become commonplace.

The Church, too, was becoming a great landowner, not merely through royal grants but also by private gifts, legacies of land to ensure the perpetual saying of masses, transfers from Indians and purchases out of income. It established farms in central Mexico that were to be models for the Indians to copy, and in the north its new mission stations with farms around them continued to push the frontier onward when the impetus from mining weakened. The Church estates continually expanded, for none could be sold and fresh legacies were added in each generation. At the end of the seventeenth century a third of the estates, both in Mexico and Peru, were in the hands of the Church, and, beneficial though Church influence had been in its early days, long-continued wealth brought its abuses.

Society was therefore becoming more varied during the seventeenth century. Village Indians, peasants owing labour and tribute to *encomenderos* or the crown, guarded by priests and to some extent by the courts, largely gave way to an Indian wage labour force, sometimes savagely exploited as in the textile workshops and some of the mines, but usually tolerably paid and even recovering a former security of status in the *hacienda*. At the other extreme from them were a few score of very rich Spaniards, nearly all of them normally living in Mexico City, owning great estates that were worked under the supervision of their lesser relations, with large numbers of more or less privileged Spanish and *mestizo* hangers-on and minor employees as well as Indian and Negro labour. At the same level of wealth was the small group of merchants who controlled the trade with Spain; almost all immigrants from Spain who were brought over as youths by merchant relatives, graduating in a closed circle of Spanish merchants, retiring with fortunes into the landowning class but first closing the circle again by bringing fresh youngsters from Spain to constitute the next generation of merchants. These landed and mercantile aristocracies dominated the colonial economy, maintained close associations with the governing circles and were able to exert great influence on the underpaid government officials who came out from Spain to regulate all activity in the New World. The government independence that had been a virtue of the old administration was rapidly eroded during the seventeenth century as great wealth exerted its influence in America and confidence evaporated in Spain. Between the extremes of poor Indian and Spanish aristocracy was a rapidly growing middle rank; the surviving modest planters and farmers – far more

in Peru than in Mexico; merchants below the wealthy ring of monopolists that controlled the import trade from Spain; workshop
owners, skilled craftsmen and junior officials. And into these middle
ranks was creeping a growing number of people who were neither
Spaniards nor Indians, but of mixed race.

For America was rapidly changing its race composition; the
sharp division between Spaniard and Indian was being eroded by
miscegenation. Few Spanish women came to the New World –
perhaps one to every ten men – and among the African slaves, too,
there was a big preponderance of men. In central Mexico and the
Caribbean lands in particular there was a wide mixture of blood,
mostly Spanish and Indian but with an important African contribution. A whole vocabulary of new terms appeared for the different
mixes; the well-known and common *mestizo, mulatto* and *zambo*
(white/Indian, white/African, Indian/African) fading away through
a whole range of complicated interbreedings to the indefinite
saltra-altra and *no-te-entiendo*. The pure-blooded Spaniards – including those *mestizos* who could pass as Spanish by appearance or,
occasionally, by virtue of their wealth – remained dominant. There
was no more than a trickle of Spanish immigration – of officials,
merchants, priests, lawyers and specially needed artisans – for after
the first hopes of conquest and of early mining there was nothing to
attract the ordinary Spaniard who had no well-entrenched connections in the New World. By the end of the century Spaniards from the
homeland, whether officials, monks and friars, or merchants, were
coming to be resented as outsiders, and the ranks of colonial-born
were closing against them. The authority of the Spanish crown over
the Indies was accepted universally and without question; but those
who represented it, except the viceroys themselves, could be despised
and their intentions perverted to serve the ends of the native-born.

The social differentiation against the Indian was being weakened.
He had undergone a transition from the status that was allotted to
him by the first Spaniards in the islands, of an animal to be driven to
his death by unrestricted forced labour; first to the serf of the
encomendero whose 'introduction to orderly habits of industry' in fact
put the Indian into complete subjection; to the protected serf, as the
crown step by step whittled away the *encomendero's* powers, from the
ineffectual Laws of Burgos (1512–13) to the gradual enforcement of
the New Laws of 1542; to the place of a labourer working compul-
sorily as he was directed by officials, hired out for *repartimiento* and
mita services after 1549. In the late sixteenth century this forced

labour was still widespread, but under official control, and it was further limited at the end of the century. *Repartimiento* was finally abolished in Mexico (except for public works and mining) in 1609, and the free Indian labourer replaced all these earlier varieties of worker.

This process of change was due in part to the desire of the state to treat its subjects equally and to break up feudal bonds, and to the conscience embodied in the Church at its best. But it also owed much to the growing scarcity of labour, which caused the mines to bid for the Indian worker with relatively high wages and forced other employers to follow suit; and to his replacement in some fields by a worker to whom the crown had no sense of obligation as a subject – the Negro slave, imported from Africa to work as domestic servant, as an urban tradesman or as a plantation labourer. But just as in Europe the ending of serfdom was not an introduction to a new heaven for the poor, nor the free wage contract a passport to a life of ease, so the economic realities facing the Indian in the New World transcended political and social changes. The facts of economic power, of highly concentrated property ownership, remained. It is true that the freer-working market forces as population reached its lowest levels around the end of the sixteenth century enabled the wage-labourer to secure a marked improvement in his conditions. The response of plantation owner, of miner and of *haciendista*, however, was to find a means of ending this freedom in the labour market, so that the Indian or *mestizo* could again be exploited without much check, as he had been under a compulsory labour system in its early days. The extent of their success is in dispute; but during the seventeenth century large numbers of wage-earning Indians came to be tied into a system of debt-bondage.

The Indian, brought from his village to mine, factory or plantations, found that in his new surroundings he had new needs to satisfy, and at first he lacked the means. His new employer was willing to advance him money or goods to secure these needs. The Indian fell into debt from the beginning of his employment, and was likely to build up this debt to proportions that he could never expect to pay out of his wages. Then he was unable to leave his employer; he was tied to his workshop or mine or *hacienda* by debt-bondage, or as it was there called, *peonage*. This condition of the labourer was so obviously open to exploitation that the government intervened against it, but with little success. The regular practice in the late sixteenth century of selling 'free' Indian labourers along with the estates on which they were settled was prohibited by the crown in 1601 and 1609, but it continued; a succession of orders from 1560 onward forbidding or strictly limiting cash advances to Indians, the first step into debt slavery, were fruitless. The long and tortuous struggle of crown and Church against the excesses of early forms of Indian exploitation had been successful; but the realities of the relation between the poor and the rich are not so easily effaced. With the generalizing of *peonage*, the lower levels of *hacienda* society were established in a pattern that has persisted in Mexico into the present century. Yet on the other side, the *hacienda* offered the Indian security; not just the meeting of his material requirements, but protection from all the Spanish pressures that still, despite all the efforts of the state, beat upon Indians remaining in the villages. It was a patriarchal social nucleus, replacing the old social nucleus of the village, and having the virtues as well as the vices of its type.

The history of Spanish America for most of the sixteenth and seventeenth centuries can be written in terms of Mexico and Peru. The sugar colony on Espanola, the fortress of Havana where the convoys gathered, the pearling beds of Margarita, the little trading post on the river Plate, even perhaps the gold-mining valleys of Colombia, all these were peripheral, having little weight in the imperial economy, supporting only tiny Spanish populations and – except where the defence of the convoys was involved – neglected by the crown. From the end of the seventeenth century, however, this history changes; these areas began to flourish, to attract planters and traders, capital and slaves and a strengthened officialdom; they entered the Atlantic economy in an important way, supplying great amounts of their own commodities to Europe. The huge Latin American continent developing varied economies can no longer be treated as a whole; and in a few pages the reasons for and the course of its new development can only be lightly sketched.

Caribbean and North American plantation agriculture, developed by English, French and Dutch during the seventeenth century, had found an enormous European demand waiting to be tapped by modestly priced additions to diet. Entirely new tastes appeared, for tobacco and coffee, while old ones were spread through new strata of the population by cheaper supply, notably of sugar and rice. The Spanish colonies took some part in this, supplying Spain with much of its sugar, but most Spanish Caribbean production went into the Mexican market, and was barely adequate for this.

The small settlements were almost unprotected and were open to buccaneering or privateering attacks through most of the seventeenth century. The government-supported privateering that had grown up during the religious wars of the sixteenth century died away but it left behind a legacy of outright piracy. Piracy received a powerful reinforcement in the 1640s from Spanish efforts to clear some islands of *boucaniers* – stateless men, runaways from ships and colonies – who lived off wild cattle in the remoter parts. The clearances simply drove many of them, as desperate outlaws, to the sea; and the new Dutch, English and French settlements on Curaçao, Jamaica and St Domingue offered them secure markets for their booty. They seized small ships engaged in coastal trade, raided small towns and isolated plantations, and so made regular agriculture and trade close to the Caribbean coasts very perilous. Eventually they began to interfere seriously with English and French interests, and this led to the closing of bases to them in the 1680s. Deprived of outlets for ordinary booty, they very rapidly declined and a degree of order and stability returned to the Caribbean. Once this was achieved it was possible for Spanish plantation agriculture to begin flourishing in the islands and along the coastlands.

The second requirement, after peace and order, was a large labour supply such as the English and French plantations had at their disposal. African slaves had been working sugar plantations in Espanola since 1518, but their numbers were limited by the strict control of the slave trade, confined to monopolists licensed by the Spanish government who brought slaves from the Portuguese trading stations in west Africa. In the 1620s, however, the Dutch swept the west African coast and thrust the Portuguese out of most of their slave trading posts. For thirty years the Dutch controlled the slave trade, and only relinquished their grip in the 1660s to the English and French. As the Portuguese were unable to supply slaves to Spanish America legally, a great illegal trade grew up, first in Dutch and later in English hands, and the Spanish colonies were able to get slaves much more readily. When the slave trading contract for Spanish America was granted to the French Guinea Company in 1702, and to the English South Sea Company in 1713, the whole situation had already changed, and these French and English contractors were falling in with a Spanish regulative system that was obsolete. During the long years of illegal trade Spaniards had become accustomed to buying slaves from small vessels in all the little ports round the Caribbean, rather than in the official market at Porto Bello, where they passed through the hands of a ring of wholesalers who took their profit. This illegal trade continued and even expanded in the eighteenth century alongside the revived legal trade, with a flood of slaves pouring in through English Jamaica, French St Domingue and Dutch St Eustatia and Curaçao. It was large enough to provide the essential labour supply for a greatly expanded plantation agriculture, the basis of Spanish as of French and English Caribbean prosperity in the eighteenth century.

Finally the plantations, having been secured from raiding and given an ample and continuing slave supply, were offered an expanding market in a Spain that was recovering prosperity during the eighteenth century, and a mainland empire whose population and wealth were growing very fast. Puerto Rico, and above all Cuba after mid-century, became the largest of all sugar producers, supplying not only Spain but also, through Barcelona, other Mediterranean markets. A second major export was cocoa, the distinctive product of the Spanish colonies, which had long been produced in southern Mexico for local consumption but spread fast in Venezuela and Colombia in the eighteenth century as a crop for export to Europe. But these were only the leaders among a range of tropical products; indigo, cotton, coffee, dyes and drugs of many kinds poured out from Spanish America in the eighteenth century.

At the other end of South America, the long neglected river Plate region was slowly drawn into the circle of commerce. Its early neglect had been to some extent deliberate; it opened a back door to the Peruvian mines, and the town of Buenos Ayres was founded in 1580 with the intention of stopping an illicit trade by Portuguese, rather than to be an active centre of trade itself. It continued, nevertheless, to be a place for the illegal shipment of silver. Far inland, meanwhile, small pastoral settlements were being built up by Spaniards who went in to exploit the vast wild herds of cattle that had grown up since the earliest arrivals. There were settlements in Paraguay as early as 1555, despite harassment by Portuguese coming down from the Matto Grosso plateau; and in the seventeenth century there was fresh pastoral development under the eastern foothills of the Andes, around Tucuman, Mendoza and Cordoba, finding a market on the Peruvian plateau. This scanty ranching population, spreading across vast areas of pampas, was responsible during the next two centuries for great quantities of hides that were sent to Europe, and supplied meat, hides and tallow to the Portuguese towns and plantations along the Brazilian coast.

A parallel development on the western side of the Andes linked this, too, more closely with the river Plate than with the isthmus and the Caribbean to the north. The Spaniards in Chile, where wheat, vines and fruit flourished, built up a prosperous community, for which the river Plate provided the best outlet until in the 1720s shipping began to go regularly round Cape Horn directly to Chile and Peru. The importance of Buenos Ayres was reluctantly accepted by the government, which in 1702 designated it as a port of entry for slaves under the French contract, and this position was confirmed when the contract was transferred to the English South Sea Company in 1713.

Less spectacular than these new developments around the Caribbean, but outweighing them in importance, was the re-expansion of the Mexican economy, based upon the growth of population and the recovery of silver mining. The advance of Mexican population, from no more than one and a half million in the early part of the seventeenth century to nearly six million at the end of the eighteenth, must be ascribed to natural increase among a people at last broken in to a new set of diseases and living conditions, with a stable society into which most of them had been born. Perhaps a fifth of the six million were whites or passed as white, the remainder being Indians or of mixed race. The rate of growth of numbers during the eighteenth century is an indication that the pressure of extreme poverty had been lifted; and Mexico was indeed prosperous, with expanding industries and a continuing modification of agriculture, now introducing wheat farming on a large scale, and new crops such as potatoes and bananas. Equally important, however, was the recovery of silver mining after 1660, passing its old peak production by 1690 and then doubling its level of production again by 1770. This was due neither to technical advance – which was not important before the middle of the eighteenth century – nor to the discovery of entirely new deposits. It came from the reopening or more vigorous exploitation of old mining areas – notably Guanajuato and Parral – under the influence of stable prices in Europe, and of the flood of gold arriving in Europe from the deposits discovered in Brazil in the 1690s, which raised the value of silver in relation to gold. Nevertheless, the old domination of the economy by mining did not return; Mexico was now largely self-sufficient, with a diversified production for a population nearly as large, at the end of the eighteenth century, as that of Castile. Peru (which in its widest sense, with present-day Bolivia and Colombia, had over five million people at the end of the century) had similarly developed a balanced and largely self-sufficient economy; mining recovery came late there, in the 1740s, and was not so pronounced as in Mexico.

The economic history of Spanish America during the eighteenth century becomes the history of particular areas that became countries after Spanish rule was overthrown. The continent was developing a number of economic centres, with variations among them as great as those between the English North American and Caribbean colonies. Apart from the Caribbean coastlands with their need for European markets, they had ceased to have a strong economic dependence on Spain; but none of them exhibited any strong urge to political independence until very late in the eighteenth century. The stationing of Spanish regular troops in the New World from 1764, and the institution of a number of administrative and financial reforms, did begin to cause some questioning of the value of the colonial link with Spain. Yet this aroused no great interest, for the colonial-born Spaniards had been remarkably successful in frustrating any metropolitan ambitions that clashed with their own. Spanish government eventually came to be seen as an irrelevance that might be pushed aside rather than as an impediment that threatened them, as the English colonists had felt themselves threatened. But action came only in consequence of the external shock of the Napoleonic wars that broke, for a time, the legality of Spanish government. To the end of the period with which we are here concerned, the Spanish Empire looked as eternal as Spain itself.

Brazil provided none of the drama of early Spanish America. There were no great empires, no masses of peasant cultivators, no treasure hoards or accessible mines of silver or gold; but an immensely long coastland of forest, the great river Amazon opening to the endless forest of the interior, and a thin population of primitive Indians. A useful small trade in brazil wood could be carried on with the coastal Indians in the north, but beyond this there was nothing to attract Portuguese settlement. In the sixteenth century they were fully occupied in developing their Indian Ocean trade and the sugar of the Atlantic islands, and the modest steps taken by the government in 1530 to encourage some Brazilian settlement were intended merely to ensure that Brazil was not seized by another power in default of Portuguese occupation. From the 1530s, however, a string of settlements was set up along the coast and the opportunities for the production of tropical products began to appear attractive. Sugar production grew steadily in the Pernambuco and Bahia areas, though for some decades it was held back by the crown because of its competition with Madeira and São Thomé. But it was an efficient production, for in order to overcome Madeira's advantage of proximity to Europe, Brazilian producers pioneered large-scale capitalist production of sugar. A big stimulus was given after 1580 by the migration of large numbers of Portuguese Jews, who feared the Inquisition in a Portugal that had come under the Spanish crown, and in the last decades of the century sugar output was expanded very rapidly, surpassing that of all the Portuguese island possessions. Advanced production methods in Brazil cheapened sugar so that rapidly growing quantities could be sold in Europe. There was no serious labour problem, for the Portuguese were accustomed to using slave labour and had control over the great sources of supply of slaves in Africa. A prosperous colony grew up, with some twenty-five thousand Europeans in 1590, and it brought wealth to Portugal, for all the trade was channelled through the mother country and paid considerable taxes to the crown. The trading profits, however, went largely to Dutch merchants, who handled the sale of the sugar and carried most of it from Brazil in their ships. It was this close Dutch connection with the sugar trade that brought them to attempt the seizure of the Pernambuco region of Brazil between 1621 and 1654; and their failure, and the emigration of many Dutch settlers from Brazil to the West Indies, helped to bring about a formidable competition from Caribbean sugar producers after 1660.

During the seventeenth century the greater part of the European population of Brazil, and its African slaves, was concentrated in the sugar-producing region along the coast, from north of Pernambuco to a little south of Bahia the capital, though there were pockets of sugar production much farther south. At the mouths of the Amazon were small settlements engaged in tobacco and cotton production, while along the southern coastline, nearly to the mouth of the Plate, was a scattering of settlements producing a little sugar, and some wheat in the uplands, with small harbours serving as outlets for cattle-ranching in the interior. Around São Paulo the farmers and ranchers, unable to afford Negro slaves, raided the Indian tribes of the interior; and between 1580 and 1654, when war obstructed the Atlantic slave trade, they were able to sell Indian slaves in Rio de Janeiro and farther north.

A century of growing Brazilian prosperity based on the production of sugar closed in the 1670s. Although the peak of production was reached in 1688, producers' incomes had already fallen heavily as competition reduced prices, and the industry's crisis dragged down not merely the Brazilian but also the Portuguese economy. The trading towns and the handicraft industries that served the planting community were all threatened. There was some expansion of cocoa and cotton in the tropical coastal area – tobacco was suffering, like sugar, from low prices – and in the south cattle ranching was expanding rapidly; but Portugal had to tighten its belt. Protectionist legislation was introduced to encourage Portuguese industry to replace imports of foreign manufactures, and luxury expenditure was discouraged, but nevertheless the Portuguese currency had to be devalued in 1688 and again in 1694.

The slave-raiding expeditions from the São Paulo region – the *bandeiras* – widened the range of their operations as they destroyed nearby Indian communities. After the union of the Spanish and Portuguese crowns in 1580, the old Spanish-Portuguese demarcation line down the 46th parallel of longitude seemed irrelevant, and the *bandeiras* pushed far to the west of it into the uplands dividing the Amazon and Plate basins, and down the valleys of the Parana and Paraguay rivers. They sought slaves, herded cattle, and here and there settled briefly to plant crops, coming into contact and clashing with Spanish ranchers coming up from the south. In this far interior they found gold, first at various points in Minas Geraes in 1693–5, and then in a whole series of strikes farther to the westward during the next forty years. To these were added the discovery in the same area, in 1728, of the world's largest diamond mines. The economy of Brazil was transformed and Portugal's wealth derived from colonies was restored.

The gold discoveries were on a huge scale, and each of the major strikes caused a rush of prospectors from the coastal towns and then from Portugal itself. Towns and the farming districts that supplied the plantations and the mines were denuded of people, and the prices of foodstuffs soared. As in Mexico long before, the mining districts created demand for food, stores, and above all carrying services. There was great employment in all these and many traders made their fortunes by supplying the mines rather than working them. Cattle ranching expanded, the southern towns grew, and the whole weight of the Brazilian economy shifted southward away from the sugar-producing region where it had been concentrated so long. This change was symbolized by the shifting of the capital from Bahia to Rio de Janeiro in 1762.

Through the first fifty years of the eighteenth century an average of some ten thousand kilograms (350,000 ounces) of gold came annually from Brazil in the official shipments – the year-to-year figures fluctuated enormously. This was not greatly less in value than the Mexican and Peruvian bullion of the late sixteenth century. It provided much less employment in Brazil simply because it was gold rather than the bulkier silver, and its discovery came to an economy which was already quite highly developed. It did not, therefore, have the same weight in the economy as Mexican production had done. Nevertheless, it enormously enriched Brazil, brought about a great addition to its population, and caused the diversification of its economy in the south to feed and supply the mining and trading centres. In Portugal, gold supported royal and ecclesiastical extravagance but had little inflationary effect because so much of it went out to pay for foreign manufactures (to the detriment of native industry); while a very rapidly expanding European economy in the eighteenth century greedily absorbed the addition to its currency that Brazilian gold made possible. In the early 1760s, however, gold mining passed its peak; though it remained important, a more varied plantation economy, with rapidly expanding cocoa, cotton and coffee production was overhauling it in the last decades of the century.

Colonization brought benefits to Portugal; crown and nobles, receiving colonial revenues, pressed less hard than elsewhere on the peasantry, and a mercantile middle class grew up which was considerable in relation to the country's size. But the gains began to fade away after the mid-eighteenth century. Portugal was left a backward, undeveloped country, its industry stunted by long dependence on the sale of Brazilian produce that had made foreign manufactures easy to obtain. The response of the government to the fall in gold shipments in the 1760s, as to the decline of earnings from sugar in the 1670s, was a new campaign to promote native industrialization, which had some modest success. Portugal was by now much poorer than the Brazilian colony, with its wide range of export products in sugar, coffee, cotton, cocoa, hides, diamonds and gold, its thriving towns and its artisans and trading classes; but eighteenth-century Brazil accepted a connection which drained an appreciable income each year to the mother country.

11 *The Rise of the*
Dutch Commercial Empire

Much of the trading activity of north-western Europe in the middle decades of the sixteenth century had been focused upon a single city, Antwerp. From the war that ruined it emerged a small nation, the United Provinces of the Netherlands, that captured a far wider range of European and extra-European trade, and in the seventeenth century dazzled every observer with its economic achievements.

The economic division of the Netherlands before and during the period of Habsburg rule was not along the east–west line roughly defined by the lines of the great rivers that became the boundary between the independent United Provinces and the remaining Spanish Netherlands. It was a north–south line, dividing the four manufacturing and trading provinces of Flanders, Brabant, Zealand and Holland from almost exclusively agricultural eastern provinces which were dragged economically as well as politically at the heels of their neighbours. Brabant, Holland and Zealand were less rich than heavily industrialized Flanders but all four provinces lived by trade, shipping, fishery and industry rather than by agriculture.

The origins of the intense maritime and trading activity of Holland and Zealand lay in a remote past. Fisheries and the trade in salt and salted herrings had taken them into the Baltic where they began to act as general carriers and traders. Their great medieval neighbours, Bruges and Antwerp, were not rivals, for their trade was largely in the hands of foreigners who had no special interest in promoting the use of Flemish shipping. These merchants trafficked in valuable goods – woollen cloth, spices, copper, silver and metalwares – which needed only a few ships, and those small enough to use the Scheldt, a river so muddy and cluttered that much cargo was loaded into and out of lighters at Arnemuiden roads. Far from resenting the entrance of Dutch shipping and merchants to the Baltic bulk trades, which were above all in corn and salt, native and foreign merchants at Antwerp provided much of the capital the Dutch employed. But the great power in the Baltic was the Hanseatic League, which had successfully resisted the efforts of English, Danes and Flemings to encroach on the business of its member-towns during the Middle Ages. The divisions of interest among the Hanse towns, however, weakened opposition to early Dutch intrusion into Baltic trade. The richest of the Hanse towns – Hamburg, Lubeck, Bremen and Rostock – earned most of their profit by an intermediary trade between the Baltic and the west, sending Flemish cloth from Bruges into the Baltic and returning Baltic furs, copper and wax that had come to them in Baltic trading. The bulk trades in salt, herrings, timber and corn that the Dutch entered into in the fifteenth century did not greatly interest them. But more easterly Baltic cities, such as Danzig, Konigsberg, Reval and Riga, were the direct sea outlets for the agricultural and forest products of Poland and Livonia, and sold western goods in return for these. These eastern towns had a monopoly of trade with the farmers and nobles of the interior, and when Dutch ships appeared in Prussian and Latvian harbours with salt, herrings and wine to exchange for corn, flax and timber, the towns' ·merchants at first attempted to drive them away. But the Prussian and Polish landowners welcomed competition among merchants and were anxious to deal with the newcomers; they put what pressure they could on the towns to allow the trade, even to the extent of bypassing the towns and bartering directly with Dutch shipmasters in creeks and villages. The town authorities had to give way and allow the use of their facilities by the Dutch, and after the middle of the fifteenth century much of the trade between western Europe and the east and north Baltic came into their hands. The Dutch sailed straight out through the Sound with their cargoes; they had little use for the services of Lubeck or Hamburg. Lubeck could look out with some equanimity on Dutch vessels sailing past carrying salt and herrings, because all Baltic markets wanted to import woollen cloth, and the Hanse, closely connected with Bruges, the port of the Flemish cloth trade, was best able to provide it. But the growth of the Dutch and English cloth industries late in the fifteenth century and the rise of

Antwerp, where the Hanse carried less weight than at Bruges, wrested this last weapon from the Hanse. Finally, they were unable to drive the Dutch out by force of arms, for the Dutch allied themselves with the Danes, who had long resented the Hanseatic monopoly and had earlier fought it alone without success. By 1500 the Dutch had become leaders in the Baltic trade and were steadily increasing their share of it.

The Dutch were not merely traders; they also had a considerable industry. Cloth-making had been developed in the towns of Amsterdam, Haarlem and Leyden, which were given privileges by the counts of Holland and attracted refugees from civil wars in Flanders. As Flemish industry turned its attention to worsteds in the late fifteenth century, Leyden concentrated on heavy cloths, and competed with England in the markets that served Baltic and Rhine routes. Early sixteenth-century Holland and Zealand, therefore, were increasingly urban; the villages were left to coastal fishermen and to cultivators who were adapting their production and methods to the demands of the prosperous towns. There was already a host of towns of middle size: Leyden, Haarlem and Delft, manufacturing centres; Brill, the largest of many shipbuilding towns; the Rhine port of Dordrecht; Enkhuizen and Rotterdam, the chief centres of the North Sea fishery. As late as 1514 Amsterdam was less wealthy than Leyden, Delft or Haarlem, if the tax lists can be believed, but in the middle decades of the century the rapid growth of the trading side of Dutch affairs, whose centre was Amsterdam, carried it to a modest pre-eminence.

This economic expansion took place within an antiquated political structure. The duchies and counties that made up the Netherlands passed by marriage to the imperial house of the Habsburgs, and eventually descended in 1555 to the monarch best known as Philip II of Spain, whose interests spanned the world from Peru to the Philippines. Burgundian and Habsburg rulers had tried to bring some uniformity to the rule of their mixed Netherlands inheritance, but with little effect beyond stirring up among the local nobility some consciousness of a common culture not shared by these alien rulers. None was so alien as Philip II, who after the first years of his reign never set foot in the Netherlands; and none was more anxious than he to make government uniform, efficient and obeyed. A slowly growing nationalist feeling, fanned by his actions, was reinforced by the emergence of a new religious zealotry. Calvinism, spreading from France in the 1550s, took a hold not just on townspeople and artisans but also on the politically conscious gentry, because it became associated with nationalist resentment at rule from Spain, and dislike at bearing the burdens of Habsburg dynastic wars. Savage Spanish repression of the new religion after 1567 led to a full-scale war of national and religious freedom, beginning in 1572 and resulting in 1609 in the effective independence of the United Provinces.

This war was fought largely on the territory of the southern Netherlands, which struggled as vigorously as the north for independence until 1579, and both before and after that date was trampled by the contesting armies. Holland, on the other hand, after the first stages of the war was protected from the devastation of combat on its own territory by the tangled waterways of the Mass/Rhine delta. Years of fighting and quartering of troops in the south decimated the population, ruined towns and industry, and destroyed livestock and farm buildings. Antwerp was sacked by mutinous Spanish troops in 1576, and its overseas trade brought to an end in 1585 when the Dutch captured both banks of the Scheldt below Antwerp. Though it recovered after 1609 to be an important centre of regional trade, and remained a financial power of some magnitude, its unique domination of the commerce of western Europe was lost. The ruin of south Netherlands industry and the collapse of Antwerp's trade, contrasting with the comparative security of the north, added an economic to the religious motive for many scores of thousands of refugees who fled to the northern Netherlands. Parma's government in the south even encouraged migration in 1585–7 and allowed refugees to take property with them; and while Calvinists fled north, few Catholics moved south. The scale and quality of this migration transformed Holland. Amsterdam was filled with merchants and the industrial towns with artisans. Half the earliest depositors in the Bank of Amsterdam, in 1609–11, had come from the southern Netherlands; forty years after the peak of the emigration more than a third of Amsterdam's population were immigrants from the south or their descendants. Moreover, a small movement of refugees from the southern Netherlands to other parts of Europe – to London and Stockholm, to Hamburg, Danzig and Leghorn – opened new opportunities for trade; the most natural trading connections of these emigrants were often with old acquaintances or relatives who had settled in Amsterdam. These personal links with trading cities abroad were important influences helping Amsterdam to become a new commercial centre for the west.

A huge leap in Dutch economic power therefore took place in the 1590s, supported by the refugees who had come in from the south, secured by the wearing down of Spanish military effort, and carried forward by the great boom in western demand for Baltic goods in the years 1589–98 and the rise to its peak of the inflow of silver from America that eased the working of the European economy. With few opportunities for investment in land, the immigrants poured their capital into trade, shipping and manufacturing, seizing opportunities that were opening both in the expanding bulk trades and in the extra-European world. In these years, therefore, the conjunction of new resources and of opportunities for their use in ways familiar to Dutch enterprise began the snowballing accumulation of Dutch resources and advantages – in capital, trading connections, commercial and industrial skills. The increase of Amsterdam's population from thirty thousand in 1585 to 105,000 in 1622 is indicative of the pace of commercial change. The Netherlands had emerged into its golden age, in which for more than half a century the rate of growth of its economy outstripped all others, establishing so strong a Dutch primacy in many fields of commerce and finance that it could only slowly be eroded.

Despite these accretions, Dutch commercial strength continued to be based on its grip on northern trade, still growing rapidly through the first half of the seventeenth century. Western Europe imported well over a hundred thousand tons of grain in almost every year of this period, the level continuing to move upward until about 1650. But other demands for Baltic and Norwegian products were rising even more rapidly. The first was for timber and such by-products as pitch, tar, turpentine and potash, chiefly for use in house- and ship-building. Timber supplies accessible to navigable water had become depleted in western Europe during the sixteenth century; and it was cheaper to bring timber five hundred miles by sea from Norway than to haul it twenty miles overland. The Low Countries had destroyed most of their trees to make farmland, southern England was going the same way, and France's remaining forest resources were largely in the mountains of the far interior, not badly served by rivers but no more accessible to the west coast than Norwegian timber was. The Dutch themselves had to import great quantities of timber since their forest area was small and their ship-building industry the greatest in Europe. Their big timber trade enabled them to design special ships for timber-carrying and to create a saw-milling industry (driven by windmills) round the

Zuider Zee, producing planks and balks in great quantity in standard sizes, which they held in stock for home use and export. Pitch, tar and turpentine brought from Finland, and potash from the German coast, were smaller in tonnage but had a higher unit value than timber. Netherlands enterprise introduced advanced techniques to the Swedish iron-making industry in the 1630s and the Dutch handled the early trade in its product, cheaply made from high-grade ore and easily accessible timber, which captured western markets.

These trades, requiring the movement of several hundreds of thousands of tons of goods out of Baltic and Norwegian ports each year, and the carriage in the other direction of salt, herrings, wine, cloth, colonial products and a variety of other things from Amsterdam and the south, provided employment for a great Dutch shipping industry. In the mid-seventeenth century the Dutch carried perhaps ten times as much out of the Baltic as any competitor (counting the Hanse towns as single units), and were alone in employing enough ships to profit fully from their specialization by type. The type of ship known as the *fluit* or fly-boat, developed in the 1590s, and its successors, built to suit the bulk trades of the relatively safe waters of northern Europe, could sacrifice speed, manœuvrablity and defence to maximum cargo space and easy handling, and were therefore cheaply operated by small crews in relation to their carrying capacity. They were also cheap to build, because they were simple, their numbers made possible some degree of standardization and they had the use of the great timber yard facilities of the Zuider Zee area. Economies in transport charges made a decisive difference to the price at which most northern products could sell in European ports. The cost of carrying a cargo of timber from Norway to Amsterdam was almost as great as the original value of the timber, while in the carriage of Danzig corn or Swedish iron the freight could add between a quarter and a half of the original cost. Until other countries built ships on the same lines as the Dutch – as Hamburg and Bremen did from the 1620s – or acquired large numbers of Dutch ships as the English did after mid-century, they could not compete with the Dutch in the principal northern carrying trades.

This did not end the Dutch advantages. From the 1580s they had been settling permanent factors for their merchant houses in the major and many minor Baltic ports, dealing all the year round with produce that had seasonal peaks of production; ready to hold stocks, to extend credit, to collect debts, to take orders for western goods and arrange their distribution. This was a big advance from the days when chaffering Dutch shipmasters hurried to exchange their salt for Konigsberg corn before the ice froze, though in small ports of the Finnish coast this shipmaster trading continued through much of the seventeenth century. The Hanseatic towns now accepted a secondary role in Baltic trade, though they benefited from the growth in its total volume and from the frequent involvement of the Dutch in wars in which they themselves remained neutral. The Dutch were able to supply the full range of Baltic purchasers' needs, and it was difficult for outsiders to break into this entrenched position. The English, represented in only a handful of northern ports before the middle of the seventeenth century, found it difficult to hold their existing small share in Baltic trade.

The scale of these trades made it possible for Amsterdam to develop a complex of marketing, warehousing and financial facilities that made it an unrivalled entrepôt for the west. The Netherlands themselves were large buyers, and much of European trade was carried on in their ships. Amsterdam was a natural warehousing place, for the last Dutch ships each year carrying wine, salt and spice cargoes came up from the south too late for their carriers to get into the Baltic and out again before the Sound froze; and Baltic corn came out in an autumn flow in advance of European requirements that were spread over a whole year. The growth of entrepôt functions was cumulative; as Amsterdam stored great quantities of food and became a resort for buyers, sellers of all kinds of goods found it increasingly necessary to offer their goods for sale there. Stock-holding was relatively cheap when Dutch interest rates were low; and commodity markets were organized for the sale of goods unseen, by sample (as in the corn trade), or for future delivery, and for taking options to buy or sell. In this sophisticated market speculators in commodities operated alongside the strict traders. The alarm and resentment at Dutch success felt in England and France around mid-century was largely due to the growing practice of their merchants buying timber, iron and hemp at Amsterdam rather than in the Baltic.

Northern commerce provided the Dutch economy with its underlying strength and its most distinctive character; but Dutch ships and traders were seen throughout Europe and beyond it. The Dutch controlled much of the trade of the west coast ports of France until after the middle of the seventeenth century, and their Baltic trade for much longer. Spain and Portugal could not survive in peace or war without the corn and other Baltic produce brought by Dutch shipping, and Spanish silver was carried away in great quantities to Amsterdam, which by mid-century had become Europe's chief bullion market. The Dutch were active in the ports of Italy and the Levant, but their ships were not well suited to operating in waters infested by Moorish corsairs, and here English, French and Italian traders were able to hold their own. They traded, too, up the Rhine waterway to Cologne and Frankfurt and beyond into central Europe, sending Dutch and English cloth, and colonial goods such as sugar, spices and tobacco in return for wine, linens, ironwares and zinc.

Beyond Europe, the Dutch forced their way into new trading spheres. The Portuguese monopoly in East India trade had been maintained for a century because of the length and difficulty of the voyage and Portuguese success in hiding its secrets. Amsterdam could not easily succeed to Antwerp's role as the northern market for spices while Portugal and its possessions were subject to the king of Spain and Dutch privateers were harassing the East India-men on their way into Lisbon. The sea war in the Atlantic, in fact, caused a steep decline in the Portuguese East India trade in the last two decades of the sixteenth century, and the old trade through the middle east recovered, to the profit of Venice. Dutch efforts in the 1590s to open an eastern trade round the north of Russia, avoiding conflict with the Portuguese, were unsuccessful; but at the same time they were collecting information about the Cape route and the Indian Ocean. This was published in Amsterdam as it became available; Plancius's charts in 1592, Linschoten's *Itinerary* in 1596. On the basis of this information, a trading voyage was sent to Java in 1595, and though unprofitable it showed that successful ventures were possible. At once there was a rush to enter the trade; fourteen private fleets, with sixty-five ships in all, set out from Holland and Zealand in the four years 1598–1602. The obvious dangers of a number of rival Dutch groups competing with one another and with the Portuguese in distant Asian lands caused the government to charter the United East India Company in 1602, with a large capital and a monopoly of the trade.

The reasons for Dutch success in the east were largely political, though they owed much to economic strength, and particularly to the ready provision of capital and maritime organization. The Dutch entered the Indian Ocean equipped to fight, whereas the Portuguese had long felt secure there and operated with nearly defenceless ships. It was easy to secure a foothold against such weak European opposition, and then to put ships, seamen and soldiers into the Indian Ocean on a scale sufficient on the one hand to seize Portuguese bases and exclude the Portuguese and English from the most valuable places of trade, and on the other to terrorize island rulers into acquiescence to Dutch terms. The greatest profits were to be made in the Spice Islands of Tidor and Ternate. These were the islands that produced the most valuable spices – cloves, nutmegs and mace – and they were small enough to be dominated from the sea. The strongest sea power, keeping out all others, ensured its traders the gains of monopsonistic buyers and monopolistic sellers. Though the Dutch ranged all over the Indian Ocean, and entered the Red Sea and the Persian Gulf, the Indonesian islands were from beginning to end the main centres of their interest. The English and Portuguese were left with a mainland trade – above all with the various parts of India – where no more than ordinary trading profits could be made in territories under strong rulers. The Dutch had a near monopoly of the sale in Europe of the most valuable spices, which always constituted about a quarter of their trade; but they had a large share of the pepper trade in the first half of the century, and added cotton and silk textiles towards its end. Though the East India Company did not compete in tonnage with the Baltic trade, it soon approached it in terms of value (on the import side) and may have passed it after mid-century.

For a time the Dutch also played a part in American development, though they never had substantial colonies of their own. The Spanish Empire on the mainland was too firmly established to be challenged by a maritime power, but the sugar plantation region of Portuguese Brazil, whose produce was regularly carried to Europe in Dutch ships, offered a more accessible prize. In 1621 an aggressively Protestant government in the Netherlands gave its support to the efforts of a new monopolist company, the West India Company, to carve a Dutch place in the New World. It waged a long struggle for Brazil, but was defeated in the end because of the persistent opposition of the settled Portuguese colonists. In their concentration on Brazil the Dutch neglected possibilities of settlement in the Caribbean, and by the time they abandoned the Brazilian venture in 1654 they no longer had an unchallenged maritime power in Europe and were obliged to submit to the constraints of English and French colonial policies in the West Indies and North America. However, they had secured the islands of Curaçao and St Eustatia, through which they carried on trade with the larger colonies of other nations, and a northern mainland settlement, called New Amsterdam, on the Hudson river. Finally, Dutch power had been exerted in Africa. Brazilian colonization required slaves, and the Dutch, who had been trading peaceably on the Guinea coast since before 1600, carried their Brazilian aggression across the Atlantic and swept the Portuguese out of their main west African strongholds, Elmina in 1637 and Axim in 1641, and occupied Angola from 1641 to 1649. For more than thirty years they were the principal suppliers of slaves, not merely to Brazil but also, through Curaçao, to the Spanish mainland and to the English and French West Indies.

In one sphere after another – the Baltic, the Iberian peninsula, Asia, America, Africa – the Dutch traders for a time outdid all others. They reaped the gains of trading and carrying for all Europe – for friend and foe impartially – and accumulated capital for the further extension of their enterprises and the beautifying of their cities. Their legal system facilitated investment in small partnerships, whether permanently in ships and trading houses, or temporarily for particular voyages or transactions, and the savings of many kinds of people, rich and less rich, therefore flowed into productive uses. The creation of the East India Company called for a financial market in which its stock units could be bought and sold easily, and techniques were developed for trading and speculation in these stocks and the bonds of towns and provinces, so that stocks and bonds could be readily turned into cash. The multiple currency authorities and private banks of the United Provinces proving inadequate to serve an international trade network, the Exchange Bank of Amsterdam was founded in 1609 by the municipality. Its foundation was intended to take out of the hands of private dealers the function of exchanging Dutch and foreign coins – which they had made use of to cull out and export the better coins. In this purpose, of improving the currency circulating within Holland, the bank was not wholly successful and the bank's standard monetary unit, the *florin banco*, normally stood at a premium over coin. But the bank also accepted deposits and facilitated transfers between customers' accounts. This transfer business turned out to be the bank's most useful function, providing means for easy settlement of debts in an unchanging monetary standard to which real money in Dutch and foreign coin could be related in value from day to day. It relieved the strain on money supply by making its physical transfer unnecessary in transactions of any size. The bank did not lend money to customers, directly or by bill discounting (a separate municipal Loan Bank was set up for this in 1614) but it presently began to use its mounting reserves clandestinely in loans to the East India Company and the Amsterdam municipality. Similar though smaller banks were established at Middelberg (1616), Delft (1621) and Rotterdam (1635).

In a land of fast-growing population and prosperity, agriculture and industry flourished. Reclamation of the great areas of lake and marsh that still remained in the northern Netherlands was resumed towards 1600, when the territories of the United Provinces were clearly safe from the Spaniards. Dutch engineers and skilled workers sought similar employment all over western Europe, draining large areas of English fenland and French marshes in the first half of the seventeenth century, and later extending these engineering operations into the German lands and central Italy. With growing yields to cornland, and cheap Baltic corn readily available, the emphasis in the Netherlands was on market gardening for vegetables, on horti-culture, and on such specialized crops as hops and tobacco and industrial raw materials like flax and madder, while much land was devoted to fattening cattle brought from western Germany and Denmark.

Trade assisted the expansion of many branches of industry. English broad woollen cloths were dyed and finished in some quantity at Amsterdam, and this activity was only checked because towards mid-century the Dutch broadcloth industry at Leyden was capturing much of the European market for cloths of this type. Haarlem's linen-finishing and bleaching industries processed the cheap Silesian linens that Dutch traders began to bring in before 1600; and the south Netherlands linen industry, that rose on the ruins of the old woollen manufacture a few years later, also looked to the Haarlem finishing trade. Many new industries were intro-duced by immigrants from the south; worsted manufacture, print-ing, sugar-refining, tobacco-cutting and glass-making. Trade required a great shipbuilding industry, and this in turn sawmills, ropewalks, and iron foundries that processed raw materials coming into Holland, and found export markets. The herring fishery, much enlarged, was still with its connection with the salt trade one of the bases of Dutch predominance in the Baltic. The herring shoals had moved to the Scottish and English shores of the North Sea, where the presence of a huge Dutch fishing fleet, employing over thirty thousand fisherman throughout the summer, was a constant source of friction with the English. Trade, industry, shipping and even fishery were town-based. Though Amsterdam was much the largest city from the time of the immigration in the 1590s, it did not stand out from others in size as Paris did in France or London in England. Its 120,000 inhabitants towards mid-century compared with Leyden's forty to fifty thousand, and Delft, Rotterdam, Haarlem and Dordrecht were not far behind. Amsterdam was far the most important centre of international trade and of finance; the others were industrial or fishing towns, or internal trading centres. Half the population of Holland was urban – but of course Holland was far from being all the Netherlands. It was this urban character, which it had in common with the southern Netherlands, that had helped to make Holland (and Zealand to a lesser degree) a breeding ground for religious dissent in the sixteenth century.

The relationship between reformed religion and capitalist advance has been the subject of endless discussion, set out in a variety of forms beyond the obvious one of the effects of religious migrations. Calvinism was the dominant religion in the United Provinces, but its influence on the state fluctuated during the seventeenth century, while state policy wavered between maintaining the rights of non-Calvinist minorities and overriding them. There was a sharp division, which broke out from time to time in savage internal conflicts, between the extreme and intolerant Calvinists, intransigent ministers backed by the artisans and small gentry and supporting the executive authority of the Prince of Orange and policies of continuing war with Spain, and on the other side the moderates, tinged with the reproach of deviating from the true faith, or at least with tolerance of others, who found their strength in the merchant oligarchy whose representatives usually ruled the state. Extreme Calvinism, which had some grip on government between 1619 and 1650, and again briefly after 1672, was narrowly bigoted, attached to medieval ideas about merchant prices, profits, usury and monopoly; it was potentially a force wholly unfavourable to economic enterprise. But the Calvinist elders did not interfere directly in economic affairs; if the state permitted interest, encouraged monopolistic enterprises in the East and West India trades, or acted for the benefit of merchants, the ministers of religion might admonish members of the government and even exercise some sanctions against them, but they did not claim a right to forbid.

On a more worldly plane, it may be that in the long run a doctrine which held worldly success to be evidence of God's favour was one that promoted diligence in work. Moreover, the new authority given by the reformed Churches to the inner convictions of the individual, as distinct from the authority of ideas handed down from above, enabled men to make up their own minds what was right; and in groups of like-minded people, similar developments of inner conviction – which could be self-interested though they were genuinely oblivious of it – would make the conviction more powerful. Like-minded congregations in their turn could make their impact on the thought and preaching of a religion which did not, like the Catholic Church, have the backing of fifteen hundred years of authority to give some rigidity to its dogmas; and the moderate Calvinism of the Dutch merchant class did not keep its dogmas constantly pure in the fires of fanaticism. It can hardly be doubted that, once past the stage of the zealots and first-generation converts, religion was much influenced by the society that surrounded it. Much more striking than any one clear relation between religion and capitalism is the fact that reformed religion of one kind or another supported totally different social implications in different milieux: socialism among small craftsmen and wage-earners who became the Anabaptists of south German towns, and the breakaway sects that supported the Levellers in England; an anti-business ideology comparable to that of medieval Catholicism among small gentry heavily indoctrinated with strict Calvinism in New England and the Netherlands; and a recognition that business success was a revelation of virtue, and its commercial morality therefore an acceptable one, among greater and lesser merchants of London and Amsterdam and the preachers – sometimes designated Arminians – whom they listened to. The general economic attitudes of the dominant groups in Holland and Zealand had been formed by many generations that had participated in commercial enterprise or lived in the vigorous trading community of Antwerp which had been learning Italian and German trading practices. Traders coming into contact with a variety of ideas, practising methods sometimes frowned on – though not suppressed – by old religion, were more ready to be tolerant of religious unorthodoxy. When the new religion flared in the sixteenth century, among workers and gentry who were much less sophisticated, the tolerant in the Netherlands and elsewhere were compelled to take sides on the religious persecution of their fellow-nationals. They stood on the side of religious freedom, and therefore in the last resort on the side of the persecuted; but they did so with some reluctance, and fearing – rightly – the excesses of the persecuted when it was their turn to persecute. Amsterdam, the last by several years of the Dutch cities to declare for the rebellion, held out more from distaste at the intolerant spirit among the rebels than for love of Spanish rule; it came in eventually only under coercion from a surrounding countryside that had long since risen.

Whether the Amsterdam merchant was made by, or was the maker of, his religious beliefs, his attachment to business had reasons special to the Netherlands. The thriftiness of the Dutch has often been exaggerated – the great burghers lived in immense pomp and luxury – but there was unquestionably little room in Holland for the spendthrift, disaccumulating, landowning courtier, who in England and France was envied his high place in the social scale. Nor was there in Holland, as in France and Spain, the opportunity to buy public office as a means of seeking not only stable income but also social status. In Holland and Zealand the purchase of landed estate did not, as in most places in the west, offer a regular means for a merchant to raise his family into a superior social class that turned its back on business. There was not much rural land in Holland and Zealand, and the eastern provinces of the Netherlands were culturally another country, Lutheran and Catholic rather than Calvinist, whose rural gentry had no great standing in Dutch society. The fatal urge to possess land for social status, that caused English, French and Spanish merchants to withdraw their accumulating fortunes from trade, was little felt in Holland; nor was there the disaccumulating landowning class whose wasteful expenditures were financed by the sale of land to accumulating merchants. At the apex of Dutch society were rich townsmen; if a few of them were able to buy estates on land reclaimed from the sea, their prestige nevertheless remained that of an urban patriciate. The government of the towns, and through them of the provinces of Holland and Zealand, was normally in the hands of such men; their urban occupations were the basis of most political influence as well as of economic power. The first consequence, a good one, was that many merchants brought up their children wholly to trade; despite the great town houses and their magnificent furniture and paintings, much of the capital made in trade was passed on in trading firms from generation to generation. Dutch merchants, therefore, often started life rich; an immense advantage over their English or French counterparts, struggling young men with small capital who had watched their uncles' mercantile fortunes laid out to support the dignity of cousins seeking to justify knighthood or barony by the extent of the acres bought for them. A second consequence, which was less wholly good, was that capital overflowing from trade, with few landed outlets, went largely into government and municipal loans – English as well as Dutch – and into financial operations that were often purely speculative. The turn towards finance, experienced in a different way in sixteenth-century Antwerp, was repeated in seventeenth-century Amsterdam with heightened sophistication in a market more highly organized for short-term speculation. After the middle of the seventeenth century, as wealth continued to accumulate while the pace of growth of maritime and commercial enterprise slowed, the commodity markets and the stock market that had been useful among Dutch institutions degenerated into being largely centres of gambling.

In the first half of the seventeenth century the progress of Dutch commercial power, though hampered by the Thirty Years War, carried the Netherlands ahead of all rivals as a trading and carrying nation, and laid a foundation of wealth on which its financial role in Europe was being built. The high point may be put at the year 1651, which was marked by the ending of the long expansion of the Baltic grain trade that had been one of the essential elements in Dutch economic success, and by the passing of the English Navigation Act, the first serious political reaction in Europe to that success.

The decline of the corn trade has been discussed in chapter 7; it is sufficient to repeat here that the tonnage of grain carried out of the Baltic fell from an average of sixty-eight thousand a year in 1600–49, to fifty-six thousand tons in 1650–99 and thirty-two thousand tons in 1700–49. It was the first of a long series of blows against the Dutch trading position in the north. After 1660 the exhaustion of some of the Norwegian forests that were most accessible to the sea led to a movement of the timber trade into the Baltic. Though most of the Baltic timber trade, too, was initially in Dutch hands, the building of sawmills on Baltic rivers – with the aid of Dutch and presently English capital – enabled Baltic producers gradually to open a direct trade with many markets, bypassing the Dutch sawmills. There was a steady erosion of the special advantages of the Dutch in Baltic trade. Vessels of economical Dutch types were being built in German ports by 1620; some were purchased by other nations; enormous numbers were captured by the English during

their three wars with the Dutch between 1652 and 1673, largely re-
stocking the English merchant fleet; and before the end of the
century they were being built in shipyards all over western Europe.
From a little before mid-century the English were settling factors
and securing trading connections with ports of the north and east
Baltic, where producers were becoming aware of the value of the
English market. Swedes encroached on the Dutch carrying trade,
building up a herring fishery from Marstrand on the Skagerrack
that provided a basis for Baltic carrying. These slowly made their
impact on Dutch trade in the Baltic; their share in the total fell only
gradually in the later seventeenth century, but it went down
sharply after 1720. For nearly two centuries before 1720, three-fifths
of the salt carried into the Baltic had regularly been brought by
Dutch ships; the proportion then fell rapidly and by the 1770s was
no more than one-third, whilst much was now brought into the
Baltic directly from southern Europe rather than from stores in
Holland. Similarly the Netherlands had provided more than three-
quarters of the herrings carried into the Baltic before 1660, but the
proportion fell gradually, and after 1740 dramatically, to no more
than a fifth as Swedish competition captured markets. And finally,
in the other direction, while the Dutch nearly maintained their grip
on the declining total of grain shipments to the west down to 1720,
still carrying 80 to 90 per cent of the total, their share fell heavily
after that date and was down to less than 50 per cent in the 1770s; in
this field they had been replaced by Scandinavian, German and
Scottish carriers.

These decisive changes in the Baltic trade owed little to political
factors; they represented the slow breaking up of an artificial
position the Dutch had been able to build when the only opposition
came from the German trading towns. In other directions, however,
political power had great influence. The ending of the English civil
wars and of the Frondist revolt in France left behind strong governments that were ready to support their mercantile classes against
any supposed Dutch infringements of their trading spheres. Both
the English Navigation Acts of 1651 and 1660, and the corresponding French ordinances of 1664 and 1673, were intended partly
to exclude the Dutch from trading in or sending their ships to and
from the American colonies of these countries. These measures
were successfully enforced despite the hostility of colonial planters
who wished to see the Dutch competing to carry their produce. At
the moment when colonial trade was attaining some importance,

the Dutch, who had played some part in creating it, were driven away. The English measures went much further, banning Dutch vessels from participation in trade between England and any other country but the Netherlands and prohibiting the import of foreign goods from Holland. This ensured that the rapid expansion of English demand for Baltic goods over the next century resulted in a trade carried on by English merchants in English or Baltic ships rather than by the Dutch. French tariff measures with similar objectives, however, failed to exclude the Dutch from French trade with the Baltic. In America, the year 1654 saw the final expulsion of the Dutch from Brazil, where for a quarter of a century they had struggled to build their own plantation colony; and in 1664 their trading base at New Amsterdam was taken by the English and renamed New York.

Political power played an important part, therefore, in slowing Netherlands development. Concentrating their extra-European efforts on objectives that could be secured by sea power, the Dutch left to England and France the ultimately more rewarding exploitation of the land masses in America and Asia. The Dutch were in most spheres the greatest beneficiaries from unrestricted trade; but when the benefit to them became too obvious it aroused the resentment of the mercantile classes of other powers, and the fears of their governments, and these were able to assert their will in restrictive economic measures that the Dutch could not effectively challenge. They submitted to the effects of the English Navigation Acts and their French counterparts because they had not the power to enforce their withdrawal, as was shown by the first Anglo-Dutch War in 1652-4. They permitted the growth of a great English power in the Indian Ocean because the Indonesian monopoly occupied most of their efforts, but also because of their need, after 1677, for English political support in Europe.

In the period when the economic future of the Netherlands hung in the balance, prolonged wars with the French tipped the scales against them in another way. These wars – in 1672-8, 1689-97 and 1702-13 – encouraged the development of Hamburg, the universal neutral, which was able to offer most of the shipping services and entrepôt facilities which the Dutch could only supply at high cost while they were engaged in a great maritime war. Hamburg, always an alternative centre for trade between England and central Europe, was rapidly outdistancing Amsterdam in this role during the eighteenth century; the Leipzig Fairs, whose prosperity depended on the exchange of western cloth for linen from Silesia and copper and silver from Saxony and its neighbours, focused their interest on Hamburg. During Franco-Dutch hostilities Hamburg attracted to itself much of the trade in French colonial goods, building sugar refineries and dealing in French coffee and indigo for all northern Europe, and it expanded this role throughout the century. Its freedom from war enabled it to keep down the levels of taxation on trade, and this added further to its attractiveness. Amsterdam had no rivals in 1640; a hundred years later it had two – London, which had developed independently on the basis of Britain's own trade, and Hamburg, which had seized important sections of Amsterdam's entrepôt trading.

All this is easier to see now than it was then. Most contemporaries thought that Dutch power was waxing all through the seventeenth century; and indeed absolute decline may not have come before 1720. But from the 1650s the Dutch economy was no longer expanding at a rate that outstripped all others. Both the English and the French doubled their trade and shipping between 1660 and 1690, and the wars after 1689 revealed that England had a far greater capacity than the Netherlands to take the accompanying disturbances to trade in its stride.

Foreign eyes were concentrated on Amsterdam, whose financial operations on behalf of all Europe,.and whose trade in high-value goods from the Indian Ocean, was still expanding. The great capital accumulations of seventeenth-century Amsterdam were flowing out in loans to governments and investment in business abroad, and Dutch financiers were as familiar in western cities in the eighteenth century as Dutch engineers had been in the seventeenth. But when peace came in 1713 the future looked less rosy to the smaller shipping, fishing and manufacturing towns, with the decline of the bulk trades and Holland's entrepôt role, and fierce competition from rural woollen and linen industries growing in Germany as well as western Europe. By the middle of the eighteenth century the Dutch played only a small part in the Atlantic economy; they were driven back on their early functions in European trade, where they were faced with far more powerful competition than before, and on the financial role made possible by their immense capital resources. Like the Italians, Germans and Spaniards before them, they had dropped out of the race for the economic leadership of Europe; this lay between the two countries that were now close economic and political rivals, Britain and France.

12 England: The Untroubled Island

*E*ngland escaped the worst of the disasters that overtook much of Europe during the sixteenth and seventeenth centuries. It suffered no famine of great consequence; epidemics, though severe, were less devastating than the worst on the continent; no foreign armies overran it, and its civil wars did not carry with them the extreme savagery and destruction of those fought in the name of religion. Yet it had to face the same problems arising from population growth that defeated the economies of Spain and France. From the low point of some two and a half million in the middle of the fifteenth century numbers rose, with minor setbacks, to approach five million by 1620. Expansion was slowed in the second quarter of the seventeenth century by migration, by a series of plague outbreaks, and perhaps by a weakening of the resistance of the poor to disease in a period when the rise in food prices had outstripped incomes; but it continued at a modest pace through the latter part of the seventeenth century. The rapid increase of population, however, had come to an end, and it was not resumed until the 1740s.

In the middle and later seventeenth century, agricultural improvement carried on faster and more consistently than elsewhere in the west (apart from the Netherlands) partially accounts for the success in feeding the English population. But, unless the extent of early improvement has been seriously underestimated, it cannot account for England's relative success in coping with sixteenth-century population growth. In chapter 7 it was explained that the grip of the peasantry on the land in France and England was exceptionally strong in the sixteenth and seventeenth centuries. Keeping this in mind, we must differentiate between France and England in another respect, the size of peasant holdings. An important feature of the English agrarian economy was the relatively high average size of the peasant landholding; and this provided the basis on which it was possible to sustain some agricultural advance even before landlord pressures towards the consolidation of holdings became strong. It is extremely difficult to make international comparisons of the average size of peasant holdings, because of different treatment of those who were on the peasant-labourer margin. French statistics show that two-thirds of the peasants of northern France towards the end of the eighteenth century had holdings of less than one hectare (two and a half acres); but these evidently include every landholder down to those who were really labourers but had a small patch of ground they intended to cultivate themselves. English writers, producing less comprehensive statistics, concentrate on peasants who were wholly engaged in working on their own land, or for whom labouring and industrial by-employments were entirely subsidiary, and treat the tiny landholder as being primarily a wage-earner. For Labrousse, the French eighteenth-century peasant with twelve and a half acres was firmly established with a secure subsistence, even if his other earnings were trivial; only 16 per cent of the peasants in the north – at the end of a phase in which the number of relatively large holdings had grown – had this amount of land. Many studies from southern and midland England indicate a view that in lowland England the full peasant holding, common in every village, was in the neighbourhood of twenty to twenty-five acres; in the *Agrarian History of England and Wales, 1540–1640*, a thirty-acre holding is used to illustrate the profits of a typical peasant.

The reasons why English landholdings were relatively large are complicated; they rest on the relations between forces that distributed demesne lands among the peasantry during the fourteenth and fifteenth centuries; the differentiation that grew among the peasantry as a result of growing commercial opportunities and pressures; and the English customs of inheritance It was in these last that a vital difference existed between England and the continent.

In England, as elsewhere in western Europe, the unprofitability of demesne cultivation in conditions of low demand and labour shortage during the fifteenth century had caused lords to abandon farming and grant much or all of their demesne land out to tenants. Some of these grants were leasehold; many were made on the customary tenures that became copyhold – though the validity of their copyhold status might be challenged much later if the origin of the grants could still be identified in manorial documents. The fortunate or able peasant, or one with several strong sons coming to manhood, could take up a patch of demesne and work it successfully, earning profit with which he could buy more land from his less successful neighbours, and ending his life with fifty or even a hundred or two acres and employing some wage labour. A real differentiation was emerging among the peasantry in the fifteenth and early sixteenth centuries, less by pushing some down into extreme poverty than by the growth of a group of relatively rich peasants, who were designated 'yeomen'. Within the tight limits which the working of land in the open field system imposed over much of the country, they were able to use their resources to experiment with new methods of handling crops and animals, or to attempt to follow the demands of the market. They often bought up strips in the open fields in order to create consolidated blocks of land they could work more easily, and when it was possible they enclosed these and, with the landlord's connivance, patches of waste land. If they were efficient, they were likely to secure further land that reverted to the lord through failure of heirs to holdings or termination of leases, because they could offer high rent to him.

A development of this kind can be seen in other countries; but large holdings were easily fragmented by division among sons and their descendants over three or four generations. In England this fragmentation was held back by the strength of the custom of primogeniture, which appears to have been the normal form of inheritance over most of lowland England. Inheritance has not been thoroughly investigated except at the level of the landlord class, but the generalization seems to be applicable to the peasantry. It was perhaps encouraged by the continuing importance of copyhold tenure, with its feudal origin in lands that had services attached to them which lords had not wished to divide. Whatever the reasons, partible inheritance, which was very common in France (among a variety of inheritance customs) had little hold in England. The younger sons of prosperous yeomen were likely to be sent off into the Church, or given some small start in trade, rather than kept with a share of the family holding. At a lower level, small peasant holdings also were usually kept intact, younger sons becoming labourers, or in periods when population was rising fast going to seek work in the towns rather than being given shares in the family holding. As a generalization with innumerable exceptions, we may suggest that in England rural population growth was accommodated by turning younger sons into wage-earners; on the continent by dividing holdings and making small peasant holdings that were unviable, so that their occupiers had to be part-time workers for wages.

If, therefore, the majority of English peasants in the middle of the sixteenth century grew crops mainly for the subsistence of their own families, it was a modestly comfortable subsistence they were accustomed to, leaving some margin for purchases beyond the village, and for a tightening of belts without actual starvation when the harvest turned out a poor one. Among the peasants was a strong leavening who were already turning into small capitalist farmers. In the last thirty years of the sixteenth century those who were able to keep their holdings on reasonable rental terms gained from the rise in corn prices, and the ranks of the capitalist farmers filled still further; the burdens of those years fell on the very smallest peasants who grew almost entirely for subsistence, and above all on the increasing mass of the wage-earners.

Two sets of obstacles faced those who saw opportunities in making changes to improve the cultivation of land or the keeping of animals. One was the form of agrarian organization known as the open field system, in which peasant land – whether owned or leased – was occupied in scattered half-acre strips in great open fields that were worked on a communal basis. These open fields still covered most of midland and large parts of eastern and southern England in the middle of the sixteenth century. The other was a tenurial organization that made it difficult for landlords to exert pressure on their tenants to take advantage of economic changes, or to divert land at all rapidly into the hands of the more enterprising peasants.

The problem facing the innovator in the open field village was that cultivation was usually carried on in ways and at times agreed communally among the peasants of the village. It was rarely possible to cultivate isolated strips independently of these arrangements, but if a yeoman could gather some of his strips together in one block, by purchase and exchange, he might get permission to enclose them and work them independently. To change open field arrangements more fundamentally required interference with the tenurial system itself.

Most farmers in Elizabethan England were in principle tenants of some sort, either leaseholders or copyholders. Leases were generally for very long terms – commonly for three lives – and gave complete legal security during tenure; copyhold was usually for life, and an absolute right of inheritance by the next of kin was normal – though far from invariable – on payment of one or two years' rent as an entry fine. There were very short leases, yearly tenancies, copyholds that did not carry the right of inheritance, and at the other extreme there were freeholds; but none of these was very widespread. Modern writing has on the one hand shown the extreme difficulty of making a successful legal challenge to tenurial arrangements (and so to improve the income of landlords) except at very long intervals; and on the other hand that landlord incomes did in fact rise steeply between 1580 and 1620. Many landlords still had home farms from which they sold produce; far more had retained some grazing rights for animals on the village commons; most had some saleable woodland. Income from all these was greatly augmented; but in addition rentals were steeply increased despite the difficulties of tenure. If the legal position of tenants was as strong as it appears, the implication is that landlords were able to get round it by exerting pressure on their tenants at points where their legal position was weaker – and so compelling concessions from them – and even by using completely extra-legal means.

The landlord was not, of course, entirely without legal resources. Some of his leases fell in; copyhold tenants died without heirs; tenants defaulted on their obligations. A mid-sixteenth century writer declared, however, that no more than a third of a landlord's estates would come into his hands in this way in the course of his lifetime. Much copyhold had an uncertain title, for the essence of the tenure was that it should have been made 'beyond the memory of man', and many original grants of demesne made during the fifteenth century could be identified, a hundred years later, in the court rolls of the manor. In such cases they were not copyhold, and the unfortunate landholder found himself reduced to the position of a tenant at will. There were copyholds, too, that could be subjected to very heavy, and perhaps prohibitive, entry fines at the death of the holder. Beyond this there was a range of possibilities for the landowner who was determined to push his income up at least in line with prices, or to get some of the benefit of the great rise in corn prices if he was ambitious. The elderly peasant of 1597, selling his surplus corn at four times the price it would have realized when he was a young man, might be susceptible to quite a gentle suggestion that he should pass on some of his gain by paying more rent to his landlord. The legal rights over the village common and waste were usually ambiguous, and a landlord might introduce large numbers of his own animals on to them, threatening an over-stocking that would harm the balance between crops and livestock that was so important to most of his tenants, and use the leverage to bargain for a change in terms for the tenants' arable holdings. The sheer power of the landlord as the local member of the governing class, as justice of the peace, commissioner for the assessment of direct taxes, responsible for compiling the muster for military service overseas, power which was used ruthlessly to secure votes for the candidate he approved in parliamentary elections, must have been used sometimes to further his economic interests in the village. By one means or another, rentals were raised; the total yield of rents and entry fines, which lagged behind the general rise in prices until late in the sixteenth century, put on a spurt and recovered the lost ground by about 1620, and probably continued for a time to make a further gain.

Associated with the raising of rental incomes was change in the form of tenures, which in the long run had far greater effects. Long leases were being replaced, as they fell in, by short leases (commonly, in the seventeenth century, for terms of seven years) so that the possibility of rapid adjustment of rents was preserved. Even more important was the replacement of a great many copyholds by leases. During the sixteenth century the position of the copyholder in relation to his landlord was very much strengthened by a series of legal decisions in the royal courts, and in time copyhold tenure came to be regarded as giving the same absolute security as freehold. But this change took place in a period in which copyhold – the principal English peasant tenure in the middle of the sixteenth century – was being reduced to small proportions. A certain amount simply became freehold, in recognition of the rights the tenant had acquired. But the same landlord pressure that pushed up rents also secured the transformation of a great amount of copyhold land into leasehold; copyhold peasant was being turned into leasehold farmer. By the latter part of the seventeenth century leasehold had replaced copyhold as the normal form of tenure.

The landlord who somehow managed to push up his rents was

simply securing his share of an income from agriculture that was rising because of the advance in prices. Once the landlord had his land in short leases, however, he was able not merely to seize some of the extra income that was coming to his tenants, but also, if he thought fit, to press his tenants to change farming organization and methods. He could thrown his support behind the enclosure of parts or the whole of the open fields, if some of his tenants were willing to operate enclosed farms; divide up the useful part of the commons; evict the incompetent farmer and add to the lands of the competent; build up large farms and encourage the direction of farmers' resources to new kinds of produce. He could thus exert a powerful stimulus towards improving the productivity of the land. Everything depended, however, on the existence of a few prosperous and enterprising farmers; and in practice it was probably the expressed desire of such farmers to get more land into their own hands, and their offers of attractive rents for it, that induced landlords to make the attempt to bring holdings back under their own control. On the other side, landlord pressure and the readiness of larger farmers to pay high rents drove many small peasants into the abandonment of their holdings, to become wage-earners or vagrants.

The growth of London's population increased the opportunities for profitable specialization. From no more than fifty thousand people in Henry VIII's reign, its numbers rose to two hundred thousand people at the beginning of the seventeenth century and some six hundred thousand at its end. In the later sixteenth century London had outgrown the supply of foodstuffs from the upper Thames valley, Essex and Suffolk, and was beginning to draw corn from all the eastern and southern counties that were accessible to the sea. Before 1600 land in the city's immediate neighbourhood was being turned to a highly labour-intensive cultivation of fruit and vegetables, drawing some inspiration from the methods of the market gardeners round the Dutch cities. In the seventeenth century its meat came from cattle that had been reared in Wales, Scotland or even Ireland and fattened in the midland counties and Essex; its cheese was brought from Cheshire and Staffordshire, and its butter from Yorkshire and Lincoln.

During the sixteenth century much of England's growing demand for corn was met by extension of the cultivated area. The long phase of conversion of land from arable to pasture that had been going on through the late Middle Ages came to an end about 1520, under the influence of pressure on corn supply and rising corn prices, and it reappeared only in conditions temporarily favouring pastoral production in the 1540s and early 1590s. Through most of the century there was a fitful and fluctuating movement towards increasing the arable area, and towards bringing more of it into enclosed fields. Enclosure and larger-scale farming enabled this change to be associated with improving methods, here and there as early as the 1570s; but the big turn towards convertible husbandry (discussed in chapter 7) took place during the second half of the seventeenth century under the influence of the check to corn prices. After the middle of that century all fears of corn shortage disappeared; corn imports, which had mounted to large proportions during the deficit years of the 1620s and 1630s, became rare; from 1660 there was occasional corn export and in 1690 fears of the effect of low grain prices on the farming community led to the introduction of bounties for the export of corn. Plentiful corn supplies and the decline in prices encouraged a widening specialization rather than a return to the old staple, wool, whose price was also depressed. Livestock farming was aided by the coming into use of feeding stuffs with better nourishing qualities, such as white clover and sainfoin, and more slowly of turnips and potatoes.

It seems likely, nevertheless, that agricultural incomes tended to decline in the later seventeenth century. Both corn and wool prices were sluggish, except in wartime, for a hundred years after 1660; the rapid rise of the sixteenth century was a distant memory. Rents were tending downward after 1660, and after 1692 a land tax at 20 per cent cut deeply into landlord incomes. The average income of farmers may nevertheless have been increasing, because there were fewer of them; the tendency to enlargement of farms and the replacement of small peasant by capitalist farmer was still pursuing its course. But the drive to break up what remained of open field farming was less vigorous than it had been in days when rising prices made it essential for landlords to raise their incomes, and demand for land gave them the opportunity to do it.

The Civil War, and even more the overthrow of James II in 1688, restored the political power of the landlord class that had been briefly threatened by royal absolutism, and the political developments that followed gave the greatest landlords a larger real power in the state than they had ever had. Alongside this incentive to build up great estates as a route to political power, developments in the law assisted the beginning of a remarkable change in the structure of the landlord class. In the middle of the seventeenth century lawyers worked out a device, the strict settlement, that made possible the creation of entailed estates, despite the hostility of English law to them; and at much the same time mortgage was so modified as to remove its extreme danger, which was of the loss of all lands mortgaged even when there was default only in a small payment. Increasingly conscious of their status in society, the larger landlords set about building up their family estates by purchase (if necessary with money borrowed on mortgage) and by judicious marriage of their children into other great landed families; and they ensured that their estates should not be broken up after their deaths by means of strict trusts that entailed the whole of the land on the heir of the eldest son, so that the latter was unable to sell it. The size of the largest landed estates grew very rapidly during the first half of the eighteenth century, while owners of smaller estates and freeholdings were selling out under the pressures of stagnant rents, low prices and the land tax. Moreover, many people who inherited small estates became willing to sell land, once an alternative form of safe and socially respectable investment offered itself, after 1692, in the government's long-term debt. In the early eighteenth century, therefore, England was moving steadily towards a society of great landowners, large farmers and a proletarianized labour force. There were still very extensive peasant survivals, and a mass of smallholders who supplemented their incomes by wage-labour. The extinction of the English peasantry, however, was very far advanced before the middle of the eighteenth century; it was a process that had been at work, gradually, for more than two hundred years.

If the English economy was mainly agricultural, industry was nevertheless important, growing and from the end of the sixteenth century becoming much more varied. The dominant industry throughout was the manufacture of woollen textiles, but others that had been insignificant grew to a respectable size alongside it by the beginning of the eighteenth century.

In England, as elsewhere in western Europe, woollen cloth production had always been widespread; almost every house had once had its spinning wheel, every village and small town its weavers. This local production remained the main provision for the poorer people, and particularly for those in the more remote districts, until far into modern times. Its place was gradually taken by the growth of production in a few areas whose specialized qualities of cloth found regional, national and international markets. The products of particular regions may first have gained wide reputation because of the quality of their local wool supply, but concentrated production encouraged the development of higher skills, and made possible large-scale organization under merchant-employers who put out wool, yarn and unprocessed cloth to a wide circle of out-workers performing individual operations. The market for their produce widened beyond the rich to the middle class and by the eighteenth century even to fairly poor people in the towns. By the beginning of the sixteenth century this development to a large scale was already in the past; in Wiltshire, Gloucestershire and East Anglia there were very large concentrations of textile workers, while a number of other areas had smaller sections of the industry, some on the brink of decay, as in Berkshire and Kent, others in Devon and Yorkshire becoming ripe for fresh expansion. From the middle of the sixteenth century the fortunes of the various sections of the industry depended on their capacity to adapt to new fashions in textiles, to changes in the type of raw material being produced, to differing levels of wages between regions, and to subtle changes in existing forms of organization, rather than on big organizational or technical advances.

Nevertheless, the industry underwent great changes between the sixteenth and the eighteenth century. The most important of them was the spread of worsted manufacture. Worsted-making, which had become the main occupation of the Flemish industry by the early sixteenth century, was firmly established in England by the Flemish and Walloon refugees who came into the south-eastern towns from the 1560s onward. The product found a ready demand in England and, in the seventeenth century, in markets of southern Europe, and revived the textile industry first in the Norwich area and then during the seventeenth century in Devon. The switch from the cheaper varieties of heavy woollens to worsteds may in any case have become necessary because of a decline in the production of the types of wool on which the older industry had been based (due, apparently, to the better feeding of sheep which caused them to grow longer, coarser wool). Quite rapidly much of the market for the cheaper varieties of the old heavy cloths was lost to these worsteds. By the beginning of the eighteenth century the old-style woollens had been almost confined to a prosperous Wiltshire industry producing very high qualities, and a low-grade production alongside worsteds in Yorkshire. More and more of the smaller producing areas faded away, and a woollen and worsted industry far more productive than it had been a century before was in 1700 concentrated in Devon and Wiltshire, Yorkshire and the Norwich area, with a manufacture of worsted stocking round Nottingham.

This turn from heavy woollens to worsteds was the first of the major changes in textile fashions, and a continuing stimulus was given to it during the seventeenth century by devising new types of worsteds, with a whole range of new names appearing and falling out of use. But competition from other textiles was growing. Linens were little produced in England, but there was a rising demand for fine linens which were imported from France and Flanders, and for coarse linens from Germany and Holland. They constituted, in fact, the largest single element in the whole of English import trade, and the government made successful efforts during the first half of the eighteenth century to replace them by supporting the growth of Scottish and Irish linen manufacture. A new element, however, was introduced by the appearance of Indian and Chinese textiles, mostly cottons but including cheap silks, which had an immense vogue towards the end of the seventeenth century. This influx of oriental textiles created alarm throughout Europe, for it threatened all the textile industries. England introduced legislation to stop the import, and although smuggling still brought in a large supply the fierceness of the competition was abated, while the small English cotton industry was stimulated to seize some of the market that had been revealed by the imported oriental cottons. Finally, growing wealth fostered the wearing of silks, most of which were imported from France and Italy. During most of the seventeenth century England had only a tiny silk industry, almost confined to making ribbon. The industry was given a new impetus by the growth of Anglo-French commercial rivalry. In 1678, as an act of commercial war against France, the import of French goods was prohibited; after the prohibition was lifted, prohibitive duties were imposed and maintained for a century. Sheltered by these measures, and given technical support by the immigration of Huguenot refugees in the 1680s, the English silk industry was rapidly expanding round the turn of the century. The growth in the variety of available textiles – both in home and foreign markets – gave the first serious and prolonged check to the woollen industry that it had experienced since the Middle Ages. It had expanded, if fitfully, for over two hundred years, but it faced a pause in growth in the decades round 1700.

The other large English industries are little documented The largest in terms of employment and output, after woollens, were leather-working and building, but they were dispersed as the woollen industry had been in more remote times, and remained so throughout the period. The cordwainer was the craftsman found in every village, since house and farm needed simple leather goods; tanning was a local town craft; but there was a specialized industry making high quality gloves, saddlery and shoes in London.

The metal industries, which had been very small in medieval England, received their first impetus during the sixteenth century. The refining of metals was deliberately supported by Henry VIII and Elizabeth I, who wished to have a native iron- and brass-making industry for ordnance. Techniques were learned from the advanced iron-makers of the Liège area, and from German miners who were ready to migrate as their copper and silver mines declined after mid-century. By the 1560s the English iron industry was meeting most of the simpler demands and iron production continued to expand until the eve of the Civil War, by which time it was encountering new competition from imported Swedish iron. Iron-making thereafter grew very little until the middle of the eighteenth century, but on the basis of home-manufactured and Swedish iron the making of iron wares was steadily developed, creating big concentrations at Birmingham, specializing in small arms, and Sheffield, producing edge tools, before the end of the seventeenth century. Birmingham became the centre of a group of industries making metal goods not only of iron but also of brass and pewter.

Other industries were promoted by the immigration of two waves of Protestant refugees from the continent: Flemings and Walloons in the 1560s and Huguenots in the 1680s. The Flemings were chiefly responsible for the introduction of worsted manufacture, but also improved paper-making and brewing; the Huguenots, in addition to making broad silk fabrics, improved paper-making once more, had some part in the creation of a linen industry in northern Ireland, and fostered a number of minor luxury industries. Finally, the expansion of the geographical sphere of English overseas trade brought in new commodities which had to be processed – sugar, tobacco, coffee – and these were the foundation of industries in the port towns.

The woollen, cotton and metal industries were dispersed in a number of regions throughout England, and London had no specialist industry with which it is associated. It was, however, one of the chief industrial areas of the country in the seventeenth century, with a great variety of small industries, and was an important beneficiary from the immigrations of refugees. The growing concentration of luxury spending in London encouraged the settlement there of an enormous variety of luxury trades – such crafts as those of the swordsmiths, coachmakers, glovemakers, silkweavers, tailors, clockmakers and jewellers. They were small crafts, with a small number of skilled men in each of them; trades of master craftsmen dealing directly with their customers and employing a few journeymen and apprentices; but in total they were the support of many thousands of London families. A second group of industries depended on London's port and shipping. The Thames was still the country's leading shipbuilding centre during the seventeenth century, though its relative importance was declining, and London had to provide large facilities for ship repairing and fitting out. Sail-making, rope-making, anchor-making and a host of other industries serving ships were carried on; river craft were built and maintained, not merely for the carriage of goods but also to carry passengers by the easiest way through much of London, the river. London's greatness depended on the presence of the court, which attracted the spending of wealth, and on the port, which handled hundreds of thousands of tons of goods each year; these activities were on a scale large enough to make London a great industrial city.

The woollen industry, dominating English manufacturing, also accounted for much the greatest part of English foreign trade – some four-fifths of it during the first half of the seventeenth century. English cloth was sold throughout Europe, and beyond it in limited quantities in western Asia and north Africa, and in Spanish America. Until well into the seventeenth century, however, most of it was marketed on the continent through one of the ports of north-western Europe; almost exclusively through Antwerp until 1563, and thereafter in a succession of cities – Emden, Stade, Hamburg, Middelberg, Dort and Amsterdam. The growth of the cloth export trade had been associated with the rise of Antwerp and of the facilities it provided for dealing with merchants from many nations; but beyond this Antwerp had come to provide the craftsmen who dyed and finished English cloth to European customers' requirements. When the Antwerp connection broke down, therefore, it was not easy to sell directly to the customers it had served. To some extent these cloth-finishing facilities were replaced in Hamburg and in the

Dutch towns, but the export trade suffered considerable difficulties until in the 1620s good quality dyeing became firmly established in England.

The difficulties of trade with Antwerp once war engulfed the Low Countries in 1572 caused strong efforts to open direct connections with markets that would take English finished cloth – mostly the cheaper varieties, among which kersies predominated. In the late sixteenth century, therefore, Baltic and Mediterranean trade was expanded; but the great change in the pattern of trade came only after the 1620s, when the Thirty Years War ruined some of the best markets for the older types of cloth, while the decline of Italian and Spanish industry opened large markets for English worsteds in southern Europe.

The fall of Antwerp made it necessary to import many goods directly from their places of production, which had formerly come through Antwerp. The establishment of trade connections with Turkey in 1580, and with India and Indonesia after 1600, were both designed more for the purpose of securing the supply of Asian spices and drugs than to promote exports. But this was not England's only entry to extra-European trade. The colonial settlements across the Atlantic began to produce commodities for sale in Europe, tobacco and furs from the 1620s, and sugar from the 1640s. After mid-century these trades took an important part in English commerce. Tobacco became a major article of trade, both for home consumption and re-export, and the English West Indian islands captured and greatly expanded the north European market for sugar that had been served by Brazil. After 1660 England became the entrepôt through which much of Europe's supply of tobacco and sugar was channelled; whilst the consolidation of the East India Company's trade produced a supply of pepper and of textiles that left great quantities for re-export. By 1688 the re-export of colonial and Asian goods accounted for more than a quarter of all exports from England.

The most attractive prospects of trade beyond Europe appeared at first to be in Asia, the established producer and trader in a range of goods that Europe needed. But in the very long run the expansion of this trade was limited. The demand for spices had always been quite adequately met in Europe, and was rather inelastic; while the import of cheap oriental textiles, which were found in the second half of the seventeenth century to have an almost unlimited European demand, threatened the powerful interest of European textile manufacturers, which was strong enough to secure the banning of their import from every country except Holland. A big new expansion of oriental trade had to await the growth in the popularity of tea in the eighteenth century.

America, on the other hand, offered trading prospects that were at first very limited but were capable of continuing expansion because it provided new products that attracted a popular demand, or old ones at costs that were far below those of the traditional producers. Sugar consumption was greatly increased during the seventeenth century by the cheapness first of Brazilian and then of West Indian sugar. Tobacco had been a luxury at the beginning of the century; Virginia produced it cheaply, so that by the end of the century it was a solace of the poor in every country, selling a ton for every pound sold in 1600. These two commodities provided the main basis for colonial expansion, on the basis of which American far outstripped Asian trade with England well before the end of the century. The growth of American earning power from these sales, meanwhile, had begun – as yet in a small way – to make possible export of the products of many minor English industries, especially of metalwares, silks, hats and leather goods.

Changing patterns of trade helped foster new economic thinking and even new policies of government. The prevailing economic ideas were moving during the century from 'terms of trade' considerations to emphasize the importance of the 'balance of trade'. The predominant view of the Middle Ages and the sixteenth century had been that there was a more or less fixed overseas demand for English goods, and that the aim of policy should be to secure the best possible selling prices (and the lowest possible buying prices for imports) and the concentration of as much as possible of the profits of trade in English hands. To secure these ends the older trades – and above all the great trade with Antwerp – were entrusted to merchants who accepted the supervision of an organization chartered by the crown, the Merchant Adventurers Company of London, which was given monopoly rights, with some concessions to much smaller and later companies in the provincial ports. An effort was made to extend this control to new branches of trade in the later sixteenth century – companies were set up for the Baltic, Levant, Morocco and Russia trades – and some of these functioned effectively in the seventeenth century. But the enormous expansion of the unregulated Iberian trades after 1604, and of colonial trades towards mid-century, alongside the stagnation and even decline of the Merchant Adventurers' trade, made nonsense of this policy. The regulated company, with its complicated organization and its monopoly rights, was increasingly seen as an anachronism, while the state, which had seen these companies as a means for exercising its own oversight of trade, gained confidence to do this through its own legislation and the officials who enforced it. Low prices to expand export trade, rather than high prices to conserve the profits of a limited trade, were seen as desirable, and the mechanism of company regulation was largely dismantled in the second half of the century, the greatest breach being made in 1689 when the monopoly privileges of the Merchant Adventurers' Company were ended. Thereafter nearly all trade was carried on by individual merchants free of regulations, or by great joint-stock companies whose capital was gathered to meet special needs in difficult or dangerous trades in the Indian Ocean, the Canadian Arctic and the west coast of Africa.

Sixteenth-century England, emerging from feudalism, hesitated on the brink of royal absolutism – and turned away. The power of the great nobility, which had rivalled that of the king, had been weakened by prolonged civil wars, exactions and forfeitures in the fifteenth century; and the Tudor monarchs found sources of new support in classes yearning for stable rule, and from religious reformers who could not afford to weaken a crown that was the guarantee against the return of Catholicism to England. The twin rocks on which, in spite of this, the possibility of absolutism foundered in England were the long-standing right of Parliament to determine new taxation, and the absence of an armed force under royal control that was strong enough to override that right. When it needed extra revenue, the crown had to secure the acquiescence of some considerable part of the propertied classes from which that revenue would normally come. Under a king of exceptional prestige and determination, Henry VIII, bolstered by wealth from ecclesiastical confiscations of the 1530s, absolutism came very close, but he spent all his wealth and much more in the 1540s, and left feeble successors behind him. Elizabeth I, under the threat of Catholic claimants to the throne, and at war through all the latter part of her reign, had to muster some national feeling behind herself and to give way at times on issues that made her unpopular. Charles I brought opposition to a head by his cleverly justified means of raising money that were against the spirit of the constitution, as many Englishmen understood it, for his methods were seen to be laying the foundation for absolutism. But the Civil War was not decisive, and James II, beginning with an immense fund of the goodwill of those who wanted stability before almost anything else, seized on the one combination of policies that could override even this feeling; a drive towards absolute rule supported by a standing army, and the forcible return of his countrymen to the Catholic religion. His successors had their standing army, but for over half a century they were conscious of dubious title to the throne and plagued by fear of Jacobite insurrection. They accepted complete financial dependence on Parliament, which had as its consequence the growth in power of ministers who needed to maintain the support of Parliament as well as of the crown.

It was England's great good fortune, therefore, that it could rarely be governed according to the whim of the crown supported by a narrow group of nobles and officials propped up by an army. Whether the crown wished to pursue its personal tastes against people of all classes – in the matter of Church of England doctrine under Charles I or return to the Catholic Church under James II – or to fulfil a role as protector of the poor against the powerful, as in the enforcement of anti-enclosure legislation or the provisions of the poor law, it had to tread carefully or it would encounter dangers. This made for weak government when the crown and its leading subjects could not reconcile their differences, in parts of the reigns of James I and Charles II, but it provided very long periods of government that was stable and to some degree attuned to the prevalent opinion of the well-to-do, particularly on economic and social questions that did not involve matters of high principle. Though there was a multitude of plots against governments, many local risings and some serious rebellion, only the seventeenth-century Civil War had any prolonged disruptive effect on society and economy. From this war, moreover, there emerged on both sides an even stronger conviction of the harm done by extreme attitudes on either side that would threaten the kind of relation in which peace and order could be maintained. Finally, the financial check held back the crown from costly expenditure in wartime; the vast and ruinous outpouring of treasure which Philip II and Louis XIV were able to continue over long periods was not matched by any English monarch until the responsibility for war became largely a parliamentary one after the Revolution of 1688.

English government was cheap in peacetime, and even in war,

down to the 1690s. While in Spain Philip II may have absorbed 10 per cent of Castile's national income to pay for his wars in the 1580s and 1590s, it is doubtful whether in the same years Elizabeth I, at her wits' end to meet war expenses, took more than the 3 per cent of national income for them. The burden was heavier during the Civil War, but it never before 1690 attained the levels that were regularly borne over long periods in France and Spain. Moreover, there was no personal taxation except in wartime (apart from the light and irregularly levied hearth tax between 1661 and 1688); and no exemption from taxation for the nobility. On the contrary, personal taxation was generally on landownership; nothing more sharply distinguished English from continental governments than the way in which the incidence of taxation fell. The taxation of the worker and producer, a heavy burden and a powerful disincentive to effort in continental countries, hardly existed in England. England was fortunate, therefore, in its form of government; the vaunted efficiencies of absolutism passed it by, to its advantage in these centuries and in the longer run. On the whole, its people were able to pursue their occupations without political interruptions; and this was perhaps the most basic of the advantages England had in its economic development over the sixteenth and seventeenth centuries.

13 France: The Unsteady Giant

The basis of France's political strength was the size of the population with a common language and culture embraced within a single political boundary. Nearly half the people of western Europe were Frenchmen living on French soil; eighteen to nineteen million of them in the late sixteenth century, around nineteen million (in a considerably larger territory) towards the end of the seventeenth. There was no other national concentration of this kind west of Russia; England and Wales only crept past five million late in the seventeenth century, Castile at its peak had no more than seven million people, and the Dutch Netherlands two. The great numbers of the German- and Italian-speaking populations farther east were divided among a multitude of small states, a few genuinely independent but most of them clients of greater powers. French unity, however, was much more striking in the political than in the economic sphere. Its economic regions had very different resources; communications between them were poor, and tariff and toll barriers divided them as much from each other as most were from foreign countries, until Colbert overhauled the tariff system in 1664. The chronology of prosperity and depression, of population advance and decline, shows great differences between the north and the south of France, and between the Atlantic and channel coastal towns and rural manufacturing regions and the eastern interior. Generalizations about French development are constantly subject to contradiction from the experience of particular areas.

Most French economic historians set their history within a framework of sixteenth-century economic advance and seventeenth-century economic decline or at best stagnation; indeed, they write of 'the tragic seventeenth century' or the 'crisis of the seventeenth-century', referring to a period running from 1630 to 1730. The beginnings of economic advance go back to the decades 1450–80, when France was emerging from the long European malaise of the late Middle Ages, and from its own particular affliction, the Hundred Years War with England that had repeatedly devastated great areas of the country until it was ended in 1453. Thereafter the loss of population was gradually recovered and empty and abandoned lands and villages were reoccupied – a process which in Burgundy and Picardy went on until late in the sixteenth century. There was a prolonged industrial expansion especially in the north and east, and the creation of hundreds of new fairs reflected the growth of internal trade. This recovery had not quite reached its natural limits when the beginning of the religious wars in 1562 began to disturb parts of the country; prosperity faltered in the south in the 1560s but advance continued in the Paris region, and probably in most of northern France, until after 1580. When Henri IV secured a general peace in 1598 a new period of industrial expansion was ushered in that was halted by the beginning of a period of renewed wars and internal conflicts between 1626 and 1659.

The general economic expansion that ran without much interruption for a hundred years from the late Middle Ages was associated with rapid population increase; by 1580 there may have been half as many Frenchmen again as there had been a century earlier. In much of France the land filled up to support the maximum numbers its existing agricultural techniques would bear. War intensified the already growing difficulties of feeding the population, but it was not merely war that caused the slowing of expansion. The birth rate was declining in some localities soon after 1560, and generally by the 1580s, and there was no full recovery to the old level of births until well on in the eighteenth century. The lowered resistance of the poor was tested by the reappearance of plague, which raged through many years of the 1580s and returned in the wake of the harvest failures of the 1590s. A heavily reduced population again had room for expansion in the quiet years after 1600, with some recovery of birth rates in the 1620s, but in the second quarter of the new century all the adverse influences returned together; famine, plague, and the devastation of external and internal war. After 1626 northern France was repeatedly invaded from the Spanish Netherlands, and eastern France from the Rhine valley, while the great port of La Rochelle underwent a prolonged siege. Serious epidemic returned in 1619 and struck repeatedly during the next few decades, particularly in 1627–31 and 1636–9; the whole country except the Mediterranean south was engulfed in the catastrophes of 1648–52 when famine and epidemic raged alongside the Frondist wars; and there was a final if more localized burst of serious famine in 1659–62. The losses of those years, and particularly of 1648–52, reduced French population to a level far below its old peak of 1580 or 1630.

Many of the setbacks that afflicted the French economy must be attributed to the character of French government; its extreme weakness during much of the period 1560–1660, and the reaction against the consequences of this weakness.

The great nobles of the sixteenth century were territorial lords commanding the allegiance of men over large areas of France, and they were able to rally forces round themselves and bring pressure on kings. The long series of religious wars that so damaged France between 1562 and 1598 was largely fought by noble factions that drew support on one side from Huguenot fanaticism, on the other from Catholic reaction and the external support of Spain, but both depending heavily on the clients and resources of their noble leaders' home territories. The wars were prolonged because the crown was unable either to suppress the struggle or to decide finally between the contestants. At last in 1594 a strong king, Henri IV, was able to begin reconciliation of the genuinely religious participants, to rouse national feeling against Spanish intervention, and so to bring the nobility to heel and end the war. He created a strong government under which France prospered, and after his assassination in 1610 his work was consolidated by Richelieu, the able minister of Henri's weak successor. Richelieu's purpose, however, was to reassert France's place in the affairs of Europe, and he led France into the Thirty Years War in 1624. Prolonged war – which eliminated Spain from the ranks of the great powers – was enormously costly, and steeply increasing taxes on both peasants and townsmen built up widespread resentment. In the years 1648–53, nobles who were seeking for the last time to recover their independence from the crown secured the support of discontented urban classes and the urban poor – above all the Paris mob – in the series of risings known as the Fronde. These years mark the low point of the French economy in the seventeenth century. In the aftermath of the Fronde, Louis XIV built on the order and confidence that Henri IV had begun and developed an intensely absolutist rule. The nobility, discredited and deprived of power, was allowed to maintain most of its old tax exemptions, was bolstered with sinecures and privileges, and renewed in each generation by creations from the ranks of financiers, tax-gatherers and officials who had built up fortunes in office. With the nobility either crushed or pacified, the king was able to pursue his own policies, leading France into great and costly wars in which French resources were poured out, taxes nearly doubled, French territories invaded deeply in the north and east, and colonial possessions lost.

France was overwhelmingly rural and indeed agricultural – despite the wide range of employment in rural industry. The agricultural basis seemed incapable after the 1560s of supporting more than a generation or so of rapid population growth without running into disaster. In agriculture, however, it is least of all possible to speak of France as a whole, and we must examine the different experiences of broad regions, and above all those of the cornlands of the north, and of lands with a more mixed agriculture that came within the fringes of Mediterranean climate in the south.

The plains and low hills of France from the Loire valley northward, densely populated and indeed overcrowded, contained a large proportion of France's population. Here peasant holdings were tiny – two-thirds of them less than two and a half acres, though they were supplemented with rented land – whilst pasture and common was very scarce, so that few animals could be maintained. The peasants of this region were heavily preoccupied with corn production; but yields were very low because of lack of manure. Few peasants had much surplus corn to sell except in the years of exceptionally bountiful harvest; while in bad years they went hungry and even starved. Most had patches of garden where they grew peas and beans and roots, and kept a vine and one or two fruit trees; they usually reserved a little land for saleable crops to pay rents and dues – notably hemp, or in suitably wet country flax. Nevertheless, the small peasants depended heavily for survival on earnings that did not come from the land; on wage labour for larger farmers, on carrying, charcoal burning and other work in the woods, and above all on the industrial by-employments in linen and woollen manufacture that their families could find in much of this region. The greatest part of the arable land was cultivated in strips in open fields, with a three-yearly rotation that left one-third of the land fallow each year. After the 1580s little fresh land of any value could be taken into cultivation without encroaching on the already scanty commons, so there was much division of peasant holdings and an intense competition for rented land that pushed rents up steeply in the first half of the seventeenth century. Nevertheless, many of the young men could secure neither holdings nor regular employment, and had to move to the towns to seek work. This was the region that suffered most severely from inability to adjust its production to population growth except over quite short periods. A generation of over-full farm-houses, or of further subdivisions of holdings, eventually faced a year or two of exceptionally bad harvests without sufficient reserves, and was sharply reduced in size by famine, accompanied by disease. With the land so emptied the survivors had a few decades of easier conditions, and then the growth of population brought crisis again. This was a sequence that was repeated time after time between 1580 and 1710.

The southern lands – Languedoc, Provence, Dauphiné – approaching the Mediterranean and a drier, sunnier climate, were less suited to corn both by the uncertainty of rainfall and the difficulty of terrain. Much land on which corn was grown was of poor quality, normally kept as rough pasture but cropped one year in five, eight or ten; that is with no regular rotation, and with adjustments to the rise or fall of demand by small changes in the frequency of cropping. Corn was grown at times wherever land was suitable and could be watered naturally or by irrigation, but the average peasant had a variety of products. He grazed sheep and goats on the un-cleared hillsides, providing wool, milk and occasionally meat. He grew vines, olives and fruit on hillside terraces or in enclosures, and was heavily dependent on the market conditions for these products. Except in the most bountiful years he bought corn to supplement his own harvest, and the region imported a large quantity from northern France in those periods when it had a surplus, or even from the Baltic. The land was emptier than the north, though much of it was infertile or inaccessible and the livings obtained from it were poor; if life was normally hard, the periodical squeeze-out of excess population did not operate so mercilessly here. Through two hundred years from 1480 to 1680 (with some interruption during the religious wars) the rural population was able to expand slowly because younger sons of peasant families could still go out and make themselves holdings, bringing marginal grazing lands into cultivation, terracing hillsides, making small irrigation works and enclosures for olives and vines. They were favoured by the growing European demand for these semi-luxuries; but as increasingly unsuitable land was pressed into cultivation the inevitable limit of this process was reached around 1680, when serious food shortages developed in the south, and many of the peasantry fell into debt and their land was sold.

In the wooded districts of the west – Brittany and western Normandy – there was a distinctive rural economy, in which corn-growing peasants kept far more animals than those in the rest of northern France. The best land was under corn, with a patch for hemp; but beyond this each peasant had substantial grazing land, parts of which he burnt over occasionally and replanted with corn for a year or two. Most households had cows and sold butter and cheese, whilst nearly all were able to supplement income by work in the linen industry. This was an area of modestly prosperous peasants, and here too the pressure of population was slower to make itself felt than in the great cornlands.

Peasant poverty is spoken of in the history of every country in the pre-industrial age as a matter of course, and it is all too easy to think of the mass of peasants throughout Europe as living in an undifferentiated condition close to a common subsistence level. But there were, of course, great differences even between the *average* living standards of the peasants in different countries and regions; due not merely to the variety of pressures of landlord and state, but also to the size of farms (a function of inheritance laws and social attitudes as well as economic pressures) and the intensity and modernity of their cultivation. By the middle of the seventeenth century the weeding out of the poorer peasants and the advancement of other peasants into modest farmers had gone much further in the Netherlands and England than in either France or Spain. French peasants were poor not merely in the sense that they were poorer than their English and Dutch counterparts. In an absolute sense they were poor (as the English were not) because they were unable to assure themselves regularly of the minimum needs of life, and therefore suffered, from time to time, a massive mortality. Peasant poverty, in this extreme form, was the basic weakness of the French economy.

Contemporary estimates of peasant income, dubious as they are, show such great differences that it is hard to believe they are wholly misleading; and they reflect the consequences of very small peasant holdings in France, and the lowness of French agricultural productivity. In England, taking the categories of freeholders and farmers (covering 31 per cent of the population) in Gregory King's estimate for 1688, the average income is £51; extending this to include the category of cottagers and paupers, which includes many people who would be classified as peasants in France, the average income (covering 55 per cent of the population) is £27. In France an estimate for 1701 gives a corresponding figure of peasant income of 200–300 livres, the equivalent of £9 to £14. A still more tentative estimate for the peasantry of New Castile in 1630 gives a figure of 60 ducats, about £17.

The movement of grain prices in the markets may be a good indicator of the problems of a market-oriented economy; it throws much less light on those of a country whose peasantry was still largely devoted to subsistence farming, and living very close to minimum levels. A great part of the corn produced in France never appeared on the market; in most years market prices reflected quite limited transactions in corn, but in very bad years a host of new buyers appeared, the peasants who normally fed themselves but were now short of corn. Consequently there were enormous differences in prices between ordinary and very bad years, and catastrophes occurred from time to time during the decades around 1700 when the long-term course of corn prices had seemed to suggest the corn supply problem was being mastered. This continued peasant poverty delayed agricultural improvement, held back the emergence of a large market for industrial products, and ensured that the penalty of a bad harvest was not merely worsened hardship but famine.

France suffered from too slow an improvement in agricultural practices; but nevertheless there was change. Here as elsewhere, discussions in terms of the yield of corn crops obscure the diversification and expansion of agricultural production. This diversification was slowed in the decades around 1600 when population pressure was becoming exceptionally heavy and required more concentration on corn, but it then proceeded, through bad periods as well as good, accelerating as corn prices fell away after 1662. Over and beyond the reparation of the damage of the religious wars, there was a considerable investment of urban resources in improvement during the first quarter of the seventeenth century, especially in the neighbourhood of the rapidly expanding city of Paris. Market gardens came to circle the city closely on the south; and farther out to the south and west, landholdings were thrown together to provide pastures for fattening cattle driven up from their rearing grounds on the heights above the Loire valley. On the north

side some large wheat farms of two to three hundred acres were
built up by capitalist farmers taking their example from the handful
of ecclesiastical home farms in the area. Rents rose steeply in the
Paris region, more than doubling between 1610 and 1670 under the
influence of the competition for holdings, particularly by bourgeois
and richer peasantry trying to build up large compact farms. Nor
was change entirely confined to the Paris region. There was much
drainage of coastal marshland in the south-west; seigneurial clearances of heath in Poitou to produce new *métayage* holdings which
they stocked with animals for mixed farming; and clearance of
forest for cornland in central France. In a wide area serving Paris,
pasture areas were being extended to support speculative stock-
rearing for the Paris market. In the south a steady ploughing up of
marginal land for corn and the extension of vineyards went on into
the 1670s, long after stagnation had set in over much of the north.

This expansive movement came to an end for a time in the 1630s,
in the cornlands of northern and eastern France. The devastation of
renewed foreign war ruined many peasants, and its risks made agricultural investment less attractive to urban capital. The condition
of the peasantry was seriously worsened by the reform of taxation
and of the tithe system under Richelieu. They had been relieved of
much of the real burden of old, fixed seigneurial dues by the long
rise in prices, and of tithe by the disrepair into which its collection
had fallen during the religious wars. Between 1620 and 1640, however, Richelieu vigorously reshaped the tax administration, raised
the level of taxes very sharply, and reactivated the collection of
tithes. A great part of the tax increase fell on the peasants; the old
seigneurial burden was replaced by a fiscal burden. Moreover, the
landlords found opportunities to replenish their incomes. Though
most peasants owned some of the land they used, they normally
supplemented this with plots of rented land, and in the period of
rising population to the 1630s the landowners, many of them now
town merchants, lawyers and officials, were able to push up the
rents of the land they let out. Finally, and perhaps in the long run
most important, the wars themselves caused many peasants and
village communities to fall into debt in attempting to meet dues and
taxes when their crops and property had been destroyed, and in
borrowing to replace stock that had been killed or driven away.
Much peasant-owned land was sold to creditors in the 1650s and
1660s in order to liquidate these wartime debts.

The early seventeenth-century changes, promising though they were, were limited in scope. They left France still a country of poor peasants, who were to be further impoverished in many areas by invasion and civil war. Prosperous and well-equipped farmers of large holdings – known in the north as *laboureurs* – while increasing in numbers, remained rare in most villages. Holdings were generally very small, ill-equipped, adequate to sustain the peasants only with the assistance of wage-labour on others' farms, or industrial by-employment, and easily tipped into shortage and debt by two or three bad harvests or a single encroachment by marauding soldiers. The landlord, rarely resident, left it to his agents to squeeze what they could from the tenants, whether from rents or from making the most of old seigneurial rights, and he invested in improvement only in the most propitious circumstances. The peasant of the mid-seventeenth century, his land producing a low return, and with taxes, tithes and rent taking a third or even a half, of his income, had little opportunity to accumulate capital, or to offer a useful demand for the products of industry.

In the early stages of France's recovery from its late-medieval depression, much of the new industrial growth was in eastern and southern France, aided by a large immigration of Italian and Spanish artisans and traders. Silk weaving was developed at Tours and after 1536 at Lyon, fine linens in the Reims area, tapestry-making at Paris and Orleans, a new woollen manufacture in Languedoc, and iron manufacture on a small scale in many parts of eastern France, particularly Dauphiné. But over the whole period of the sixteenth and seventeenth centuries the most important developments were in the linen and woollen industries, first in the towns of Picardy and Normandy but increasingly in the countryside. Textiles were expanding in northern France not only by moving from town to country but also by spreading out geographically; woollens from Picardy and the Cambrai area where they had long been settled, eastwards into Champagne and westward into Normandy, while linens extended still farther into Brittany, Maine and Anjou. The towns remained important industrial centres, but by the middle of the seventeenth century the early processing and weaving of coarser and middling fabrics in both linen and woollen industries was almost entirely rural. These rural industries, using the resources of town finishing trades and town markets, had by 1650 pushed far beyond serving merely local demands or sending goods abroad through convenient ports. Despite all the difficulties of internal transport they had created a national market for their products in France, so that, for example, cloths made in the area of Beauvais or Mans were sold in every corner of the country.

The seventeenth century witnessed the appearance of changing fashions in textiles; not merely the turn from woollens to silks, linens and presently cottons, but also the acceptance of an increasing range of types of woollen cloth. The chief sufferers from this were the producers of heavy high-quality cloths, who faced increasing competition for a market that ceased to expand. At the beginning of the seventeenth century the towns of Normandy and Picardy were still major centres for weaving and finishing these cloths, though spinning was entirely rural. The technically conservative urban artisans in these heavily regulated trades were unwilling to change the methods, organization and fabrics they knew; and they could not stand up to the competition of innovations produced by the new Dutch industry at Leyden or the English makers in Wiltshire. The French home market was invaded by these foreign cloths, and they were only checked by Colbert's imposition of very high tariffs in 1664. Behind this tariff barrier he attempted to stimulate the industry by subsidizing the immigration of Dutch and Flemish weavers and entrepreneurs into Normandy. Pressed by its difficulties and encouraged by state assistance, the industry slowly changed its structure and its products. By 1680 the independent town craftsman had generally been replaced by the small workshop in which a single master, backed by merchant finance, employed several journeymen; and he made his production flexible by giving out some work to rural labour. The towns abandoned the more standardized products to rural makers, and began to produce new fancy woollen mixtures, incorporating silk, camel- and goat-hair, and with these luxury products went on to a steady expansion in the eighteenth century.

The rural industry in Picardy had turned over to making cheap, light woollen cloths or worsteds during the sixteenth century, and this manufacture flourished, developing a big export to Spain. Its centre, however, was a border area particularly prone to invasion. The great industry of the Hordschoote region, making the popular light cloths known as says, was severely damaged by the religious wars and the Spanish invasion of the 1580s and 1590s; recovering a new prosperity in the first quarter of the next century, it was again destroyed by war after 1630. But the industry revived once more in the decades of stability after 1660, extending into

Normandy and Champagne, and producing still cheaper varieties of cloth. On the other hand, the Languedoc industry which captured Mediterranean markets during the sixteenth century was so badly weakened by the troubles of the 1640s and 1650s that even a massive concentration of state assistance in Colbert's time put it only precariously on its feet, and full recovery was delayed until well into the eighteenth century.

The leaders of the European woollen industry, in fact, were now the Dutch and English, while new competition was appearing late in the seventeenth century from the rising Silesian industry. The French could not excel at everything, and the speciality in which they now led Europe was linen, especially fine linens and best quality canvas. The French industry first grew to importance in Picardy (where it began with labour released by the decline of the woollen industry at the end of the Middle Ages) and spread southward from there. During the sixteenth century it was able to replace imports from the Netherlands; its quality was improved after 1600 by the introduction of Dutch bleaching methods and the best French products forged far ahead of their rivals. The industry originally used flax grown in the lower reaches of the river valleys of the west, but even before the end of the sixteenth century it had to supplement these native supplies by large imports from the Baltic. The best quality linens were made in the area behind Rouen and exported through it; they had no competition except from Flanders. Brittany had a varied linen production, largely serving the home market but also exporting through Nantes and St Malo, while Anjou's chief product was canvas. Everywhere the industry was one of rural outworkers taking their materials from merchant organizers; and it gave double support to rural population as an employer of labour and as a consumer of a readily grown flax crop. The industry, situated close behind the ports of the channel coast and the Atlantic, was strongly oriented towards exporting. Though badly hit by the mid-century wars, it was firmly set on a path of long-term growth, well able to cope with Dutch and German competition, for the European demand for linens was still rapidly expanding.

The silk industry, exceptionally among textiles, was an almost wholly urban one. Its centre after the middle of the sixteenth century was Lyon, well away from the main currents of war; and its competitor was not one of the freely reorganizing countries of the west, but an Italian industry that was old and inflexible in its ways.

The industry at Lyon therefore flourished almost throughout the seventeenth century, diversifying its range of products into damasks and brocades to attract new customers. During the four mid-century decades that were disastrous to much of French industry, the number of silk workshops in the Lyon area actually doubled. The organization of the industry changed; it was brought largely under the domination of the merchants who imported silk from Italy. The master artisans were reduced to the situation of dependent workers, though they still held to their own workshops and employees and maintained some influence through control of the gilds. Finding most of its customers among the rich, the industry was less affected than others by changing tides of prosperity, and it widened its appeal as some of the middle classes came to have aspirations to luxury.

Beyond these industries, which served national and international markets, industry was generally scattered in small units and narrow producing areas. In such a large and thickly populated country the total output was large, but it is hard to measure or even see its approximate size with any clarity. The modest sixteenth-century expansion of the metal industries, and of the iron industry in particular after the introduction of the blast furnace, was checked in the following century by the expansion of Dutch trade in German, Lorraine and presently Swedish iron and iron goods. It remained a small-scale industry, generally with old-fashioned methods, in many of the well-timbered areas of France, to be given some stimulus after 1661 by Colbert's subsidization of selected enterprises in Dauphiné, Burgundy and Languedoc. Beyond this, even such well-known industries with export markets as chemicals, paper, glass and fine leatherware were small.

There was an old tradition of government regulation of urban industries, both through the general regulation imposed by municipalities with the backing of royal authority, and through the strictly controlled gilds that had been created in many towns – again with royal support – and regulated entry to trades and work within them. The check to industrial growth after 1630, and especially the difficulties of branches of the woollen industry, caused government to return to industrial protection in 1648. After 1661 the royal minister Colbert set out more systematically to develop some branches of French industry. He believed that French manufactures had been losing something of that feeling for quality that had enabled them to compete with the Italians in the luxury market in the sixteenth century. The highest quality goods would always be sought, at almost any price, by the wealthy at home and abroad, and he sought to create a new French reputation for them. Some kinds of manufacture were set up in state workshops – Gobelins tapestry or Van Robais woollens; some left in private hands but given temporary monopoly advantages and subsidies, and put under strict regulations to be minutely observed under the eyes of government inspectors. The policy had some success in raising the international esteem of the best French products, in aiding the recovery of the fine-woollen industry of north-western France and setting the Languedoc woollen industry on its feet, and in establishing cannon foundries. In these advantageous respects it outlived Colbert; but it left behind also his legacy of detailed control, meticulous inspection and reliance on privileges that added to the rigidity of French industry and in the long run to its weakness. In any case, Colbert's work had less influence on the recovery of 1660–90 than the reorganization forced upon industries by the difficulties of mid-century, which bore its fruit in a generation of comparative peace, population growth and trade expansion. The move of industry into the countryside accelerated, and craft conservatism was broken down by merchant pressures exercised directly on producers to get more saleable products. In the advancing industries there was a general tendency towards the replacement of independent craftsmen by sharply divided groups of merchant capitalists on one side and dependent wage-earners on the other. In the rural districts merchants dealt directly with the workers, but in the towns they exercised their influence on production indirectly through their dominance of modestly prosperous but dependent workshop owners.

The impact of the new currents of trade that began to flow through Europe in the late fifteenth century had been felt chiefly on the periphery of France. The north–south route through the Rhône valley gained renewed importance, and Lyon became the most active financial centre of the west outside Italy. Marseilles and Toulouse flourished on expanded trade with Spain, and the connection of northern France with Antwerp was strengthened. But France's size, population and natural resources enabled it to be remarkably self-sufficient. At the beginning of the sixteenth century France's only major foreign supplier was Italy, from which it imported fine silks and other fabrics, spices, drugs and dyestuffs. The encouragement of the new silk industry at Tours and Lyon, and the opening of direct trade with the Turkish Empire in the 1530s, were attempts to reduce this trade, for there was no corresponding French export to Italy.

After the earliest decades of the sixteenth century, however, the expansion of overseas trade was associated with the rise of the western ports. On the channel coast Rouen connected Paris and northern France with the trading metropolis of Antwerp, and was in fact a satellite of that city, with its business carried on largely by Italian and Spanish commercial houses. The small ports of Normandy and Brittany had old-established fisheries, and after 1520 were turning particularly to the Newfoundland fishery, sending hundreds of vessels a year after mid-century. There was a large coasting trade, connecting the ports at the mouths of the great rivers that led into the interior. Bordeaux and Rochelle exported great quantities of wine to England and the Netherlands; Morlaix and St Malo, as well as Rouen, sent linens to Spain, and great fleets came to the Biscay coast to lade Brouage salt for the Netherlands and the Baltic. The bulk trades were largely in foreign hands; English and Dutch ships carried away the wine, and Dutch and Hanseatic ships the salt, which accounted for most of the tonnage of French exports. But the valuable trade was with Spain; indirectly through Rouen and Antwerp, to Catalonia and Valencia through Marseilles, and directly to the rising markets of Castile through Morlaix, St Malo, Nantes, Bordeaux and Rochelle. This rapidly expanding Spanish trade particularly benefited the linen industry of Maine and Anjou, which found its main outlet there; but woollens, corn, woad, ironware, paper and other goods were also sent to Spain. The linen trade was largely in the hands of Spanish merchants settled in the western ports, and it was from them that the French at St Malo, Nantes and Bordeaux learned modern Italian commercial techniques.

Overseas trade suffered more from war than most sections of the economy. It seems likely that in the early years of the 1560s, before the wars of religion, a trading peak was attained that was only briefly reached again in the early seventeenth century, and then lost until after 1660. The sieges of Rouen and Havre in 1562–3, of Rouen again in 1591–2, and the blockade of Bordeaux in 1592–5, accentuated the trading difficulties that wars in their immediate hinterland created, though the troubles of each particular port brought short surges of prosperity to the others. From the 1570s Moorish piracy in the Mediterranean and Dutch and English competition began to whittle away the trade of Marseilles. The early seventeenth-century wars hit the ports less directly (though Rochelle underwent a long siege in 1626-7) but they again suffered from the damage done to industry in the north, and from the breach of relations with Spain.

After 1660 the western ports entered a flourishing period. The total tonnage of French merchant shipping doubled in the next thirty years, with Rochelle, Nantes, St Malo and Bayonne in the lead. This is paradoxical in a period in which the main export trades were not doing well, the linen export to Spain showing a falling tendency and the Levant trade still in the doldrums. The ports and their merchants flourished because Frenchmen took over some of the old bulk trades from foreigners, and above all because colonial trade expanded very rapidly. The Spaniards who had led the commercial life of the western ports were being replaced, in the early decades of the seventeenth century, by Dutch merchants, and in its middle decades most trade and shipping in the west was in Dutch hands. Colbert not only gave France industrial protection by the tariffs of 1664 and 1667, but also proceeded to squeeze out the Dutch traders and carriers. Shipping was promoted by subsidies for building and purchasing ships and encouragement for Dutch and English shipwrights to practise their craft in France. In 1673 a decree excluded foreign ships from participating in French colonial trade.

At the centre of the new trade expansion was the West Indian trade, of which Rochelle and Nantes were the chief beneficiaries in this period, with St Malo and Bordeaux some way behind. St Malo was the centre for the Newfoundland and St Lawrence fisheries, and for Atlantic whaling. The French Atlantic ports, their populations growing fast, became prosperous from Europe's growing demand for tropical products, and called on French industry for manufactured goods to send to the colonies in return. A large shipping industry was built up, largely based on this colonial trade from which the Dutch were excluded; with the single important exception of Baltic trade, the Dutch had been replaced as carriers for France before 1690. Overseas trade was severely set back in the war of 1689-97, when ports were closed and great numbers of French ships were captured; but it recovered and after 1702 was supplemented by a brief but splendid burst of direct trade with Spanish America. St Malo, whose cod fishery had first given it a close connection with Spain, was the centre of this new trade, its ships even penetrating the Pacific; and when Spanish-American trade with

France received its severe setback in 1713 by the peace treaty that handed French privileges to the English, St Malo rapidly lost the importance it had briefly held. But in France, as in England, this commercial expansion had only a very limited industrial impact; there was an expansion of trade passing through the country, of shipping and of commercial capital rather than of industry.

The view of French economic history that sees the period 1630–1730 as one of 'general crisis' – fitted, despite difficulties of chronology, into a general European crisis – is essentially a price-history one. It is associated with Simiand's application to long historical periods of the theory that falling prices, or prices maintained at a low level, are associated with depression and stagnation. The economic weakness of the second quarter of the seventeenth century was not, however, continued, and the remaining eighty years down to 1730 are on the whole years of recovery in which serious brief setbacks were experienced, rather than of overall stagnation. Moreover, there is only a slender link between the histories of the different regions of France; the thickly populated north running into subsistence crises and problems of foreign industrial competition in the 1630s, the Atlantic coast emerging in the 1660s into a bounding prosperity, the southern provinces with their economy expanding until after 1680 and then going into a precipitous decline that was only partially stayed by industrial revival.

There were no serious wars on French soil for half a century after 1653. Plague never struck universally after 1655; the last widespread epidemic in 1668–70 was a comparatively mild one, and it then almost disappeared until its last fling at Marseilles in 1720. The decline in corn prices after 1662 suggests that the desperate shortages of the earlier part of the century had been overcome, though there were setbacks in periods of dearth, in northern France in 1678–81 and in the south in 1684–7. The years 1662–90, in fact, saw low food prices, a marked revival in many branches of industry and the establishment of new ones, and an enormous expansion of overseas trade partly based on colonial development.

Once security returned with the ending of the Frondist wars in 1653, slow development had recommenced in agriculture. There was a concentration of wine production for the market on particular areas: Auxerre, Beaune, Orleans, Poitou and Charente distributed their produce widely through France and expanded their vineyards to cope with increased demand. The north-western

I

region gradually abandoned its inferior wine production for cider. Rapid expansion of the linen and canvas industries after 1660 encouraged peasants in the north-west to reserve more of their land for growing flax to secure a cash revenue. In south-western and central France, new field crops were introduced; of buckwheat – grown on lands that would bear no other cereal – and of maize, which was high yielding and used for fodder, helping to make possible enlarged cattle herds. Similarly in the pastoral areas that served Paris, the introduction of sainfoin and other artificial grasses supported larger herds. Only in a few cases, however, did the turn away from corn to other products involve the extension of mixed farming that would improve corn yields. The convertible husbandry that elsewhere in western Europe was breaking the vicious circle of few animals and low corn yields was rarely adopted in France.

Corn yields remained low according to the available data, though these are scattered and not wholly conclusive. The averages that have been computed are very heavily influenced by the scattering of bad harvests among them; thus the catastrophic years 1643–51 reveal such a mixed bag of influences – war, bad weather, Fronde and plague – that the basic causation is not easily disentangled; and the 'low yield' period 1687–1715 is one in which three or four years' bad harvests pulled down the average levels of more than a quarter of a century in which the return was generally reasonable. It is possible, as some writers suggest, that periods of particular difficulty for French agriculture are related to climatic cycles of thirty-five to forty years' duration; but final judgement on this must be reserved until the existence of such regular short-term climatic movements has been confirmed and explained.

Cereal prices were generally declining from 1662 until the mid-1680s, and after that date remained at modest levels in most years, rising to extraordinary heights in the years 1692–4 and 1709–10. This was an unfavourable situation for corn production; long-sustained low prices discouraged investment in building up large and efficient cereal farms, while the occasional dearths that temporarily favoured the very large producers were disastrous to small peasants whose surpluses were wiped out so they had to borrow if they were to survive. The level of rents was creeping downward for well over half a century after 1670, giving some relief to those who cultivated leased lands. Cereal production was undoubtedly being expanded, for the slow decline of prices was going on alongside a rising population until 1692; while it seems unlikely that the rise in corn production towards the middle of the eighteenth century could have come about quite unheralded by earlier improvement.

Industrially, the decades after 1660 saw the recovery of rural industries that had been overrun by war, and the building up of selected industrial sectors by government efforts. This received some support from the increased purchasing power, released by cheap food, in the hands of townspeople, and more plentiful marketable surpluses at the disposal of many peasants. Paris was the great consuming centre of France, but never its economic centre of gravity; the latter might have been found in the industrial areas of the north-west set amidst a thick peasant population, or in the Rhône valley; but at the end of the seventeenth century the most rapid economic advance was in the Atlantic ports of St Malo, Nantes, Rochelle and Bordeaux.

Post-1660 prosperity received a serious shock with the persecution of the Huguenots in the 1680s, in consequence of which some two hundred thousand people are said to have emigrated, a large proportion of them townspeople of the west and south-west – merchants, artisans, lawyers, mariners. The beginnings of agrarian depression in the south were followed by the deficient harvests of 1684–7, threatening the return of general food shortages and showing that France had failed to break out completely from the subsistence cycle. Then in 1689 came renewed war, pursued on a tremendous scale and continuing with only a brief interval until 1713. Taxation was enormously increased – at its peak absorbing possibly 15 per cent of national income – and as always most of it fell on the rural poor and the peasantry. This new taxation imposed a crushing burden on an already weakening agrarian base. The famine disaster of 1692–4 was probably the most destructive in three hundred years; that of 1709–10 was equally deadly in many regions, though it did not strike the whole of France. Between 10 and 20 per cent of the French died in these two brief periods. The disaster was not merely rural, for the cutting-off of demand as people used all their money to buy necessary food created heavy industrial unemployment, and this joined with famine and the migration of rural labourers to bring hardship and pestilence to the towns. Overseas trade was stopped by wartime blockade for long periods, particularly in the 1690s, and was always hampered; many thousands of ships were lost to English and Dutch privateers.

Even when the wars were over their baleful effects were felt; the attempt to liquidate the legacy of crown debt by means of ingenious financial manipulation devised by John Law was ahead of its time and brought about a huge financial and commercial crisis in 1720. This held back advance for some years, and prevented the proper development of French banking institutions for more than half a century. England had lagged far behind France, industrially, in 1600; it was able to progress more rapidly and uninterruptedly during the seventeenth century. By 1730 it was – allowing for its smaller size – far in advance, and had encroached on fields where French supremacy had once been quite unchallenged.

14 *Capital, Credit and Financial Institutions*

Modern writers have examined two aspects of capitalism in the period between the fifteenth and the eighteenth century. One is the concept of the 'spirit of capitalism', which will not be pursued here because it is concerned with the response to the increasing importance of capital in productive relations, rather than with something preceding or causing this development. The other is the growing importance of capital-using types of commerce and industry, and the extension of capitalist-wage-earner relationships to larger sections of the population.

There are ambiguities in the economist's view of capital which have particular importance for the pre-industrial age. In the first place, land is often treated as something distinct from capital, though it is fully recognized that cleared and cultivated land derives much of its utility from having been cleared by human efforts which amount to capital investment. It may be convenient to view land as a distinctive form of capital stock; but investment in the improvement of land competed in every year with other uses for new savings, absorbing a very large part of new capital accumulations. There was heavy investment in the enclosure and preparation of vineyards in Andalusia, clearing of woodland to plant tobacco in Virginia, enclosure and ploughing up of pasture in England, building of irrigation systems for new smallholdings in Provence; and on a more spectacular scale polder-building in Holland, fen drainage in eastern England and south-western France, and swamp clearance and irrigation works in St Domingue.

Again, the position of the domestic house and mansion in relation to definitions of capital is ambiguous; but a large part of every year's savings went into new buildings. The intense urbanization of the sixteenth and early seventeenth centuries, revealed by town maps and illustrations as well as by population statistics; the aggrandizement of the country residences of the rich in England and France and the town houses of the Dutch bourgeoisie, in the seventeenth and eighteenth centuries; the wave of rebuilding of ordinary houses in rural England between 1570 and 1640; these required new investment on a grand scale. Much the greatest part of net investment in the sixteenth, seventeenth and eighteenth centuries went on land improvement and building; a far smaller part supported the expansion of commerce or industry. (It is possible that this statement is not true of Brabant and Flanders in the sixteenth century or of Holland in the seventeenth.) The increase of total capital employed in industry and commerce, important though it was to the changing pattern of economic life, absorbed only a small part of all savings; so far as there was at any time a national problem of shortage of industrial and commercial capital – as distinct from individuals' problems of raising capital – it was one of winning a slightly increased proportion of gross savings away from other uses. The situation in the nineteenth century, following the Industrial Revolution, was quite different; industrial capital then became associated to a great and growing extent with fixed equipment – factories, machines, ships, railways. Before the eighteenth century much of the modest body of fixed equipment that existed was owned not by people normally thought of as capitalists but by employees with their own looms or tools, who worked for masters in their own cottages. Finally, turning to employee–employer relations, the number of dependent wage-earners was growing in agriculture as well as in industry; and in England and Spain, at least, it is likely that the growth of absolute numbers in the wage-earning class was attributable chiefly to agriculture.

Industrial and commercial capital, on the whole, existed in the form of stocks of raw materials and finished goods, and of work partly completed. Indeed, it is difficult to distinguish between commercial and industrial capital; 'merchant-organizers' provided raw materials and semi-finished goods to successive groups of productive workers in an industry, organized the smooth flow of production, sold the finished product and supported all this with a sufficient provision of capital. The putter-out in the Wiltshire woollen industry had to pay wages, week by week, to workers whose product might not be sold for some months after production was started. Even the forge owner in Dauphiné with valuable fixed equipment was likely to have stocks and unfinished work totalling a greater value. From the individual's point of view there was another vitally important element in capital – the credit he extended, partly counter-balanced by the credit he received for goods he bought. In the aggregate, however, this simply determined how capital need was distributed within the nation.

In overseas trade, again, capital was largely in stocks of goods afloat in ships, or in warehouses, though from a national point of view the extension of credit to overseas buyers, or the lending of money to producers of goods to be imported, did involve investment and the export of capital. Internal trade generally required more modest capital, and was largely supported by credit from industrialists. There was, however, a special case of agricultural stockholding, which was important because of the great size of the agricultural sector. Much capital was provided, in a sense that is not usually taken into account, by peasant and farmer; that is, the holding of enough of last year's produce to keep his family going until the next harvest (the financing, in other words, of 'work-in-progress' in the form of growing crops and animals). So far as agricultural produce came on the market, however, it was financed by merchants, who usually paid promptly when they bought it from the producer and sold on credit when the market seemed right. Merchants of one kind or another financed the holdings of agricultural stocks for the whole period between one harvest and the next; and the total of these was very large.

The total requirement for industrial and commercial capital was modest, if we leave out of account the equipment in the hands of cottage outworkers and the food stocks of the peasants. It was a requirement, however, that grew in this period much faster than national income, faster even than the growth in the value of industrial production or of trade. *This* was the growth of capitalism: the *relative* growth within society of the particular forms of economic activity in which capital and capitalist relations were essential. The combined capital needs of trade and industry, so hard to distinguish from one another, grew fast in the Netherlands in the sixteenth and the first half of the seventeenth century; in England in the economic expansion from the middle of the seventeenth century; and in France to some extent during the commercial growth of the period 1660–90, but above all in its eighteenth-century industrial expansion.

Beyond the expansion of industry there was the expansion of capitalist sectors within industry. Earlier chapters have shown how in most countries (Spain appears an exception, but this may simply reflect our lack of knowledge) responsibility for the finance of production was in one industry after another being shifted from the craftsman to the merchant capitalist. Far advanced in some of the textile industries before the end of the fifteenth century, notably in Flemish and English woollen manufacture, it was spreading into Picardy linens, into the Sheffield cutlery trades, into Lyon silk, into mining. In all these industries and many others the provision of capital was becoming a function of merchant organizers in place of independent workers or small working capitalists. This concentration of capital in merchant hands went much further towards creating capitalist relationships in industry as a whole than did the modest building-up of fixed plant in small industries like mining, metal-refining and soap boiling – at least until the eighteenth century. True capitalist relationships were developing, between rich capitalists and poor wage-earners; control of production was coming into the hands of people whose interest was in selling and in making profits related to money laid out, rather than in producing goods to traditional standards.

There was a similar expansion of the need for capital in commerce, both internal and external. A striking feature of English development in the later seventeenth and eighteenth centuries was the increased marketing of agricultural goods; but this process had been going on in many parts of western Europe much earlier, with the growth of agricultural specialization and regional markets. The peasant or large farmer, selling his produce in the market, transferred the problem of financing stockholding to the merchant; and ranges of merchant intermediaries grew up between the producers and the final consumers, the total capital they employed expanding enormously. There was an increase, too, in merchants' stockholding of manufactures. When, for example, a national market began to emerge in seventeenth-century France for the cloth of Reims or Beauvais, which had previously been sold within a much narrower area, a new need for capital was introduced. A larger quantity of cloth would always be in transit at any given time, simply because to move a bale from, say, Beauvais to Grenoble took several weeks; and the Grenoble retailer, who could not replace cloths quickly, had to hold big stocks. The supersession of local markets by regional and national ones, in an age of very slow communications, required a big accession to merchants' capital.

The expansion of international trade – and above all the appearance and rapid growth of trade beyond the oceans – multiplied capital needs in a number of ways beyond the sheer growth in the value of trade. First, the distances involved in international trade were being lengthened. It is true that even in the eighteenth century a very large part of international trade was carried on between Hamburg and London, St Malo and Cadiz, Lisbon and Amsterdam; but from the time of the fifteenth-century discoveries an increasing share of it was over very much longer distances. From the Spice Islands to Amsterdam, from Vera Cruz to Seville, from Bahia to Lisbon, from Chesapeake Bay to London, from Guadeloupe to Nantes, were obviously longer voyages; but within Europe, too, English and Dutch ports were carrying on much more trade with the farther corners of the Mediterranean and the Baltic in the seventeenth century. Goods spent more time in ships' holds; factors and agents in America or India, where ships came regularly once a year, had to hold larger stocks of European goods than those who worked in towns supplied by weekly shipments across the North Sea and the channel. More ships were needed, and bigger ones costing more per ton to build. For these reasons alone the capital needs of overseas trade expanded fast.

Within Europe a great part of trade was in manufactured goods, and merchants were given credit for goods they bought at both ends of their trading connections. They might usually expect to sell goods and collect the proceeds before they paid for them; they needed capital as a reserve to meet other obligations if sales were slow, rather than to finance large regular commitments. But imports from more distant places were generally of agricultural and forest products, commonly bought from producers or from small traders with few resources. The crop of tobacco or sugar or silk or flax was bought to be shipped to Europe as soon as it became available; the grower was usually paid at once in European goods, slaves or occasionally cash. The burden of holding stocks, at sea or in warehouses, through the year until the next crop was available, was carried by the European merchant. Finally, many European merchants were gradually drawn beyond this into extending credit to overseas suppliers; into providing European goods before receiving the commodities contracted for; and thus going beyond the holding of one year's crop to financing the growing of the next year's – with a tendency for the debts to get out of hand and become much bigger still. This happened not only in colonial trade, but in Mediterranean fruit and wine, and in Baltic timber and iron trades.

In all these ways capital investment in overseas trade was growing very rapidly in England, the Netherlands and France in the seventeenth and eighteenth centuries. The burden was not borne wholly by the merchants; there was a general lengthening of credit terms in the course of the seventeenth century, from a common one, two or three months at its beginning to six, nine, twelve months or more at its end. This may plausibly be associated with the lengthening of trade routes. Much of the burden of providing capital might in this way be transferred back down the line of merchants to the man who did not live by credit; that is, normally, to the manufacturer who paid out wages in cash.

The sources of savings cannot be pin-pointed in any precise way; people in all the well-to-do sections of the community saved. Savings came principally from people who were newly rich, whose spending habits had not kept pace with their rising incomes. Those who were habituated to wealth had generally become landowners; in England they were normally living in the countryside, in Spain and France they were often town-dwellers, but all of them lived in great and expensive state; it was derogatory not to keep the big house with open hospitality, many servants, carriages and horses that seemed appropriate to their status in society. As generation succeeded generation this extravagant expenditure was more likely to expand than to contract, whatever the movement of the corresponding income, and few great houses passed through many generations before the head of one of them found his debts compelling him to sell land.

The peasantry always included a small minority of the fortunate and thrifty who accumulated rapidly, and there were short periods of widespread peasant prosperity in which many saved. In the long run, however, it seems likely that the peasantry tended to spend beyond its income and be compelled, eventually, to sell land to meet its debts. It would otherwise be difficult to account for the erosion of peasant landholdings through sales to landlords, and particularly to town merchants and officials and professional people. To some extent, it is true, the disappearance of peasant land was due to individual peasants taking themselves and their land out of the peasant class into the gentry.

The great purchases of land by the rising classes, by merchants, officials and the saving landlords and peasants, which caused most land to change its ownership once, and much of it two or three times, in three centuries, were made from landowners and peasants who had spent beyond their incomes. These land sales were the consequence of years of generations of dissaving by the owners or their ancestors, and a very great part of saving was cancelled out by this dissaving. The merchant buying land was, from his own point of view, making an investment; but from a national point of view his cash was setting off someone else's debts, and the one real capital asset, the land, was unchanged by the transaction.

The sources of saving were mainly among those people who were economically active and who had opportunities to enlarge their incomes greatly during their working lifetimes; these were usually merchants, professional men and officials, and they often put some of their resources to financial business once they had become really wealthy. Most merchants who ended life with large fortunes started with quite small incomes. This was because, outside the Netherlands, prosperous merchants safeguarded their families by buying land and government securities, and had ambitions to give their eldest sons the high social status of idle gentlemen rather than expecting them to carry on a family business. Merchant houses were constantly being founded by younger sons or nephews of the rich, or elder sons of the less successful, who were provided by parent or uncle with small but usually adequate capital. Supported by the trading connections and goodwill built up by their families, or by apprenticeship to houses of standing, they had no difficulty, if they were reasonably competent and thrifty, in earning good incomes and quickly accumulating more capital. In the same ways the professional man, the lawyer, physician or higher government official, coming from similar origins, could expect his income to rise rapidly in the course of his working life. In such groups of people, rising incomes were normal; among landowners, peasants and artisans, long-run stability of income (whatever the short-term fluctuation) was expected, and though many improved their incomes, the kind of expansion of income that merchants commonly achieved was impossible.

Professional men obviously did not need much capital to carry on their occupations, once their parents had provided them with the training and whatever form of entrance fee was necessary. Nor, strange as it may seem, did most merchants. On the whole, trade was financed by credit from industry; the merchant's capital was needed to bridge securely any gap between the credit he received and the credit he gave; to ensure that he would be able to meet the flow of payments due from him even if the flow of anticipated receipts was briefly halted. Except in the East India trade (which was company-financed) and in the English and Dutch Levant trades that handled valuable goods at the end of a long voyage, a great turnover could be supported by very small capital; many tens of thousands of pounds a year of sales by a capital of a very few thousands – even, taking some risk, with no capital at all, if the trader's credit was sound. The records of rich English, French and Spanish merchants who made their fortunes in trade in the late sixteenth, seventeenth and eighteenth centuries all show that they kept only a small part of their capital in continuing trade, and the remainder was employed in lending, or investing in land. The withdrawal of capital from trade into landed estates was not undertaken wholly because of the prestige of landowning; a place had to be found for surplus funds that could not be employed even by a very large-scale trader.

There were, it is true, some indirect ways of investing in trade. A number of joint-stock trading companies had stocks that could be bought; the important ones were the Dutch and English East India Companies but there were several less secure and generally unprofitable companies – the Dutch West India and the English African Companies, a number of French companies and in Spain in the eighteenth century the Caracas Company. In Holland and France it was possible to invest in trading partnerships on a limited liability principle, which English law did not allow; but on the whole, as capital became more plentiful, the available opportunities of this kind were in short-term syndicates of a speculative kind. Marine insurance syndicates gave similar opportunities of deriving some profit from a form of commercial speculation; they required, not capital, but the ability to produce capital if a loss was incurred.

The great outlet for savings in every country – with a limited exception for Holland – was the ownership of land and buildings, which conveyed social prestige and often some political power. The land market was limited, in the Netherlands, by the small area of the country, and elsewhere by the practice of entailing estates, carried on in Spain from the end of the Middle Ages and in England

and France from the mid-seventeenth century. Nevertheless, the determined aspirant could find some land to buy, from owners of unentailed estates or from peasant proprietors. The land remained the same under its new owner, unless, of course, he invested additional capital in its improvement. It was a safe form of investment, and offered the possibility to a determined new owner of markedly improving the income with no real risk of loss. A half-way house to buying land was lending on mortgage, but apart from the specialist moneylenders few people engaged in this except among the circle of their own close acquaintances.

The larger fortunes that individuals accumulated, if they were not invested in land, went into lending, and most commonly into lending to governments. Government borrowing took two forms. One was the securing of quite small sums from large numbers of prosperous people; this was the means by which Spanish *juros*, French *rentes*, and Dutch annuities of the sixteenth century and onward were recruited. The first two, it is true, often represented involuntary lending; the Spanish and French crowns repeatedly made unilateral declarations that debts they had incurred for goods and services should be transformed into these long-term interest-bearing loans; later, they reduced the promised interest rates. But many people bought these bonds voluntarily, for they provided interest rates that compared quite well with the returns from land-owning. In each country a market developed where these bonds could be bought and sold, and no doubt they changed hands in the same way as land, new savings being used to buy them from sellers who had overspent their incomes. In England the peculiar relationship between crown and Parliament in financial matters before 1689 prevented both long-term borrowing and, generally, the forced transformation of floating into long-term debt. From 1692, however, long-term debt was created in great amounts, and once established it was attractive to investors, offering the same kind of security as the Dutch state debt.

The man who invested in a national debt was enabling the Spanish, Dutch or French Government to overspend its income, generally by money poured out unproductively on munitions and the pay of troops. This overspending was met, on the whole, from the new savings of people who had accumulated the money they earned productively. There was a different and older way in which governments secured finance for their deficits, through the operations of small numbers of specialist financiers, using their own money or the deposits of other people that had been entrusted to them. The Italian and German financial houses that supported the French and Spanish crowns in the sixteenth century; the English customs farmers and goldsmith bankers of the seventeenth century; the French tax farmers of the eighteenth century; all these were men who made huge fortunes from government finance. They lent at high rates of interest, since governments were not affected by laws that limited interest on private loans; they secured all kinds of concessions in trade, colonial grants, office or other privileges; they were often able to buy up at a discount government paper obligations whose owners despaired of quick payment, and get them paid quickly through their own close connections with Treasury officials. In the long run they lent largely from fortunes they had accumulated from the interest and profits of past loans. The greatest fortunes of their day were made in this kind of government finance; but financiers were exposed to all the enormous risks of government default, and most were sooner or later ruined by it.

The market supply of capital was rapidly becoming more abundant in the seventeenth and most of the eighteenth centuries. This abundance reflected accumulation catching up on the limited needs of an age which had little use for fixed capital outside agriculture. There was much literary comment on the improving supply of capital in England and France from the late seventeenth century, but the clearest evidence is to be seen in the decline in interest rates. Ecclesiastical and secular prohibitions on interest had probably kept rates artificially high during the Middle Ages, but as late as the 1550s rates paid on private deposits by bankers in Antwerp and Lyon ranged between 9 and 12 per cent; the French, Spanish and English governments commonly borrowed at over 10 per cent late in the sixteenth century, and never at a rate lower than 8 per cent; the Dutch Government was paying 7½ per cent in 1606. Really low interest rates did not appear until mid-century and then only in Holland. With the slowing of expansion of Dutch commerce and the ending of the financial strains of the Thirty Years War, Dutch merchants employing surplus resources in finance found that their supply outran demand. In consequence, by the 1660s the Dutch borrower was the envy of Europe, with ample funds available at 3 to 4 per cent, coming down to a normal 2 to 3 per cent that was maintained through the first three-quarters of the eighteenth century. The Dutch, indeed, found it impossible to invest their surpluses at home after the end of the century, and lent abroad on a great scale, particularly to the English and French Governments. English rates came down in the wake of the Dutch; the reduction of the legal maximum from 10 per cent to 8 per cent in 1622 seems to have reflected actual rates paid, as did the further reduction to 6 per cent in 1664. By 1670 borrowers on good security could get loans at 4 to 4½ per cent in England; in the peace years of the eighteenth century the rate was 4 per cent or occasionally less. English government long-term borrowings, which started in the 1690s at levels of 8 per cent or more, on an experimental basis, soon came down; from the 1720s government stock sold in the market at rates yielding only 3 per cent, rising a little after mid-century because of the great scale to which the debt had grown. The French were still farther behind the Dutch, but their rates too showed a declining tendency with commercial interest rates coming down to 4 to 5 per cent in the 1670s. Thereafter they showed little improvement, while the yield of French Government debt, which could not be regarded as secure, never fell for long below 6 or 7 per cent.

Most business undertakings were carried on by single persons. Partnerships were not uncommon, but usually had special features. Very often they were family businesses of two brothers, or father and son; or temporary alliances between a newcomer who would shortly take over and an old proprietor wishing to extricate his capital. The scale of most businesses was small enough to be controlled by a single man, though occasionally a trader would be in partnership with his counterpart in the country he traded with. Every member of an ordinary partnership was legally liable for its debts without limit; this was a powerful reason for not extending the responsibility for the operations of a business house beyond the bounds of tight kinship, and even more for not investing in partnerships except when the investor himself could take a full part in management. It was the reason, too, for withdrawing completely from business and investing in landed or other security when active participation ceased. Outside England, it is true, some use was made of the Italian *commenda* form of partnership, which enabled one of the partners to assume only a limited liability for its debts; it was much used in early Spanish-American trade, and was legalized (as partnership *en commandite*) in France in 1673, after which it was not uncommon in French long-distance trading ventures.

In every country some large or very risky enterprises called for a larger gathering-together of capital than a single person or a handful of partners was willing to provide. For these purposes the joint-stock company was created. The outstanding examples were the companies formed for Asian trade, which were invested with responsibility in dealing with governments beyond the range of European diplomacy, and needed capital for very long trading voyages, the maintenance of large permanent establishments in the Indies, and the handling of very valuable goods, including large amounts of bullion. The Dutch *Vereenigde Oost-Indische Compagnie* of 1602, the English East India Company of 1600, and the French *Compagnie des Indes Orientales* of 1664, were all of this type, gathering together great masses of capital and receiving national monopolies of trade beyond the Cape of Good Hope. But joint-stock companies were not created simply for economic reasons. Many had as their main purpose the securing of monopolies, trading privileges or state support that would not be given to individuals. The many companies founded in the Netherlands, England and France for West Indies, Russia, Levant or Africa trade had mixed justification, possibly requiring capital raised by joint stock at their inception; but once these trades had been made open they were operated more successfully by individual traders than they had been by the companies. Besides the East India Companies, the one other great and successful example of joint-stock enterprise was the Bank of England of 1694, which set out to create confidence and attract deposits by exhibiting a huge capital backing. Many minor examples of joint-stock organization can be found in industry, particularly in mining companies in England in the 1690s, and in France during the eighteenth century; but joint-stock enterprise was not of great economic significance beyond the East India trade and banking.

The subject of capital cannot be left without some consideration of paper instruments for transferring money, and credit and banking.

Much the most important of all paper instruments was the bill of exchange, which was devised in medieval Italy and remained an essential tool of international trade down to the present century. It was brought into use to solve two problems for international traders: to avoid the necessity of carrying gold and silver over long distances in a disorderly Europe, and to avoid also the need for identifying coins of a variety of mints – both official and counterfeit. In the sixteenth century the bill of exchange operated in the following way. Dominguez, a wool dealer in Burgos, having sold wool to de Roover, a merchant in Bruges, at a price in Spanish *maravedis*, wanted to receive payment in Burgos. De Roover went to an exchanger, Pirenne, in his own city and paid him an equivalent sum in Flemish pounds and groats. Pirenne then wrote a letter in a special form – which was a bill of exchange – to an exchanger, Carande, who was his business connection in Burgos, telling him to pay the Spanish equivalent there to Dominguez (at the same time informing Dominguez that he had done so) and Dominguez collected the money from Carande on the due date. The bill of exchange was always payable after an in'erval, to allow time for its carriage and for the recipient to prepare himself to pay.

Bills of exchange were originally handled by exchange dealers and were often written out by them, because they were currency experts and had international connections; but some of the greater merchants did their own business of this kind and might extend their facilities to other merchants so becoming dealers in bills of exchange. As long as the exchangers met from time to time to settle the balances between them on multitudes of bill transactions in both directions, there was no need to ship large amounts of silver coin about Europe.

The bill of exchange came into increasing use in north-western Europe from the middle decades of the sixteenth century. It was a great convenience to transmit payments by bill of exchange between London and Antwerp; though the total trade in both directions may have roughly balanced, the trade of particular merchants did not necessarily do so. In many trades between individual countries, however, there was a big difference between the values of the two sides of the trade. Already Italy sold far more to France than it bought in exchange; a big transport of French silver into Italy would have been necessary had not bill transactions at Lyon settled the national balances out of the surplus on French trade with Spain. Similarly, the expanding purchases of England, France and Spain in the eighteenth-century Baltic were met not only by the shipment of goods that gave rise to mutually cancelling bill transactions, but also by bills drawn by Baltic merchants on Amsterdam, which had a surplus on its trade with the Baltic and a deficit on trade with England and the south. The cycle of English and French trans-Atlantic trade depended on the ability of North American traders selling in the West Indies to draw bills on London on the surpluses earned there by West Indian planters. Multilateral trade, that is trading in which each country achieved a balance between imports and exports only in its total transactions, and not in transactions with each country, developed very rapidly after the middle of the seventeenth century; it would have been very difficult to operate without these clearing arrangements through bills of exchange.

The bill of exchange had far less importance as a credit instrument than as a means of exchange in industry and commerce. In purely financial loan business – to finance speculation in commodities or to meet the temporary borrowing needs of the rich – the bill operated usefully to conceal interest charges. But in commerce, credit long preceded the use of the bill of exchange and was normally managed without its use.

Commercial credit is the transfer of goods or services without simultaneous payment for them. Two new elements were brought to it by Italian merchants in the late Middle Ages; systematic book-keeping, and the bill of exchange. Book-keeping was not essential until credit was given; but once great numbers of credit transactions were taking place, they had to be recorded by a system whose accuracy was assured by its self-balancing character. Most granting of credit was simply recorded in the merchants' books of account, with no separate formal acknowledgement or written promise to pay by the debtor. When large-scale credit trading ceased to be virtually an Italian monopoly, the book-keeping system was learned and practised in Spain and the Low Countries, and in the sixteenth century in France and England.

The bill of exchange formalized a debt and the time and place of its payment; no debtor would wish to be tied down by it. It did not offer much extra security to the seller of goods on credit, if he was satisfied as to his debtor's credit-worthiness; and he was unlikely to raise money, by selling it before the due date for payment. For the ordinary commercial bill – as distinct from a bill payable by a financier or exchanger – was not, in practice, easy to sell. In the hands of the named payee it was a secure instrument for collecting from the designated payer (and from the drawer), but endorsement to authorize another party to collect the money was full of legal difficulty until well after 1600. Transfer by endorsement was practised in Europe as early as the 1530s, by professional financiers who were in one anothers' confidence and did not expect to resort to the law courts for collection. It became a well-known practice among ordinary merchants in England, the Low Countries and France only in the second quarter of the seventeenth century. Then only was it regularized by the law; in the Netherlands by a series of ordinances from 1651 onward, in France by ordinance in 1673, in England by legal decisions of 1693 and 1696 and an act of 1704; in

Spain not until 1737. These established – with some exceptions – free negotiability; the holder of an endorsed bill normally had an unobstructed title to collect payment. The date of the emergence of true discounting, the negotiating of bills of exchange before their due date at a price explicitly referred to a current annual interest rate, has been much disputed. But in ordinary commerce, as distinct from the operations of financial specialists, it does not appear to have emerged before the very end of the seventeenth century. Though old attitudes to usury had changed, governments were reluctant, outside England, to go so far as to make interest charges enforceable in courts of law; in the Netherlands only certain types of interest transactions were legalized. Discounting, which was explicitly paying an interest rate, was therefore slow to develop except in England and Scotland.

By a natural process, many dealers in bills and currency became bankers. They were professional dealers in money, making their profits legally by charging for drawing bills and by adjusting the exchange rates between currencies in accordance with supply and demand; and illegally, by carrying on loan business at interest under many disguises. They needed strong safes to hold big stocks of coin; many became rich and inspired confidence in their trust-worthiness. Merchants and others were therefore anxious to deposit surplus cash with them for safety. Their bill business, too, provided them with deposits; the buyers of bills deposited money to pay for them long before the banker had to make the corresponding out-payment; and other clients maintained deposits to ensure that their bills coming in for payment would be met. They presently began to attract still more deposits by offering to pay interest on them, for they found that it was possible to estimate the likely demands for cash over short future periods and use the remainder of the cash deposited in their hands to lend out and make profit for themselves. This was their downfall. We have seen that there was only limited scope for the use of funds in the finance of trade. The bankers' lending, therefore, was chiefly to local lords, to municipalities, and above all to the heads of the great powers, the emperor, the King of France, the King of Spain. None of these was very reliable in repayment of debt, and most of them could place obstacles in the way of attempts at legal collection, whilst sovereign rulers could block them completely. On the other hand, they could offer all kinds of concessions – mining and colonial grants, monopoly rights, contracts for munitions, in addition to high interest rates. The bankers who embarked on this path of high finance were therefore drawn in further and further, enlarging and extending their loans, driven in the end by the hope that they would make so much profit before their debtors finally defaulted that the net result of all the business would be a gain. This was generally an illusion; they lent money faster than they made profits. Periodical state bankruptcies ruined the European bankers – Italians, Germans, Spaniards – as they had ruined Italians in earlier centuries; and their depositors often lost heavily. In the second half of the sixteenth century the structure of large-scale specialist banking in western Europe was brought down by the bankruptcies of the emperor and the kings of France and Spain, and of innumerable princes, dukes and marquises.

Whatever the weakness and temptations these experiences revealed in deposit banking, the exchange and transfer functions were too important to be lost. In the wake of these bankruptcies public exchange banks were started, in the hope that they would not succumb to the same temptations as commercial ventures. The first were in Italy, starting with the Bank of Palermo in 1552; but in the north, in the vacuum caused by collapse of confidence in old banking arrangements, a new start was made by the Bank of Amsterdam in 1609. It had imitators at Middelberg in 1616 and Hamburg in 1619, while in 1751 the Royal Remittance Office was set up in Madrid with the same functions.

Amsterdam was new as a financial centre. As late as 1580 large transactions were often settled there by payment in coin. It had to handle the currency of a number of Dutch mints, and its money changers were accused of melting down the best coins and exporting the silver. The Bank of Amsterdam was founded primarily to create monetary security for the benefit of trade; the easing of transfers was seen as a secondary function but was soon recognized as the most valuable one. Being an old-style exchange bank, its earliest commercial function was as a place at which bills of exchange were directed to be paid; indeed in Holland the law required that all bills over six hundred florins be paid there unless their terms expressly declared they should not. All traders and most other people of substance found it necessary to keep accounts at the bank, using it to collect and pay bills of exchange, and make simple transfers between account holders. Rather than offer constantly changing exchange rates between each pair of currencies, the bank kept all accounts in its own monetary unit – the *florin banco* – and translated currencies passing through its customers' accounts into these. Wealth, prestige and convenience all went to make the Bank of Amsterdam a place where people deposited their surplus money. But these were the limits of the bank's commercial functions; it did not buy or discount bills or lend directly to traders, and it did not issue notes (though its deposit receipts began to circulate to some extent as money after 1658). It was an exchange bank, and so were its imitators down to the foundation of the Bank of England.

Other bankers grew up in the interstices of the system, besides those whose origins were in exchange business. Much the most important of them – though their history is shadowy – were merchants, particularly those engaged in international trade. Great merchants, with correspondents in many places at home and abroad, issuing and receiving many bills of exchange on their own account, came to act as drawers or payers of bills for others; at one time they may have handled a large part of international bill business. In the same way as exchangers, they came to accept deposits from clients, turning more towards banking functions; and some followed the same financial road to fortune and ruin as the exchangers. The German bankers of Antwerp, whose fortunes were founded in mining and trade in precious metals, were of this kind. At Amsterdam and Hamburg the success of public banks drew exchange business away from the merchant bankers but in London they continued to flourish throughout the seventeenth century. The English goldsmiths who turned into bankers were a group of this kind whose original trade, from which they made their fortunes, was in making gold and silver plate and hence trading in bullion. In eighteenth-century France merchant bankers, keeping clear of the heady prospects in public finance, provided the main facilities for handling bills and commercial transfers. From merchant activity of many kinds a flow of fresh capital went constantly into the formation of banks, and as the needs and dangers of banking operations became clearer, it was from these that most of the long-surviving banking houses in every country emerged.

Banking houses that accepted deposits came to issue deposit receipts, which might pass from hand to hand as money substitutes, as did those of the Bank of Amsterdam after 1658. But the natural development from this to bank notes – deposit receipts issued in amounts of fixed denomination, and issued as loans as well as against deposits – encountered the difficulties of the law of negotiable instruments. It is sufficient to say here that the bank note was the specific contribution of English banking to financial practice.

The English goldsmith bankers of the mid-seventeenth century had
– like some earlier financiers – issued promises to pay, payable on
demand; but after 1660 they went beyond this to make payments in
notes, that is, promises to pay, of fixed denomination. (The Bank of
Sweden did the same, briefly and to its ruin, in 1661–4.) Within a
decade these notes were widely used as means of payment within
London, and the founders of the Bank of England in 1694 expected
it to issue such notes, which would be widely acceptable because
of the bank's great capital. Despite some early difficulties, regularized by an act of Parliament in 1704, Bank of England notes started
well and their issue rose rapidly. Bank of England and private bank
notes were a large part of the regular currency of eighteenth-century
England, though they were little used beyond the London area, and
the total of notes in mid-century was about a third of the amount of
circulating silver and coin. In England alone did notes add significantly and permanently to money supply; the brief period of note
issue by the Banque Royale in France in 1716–20 ended in catastrophe that discredited bank notes there for half a century.

The new public banks of western Europe soon faced the problem
of so many earlier financiers, that of making profitable use of the
funds deposited with them. All were lured or coerced along the old
path of lending to governments, and most of them foundered on
this. The outstanding example was the Banque Royale, founded in
France in 1716 by John Law, which accepted vast sums in deposits,
issued notes, lent the greatest part of its resources to the government, and failed in the speculative wave of 1720. The Bank of
Stockholm went down in the same way in 1664; the Hamburg
Bank twice suspended payments; the Stockholm Exchange Bank
collapsed in 1745, and the Danish Exchange Bank in 1757. Depending on the state, they could not hold back from the needs of the
state. Only the Bank of Amsterdam and the Bank of England were
able to limit their state lending to a level which, given their solid
assets, was reasonable. Nevertheless, they did make very large
loans; the Bank of Amsterdam particularly to the municipal
authorities, though its difficulties only appeared after 1781 because
of excessive lending to the partly political Dutch East India
Company; and the Bank of England to the government and the
East India Company. The financial needs of the British government,
which pressed hard on the Bank of England in its earlier years, were
fortunately channelled off between 1710 and 1720 into a new financial organization, the South Sea Company; and when this was

ruined in 1720 the Bank of England was allowed to profit by the lesson, and was not dragged out of its depth in aid of government.

The role of the banks in providing capital for industry and commerce was very modest. The Bank of Amsterdam, which was forbidden to discount bills of exchange or to make private loans, pumped funds into the municipal Loan Bank but the business of the latter was principally in loans on property. The Bank of England made loans, as a rule, on the security of government stock and land; until after 1760 only a small part of its assets was in discounted bills, and most of these were government rather than commercial paper. The private banks in the City of London concentrated their lending facilities on discount business, but their resources were not very large; other London banks, and the well-developed Scottish banks, did very little bill discounting before 1750. It may be that the merchants who were beginning to specialize in banking, those shadowy provincial figures in England and France, were more active in bill discounting during the eighteenth century; but on the whole it seems to have been the late emergence of great numbers of new banks that really made the practice common. The rapidly expanding industrial production of the late eighteenth century revealed a new need for circulating as well as fixed capital, and some of the burden of providing this was transferred, by bill discounting, from the producers to the banks' depositors. In England as late as the middle of the eighteenth century the great majority of commercial bills were held by their payees until the due date for payment, or alternatively were endorsed over to their ordinary commercial creditors, who similarly held them to the due date.

On the whole, therefore, the significance of paper instruments and of banking lay in their addition to money supply, and even more to the facility they gave for transferring funds over distances and between currencies. As credit instruments, bills of exchange made only a very limited contribution to economic development before the Industrial Revolution. It was not merely the slowness of the law to regularize negotiability and discounting, but even more the lack of need for such facilities among ordinary traders, that delayed their full development as credit instruments. As to banks, the most serious obstacle to their proper development was the ease with which the state could command their concentrated resources for itself, or attract them in ways forbidden to its subjects. It is not accidental that banking advanced most securely in the Netherlands and England, where absolute government had broken down.

15 *The Tropical Colonies in America*

The regions of America that the Spaniards did not settle had neither dense native populations nor accessible gold or silver deposits. Portuguese, French, English and Dutch colonies therefore required a labour force to be brought into America to work on the land. The settlement of this labour force, and the development of the colonial economies, in all the lowland tropics occupied by these powers, went through broadly similar stages of development. First there was the struggle to produce the essentials of life. Though pioneers might have set their minds on Indian trade, brazilwood-cutting, seeking the western passage, or supporting piracy, they were compelled to devote much of their attention to growing food crops (usually manioc or maize, whose cultivation they learned from the Indians) to escape dependence on a precarious supply from the mother country. Once they had made sure of subsistence – and this rarely offered great difficulty in tropical America – the colonists began to experiment to find crops that might be sold in Europe, pulling themselves out of the struggle for bare existence and making their colony attractive to more investors and settlers. Tobacco, the early West Indian staple, became less attractive there as the price fell in the 1620s and 1630s; the colonists found a variety of other saleable crops, among which cotton and ginger were for a time the most important, and for some decades the island economies were very diversified. The introduction of sugar planting to the islands in the 1640s opened a new phase in their development. Sugar was particularly suited to growth in the

Caribbean climate, and to the vagaries of local soil and topography in many of the islands; and as increasingly efficient production cheapened sugar, it became apparent that it had a far greater potential sale in Europe than any others of the islands' products. Finally sugar production, once it had been introduced, showed a tendency to engulf whole islands in single-crop cultivation, and it created its own form of society whose stamp still lies upon the Caribbean. There were exceptions: the small islands of Grenada and Dominica had single-crop coffee economies for some decades of the eighteenth century, and colonies with great land areas, St Domingue and especially Brazil, could produce immense sugar crops while still retaining some variety in cultivation. But the value of the Caribbean colonies to Europe came to be in their sugar production. So overwhelmingly did it dominate island economy and society, so vital was it even to Brazil, that the main features of the life of Europe's tropical colonies are best set out in terms of the movement towards sugar, and the adaptation of society to the needs of its production. After 1660 England's sugar imports always exceeded its combined imports of all other colonial produce; in 1774 sugar made up just half of all French imports from her West Indian colonies; over the colonial period as a whole more than half Brazil's exports of goods were sugar. Sugar made up almost a fifth of the whole English import bill in 1774, far surpassing the share of any other commodity.

In medieval Europe sugar was an extreme rarity. An entirely new taste for sweetness manifested itself as soon as the means to satisfy it became available, and sugar contributed in the seventeenth century to the widespread consumption of new commodities such as dried fruits, coffee and tea. This new taste was first experienced among the rich, and then as cheaper sugar became available it spread through society, so that by 1750 the poorest English farm labourer's wife took sugar in her tea. The supply of sugar rose from some three or four thousand tons a year in the late fifteenth century to twenty thousand tons a hundred years later, and at the time of the American Revolution it had passed two hundred thousand tons. The growth of consumption during the seventeenth century may be partly explained by the cheapening of sugar, first by Brazilian and then by West Indian supplies; but the demand continued to grow long after the trend of prices took an upward turn in the 1730s. More than once a brief collapse of sugar prices seemed to indicate that production was outrunning demand: at the end of the fifteenth century, when Madeira, the Canaries and São Thomé were offering supplies to Europe on a new scale; in the 1680s when the massive growth of West Indian supply gave a check to the prosperity of the Brazilian plantations; and in the 1720s when Jamaica and St Domingue emerged out of the tribulations of war to enlarge the scale of Caribbean production. But time and again rising demand came to the rescue, even absorbing without difficulty the sensational rise of production when Cuba came on to the market in the 1770s; and at the end of the eighteenth century the prospects were bright enough to cause the opening of production beyond the Americas, in Mauritius, Java and the Philippines.

Discussion of the sugar islands in the seventeenth century has commonly been overshadowed by the exceptional experience of Barbados, which went over to sugar production earlier and much faster and more completely than any other island. As early as 1637 the first experiments were undertaken there with Dutch help, and in the following years some planters visited Pernambuco to learn about sugar production and processing. The great expansion in Barbados took place between 1646 and 1652, stimulated by the high sugar prices due to war in Brazil, and by some immigration of Dutchmen bringing skill, slaves and equipment, and of English royalists with considerable capital resources. Early settlers who had prospered, and Dutch and royalist immigrants, set out to build up sugar plantations from the small tobacco, cotton and food plots of the settlers, throwing many holdings together to make a single plantation. Sugar production soared, small settlers and servants abandoned the island in large numbers – mostly for other islands – and Dutch traders brought in great numbers of African slaves. By 1667 the number of proprietors of land in Barbados had fallen from 11,200 to 745; between 1650 and 1680 thirty thousand white people left the island; the number of slaves rose from six thousand in 1643 to thirty-five thousand in 1680; and in 1673 Barbados exported some seven thousand tons of sugar, roughly a quarter of the output Brazil had reached after a century of operation.

Barbados took the lead in sugar production because it was already the most developed of the English and French islands. One of the first to be settled, and always free from the danger of savage Indians – the Caribs – that beset many of the other islands, it had attracted a big early migration from England. Despite its smallness, in the mid-1640s it probably contained half the white population of the English and French Caribbean, and there was still a wave of

English royalists to come. Alone among the islands, Barbados was producing large quantities of sugar early enough to benefit from the exceptional prices of the 1650s, and many planters made profits that enabled them to expand their plantations further, so that Barbados production was still far ahead of all others in the prosperous 1660s and early 1670s. Already the island had turned almost entirely to sugar; in 1672 it was producing so little food that three-quarters of its requirements had to be imported. But Barbados paid a penalty for this precocity. By 1680 intensive sugar production was beginning to exhaust the soil of the older plantations, and soil exhaustion became general by the early eighteenth century. Thereafter the planters struggled against rising costs, maintaining sugar production by intensive and costly manuring and the employment of an exceptionally large labour force, and running into serious difficulties when sugar prices were low in the 1720s and 1730s. After 1720 there was a small continuous migration from Barbados to newly planted islands and Guiana.

The small English islands – St Kitts, Nevis, Monserrat, Antigua – lagging some years behind Barbados in turning to sugar production, missed the top of the boom of the 1650s that had brought such fortune to Barbados. As their expansion brought sugar prices down with a run at the end of the 1670s, the extreme profitability of sugar production faded before they had become as fully committed to it as Barbados. The rush towards sugar was halted, and although they contained many big plantations these islands retained, for a long time, varied economies with production of indigo, cotton, ginger, cocoa and pimento. Land under sugar was slowly extended until a new boom and rising prices in the late 1730s, caused by the expansion of English home demand, accelerated the movement towards a sugar monoculture. By the 1750s these islands were almost completely committed to sugar and had begun to experience the problems of soil exhaustion that Barbados encountered in the 1680s.

French Martinique and Guadeloupe, settled in 1635, were both held back by twenty years of war with the Caribs, the costs and hazards of which discouraged settlement. Though there were experiments with sugar as early as 1644, the real stimulus to its production was given by the arrival of several hundred Dutch from Brazil in 1654, going to the French islands because England was then at war with the Netherlands. Even then, the inadequacy of French slave supply held back expansion; in the early 1670s Barbados had four times as many slaves as both these islands together.

Sugar production, only becoming substantial in the course of the 1670s, missed the boom in prices, and the islands continued to support small planters producing cocoa, cassava and cotton. Nevertheless these islands were largely slave-worked by the end of the century, for there were now no free landholdings for white servants and the dignity of manual labour had been lowered by the entry of slaves. Soil exhaustion on the sugar plantations began to show itself seriously in the 1730s.

Sugar production on the small Caribbean islands could not, in the long run, keep pace with European demand. Brazilian sugar, though of high quality, was much more costly than West Indian, and hardly sold beyond southern Europe after the end of the seventeenth century. The eighteenth-century expansion of production took place very largely in the big islands: in English Jamaica, French St Domingue and, from the 1760s, in Spanish Cuba. The large islands had sufficient land to be able to abandon overworked sugar plantations and replant on virgin soil. Moreover, much of their varied and mountainous terrain was better suited to other crops than sugar, so that Jamaica only approached sugar monoculture very late in the century, and St Domingue never reached it.

Jamaica was at first unattractive to English settlers, for it was dangerously isolated from the other colonies and much of the most accessible land was granted in huge tracts to rich or well-connected individuals. These used large parts of their estates for cattle ranching, as the Spaniards had done before them, while they waited for land values to rise. The smaller settlers attempted cocoa production, but disease destroyed it in 1671; they had more success with pimento and cotton, and the cultivation of these continued and was expanded in the eighteenth century. Sugar production was introduced from Barbados in 1664, but it missed the years of good sugar prices, and grew only slowly until well into the eighteenth century. Jamaica's possibilities could not be fully exploited until the island was made secure, for its size and rugged terrain permitted escaped slaves to establish permanent settlements from which they harassed the plantations, and they engaged in regular war from 1730 to 1739. Until they were brought to a peaceful agreement in 1739 plantations could not spread widely over the island, and the conjunction of this peace with the early stage of a long rise in sugar prices led to a vast extension of plantations. In 1770 Jamaica provided half of all British West Indian sugar, and by that time sugar and its products made up 89 per cent of Jamaican exports.

The great advantage of all the British islands was the size of the British market that was guaranteed to them by a high import duty on foreign sugar. Britain consumed a third of all the sugar that came into Europe in the eighteenth century; its consumption per head was eight times as great as the French. For a time, after beating down Brazilian competition in the 1660s, English sugar had been the main supply of northern Europe; but once the great virgin lands of St Domingue came into large-scale production early in the eighteenth century, their competition drove English sugar out of the European market. Yet so great was demand in England alone that after a few years of low prices in the 1730s the productive capacity of the English islands was again being pressed to its limit. Even the high-cost producers were able to prosper through several decades of high prices, culminating in the 'silver age' of the planters, the interwar periods 1748–56 and 1763–76. In 1763 English producers were glad of the opportunity to begin sugar production in islands newly seized from France – Tobago, St Vincent, Grenada, Dominica – though they boggled at retaining within the protected circle of English trade the two big sugar producers of Guadeloupe and Martinique.

The largest Caribbean island after Spanish Cuba was Espanola; and even the western half of it, St Domingue that Spain formally ceded to France in 1697, was far bigger than Jamaica. The first French settlers there were buccaneers and logwood cutters, driven from Tobago after 1660 by the Spaniards. French presence in this otherwise empty corner of Espanola was tacitly accepted by Spain, and within a few years migrants – generally indentured servants – were going out from France in some numbers, so that despite the irregular political situation an ordinary colony was developing. The settlers first grew cotton, but real prosperity came to them with the expansion of indigo production towards the end of the century. Heavy investment in large and well-equipped sugar plantations was not readily undertaken while the territorial status of the colony was uncertain, but after 1697 there was a huge expansion of sugar production, and in the 1720s St Domingue overtook Jamaica. By this time, however, the decline of sugar prices was so serious that alternative products were being sought, and the introduction of coffee in 1727 was so successful that much investment was diverted to it in the 1730s and 1740s. The return of high sugar prices eventually encouraged the expansion of plantations again. Large investment in irrigation works to make use of the alluvial plains was completed in time for sugar producers to respond to the high prices of the 1760s with another big increase in production. Nevertheless, even in the 1770s little more than half the island's exports were of sugar and its byproducts, while coffee, indigo and cotton were sent out in great quantities.

Brazil alone developed away from sugar. From the latter part of the seventeenth century the continuing extension of cultivation was rarely for sugar plantations. The prosperity of the Brazilian sugar industry slowly declined after the expulsion of the Dutch; the Dutch trading connection had been lost, though some Brazilian sugar continued to be sold on the Amsterdam market for many years. For two decades English ships served the Brazil–Portugal sugar trade, but then rising opportunities in the Caribbean drew them away. The voyage from Brazil to Europe was a much longer one than that from the West Indies, and with a cheap – and cheapening – commodity the difference in transport costs was significant; the requirement that cargoes be taken first to Lisbon added to the handicaps of selling in northern Europe; slaves were dearer after the Dutch and English slave traders were excluded; and Brazilian sugar was taxed at the point of production in a way that West Indian sugar escaped. Despite the high quality of the Brazilian product, and the large area of virgin land that was open to sugar planting even within the quite narrow coastal strip between Bahia and Pernambuco where production was concentrated, the northern European market was captured from it by Barbados sugar between 1660 and 1680. Driven back on Portuguese consumption, some sale in the Mediterranean, and a trade with Peru through Buenos Ayres, Brazilian sugar production ceased to grow. As sugar prices at Lisbon fell in the 1680s to a third of their mid-century level, new resources went into the production of tobacco, indigo and cocoa, and in the middle of the eighteenth century coffee and cotton were added. All these had to meet competition from the Spanish and French Caribbean, but their production was expanded and the Brazilian economy diversified.

The last Caribbean development of sugar production was in Cuba. The Spanish islands had long provided their own needs of sugar, and sent some to the American mainland, but they had not exported to Europe since the sixteenth century. In 1762, however, an English force occupied Cuba, and for a year the island was freely open to English trade. Ten thousand slaves were brought in during that short period; an immense stimulus was given to sugar planting, and after the English left Spaniards continued to expand the plantations that had been opened. Restrictions on the import of slaves by foreigners were lifted, and the great numbers brought in enabled Cuba to enter the ranks of the sugar producers on a scale that made it competitive with Jamaica and St Domingue in the last quarter of the century.

Table 4

Estimates of Sugar Production (thousands of tons)

	Brazil	Bar-bados	Jamaica	Other British West Indies	Martinique Guadeloupe	St Domingue
1620	15					
1655		7				
1670	27					
1700		10	5	7		
1720	20	7	10	7	14	10
1740		7	17	11		40
1767		6	36	25	14	63

Sugar transformed society in every area it touched, because of the economies of scale that large productive units offered. The small producer could not compete with the large, and in suitable soil sugar planting was much the most profitable use of land during long stretches of the seventeenth and eighteenth centuries. When the land was divided into large and highly capitalized plantations, leaving little scope for the smallholder, the supply of labour coming voluntarily from Europe dried up. Moreover, once land had been turned over to this plantation organization, and a large slave labour force committed to it, even sharp changes in price relations could not readily cause it to be turned back to other uses. The sugar plantation changed colonial societies in much the same fashion that the factory for a time changed English society; the efficient scale of operation required a large concentration of fixed capital, and the owner of the capital wanted a completely subordinated and rigidly disciplined labour force.

At the centre of this was a simple fact of technology. Once sugar cane had been cut, the first stages of processing had to be carried through very quickly, preferably within a few hours. Every plantation had to have ready access to a crushing mill that could handle quantities of cane cut and brought in at a rate appropriate to the size of the plantation. Moreover, up to a certain point, this large and costly equipment became proportionately less costly as its size increased. The optimum size of mill determined the size of the plantation. The minimum size of plantation that could keep a fully efficient mill fully occupied during the cutting season varied in different islands according to yield of sugar per acre, and ease of transport; it might be as small as a hundred acres (with forty to fifty acres producing cane each year), while it was nowhere likely to exceed three hundred acres for a single mill. These were the limits of size of the operating unit, though ownership of two or three of these units by a single family was common in the eighteenth century, and Peter Beckford owned twenty-seven plantations in Jamaica in 1739. The crushing mill's capacity also determined the size of the labour force needed to keep it supplied at full stretch – which might well mean for twenty hours a day – during a large part of the cane-cutting season from January to May, as well as the number of draught animals, carts and hogsheads needed. The mills were often worked by cattle in early days, but it was more economical to use other forms of energy – as well as saving the grazing land that animals needed – so Barbados went over rapidly to windmills around 1700, Martinique, Guadeloupe and St Domingue were using many water mills in the eighteenth century, and tide mills were in use on the Guiana coast. Large amounts of capital were invested in the mill, the slaves, the animals and the large plantation itself, so the sugar islands ceased to be places for smallholders (though, as we shall see, Brazil and St Domingue found a compromise). Great plantations with rich owners, a few white or mulatto overseers, and a mass of slaves; these characterized the sugar islands and shaped their society.

In the middle of the eighteenth century as much as nine-tenths of the capital of a plantation, excluding the land itself, might be invested in slaves. Slaves were expensive, and became more so as demand rose during the eighteenth century. English traders not only supplied the British islands but were also selling more or less openly on the Spanish mainland coast, and sending slaves to St Domingue. Without the continuing slave trade, the sugar plantations could not have survived, for the common expectation of life for a slave entering a plantation was no more than ten years. The owner of a stock of a hundred slaves had to buy eight or ten a year to maintain it, and attempts to economize by driving them even harder or scamping on their provisions would simply worsen the death rate. The cost of the supply of slaves could not, therefore, be readily altered in the short run, though the larger plantations could identify and make use of specialist abilities, and minimize their labour needs by efficient management.

Only a quite rich man, therefore, could establish or buy a sugar plantation, and it was likely to be the most profitable investment such a man could make in the tropics, if he were ready to devote himself to its management. Nevertheless, there was more than one kind of organization of sugar production.

Throughout the British West Indies, as in Guadeloupe and Martinique, the typical unit was the large plantation producing for its single owner, with one or more mills, a group of employed overseers, and one, two or exceptionally three hundred slaves. The wealthy owner looked to England or France as home, and would return there if the plantation income seemed large and secure enough. A colonial sugar plantation was, as John Pinney of Nevis put it, 'a convenient source of income for a Dorset country gentle-man', which enabled him to remove himself from the heat and toil, the quarrelling of the petty island society, and the all-pervading odour of slavery. But it was the general rule that a plantation suf-fered if the closest and most dedicated supervision were not exer-cised over it; many a planter returned to England from a prosperous plantation, which within a few years was losing money. Though plantations were often run by managers, their management was interspersed with spells in which, in desperation at the decline of income, a son of the house would come out for a few years to run them for his own benefit and restore the family fortune.

In Brazil the situation was quite different. The masters of the great Brazilian sugar estates were also wealthy men, living in luxury, but they were firmly settled and regarded themselves as natives – and indeed as masters – of the country. Portugal was the place for an occasional visit, not a distant longed-for homeland. There was, moreover, a distinct form of estate operation. The landowner owned the sugar mill; indeed, the central role of the mill in the sugar plantations is underlined by the fact that he was referred to, not as the owner of the estate, but as the *senhor de enginho* – the mill-owner. This mill, with its equipment and supply

K

of cattle and slaves, was big enough to handle all the sugar the estate could produce. Much of the land on the estate, however, was put out on lease for short periods of years to small farmers – *lavradores* – who each employed a few slaves to grow cane and bring it to the mill for crushing. The farmers were obliged to clear specified areas of virgin land each year, so the estate was constantly being enlarged. The *lavrador* worked on a crop-sharing basis, commonly one that gave him the proceeds of a third of the sugar produced from his cane; and he was economically – though not, of course, socially – closer to the life of the slave than to that of his landlord. Similarly in Espanola and Cuba the mill-owner, though he generally operated a plantation of his own, leased some land to numbers of smallholders, who paid him for use of the mill with a half-share of their produce. A similar system developed in eighteenth-century St Domingue, alongside the very large estates worked entirely by their owners' slaves. The difference between these systems and those of the small islands reflects land shortage in the latter, with the absence of virgin soil to which cultivation could be moved, and the need for very intensive working of sugar-bearing land.

Many other crops were grown in the tropics for export to Europe. None of them had the same technical constraints as sugar, requiring the large plantation and its labour force, though there were some advantages of scale in indigo production, which had expensive processing equipment. Tobacco was little grown in the British or French island colonies after the middle of the seventeenth century; but in Brazil it was second only to sugar, continuing to be a crop of small cultivators employing one or two slaves, for the best qualities of tobacco required some skill and nicety of judgement in those who looked after the plants. Indigo became a major crop in St Domingue, but British island producers never overcame the endless problems that appeared in processing, and British production was eventually moved to South Carolina. Cacao (the source of the cocoa bean), which had long provided a drink that was popular in Spanish territories, found some market in northern Europe towards the end of the seventeenth century, and seemed a promising crop. But it was very susceptible to disease, which wiped it out in Jamaica in 1671, and in Martinique and St Domingue in 1715. Its production almost disappeared from the islands, but was expanded and brought fortune to mainland Brazil, Guiana and Venezuela.

Coffee, widely consumed in Europe, was all imported from Arabia until its production was introduced into the West Indies in 1727. It spread rapidly in the French islands and became their main crop after sugar, and within a few years West Indian coffee had captured the European market and was even being sent to the middle east. Coffee planting required some capital, for the plants did not offer a full crop until the fifth year of growth. Finally, cotton was grown in the islands and Brazil, sharing a modest European market with Turkish production, but its scale was very small until the rapid expansion of the European cotton industries in the 1770s boosted demand and price, and caused more land to be turned to cotton-growing.

The relative importance of the main products of the West Indian islands at the end of our period is shown in the table:

Table 5

Per cent of Exports from the West Indies, 1770

	British Islands	French Islands
sugar, rum, molasses	81	49
coffee	11	24
indigo	–	14
cotton	3	8

British concentration on sugar was even more extreme than the table indicates, for much of the coffee produced in 1770 grew in Dominica and Grenada, islands that had been settled by the French in the 1740s for coffee production; they were annexed by the English in 1763, and a few years later were in process of being turned towards sugar production.

Tobacco and cotton were small men's crops, requiring little equipment and coming to production quickly; indigo and coffee required rather more capital. But while their production may have started as the work of white colonists doing much of what was needed with their own hands, slave production overtook them almost completely in the early part of the eighteenth century. Manual labour had become associated with the degradation of slavery; even the smallholder now wanted his slaves, though he might supervise them more closely and do some work alongside them. Writers on late eighteenth-century Jamaica explained how settlers with little capital had begun their careers by planting the minor staples – cotton, indigo, ginger – before building up sugar plantations. But their 'little' capital was by this time not the year's corn of the indentured servant who had completed his period of servitude; it was 'little' in terms of the assumption that, while he would need to own a few slaves to grow any crop at all, the natural thing to grow in the island was sugar with its great capital requirement. The smallholder remained a reality in Brazil, and even to some extent in St Domingue; but the eighteenth-century smallholder in the British islands would not have been recognized as one by the Barbados settler of 1640.

The plantation colonies, therefore, concentrated their resources on the crops they found most readily saleable in Europe. These earned them far more than they needed to pay for their own consumption in the islands, and for the machinery, horses, timber, provisions and clothing for slaves and for buying the slaves themselves. English and French planters nevertheless fell heavily into debt to European creditors in the course of the eighteenth century, largely because of the heavy remittances out of plantation earnings to pay for the gentlemanly life of absentee planters, the interest on debts they fell into, and the loss of income – or its siphoning into managers' pockets – when plantations were not personally managed by their proprietors.

The colonists spent heavily in Europe on luxuries for their own consumption and on clothing for their slaves; but their two essential needs – food and slaves – could not be obtained in Europe and had to be sought elsewhere. Brazil and the Spanish islands had enough land to grow all the sugar they could sell, and to produce food as well both for slaves and their masters. Indeed, in Brazil the individual estate was normally self-sufficient in food, and might have its own craftsmen; and the colony exported sugar to Buenos Ayres, where it was exchanged for cattle and their products. The smaller English and French territories were differently placed. In the early days, the colonists had grown their own food on plots alongside the tobacco and cotton lands, and grazed animals extensively. As larger plantations were developed for sugar, the owners retained food plots (encouraging the slaves to work smallholdings of yams and maize on Saturdays for their own maintenance) but they encroached on the cattle grazing, reducing herds eventually to the essential minimum of draught animals. For a time there was an inter-island trade in meat, but by 1660 this was inadequate. An outside supply was found in Ireland; it became normal for ships sailing from England or France to call in at a south Irish harbour to lade barrelled pork or beef for the islands. As early as 1647, New England began to send food into the West Indies; in that year John Winthrop wrote: 'It pleased the Lord to open to us a trade with Barbados and other islands in the West Indies, which as it proved gainful, so the commodities we had in exchange there for our cattle and provisions, as sugar, cotton, tobacco and indigo were a good help to discharge our engagements in England.' Supplies from Ireland and America were increased as the slave population grew, sugar lands became more expensive, and the cost of using land for food crops came to be much greater than that of importing corn and meat. Plots that had been set aside for food crops were taken over for sugar; smallholders who had continued to find profit in selling provisions to the big plantations were tempted by good offers for their land to sell up and migrate to North America. By 1700 Barbados was almost completely, and other islands largely, dependent on imported foods of all kinds. The principal suppliers were now the mainland American colonies, from Pennsylvania northward. Meat, flour, butter, cheese, horses and timber were exchanged for island produce such as rum and molasses, and even more eagerly for bills of exchange drawn on the sugar planters' agents in London, with which the northern colonists could pay for their own imports of European goods. After the general peace of 1713, the expansion of agricultural surpluses in the northern colonies rapidly outran the demands of the British West Indies, and North American traders, defying the Navigation Acts, began to supply the French and Dutch islands in the same way. Thus the North American economy came to revolve around the produce of the tropical colonies – and in the main, around sugar – whilst the sugar islands in their turn depended for the lives of their slaves on continuing American supplies.

16 The British
Mainland Colonies

*E*nglish America was a land of many harbours, but its great
rivers were navigable only to a line of falls and rapids a few score
miles inland. These facts determined the shape of the settled territory that had come into existence by 1713. When an Anglo-French
peace was signed in that year, almost the whole line of coast had
been settled, but the limit of settlement stood on tidewater nearly
everywhere; no farmers were more than a hundred miles from the
coast, though trading pioneers had penetrated far inland among the
Indian tribes. In the following sixty years, population multiplying
nearly ten-fold carried settlement above the fall-line of the rivers,
penetrated the first ranges of mountains in several places, and broke
right through them into the Ohio valley in the west of Pennsylvania.
On the eve of the Revolution, the North American colonies had far
outstripped in population the British West Indies with their hundred
thousand white colonists and three hundred thousand slaves.

Virginia and Maryland were essentially tobacco colonies from the
beginning to the end of the colonial period, though their dependence on this single crop slackened in the course of time. Tobacco
production continued to expand at an extraordinary pace, from
twenty million pounds' weight in 1700 to eighty million in the mid-
1730s and two hundred and twenty million in 1775. This expansion
posed entirely new problems of both land and labour in the eighteenth century. The earliest settlements had been on the lowlands
surrounding Chesapeake Bay, and planters were reluctant to push
beyond the area that was accessible to the sea by tidal rivers and

Table 6

Population of British North America* (thousands)

	1700 White	1774 White	Negro
New England: Massachusetts, New Hampshire, Rhode Island, Connecticut	90	661	15
Middle Colonies: New York, New Jersey, Pennsylvania, Delaware	33	617	6
Southern Colonies: Maryland, Virginia, North Carolina, South Carolina, Georgia	105	898	310
	228	2,176	331

*Excluding Canada, which had one hundred thousand people in 1774.

creeks. This land, however, quickly became worked out, for the clearance of the natural forest cover to plant tobacco was usually followed within three or four years by the draining away of much of the best soil; and tobacco-cropping very rapidly exhausted the land's fertility. Every planter, therefore, tried to build up a large landholding with plenty of uncleared land in reserve, using the ample spare labour of the slack season each year to clear a piece of virgin land to which he moved some of his tobacco cultivation. By the early eighteenth century most of the tidewater land had been appropriated; a good deal was worn out and much of the remainder was embraced in the large estates of those planters who had grown rich, and had accumulated land either for future cultivation or as a speculation on rising land prices. As early as 1709 good land in lowland Virginia was selling at twenty shillings an acre, and the demand for tobacco, still growing rapidly, required the extension of planting into the hill country above the fall line, the so-called piedmont.

Pennsylvania and New Jersey were now the favoured colonies of immigration. The Virginia lowlands had growing difficulty in attracting indentured servants after the end of the seventeenth century, though land was still available for their settlement in the piedmont. The large plantations in the lowlands responded by going over to slave labour between 1713 and 1730. It was still possible, however, to operate a small tobacco holding profitably with a hard-working family and one or two indentured servants or convicts, who could be bought more cheaply than slaves. In consequence, large and small plantations were still intermixed in the tidewater lands, while the introduction of tobacco into the piedmont was principally by small producers who were able to tempt some indentured servants with the promise of their own land grants farther into the interior.

The great planters dominated society and politics in Virginia and Maryland, with their plantations of thousands of acres raising corn and cattle as well as tobacco, their hundreds of slaves, their interests in shipowning and trading and in land speculation both in tidewater and frontier areas. They were great magnates who dealt directly with the English tobacco market, scorning the use of local intermediaries. Ships from Britain came far up into the rivers and creeks round Chesapeake Bay to collect hogsheads of tobacco directly from the plantations, which until 1700 were nearly all close to navigable water. Though they first dealt with travelling merchants or ships' masters, the large planters had soon developed the practice of sending their cargoes for England on their own account, to be sold for them by commission agents in London. By 1730 nearly all their tobacco was disposed of in this way, while many of the smaller tidewater planters sold their crops to rich neighbours who included them in their own shipments. The London agents, in return, ensured that ships offered themselves for lading, bought and despatched the planters' requirements in England, and met bills of exchange the planters drew upon them. This was such an easy way of spending money in England that most big tobacco producers ran up debts with their agents (as sugar planters were doing in exactly similar relationships). These debts mounted from generation and tied the more honest planters to dealing permanently with the same London agents. On the eve of the Revolution some five-sixths of private colonial debt owed to Britain was due from Virginia and Maryland, the great bulk of it from tobacco planters.

The smaller planters preferred to sell on the spot in exchange for the goods they needed. As tobacco-growing was extended away from the banks of the navigable rivers into the back country where direct trade with the ships was not possible, English and Scottish traders came in to open stores and deal in tobacco. The movement was assisted by the colonial inspection laws of 1730 (Virginia) and 1747 (Maryland) which required all tobacco to be delivered into official warehouses set twelve to fourteen miles apart, for official inspection before export, and provided for storage in the warehouses and the issue of official 'crop' notes conveying ownership, which were used as legal tender in these colonies. The factors sold their goods for tobacco, or on the security of tobacco to come, so that many small planters ran into debt and became tied almost as closely to their factors as the large planters were to their London commission agent. The earlier factors were in the employment of Liverpool and Whitehaven merchants, but Glasgow factors were soon competing and by 1740 had outstripped all others. In 1738 Scotland took only 10 per cent of American tobacco exports; thirty years later it took nearly half of them, nearly all for re-export.

The network of waterways serving the early Virginia and Maryland plantations had discouraged the concentration of trade at nodal points, and there were no real towns in these colonies before this new form of trading encouraged their development on the fall line of the rivers. But when Baltimore and Norfolk and many others emerged towards the middle of the new century, they were not merely centres of tobacco trade. Tobacco was ceasing to be the sole trading product of Virginia and Maryland. On the one hand, the turn to slave labour could not hold back the rising costs of tidewater production; much of the profit was disappearing from tobacco planting, on land becoming increasingly exhausted by tobacco-cropping, with the price of slaves rising rapidly. The advantage of accessibility to the sea began to be outweighed by the freshness of the land to the west, once the settlement there of competing traders ensured that crops would fetch the fair market price. The larger tidewater estates had always produced foodstuffs for their families, servants and slaves, as well as tobacco. They now began to follow their northern neighbours into supplying the West Indian market, turning a larger part of their land over to food crops and livestock, and selling wheat, beef and pork to the small town merchants who would export them. On the other side, the piedmont was filling up not only with indentured servants who had completed their time on plantations, and with small planters whose tidewater lands were worked out, but also with northern farmers who had come down through the back country from Pennsylvania to seek land on which to grow wheat and rear cattle. These small general farmers, too, sold their produce in the new towns, Baltimore becoming the fore-most centre of their grain trade. By mid-century the tidewater economy was diversifying fast, and behind it the piedmont was being developed on a farming pattern more akin to that of Pennsylvania than to that of tidewater Virginia. The old planting society and the new farming society were in fact coming into conflict, for the colonial legislatures made huge grants in the back country to members of old tobacco-planting families, and the agents of these grantees often found the land already settled by men of a quite new sort, who had cleared and planted it and saw no reason to pay for the privilege.

To the south were the Carolinas, which were founded in 1670, with a generous land grant policy that brought in large numbers of West Indian colonists who had sold their holdings to sugar planters. Most of them settled down as general farmers and cattle ranchers, or traded with the Indians for deerskins. The feebler North Carolina colony remained one of general farming, though lumbering for export was stimulated by the English Parliament's grant of a bounty in 1705 to colonial pitch, tar and turpentine production. South Carolina developed slowly in the first generation, but found a profitable export staple with the introduction of rice in 1693. The cypress swamps of the coastline were well suited to its production, and there was a big market awaiting it in England and in southern Europe. This new planters' economy was unable to attract European labour for the dull and laborious tasks of the ricelands, and the slave-worked plantation took over rapidly and completely. The plantations were heavily capitalized, requiring expensive irrigation works as well as big slave labour forces, and another wealthy planter aristocracy quickly emerged. When indigo cultivation was introduced on the higher and better drained soils in 1742, and expanded under the stimulus of British bounties after 1748, it was similarly carried on by slave labour. On the eve of the Revolution the exports of the two Carolinas – rice, indigo and timber products – ran only a little behind those of Virginia and Maryland; a second pair of staple colonies was now firmly grounded in the south, with the beginnings of the Georgia settlement as an appendage. Charleston, the fourth city of British America and the only large one in the south, became the centre of social life for all the country south of Virginia.

The English colonial presence in the north was firmly established by the settling of nearly two thousand men, women and children by the Massachusetts Bay Company, at one stroke in 1629. A colony of this size was from the outset more firmly committed to making a permanency of settlement than the few score men at a time who were put ashore in early Virginia or Maine or St Kitts. By the time religious migration died down in the early 1640s New England was sufficiently populous and firmly settled to continue rapid growth by natural increase; despite the continuous Indian threat, its population passed a hundred thousand early in the eighteenth century.

New England's economic development was wholly different from that of the southern colonies. Once the first pioneering decade was past, it was essentially an economically independent if backward country, rather than a single-crop economy totally dependent on external markets. For a long time it remained in a primitive stage of settlement, its people devoting their energies to producing maize and oats or rearing livestock to feed themselves and provide raw materials for a considerable household manufacture of coarse woollens, linens and leatherware. As population grew, farmers diversified into a wider range of agricultural produce, and the towns offered some attractions to specialist artisans. But expectations grew as well, the demands of a prospering community outran the productive possibilities of household and small-town industry, and more goods had to be imported from Europe. In the early days these were such simple things as axes, kettles, knives and salt, but soon every variety of remembered European produce was in demand. The development of local manufacture outside the household was very slow in these colonies because of their own peculiar labour problem. With an open frontier, and virtually free land available for settlement, labour could not easily be held in wage-earning occupations; even the independent artisan was likely to pack up and go farming when he had accumulated a little capital from his trade. Wages and artisan earnings had to be high in the colonies to attract and keep even a minimum of skilled industrial workers.

New England settlement began to spread back from the Massachusetts coastline after 1635, entering the fertile Connecticut valley in the 1640s, and the colonists pushed on into the Hudson valley after the Dutch flag was hauled down there in 1664, and linked with Pennsylvania when this colony was established by a new wave of religious migrants after 1682. Early life was difficult in these northern colonies, with a climate harsher than the immigrants had known, and a land that over much of the original New England was stony and infertile. An immense effort of labour was needed to clear woodlands, and plant European crops of wheat (whose production ceased in New England after disease struck it in 1660) barley and oats. Eventually the cultivation of maize, learned from the Indians, provided the most important crop in the north. Cattle and sheep, in limited numbers, grazed the fallows; pigs and poultry wandered in the surrounding woods. The farms were soon producing surpluses above the farmers' needs; these found some outlet in the towns but could not be sent to Europe because the cost of shipping them across the Atlantic was too great. Unsaleable surpluses and unattainable desires; to reconcile them New England had to create non-agricultural occupations to supply some of its needs from local workers who would buy farm surpluses; or produce other goods that could be sold in Europe; or find markets beyond Europe that would take the corn, beef and pork of the farmers.

The very earliest New Englanders found an answer in the character of the continued immigration. Many of the religious migrants were well-to-do people, who brought their own families and servants and assisted other families of their own persuasion to come with them to establish working communities. They laded the emigrant ships with goods for sale in the colony, and used these to buy their flour and meat from the pioneers. When the flow of immigrants died away after 1640 there was a sharp temporary crisis of the New England economy, ruining some of the farmers who had come to rely on their trade, and causing a number to migrate to Virginia or the West Indies.

But the early projectors of northern colonization had envisaged two quite different supports for their colonies, in fur trade and fishery. In the earliest years of the seventeenth century men had occasionally wintered ashore on the New England coast to trade with the Indians; fishermen often came from the Newfoundland Banks to the inshore grounds of Maine; the Pilgrim Fathers whose ship brought them to Cape Cod in 1620 confidently expected to pay off the creditors they had left behind in Europe by means of fur trading. Though Canadian experience was to show that fur trade and fishery could not by themselves support large-scale settlements, they gave valuable support to primary farming colonies.

The French colonies on the St Lawrence existed for the fur trade. They accepted farming settlers only at the insistence of a home government that saw the need for a more broadly based colonial economy, and at the time when England conquered French Canada, in 1760, it had only some seventy thousand settlers – while the population of British North America was approaching two million. In New England, however, fur trading was the occupation of a handful of pioneers on the fringes of settlement or pushing beyond them; the settled farmer expected only an occasional windfall from trapping.

Most fur was secured by trading with the Indians – who were skilled trappers – for liquor, firearms, woollens, wampum or other goods. As farming spread, it cut down the forest habitat of both the fur-bearing animals and the Indians. The fur traders were therefore constantly compelled to push forward into new territory; they were the pioneers who discovered and opened up the interior of America. The St Lawrence river opened an easy way for French traders to the Great Lakes and westward beyond them, and south into the Ohio and Mississippi valleys. When the English came into the Hudson valley in 1664, this gave them a route into the interior for fur trading – though in time they found it more useful to trade with their French rivals at Montreal. Early in the eighteenth century, traders based on Philadelphia broke across the mountains by difficult routes; and in the south the Carolina frontier was always in contact with Indians who traded in deerskins. These avenues were not open to New England traders, whose territory was bounded to the north by impassable mountains. Nevertheless, throughout the seventeenth century, fur trapped in New England itself gave the colony a useful export trade, which contributed to building up the Boston merchant community.

The fur traders, pioneers of European advance, went up the rivers to Indian villages, and established trading posts in Indian territory. On the one hand they showed the path forward for settlement; on the other, many of them dealt unfairly with the Indians and provoked anti-European feeling. Colonial government everywhere was conscious of the dangers that uncontrolled fur trading brought to the peaceful development of the settlements behind them. The Massachusetts Bay Company, with its plans for orderly settlement in townships, discouraged individuals from setting up lonely trading stations. From 1632 it was trying to control the trade, licensing fur traders to keep undesirables out of it; after 1699 the trade was made a monopoly of 'truckmasters' in government trading posts. The first clash of English and French interests in the 1670s was in the fur trade north of the Hudson-Mohawk gap; and for eighty years there was a struggle between them, muted or violent, for the allegiance of Indian tribes and for the control of the fur trade in the interior of the continent. This area was disorganized by prolonged wars and raiding from 1690 onward, and when peace came in 1713 the New York government concentrated the trade on Albany and Oswego, where it could be firmly controlled. The traders who pushed across the Alleghanies into the Ohio valley in 1724 operated without restriction in Indian villages until the Pennsylvania government put a controlling hand on the trade in 1758. All this was on a much smaller scale than the fur trading which the French carried on through the St Lawrence, or even that of the English Hudson's Bay Company which operated in the far north from 1670. The great days of the east-coast fur merchants came after the conquest of Canada, when New York and New England capital was put behind the Montreal *voyageurs* to exploit the fur trade of the whole interior of the continent.

The sea fishery was even more valuable to the northern colonies. After the earlier years it became a highly specialized occupation carried on from a small number of harbours. The New England settlements developed inshore mackerel fisheries soon after 1620, went on to cod fishery off Maine, and by mid-century were fishing the Newfoundland Banks. Operating at first only to feed themselves, before mid-century they had begun to sell to English trading ships; by 1690 they were exporting the poor quality fish in great quantities to the West Indian plantations, where it became a major part of slaves' diet, and in the eighteenth century they were selling in the Atlantic islands and in Spain. Moreover, in the eighteenth century settlement at last got a footing on Newfoundland, where there were some seven thousand permanent inhabitants by 1750. This settlement existed largely to serve vessels that came from Europe to buy fish, and became completely dependent on New England for its rum and provisions.

These occupations, along with the shipment of masts for the British navy from the New Hampshire shore, the sale of many Massachusetts-built ships to England in wartime, and a small West Indian trade, provided export earnings that enabled the northern and middle colonies to buy their modest needs of European goods down to the end of the seventeenth century. New England's population doubled in each decade of the new century, and there was an even faster rate of growth in the middle colonies, which in 1700 were only embryonic. They could continue to develop and prosper only by finding outlets for the surplus produce of their main occupation, agriculture. The economy of the northern and middle colonies came to depend on their vast export of foodstuffs, horses and timber to the British, French and Dutch West Indian colonies. The origins of this trade lay as far back as the 1640s; but its full development to become the main support of the trade balance of temperate colonies took place in the middle decades of the eighteenth century.

On the eve of the American Revolution almost three-quarters of a million people lived in the three colonies of Massachusetts, Rhode Island and Connecticut, and a handful in the other New England colonies of Maine and New Hampshire. Most of them worked on the land, rearing pigs and cattle and growing maize, rye and oats. Yet already the two oldest of these colonies, Massachusetts and Rhode Island, had urbanized to an extent that swallowed up all their farmers' surpluses and caused them to import food. The last big reserve of cultivable land in New England, the Connecticut valley, filled up between 1720 and 1750, and migrants were streaming out of New England to Pennsylvania and beyond throughout the century. If the majority of the population still lived in the countryside, the special functions of New England among the American colonies now depended on the trade, fisheries and industries carried on by its townsfolk. The Massachusetts and Rhode Island towns, headed by Boston and Newport, traded along the whole American coast and into the Caribbean; they were the universal carriers for the colonies, and most of their earnings came from trading, carrying and insurance services. Fisheries not only fed the New England towns but provided exports that went to Spain and the West Indies, bringing back to their home ports rum, molasses and above all bills on London that would pay for English goods. Modest manufacturing industries that served many of New England's needs had begun to export to other colonies.

Boston, the great town of New England, was the principal port of entry for British manufactures into America until after 1740, and its merchants had a large and profitable business in re-selling them in the other colonies. Boston's own merchants had traded with England almost from the beginning whereas even at New York and Philadelphia the trade was handled by factors of English firms until well after 1700. Merchant wealth had diversified into shipowning, financial and insurance business, and the organization of industry on a larger scale than elsewhere. Boston's predominance was undermined in the long period of war and uneasy peace, 1743–60, which caused it heavy losses in men and ships. Philadelphia, centre of the fastest-growing colonial region, was already overtaking it; while New York, as a base of military operations during the wars, received an accession of wealth and trading connections from which it never looked back. Even minor New England ports encroached on Boston's activities; Portsmouth and Newbury overtook Boston's shipbuilding, Salem and Newport captured some of its West Indian trade, and inland areas of Massachusetts itself began to use Newport and Providence as alternative outlets to the sea.

The ships of Massachusetts and Rhode Island collected and discharged cargoes everywhere between the St Lawrence and Trinidad, carrying lumber, corn, biscuit, dried fish, meat, horses and English and colonial manufactures southward to the West Indies, bringing colonial products north, and exchanging provisions for manufactures along the North American coast itself. Rhode Island was the principal centre of the American slave trade, taking rum to Africa to buy slaves and bringing them back for sale in the Virginia and Carolina plantations. Trading, carrying and insuring earned New England money to pay for its imports from England, for its food supplies from other colonies, and for rum and molasses from the West Indies that provided the basis for further trade.

The New England towns developed manufactures, and town merchants organized industry in the countryside as well. The colonists had brought with them from England the skills of woollen and linen spinning and weaving, and a widely dispersed household industry had always supplied most of the rural needs for coarse textiles. By the eighteenth century, however, small-town merchants had taken over the organization of much of this household production, and directed it to the market. This was the principal industry, though it sent little of its product beyond New England. Shipbuilding was tending to move eastwards to sites along the New Hampshire and Maine coasts as the best coastal woodlands were worked out; but the ample inland woods provided timber for furniture-making, and planking for houses and for exports. There was charcoal for an iron industry, which had fifty bloomeries and forges; axes and scythes were produced in quantity and exported to other colonies; and nail-making had begun. Other industries were based on imports; sugar-refining, rum distillation from molasses, and candle-making from whale oil.

Connecticut was much more rural than Massachusetts or Rhode Island, with little industry apart from some iron-making on the Massachusetts border. Until mid-century it still had some vacant land for settlement; its towns were small and its farmers and stock-raisers sent their surpluses to supply Boston and New York, and to a small extent into the West India trade. Most of its imports came through Boston and New York, and it had only a modest overseas trade, and little shipping of its own. Of its three substantial towns, Middletown, Norwich and New Haven, only the last was a seaport.

The development of the New York colony was delayed by the policy of its proprietors of distributing land in huge grants – often more than a hundred thousand acres – to favoured individuals. These grantees had no means and little incentive to develop any large part of this land; but they were unwilling to sell it, preferring to wait to derive profit from the slow rise in its value, and in the meantime to lease out tracts for farms. These New York terms were not attractive to settlers while other colonies were offering free-hold land subject only to tiny quit rents. After the middle of the eighteenth century, however, New York's population rose very fast. The heavy flow of surplus population out of New England was creating a pressure of demand for land that made New York terms seem more acceptable, while the conquest of Canada from France in 1760 removed a threat that had always made upper New York an unsafe place to settle. New York City grew to importance as the trading centre for much of neighbouring New Jersey and to an increasing extent for the Connecticut valley, and it sent out flour and pork from the Hudson valley, as well as furs collected at Albany. It owned only a modest number of ships, but it had a large mer-chant class, which profited heavily from the use of the city as a supply base for the British army during the long years of the French wars.

Finally, the heart of farming America in the eighteenth century was Pennsylvania and New Jersey. With a variety of richer soils and a less harsh climate than New England, deeply penetrated by the great rivers Delaware and Susquehanna, these colonies drew in the majority of eighteenth-century immigrants; Scots and Irish in the first quarter of the century and Germans of persecuted creeds in the second, coming as indentured servants or redemptioners. The earlier arrivals built up big farms that occupied much of the land of the lower Delaware, and by mid-century newcomers were going to farm in the north and west, filling up the whole lowland and going on over the hills into the great valley of Virginia and as far as the uplands of South Carolina. In all this back country of the middle and southern colonies, wheat-farming and stock-raising were carried on by settlers with farms of a hundred to two hundred acres. Through them the economy of the north, together with its relatively egalitarian society, was extended far into the south.

The great trading centre for all this area (except eastern New Jersey) was Philadelphia, which emerged in the 1750s as the largest town in colonial America, comparable in size with the largest English provincial cities, Bristol, Manchester and Norwich. Its population rose from ten thousand in 1722 to thirty-five thousand in 1775. Pennsylvania's shipping was modest, though by mid-century there was an important shipbuilding industry whose product, using native whiteoak, was far superior to that of New England. Though Pennsylvania had no large industry beyond this and a scattered iron manufacture, Philadelphia supported a great number of artisans who supplied many of the manufacturing needs of the region. Philadelphia merchants financed country stores in the back country of Pennsylvania, encouraging the growth of such subsidiary trading centres as Trenton, Wilmington, Charles Town and Elkton; and pushing on through Lancaster into Virginia, maintained trading connections with Pennsylvania migrants in the far west of Virginia and the Carolinas. It sent foodstuffs and timber to the Caribbean, where they were exchanged for sugar, molasses and bills on London; to South Carolina for rice, turpentine and skins; and to Boston and Newport where they paid for shipping and insurance services.

The mainland colonies differed in resources even within one general climatic region; they differed too in forms of government and land-holdings; and they came under varying degrees of pressure from Indians – negligible in the coastlands, fierce and continuous on the Carolina frontier, sporadic in New York and New England. What general themes can nevertheless be discerned?

In this whole area there was a widely diffused prosperity; few were very rich and few very poor by the standards of Europe. This common feature derived from the availability of almost unlimited areas of land that was virtually free – even though in the more favoured places, close to towns and markets or the sea, land became sought after and costly in the eighteenth century. Landholdings were far larger than in Europe, a fifty-acre holding being a small one. On the eve of the Revolution the average farmer's holding in a crowded corner of Massachusetts that had been settled for well over a century was forty-three acres; the French peasant's holding was rarely as much as ten.

The land systems of the colonies showed important differences in their details, arising from the original relations of the crown and the early colonial proprietors. But whether they had become royal colonies in the seventeenth century, like New York, New Jersey, Virginia and the New England colonies, or remained proprietorial like Pennsylvania and Maryland, or South or North Carolina until 1720 and 1728 respectively, they showed (with the single exception of New York) a common characteristic; the willingness of the crown or the other ultimate proprietor of the land to alienate it permanently in small lots, reserving only nominal rents of two or four shillings a hundred acres. These alienations created, for practical purposes, freehold cultivating proprietors, sometimes of plots of a few tens of acres, but quite often of several hundred acres. In Massachusetts, and on the fringes of settlement generally, the initial allotments were made free, or at charges that merely covered some survey and legal costs; but in the eighteenth century, in areas where unsettled land was becoming scarcer, a modest purchase price might be exacted, ranging up to fifteen pounds a hundred acres for uncleared land. Long settled and cleared land bought from an existing owner, of course, cost very much more, and in the course of time land speculation came to put a price on most land that was not on the frontier of settlement.

In democratic New England, which was long governed by men who attempted to behave as religion told them was right, there was a serious effort to prevent large-scale engrossment of land by speculators. Land was first allotted to townships to be distributed equally among those who intended to settle in them. But the grants were too large to be fully occupied at once, and later generations of the townships' inhabitants came to hold their uncleared land as speculations. Moreover, as religious fervour in the governing groups gave way to commercialism late in the seventeenth century, township allotments came to include grants made to men of substance and influence in the colony, who did not intend to cultivate them but to hold them vacant until neighbouring cultivation and settlement had raised their value, and then to sell. After 1725 much of the free land still remaining was distributed to pure land speculators and the egalitarian policy finally collapsed. Nowhere else was such a policy seriously attempted; large grants were made from the beginning to men of influence, and land speculation started early.

Nevertheless, it always remained true that the genuine settler could get land on very easy terms somewhere in a colony, either by dealing directly with the crown's or the proprietor's agents, or on the colonial fringes by clearing a patch of land and establishing his farm, and later getting the land granted to him formally on the usual terms. For the genuine pioneer, who was ready to go to the frontier and clear and plant land as earlier pioneers had done, land was almost free. When in 1763 the British Government proposed to restrict the movement of settlers across the Alleghany frontier that had been opened by the French surrender of America, this was seen as an intolerable measure that would sooner or later extinguish this most cherished opportunity of free Americans, by putting a limit on the land that could be settled and so creating a land shortage.

The consequence of plentiful land was the unimportance of rent. Peasants and labourers came to America from countries where landed proprietors, Church and state between them exacted taxes, tithes, dues and rent equivalent to a third or more of a cultivator's produce: but in the new land they came to, the produce was almost entirely their own. In Europe, every thousand or two acres bore a landlord who expected a luxurious living to be provided for him from its rents; a Baltimore or Pennsylvania proprietor was happy to draw a few thousands of pounds of revenue from millions of acres of land. In America, the crown's civil administration was very small and its costs borne out of the quit rents on land grants, interest on loans to farmers, or in Virginia by a tiny export tax on tobacco, while military costs were met by the English tax payer. It is true that quarrels over quit rents became frequent in the eighteenth century, though usually as reinforcement to arguments over much wider issues of liberty of land use and extension of frontiers. The Ulsterman who had migrated through the backwoods of half a dozen colonies to the South Carolina hill country, never setting eyes on Charleston society, was naturally resentful when the agent of Lord Granville, who had acquired rights over hundreds of thousands of acres for no particular services, struggled up the trail from the nearest Carolina township and demanded a few shillings quit rent. But it was resentment at a gadfly sting that had no relation to the crushing burdens the European peasant and farmer had always taken for granted. Even the final British land settlement before the Revolution in 1774, which reiterated that settlement beyond the Alleghanies was to be strictly confined, and provided for increased quit rents and purchase prices on land still unallocated in the east, had only a trivial economic impact.

If the economic independence of the farming community was being eroded during the eighteenth century, the reasons lay in farmers' rising aspirations, in the increasing remoteness of much settlement from large markets, and in the growth of colonial commerce and financial facilities to meet these conditions. Although the supply of virtually free land constituted the fundamental basis of the prosperity of Americans, it remained true that the cheapest land was far from the places where the most civilized life could be carried on. Farmers who wished for something better than a very primitive if ample subsistence had to rely on traders to buy their produce and bring their needs. Moreover, in spite of the absence of rent burdens, American farmers, like others, could fall on hard times, their incomes fluctuating and lagging periodically behind expenditure; and in such difficulties they turned for support to the local stores, backed by Boston or New York, or even Bristol or Glasgow, merchant capital. The prosperous American farmer, like the European peasant who had been freed from feudal ties, was a desirable object for the granting of credit on the security of his land; and in America as elsewhere this could lead to the cultivator becoming permanently dependent on his creditor. As population grew, the value of land rose near urban centres and seaports, and it became attractive as an investment on which investors would expect a maximum return in rent. There was a slow differentiating tendency at work as the less able, fortunate or thrifty farmers got into debt and sold out to merchants or to their more prosperous neighbours. Much of the land gradually came into merchant hands; and more and more trembled on the brink of alienation in this way, creating dissatisfaction among the farmers and resentment at the pressures of urban interests upon them.

In the last quarter century before the Revolution, in fact, the familiar tension between merchant and farmer, debtor and creditor, was emerging – a tension that was to have its influence in the taking of sides in the Revolution itself. It had for long been relieved in some degree by the credit policies of colonial governments, whose laws on paper currency and land credit were of the utmost importance to farmers and their creditors in the American towns and in England. But the Currency Act of 1751, which strictly limited paper issues, closed an important safety valve of farmers' discontent.

The colonies had very difficult currency problems, for the British Government forbade them to mint coin, while at the same time prohibiting the export to them of English and Scots coin. How, then, could transactions be carried on at all in the colonies? They used some foreign coin that came in the course of trade. Much more important was barter, which was formalized during the seventeenth century by designating particular commodities as money, fixing prices for them at which they were acceptable for public payments. Although this raised problems of quality and transportability, it was a tolerable solution for such single-staple economies as those of early Virginia and Maryland, which accounted for all transactions in terms of pounds of tobacco far into the eighteenth century, and did not entirely abandon the system after the Revolution. But in the northern and middle colonies it was hardly better than primitive barter, and though it might work within townships, it imposed great difficulties of valuation, storage and transportation in longer-distance trade centred on the ports. There was a great extension of the use of accounting and of credit to reduce the need for the physical transfer of money or its equivalents, but the northern colonies had to find a means to institute a proper monetary system. They did so in the way that was catching hold in England during the eighteenth century, by developing the use of paper money. But in the political conditions of the colonies, where government was by popular assemblies whose majorities were often at odds with the wealthiest sections of the local communities, paper money became a weapon in economic war.

As early as 1690 the Massachusetts legislature had begun the issue of promissory notes, secured on the provincial revenue. Its example was followed by the other colonies – except Pennsylvania, Virginia and Maryland – between 1700 and 1715. These printed notes, secured on war taxation, designed to bring income to the colonial government before the taxes were collected and then to be repaid from their proceeds, were welcomed as freely circulating substitutes for regular money. When war ended and the extraordinary revenues were abandoned the original function of the notes disappeared, but the desire to continue their vicarious function as circulating media remained. The means of doing so, adopted in one colony after another, was the creation of colonial credit banks. The colonial government would print off blocks of notes, make loans in them to farmers on the security of their land, and draw interest on the loans. The farmers received money to spend at once, and the government an income (which enabled Rhode Island to avoid levying any taxes at all for thirty years), and the people of the colony enjoyed a circulating medium. The drawback was that whereas the earlier note issues had been related to a regular tax revenue, which was automatically used to retire them as it came in, the new issues were related to the nearly unlimited borrowing capacity of farmers, whose undertakings to make regular repayments were rarely met for very long before they needed fresh loans to support them. Paper money was therefore over-issued, and the value at which it was acceptable depreciated, to a greater or lesser extent, in all the colonies. These colonies had created a currency of their own, and debased it almost at once. The notes were originally issued at a notional value of eight shillings to an ounce of silver; by 1730 an ounce of silver was valued at thirty shillings in South Carolina or Massachusetts notes, and even more in those of Rhode Island. The price level, in terms of this currency, rose steeply.

Rapid currency depreciation, of course, benefited debtors; and debtors were mostly in the farming class that made up the majority of the population, while creditors (apart from the note-issuing legislatures themselves) were merchants – local ones or the factors of English or Scots overseas – or the owners of fixed quit rents. The simple banking solution to the problem of money supply was therefore involved in a political struggle. The colonial legislatures, which came into the hands of farmers by weight of their numbers, pressed on with loans and note issues; the creditors, overborne by local political power, called for help from the ultimate governing authority in London. The British Parliament repeatedly refused to allow colonial note issues to be made legal tender, attempted sporadically to get them reduced, and finally, in 1751, passed the Currency Act, which forbade land banks, required the regular retirement of existing issues, and banned all future note issues except those tied to tax collections. This brought the colonial monetary system under control; but at the cost of increasing the problems of shortage of circulating medium and farm indebtedness.

The currency struggle was an aspect of a new feature in eighteenth-century America; the emergence of the local debtor-creditor relation (farmer-merchant, easterner-westerner) that was to remain in the forefront of economic and political life down to the twentieth century. Creditors had originally been people across the sea in England, and they remained so for the wealthier tobacco planters of Virginia and Maryland. But outside the tobacco colonies, farmers' debts were largely to other Americans. Those Americans who were in debt to England were the merchants of Philadelphia, Boston, New York or Charleston, and the credit they received from London or Liverpool augmented the capital they employed in the extension of credit to small country stores, to pedlars and to farmers right up to the edge of the uncleared forest.

Tension was beginning to appear in another aspect of relations between town and country, that of consumers and producers. Most townspeople were not merchants squeezing profits from the farmer, but artisans, fishermen, labourers, professional men; whether rich or poor, they were buyers of food that came from colonial farms. The normal fluctuations of farm prices were replaced from 1763 until the Revolution by a long spell in which farm prices were high, and complaints about food prices and against the greed of the farmers were loud in the northern towns. It was possible to blame this situation on England, for after mid-century England became an occasional grain importer, while the ending of English grain exports caused Spain and Portugal to turn to America to replace their grain supply. The sudden expansion of export demand – which was not confined to corn – undoubtedly had an influence in keeping up prices and farming prosperity; but so too did the rapid growth of the colonial towns and of the West Indian market. From 1766 there was a growing agitation in the towns about high food prices, which was reminiscent of old Europe; New York attempted in that year to prevent corn exports, Massachusetts offered bounties for wheat and flour, and control over marketing procedures was extended in an attempt to squeeze out middlemen's profits. All this was yet another sign of American maturity; the urban sector was no longer so small a proportion of the whole that its food demand could automatically be met cheaply and easily.

Endless land and negligible rent generally produced ample food and the materials for some household production, and as colonial communities became larger they offered markets for more sophisticated local industries. Even the simplest communities needed some manufactures, and as the colonies matured, grew populous and variegated, the range of their wants multiplied much faster than the expansion of colonial manufactures. Free land, however remote, was attractive to people whose alternative was the near-destitution of the European peasant or labourer; but for the later generations that were in their simple terms, well-to-do, its cheapness was the counterpart of distance from markets and of the cost and difficulty of getting European goods. Within the individual colonies this was expressed in the rise in land values of the less remote land. But for the colonies as a whole, particularly the northern and middle colonies, rising consumer demand raised the problem of earning in Europe enough to pay for all the European commodities the colonists wanted. We have seen the many expedients to which this led in the early days: the fisheries, the fur trade, the sale of ships to England, the timber trade, which between them enabled Americans to pay for their imports. The basic difficulty in temperate America's external relations lay in the fact that the land was best suited to produce the bulky foodstuffs – wheat and maize, beef and pork – which until the 1760s could not bear the costs of transport across the Atlantic and still sell at prices that were competitive in Europe.

America had either to diversify or to find other markets for the production of its farms. As we have seen, it did develop some branches of industry; but free land was an obstacle tempting workers to the frontier, forcing industrialists to pay high wages to retain them and so making most American manufactures uncompetitive with imports. The balance of payments problem was solved by developing the sale of surplus foodstuffs to those colonies where the growth of tropical staples occupied nearly all the land; in other words, in the sugar islands of the Caribbean and to a much smaller extent in the tobacco and rice colonies of the American south. By the middle of the eighteenth century the international trade of the temperate colonies had come to revolve around the sugar islands.

The expanded West Indian trade of the eighteenth century was carried on by independent merchants – especially of Boston and Newport – who sent small ships, commonly of forty or fifty tons, with mixed cargoes of timber, horses, provisions and European goods. They were trading ships; the master (or occasionally a supercargo) was given almost unlimited discretion as to the places he might visit and the prices at which he might barter his cargo for a variety of island products – though normally he had to settle for molasses – and the terms on which he might accept payment in Spanish silver coin or in bills on London. Much of his outward cargo was as likely to be picked up in New Haven or Baltimore as his home port, and he was ready to go into any likely place on the American coastline to dispose of his return cargo, or even to cross the Atlantic. The Newfoundland fisheries came into his beat, for he might sell rum there in exchange for dried fish to feed the slaves. If cargo hung fire in the Caribbean, he could go to the Isle of May and set his crew digging salt, or to the Cayman Islands for turtle meat, or to the Yucatan coast to cut logwood for dyes. This was an old-fashioned form of trade, which in most of Europe had been replaced by the settlement of factors in foreign ports, and larger ships making regular voyages with masters who nearly confined themselves to the work of navigation. It was very rapidly disappearing from the American sugar and tobacco trades by the beginning of the eighteenth century, as these became large and regular enough to bear new arrangements. Sugar planters were becoming so tied to English agents that casual traders – whether American or English – found it harder to get supplies. Even rum became scarcer; the New Englanders who had based their trades in Newfoundland fish and African slaves upon supplying rum found that the increasingly strict regulation of gin-drinking in England after 1736 was stimulating English demand for rum, and for molasses to refine it from.

Northern surpluses grew far more rapidly than the British West Indies could absorb them. The population of the northern and middle colonies increased ten-fold while that of the British West Indies only trebled. As it became apparent that the British West Indies market was inadequate, Americans looked increasingly to markets in foreign West Indian islands. France, like England, was unable to supply its islands with provisions from home, and its sporadic attempts to encourage Canadian supplies had failed completely. As intensive sugar cultivation employing great numbers of slaves spread through French islands, British North America became the obvious source of food supply; and it was the only market that would take any large quantity of the byproducts of sugar production – molasses and rum. Sugar was cheaper in the French islands than in Barbados or the Leeward Islands, for production costs were lower and duties on export negligible; and the Dutch islands, where all the Caribbean nations traded, also offered markets to Americans.

American traders therefore began to frequent the foreign West Indies as early as 1700. They often found it advantageous to sell part of their cargo for cash in the British islands (or for bills drawn on the planters' London agents against their sugar consignments) and then go on to a French or Dutch island to buy molasses or refined sugar more cheaply. This trade was entirely contrary to the Navigation Acts, but it flourished unhindered until French competition began to bite into the markets of the English sugar producers in the 1720s. The agitation of English sugar planters then secured the passing of the Molasses Act (1733) which legalized the trade but imposed very heavy duties on foreign rum, sugar and molasses coming into North America. But the measure was very difficult to enforce, and although it ensured that the southern mainland colonies increased their import of British West Indian products, the trade of northern colonies was little affected. Indeed, as the foreign islands moved more intensively to the production of sugar, coffee and indigo, they took a growing share of North American output and came into the same kind of dependence on British North American food supplies as the British islands had before them.

In the half-century before the Revolution, therefore, the colonies were tied into a circle of dependence. British, French and Dutch West Indies (and to an increasing extent the Spanish islands and coastal colonies) all found the principal markets for their produce in Europe, and required in return foodstuffs, horses and timber that Europe could not provide; and British North American colonies, with a demand for European goods that they could not directly pay for, produced surpluses of food and timber that they sold in the Caribbean. Narrower specializations developed in particular goods and services; New York was the main source of wheaten flour, North Carolina of barrel staves, while Massachusetts and Rhode Island, now food-deficit areas themselves, sold their merchanting, shipping and insurance services to all these colonial trades. The intercolonial trade became essential to all the parties to it, and was carried on in war and in peace. Rhode Island skippers took their flour and pork down to French St Domingue while English and French fleets battered each other and Indian allies of the French slaughtered British colonial soldiers and settlers in the Hudson valley; and New England merchants, like those other defenders of the principle of freedom of trade, the Dutch, filled the air with bitter protest at any attempt to limit or interfere with their wartime trade. Yet North American growth was fast outstripping all possible West Indian demand. The new relation of the nineteenth century, when western Europe itself would become a food deficit area, was faintly foreshadowed by the first serious shipment of wheat from Virginia and Pennsylvania to England, a few years before the Revolution. Only Virginia, Maryland and the Carolinas were freed from this circle of dependence by the growth of a varied farming on their own soil alongside the old plantations producing for export.

In the years after the Peace of Paris of 1763, which finally excluded the French from North America, the desirability of the colonial relationship came increasingly into doubt, until the question had to be settled in favour of independence by the war of the Revolution. There was a reality in colonial oppression, though it is easily misunderstood. We need not assume that because pamphleteers and occasionally statesmen declared that colonies existed to bring advantages to the mother country, and must be regulated to do so even to their own disadvantage, things really worked that way; still less that the more extreme and vividly quotable of such views formed the foundation of policy. The results of policy differed from intentions as frequently when the intentions were bad as when they were good. Nevertheless, there was real interference in colonial economic activity, accompanied by the giving of solid economic benefits to colonists. The main framework was provided by the English Navigation Act of 1660, which (with its various amendments) effectively prohibited direct trade between the colonies and foreign countries in Europe; in return colonial tobacco and sugar were given a monopoly of the English market. These measures were probably advantageous to the colonies, on balance, until some time after the ending of the second of the great Anglo-French wars in 1713, but as American produce became more varied and its supply outgrew the capacity of the English and colonial market to absorb it, the restrictions came increasingly to outweigh the economic advantages. Other regulation of the colonial economies was of modest importance. The acts restricting colonial hat-making, iron and woollen textile industries were little observed; in any case they were counterbalanced by the bounties given by the British Government to the iron-making and some timber industries. The uncontrolled paper money issues that the Currency Act ended in 1751 would have had to be dealt with somehow; and the post-1763 taxation imposed by England was light even when it was not withdrawn altogether in the face of opposition.

In recent years interesting attempts have been made to quantify the cost to the North American colonies of British imperial policy; and the most thoroughly worked out of these appear to agree that in the 1760s the effect of the Navigation Acts, in distorting American trade, may have been to reduce the national income by some

2 per cent. The important thing here is the dating. It is very unlikely that before 1720 America lost anything by the imperial connection, even in strict economic terms. Between 1720 and 1760 it probably tended increasingly to do so. But the alternative in those four decades did not lie between British colonialism and independence, for the French presence was very strong in America and had not only closed the interior to British American advance but was attempting to roll back the frontier in places. The opening of all America to British Americans – which was essential to the colonists in the later eighteenth century – was the result of wars fought on colonial, ocean and European battlefields, and determined in favour of the British colonists not just at Louisburg and Ticonderoga, but in the defeat of France on the seas and in Europe as a European power. Such a defeat was far beyond the resources of the colonists alone. The costs of these wars were paid for almost entirely by Britain rather than the colonies, and far outweighed all simple calculations of benefits based merely on diversion of trade and military expenditures on American soil. After 1760, when the French were driven from North America – a situation formalized at the peace of 1763 – the situation was entirely changed. Thereafter direct economic loss from the imperial connection had no indirect compensation in the form of free protection from the French, and the loss grew rapidly with the widening of American resources. By removing the one essential function of the imperial connection, namely protection by one great European power against the other one that had foothold in the American continent, success in war removed the need for that connection. It removed a restraint within which anti-imperial feeling had had to operate, so that it became possible for all the minor reasons for breaking the connection, political and economic, real and false, to make themselves felt, reinforcing the great and substantial reason that the need for it was gone, and with it the justification.

17 France and England in the Eighteenth Century

In 1776 the American Declaration of Independence announced the breaking up of the colonial systems whose origin and development have been principal themes of this book; and Adam Smith published his *Inquiry into the Nature and Causes of the Wealth of Nations*, laying the foundation of modern economics with a work based on empirical study of the economy of the pre-industrial age. Adam Smith was not conscious that an extra-ordinary change in economic and social life was on the point of overtaking his country; and neither English nor French writers of the time imagined that an Industrial Revolution would within a couple of decades have caused the economic hegemony of Europe to pass decisively to England. The half century before 1776 was a period of prosperity and expansion for both France and England, and the literature of the time is full of self-congratulatory material. Statistics suggest that both French and English national income more than doubled in the first three-quarters of the eighteenth century, though these estimates probably overstate the true increase; and it is likely that in the middle decades, from 1730 to 1770, the advance was faster in France than in England. Yet the acceleration of economic growth and the mounting evidences of prosperity fell far short of the scale of change in England that was to follow 1776. They may better be compared with the expansive period 1600–30 that terminated with the downturn of the mid-seventeenth century. There was nothing new in rapid economic progress in Europe, but it had in the past come in brief surges as it did to France in the eighteenth century. The really new thing was the steep upturn in England in the last quarter of the century, which is outside the period of this book. These concluding chapters will examine the mid-eighteenth century expansion on its own merits; but it is impossible to ignore the great landmark in economic history that looms up immediately beyond the terminal date of 1776. In examining development in the middle decades of the eighteenth century, the questions must be asked whether it exhibits features that explain the great discontinuity of the Industrial Revolution that was about to occur; and whether it reveals the reasons why the Industrial Revolution came to Britain and not to France.

Rising production and national income must be seen in the context of populations that were growing fast; in England from the 1740s, in France from a trough in the 1720s. In 1690 there had been some five and a half million English men and women; their numbers had not reached six million in 1751, but they passed seven million in 1771 and eight million before 1791. In France, the prolongation of war and economic troubles prevented real recovery of the losses of 1709–10 before the 1720s; but from a low point of nineteen million the French population rose to twenty-six million in 1789 (including a million in freshly annexed territory). The renewal of population growth towards the middle of the eighteenth century, after prolonged stagnation, was the common experience of Europe. Yet there is a significant difference between the general European movement, to which the French corresponded, and the course of development in England. In England, renewed growth began in the 1740s from the highest level that had ever been reached; by 1770 it was some 50 per cent higher than it had been in 1630, and it continued to grow at an accelerating pace into the nineteenth century. In France the initial growth of the 1720s and 1730s was a recovery to old levels of population; by 1770 the numbers were only some 25 per cent higher than they had been in 1630, and in the 1770s rises in death rate began to appear in some areas, slowing the rate of growth and presently bringing about some decline of population in southern and central France. In England growth was continuous and accelerating; in France there was only a brief phase of growth matching England's, before the spectre of the subsistence crisis began to hover once more. The special problem of English demographic history, the explanation of the sustained growth of numbers continuing into the nineteenth century, which other countries did not experience, is beyond the scope of this book.

Renewal of population growth in France seems to be clearly associated with improved food supply, ending the recurrent onsets of severe famine that had afflicted France since the late sixteenth century. There was a long run of generally good harvests from 1726 until 1770 (seriously broken only in 1739–41) and this corresponds with population growth reaching its fastest rate between 1750 and 1770. The chief mechanism of growth in this period, in France as in England, was a fall in the death rate – and particularly the death rate among children – rather than more births. It showed itself in both countries in a cutting down of the occasional violent leaps in the death rate, which in previous centuries had wiped out several years' population increase once or twice in every decade; and in France in the disappearance after 1709–10 of those extraordinary demographic disasters that had repeatedly prevented population getting back to its early seventeenth-century peak. Yet English experience suggests that better feeding was by no means the sole explanation of a lowered death rate. In England the subsistence problem in its most serious form had long since been solved; people still died because they were undernourished and unable to stand up to illness, but famine had long been absent. It has been strongly argued that on the other side, better subsistence could have been expected to produce some rise in birth rates. The factual evidence on this in the eighteenth century is inconclusive, but it had some effect in France, if not in England. However, the well-attested demographic experience of the English peerage throws great doubt on subsistence explanations of population growth in this century It is unlikely that families of the nobility ever suffered from being under-fed; yet they showed the same marked fall in death rates, in the second quarter of the eighteenth century, as did society as a whole.

The basis for the rising prosperity in the middle decades of the eighteenth century lay in the unusual combination of growing populations with an agricultural production that kept pace with their needs. The more spectacular and more frequently commented on industrial expansion was dependent on this, to provide part of its market, to release labour from the land, and to feed the manu-facturing populations. In England, improvement of agricultural productivity had long been under way, with rising crop yields per acre, and great diversification and specialization of particular areas. More corn was produced, alongside a rise of animal husbandry. Its conjunction with a century of only slowly rising population after

1630 had resulted in the emergence of a food surplus, with low corn prices, culminating in something of an overproduction crisis for the more specialized corn producers in the period 1730–50. The fundamental improvements continued to spread, at a pace that accelerated after mid-century; their main features were the introduction of more flexible crop rotations embracing roots, legumes and improved grasses, which enabled the land both to carry more stock and to grow more corn. The obstacles of open-field farming and of peasant tenures were broken down more easily in the eighteenth century, as the economic advantages became more apparent and the social costs more acceptable to a government now composed of great landlords. The larger farmers, in whose hands an increasing share of the land was held, had the best opportunities to learn about innovations that had been pioneered, and had the resources to introduce them. After mid-century, moreover, rising population brought an end to the long-term stability of corn prices that had prevailed for nearly a century, and they began to move upward. This caused a renewed interest by large farmers and their landlords in expanding corn production, and the main contribution to it was made by ploughing up much of the old common and waste, particularly in the eastern counties. Thanks to the improvement of fodder crops and the bringing into use of more Welsh and Scottish highland to rear cattle for England, this reduction of commons did not prevent continuing increase in supplies of meat and dairy produce.

Change in England was associated with the rapid movement away from a society of peasants to one of middling and large farmers employing a little wage labour and producing for the market. France, on the other hand, remained essentially a country of poor peasants, with no substantial changes in rural structure, although landlords were attempting to build up larger farms here and there. Nevertheless, the years 1730–70 saw a big advance in the productivity of French agriculture. Wheat prices were low and still declining until 1760–1, more than a decade after they had started to move upward in England and Holland, clearly indicating that in an age of population growth French production was rising to match it. Writers on English agrarian history explain increases in long-run productivity by improvements in methods and organization; the French see the good years 1730–70 as essentially a good period in the climatic cycle, four decades in which years of good harvest weather were clustered unusually thickly. These differing emphases reflect, to some extent, the development of the two countries:

L

agricultural improvement was, over a very long period, much more evident in England than in France. Nevertheless, improvement *was* going on in France; and in particular, the gains of the years of good weather 1726–38 built up peasant resources and enabled some of them to expand their livestock and equipment, so reinforcing the effects of a continuing favourable climate in the next three decades. On the other side, if climatic conditions helped the peasants of northern France, they must have had some influence on the increase of English corn production. In both countries a clustering of years of good harvest weather between 1730 and 1770 supported investment in the land and improvement of methods of cultivation.

French agricultural production leaped forward in this period. Rather dubious overall statistics suggest a doubling of production between 1701–10 and 1781–90; but evidence of improvement of this order of size also comes firmly from the records of yield of tithes in many parts of France. On rented land – which on the eve of the Revolution accounted for over two-thirds of France – rents at least doubled, and in many places tripled, between 1720 and 1780. Yet peasant incomes were rising, because there was some time-lag before the diversion of their income to increased rent took effect.

Landlords had taken little interest in agricultural improvement but a combination of circumstances brought them into it after 1760. A literature of agricultural improvement began to appear in France, and in the 1760s the Physiocrats were drawing attention to the dependence of all incomes on a healthy agriculture. More important, rising corn prices gave an impetus to the ploughing up of fresh land – which in the north meant encroachment on the already very limited commons – and the state, reversing its earlier attitude, encouraged this work from 1761 onward. The enclosure of commons was often the work of landlords, their resources already enhanced by enlarged rent rolls; and their renewal of pressure on the peasantry was a factor in building up the rising peasant discontent that reached a revolutionary pitch in 1789.

Through the period 1730–70, therefore, the French economy was greatly strengthened not only by rising peasant incomes that brought more of them into the market for industrial products but also by the increase in landlord incomes and by the sustained rise in population that a more ample food supply supported. The average peasant remained very poor; but the group that had struggled beyond subsistence level to some modest comfort was enlarged. The growth of landed incomes as a whole was probably faster in

France than in England in the early part of this period, and this was certainly true of the growth of rents. After about 1760, however, the experience of the two countries diverged. In England, the rapid adaptation of capitalist farmers to a rising demand for corn increased its supply and steeply augmented farmers' and landlords' incomes. In France, the efforts of some landlords and their larger tenants made only slow headway, for the tone of French agriculture was still set by a great mass of landowning peasantry, not indeed wholly conservative but adapting itself too slowly. The peasants remained in 1770, as they had been a hundred years earlier, the brake on French economic expansion.

Regional specialization in agriculture depended on good communications to distribute its products. Few major agricultural products could bear the costs of long-distance transport except by waterways; and the risks to a region that specialized away from corn were very serious if it was not assured that supplies could easily be brought in from outside. The problem was a lesser one for England, where no point was a great distance from the sea, than it was for France; but even so the improvement of English river systems for navigation, beginning in the 1660s but carried on much more actively in the eighteenth century, was very important. The supply of the swollen city of London depended in part on food brought by river from the upper part of the Thàmes basin; and while far more food came into the Thames by sea, it had been brought down to the seacoast to be laded for London by means of the river systems. The Great Ouse and its many tributaries carried corn from much of eastern England down to King's Lynn and other ports, and a series of improvements at difficult points of this system had been made during the seventeenth century. In the north, the rivers of the Trent and Ouse basins carried goods from a huge area down to the Humber and the sea. Great extensions were made to the navigable sections of the Trent around 1700, and in mid-century Cheshire cheese was more often being carried to the Trent and by river and sea to London, than sent out westward through Chester. These river improvements were not, of course, wholly for agricultural purposes; they were designed to get lead from the Pennines to the sea, to provide cheaper transport of wool and woollens for the Yorkshire manufacturing area, to bring Cheshire salt down to the Mersey and Dee estuaries, and to open up Midland coalfields. But their principal function was carrying corn and fodder, relieving many inland areas of surpluses that had once been hardly saleable, supplying deficit areas more cheaply, and generally levelling down the price differences that corn sales showed at markets in different parts of the country. The further improvements of river navigations in the 1740s and 1760s, and the beginnings of true canal building with the Sankey Navigation of 1757 and the Bridgewater Canal of 1761-7, were prompted chiefly by the need to bring food and raw materials into the rising industrial districts of the north and to the Birmingham area. In the same period, road improvement began to strengthen the links of towns with the waterways and to speed the movement of long-distance passenger traffic.

The French problem was far greater, in a larger country, much of it very remote from the sea. Great rivers cut into it deeply, but the heavily populated north was less well served by them than the centre and the south. Moreover, to send goods down the immense stretches of one of these rivers to the Atlantic sea coast, and then coastwise and up another river, was a tremendously long and costly business. Drought made sections of the rivers unnavigable in summer, and icing was likely to be encountered in some winters. There were tolls everywhere; the river Loire had seventy-five. The great centre of circulation was the Loire, connected by road links with Paris and the east, and with the Rhône-Saône basin to the south-east; its great city and river port was Orleans. Paris secured its corn supply not merely from the surrounding countryside but from a vast area of central and eastern France served by the Loire and Seine, extending into Burgundy and Lorraine. Corn for Lyon was carried down the Saône from Franche Comté and Burgundy, and from Provence up the Loire. But much traffic was along short stretches, alternately of road and river, in the interior. Away from the rivers many villages were quite isolated, and the regular phenomenon of seventeenth-century France had been serious food shortage and high prices in one region, whilst supplies were ample no more than a hundred miles away.

Colbert, who was conscious of the need to assist development of a national market, gave most of his attention to roads. Though his funds were never adequate, it was nevertheless established in France that the creation of a trunk road system was a function of the state rather than of local administration or private enterprise. After 1738 a national plan for roads was gradually implemented, with roads radiating out from Paris to the seaports, frontiers and great towns. Road-building technique reached a high level from the 1750s, and in the third quarter of the century French roads were far in advance of English. Yet it was a road and not a waterway system, built primarily for strategic and administrative rather than commercial reasons; it greatly speeded personal travel but did little to cheapen the carriage of heavy goods, or to open up remote regions, so its economic impact was limited. The improvement of waterways was more modest. The famous and costly Canal des Deux Mers, which in 1681 was completed to link the Mediterranean with the Garonne basin, had little economic value. The important waterways were in the north, particularly those that supplied Paris and the industrial areas. In the late seventeenth century, parts of the Loire and the Seine were improved by embanking and straightening: the Loire and Seine connection was established by the Orleans Canal (1692) and the Loing Canal (1724), and the Oise and Somme were connected in 1738. The ultimate alleviation of some of the extremes of food shortage, and the improvement of rural incomes, did owe a good deal to the improvement of waterways. The weak link in French communications, however, remained the inadequacy of the pathways that connected most villages with the great trunk roads or with navigable water.

Since the agricultural sector was so large – in eighteenth-century England accounting for some 40–45 per cent of national production, and in France for some 60 per cent – the state of its health had a strong reaction on the industrial sector of the economy. Indeed, modern writers now see in the long-term advance, and the short-term fluctuation of agriculture, an important part of the explanation of English and French economic development in the eighteenth century, and perhaps in the preceding one.

The complicated relationship between agricultural and industrial prosperity is usually simplified by making two general assumptions: that agriculture was overwhelmingly dominated by corn production, and that the demand for corn was very inelastic. The first may serve, though we are conscious that it applies more closely to the densely populated parts of northern France and southern and midland England than to the hilly parts of those countries, and that in England during the first half of the eighteenth century the other produce of the land was being rapidly increased. The second assumption is attested by the wide year-to-year fluctuations in corn prices. Since corn (or its derivatives, flour and bread) was essential to people's lives, they would bid up its price very rapidly if it was scarce; but since it was the regular and least exciting food, once this necessary demand had been satisfied they spent any money they had left on other foods or on industrial products, so that a surplus of corn would cause its price to fall a very long way. Indeed, beyond the most modest deviations from average, a large corn harvest would actually produce a smaller total cash return to the producer than an average harvest would do; and a long spell of good harvests would actually depress the incomes of large corn producers. Within the limits of these assumptions, the likely consequences of the decades of good harvests that were experienced in the middle of the eighteenth century may be examined.

Better harvests changed the incomes of those who derived incomes from cornland; they sold more, at prices that were lowered, and more labour had to be put into harvesting, threshing and carrying, whether by the family or by wage-earners. Since most people derived their income from the land in one way or another – as peasants or farmers, labourers or landlords, carriers or dealers in foodstuffs – change in their incomes powerfully influenced the total of all incomes that were available to be spent not only on agricultural products but on manufactures, services and imported goods. Moreover, all but the well-to-do spent so large a part of their income on the basic foodstuffs that a modest reduction in corn prices could multiply the surpluses to be spent on other things. Transport costs, grinding and baking and traders' margins made up a large part of the final cost of flour and bread bought by most consumers, and the relative stability of these additional costs prevented bread prices from fluctuating so violently as those of corn. The disagreements among historians over the short-term impact of harvest fluctuations, and the more permanent results of long periods of low or high corn prices, arise from their differing estimates in two fields. One is the importance of the combined incomes of all those who supplied and served the market for corn, in relation to the total income of all food producers; the other concerns the patterns of expenditure of various classes within society and the way these classes reacted to changing prices. The differences reflect real and important contrasts between the social structure of England and France.

Assuming that the demand for corn was inelastic, the effect of an abundant supply on the incomes of its producers could range between two extremes. At one end was the large capitalist farmer, employing wage labour to do much of his work, and expecting to sell most of his corn on the market though he kept some for seed, tithes and his own family consumption. In an exceptionally good harvest, doubling his normal yield, he would be able to sell a good deal more than twice his normal supply on the market – perhaps two and a half times as much. However, the very heavy reduction in price, and the greatly increased cost of harvesting, threshing and carrying, caused such a farmer to suffer by a good harvest. A series of good harvests could be disastrous for him, as English experience showed in the 1730s. He was, of course, the best equipped of all farmers to divert resources away from corn production if the long-term prospects seemed bad. At the other extreme was the peasant whose main concern was to produce the corn needed to feed his own family. His rents and other outgoings were found from the proceeds of such subsidiary products as grapes, flax or pigs, by labouring for others on their land, or industrial by-employment of himself or his family. In an average year he produced enough corn to meet his family needs, pay his tithe and provide next year's seed; in a good year he had surplus corn to sell on the market, and this was pure gain for him beyond his normal condition – however low the price, he got something rather than nothing. A period of low corn prices gave him no adequate inducement to transfer resources to other production.

Obviously there was every kind of dependence on the market for corn between these two extreme types of producer; but it is important to see that, over most of the intermediate range, good crops *must* have added to peasant incomes, apart from by-employments. Consider, for example, the peasant who in an average year was able to sell a quarter of his corn crop as surplus. In a moderately bad year he would have none to spare and he might go hungry. In a very good year, in which the harvest was doubled, he could sell nearly five times as much as in the average year, and no conceivable fall in price would prevent his income being raised. Moreover, in a year of cheap corn the demand for other food products would expand and (if weather conditions favouring corn had not been harmful to them) the same peasant would get more money for his sales of this other produce. Much the greatest part of French rural production, and a very considerable part of English even in the middle of the eighteenth century, came from small and modest peasants in this intermediate range, together with the really poor subsistence peasants. Those English writers on the eighteenth century who assert that the farming community suffered from the series of good harvests lean too heavily on the experience of the big farmers; even in England the class of cultivators as a whole probably benefited from good harvests. Rural social structures in France and England differed greatly; in England in 1750 – or in 1700 or even 1650 – the admixture of large capitalist farmers was substantial. The English generalization about good harvests is closer to reality, therefore, for England than it is for France. The large farmer was a substantial customer for the products of industry, and a decline in his income would reduce his purchases; but even in England the expansion of peasant incomes might well have counterbalanced this, and in France it certainly did so. However, the smaller peasants – and particularly those in the more remote areas of rural France – would have spent their extra earnings more with the small craftsmen of their own localities than on the produce of the national large-scale industries.

What were the effects of lowered corn prices on other incomes? Half the population of England, and rather less in France, were regular wage-earners, though of course they received only a small part of the total national income. Neither in England nor in France did wages on the land or in industry fall along with food prices; and there was some increased employment to handle a bigger output. With incomes at least maintained, and the cost of their flour or bread considerably reduced, the wage-earners could buy more of other things, and their total additional demand would be large. English writers have attached great importance to expansion in demand for industrial goods from this source. However, they had other outlets for their surplus income; later experience suggests that increased real income among poor wage-earners was likely to be spent on improving the quality of their food supply, and particularly on buying more meat. Moreover, rural labourers, and even workers in small-town industry and services, were more likely to buy the coarse products of local weavers and shoemakers, and the urban poor to buy the cast-off clothing of the rich that descended through servants to the second-hand market, than add to the demand for products of the national, large-scale industries. French historians, indeed, incline to the view that this part of the population was normally so poor and underfed that its reaction to cheaper bread was to buy much more of it. On the whole it seems doubtful whether wage-earners made a large contribution to industrial demand, even in England.

Much the largest component of income that was in the hands of the rich or relatively well-to-do was in the form of rents of land.

The level of rents, when they could be freely negotiated, moved under two different influences. An expanding peasant population, with younger sons seeking landholdings, had always bid up rents competitively, and this was still happening in France between the 1720s and 1770s despite the lowness of corn prices. Men wanted livings for their families, not the right to produce for a competitive corn market. In France in this period agricultural production was greatly expanded; a little of this gain went to the consumers in lower prices; most peasants gained by eating better yet selling more, until higher rents ate into their surpluses; and their landlords presently managed to push rents up very substantially. Only a few big specializing farmers suffered. The improvement in landlord incomes – the doubling and more of rents in half a century – was probably the most powerful influence on raising the level of industrial demand in France. The other influence on rents was the ability of the enterprising, market-oriented farmer to pay; and this might well decline in a period of low corn prices. In England, in fact, the maximum level of rents was set by what the large commercial farmer would pay rather than by peasant demand; and until well after 1750 it reflected the low prices he was getting for his produce. Maximum commercial rents had some tendency to fall. The total of rental income was rising moderately, however, with the continuing process of dispossessing smallholders, breaking up open fields, and transferring inefficiently cultivated lands that had produced low rents into the hands of commercial farmers who would pay the maximum market rent. Before 1760, however, total rents were not rising at anything like the pace of those in France.

In both countries there was a considerable stratum of urban population as well as of middling peasants well above the level of the very poor. Many of them derived their income ultimately from land; the modest minor beneficiaries of the income of great estates – cousins, nieces, aunts of the minor aristocracy – living in provincial towns. There was a great proliferation of dealers, carriers and shopkeepers with the widening of market areas, and industrial producers and craftsmen were multiplying. The rise of these middle-income groups is a conspicuous feature of English social development in the eighteenth century, and it is evident, if not on the same scale, in France. If the rich landowners, traders, financiers and officials spent much of their income on services and luxury craft products, and the poor bought from local craftsmen, these middle strata accounted for a great demand for produce of good quality that was produced reasonably cheaply. The typical large-scale industries of the eighteenth century, the great rural textile industries, turned out great quantities of woollen and linen cloth, of stockings, sheets and blankets, to meet these middling demands. The spending of such people was important to the metallurgical industries, making cutlery, locks, metal ornaments and buttons; and to such industries as hat-making, soap-making, paper-making and many others. In these families in the middle ranks of society, spending patterns could be markedly influenced by the cheapening of corn; the very prosperous craftsman or shopkeeper, the low-ranking official or small professional man making £100 a year, might in a normal year spend a fifth of this on breadstuffs for his family.

Though views differ on the effect of increasing agricultural productivity on the income and spending of different social classes, they lead to the same general conclusion about the overall effect on industry. For some English historians, the good harvests and low corn prices of the mid-eighteenth century indicate a reduction in farmers' and landlords' incomes; yet they consider industrial demand was expanded because the rise of wage-earners' incomes and other urban demands outweighed the fall in rural producers' spending. For the French writers, who see farming as overwhelmingly peasant farming, good harvests indicated higher farm incomes and increasing rents; all but the poorest peasants could buy more industrial goods, and so could their landlords, while wage-earners hardly affected the situation for they lived so close to subsistence that their surpluses were always negligible. All agree, however, that good harvests were good for industry and for the economy as a whole; and looking beyond these narrow economic arguments it was obviously a better society in which the mass of the people were adequately fed and had some small surpluses. The most powerful effect on industrial expansion was exerted by the increased purchasing power of the middle incomes in England, and by this together with the expansion of landlord incomes in France. Purchasing power was released by the cheapening of basic foodstuffs and the raising of real incomes. The increased demand for foods of better quality and more varied kinds, and for manufactures and craft products, reinforced the purchasing power of cattle-raisers and dairy farmers, artisans and wage-earners and their employers; there was a multiplier effect at work, whose influence even extended to some expansion of investment.

18 France and England: Industrial Growth and Industrial Revolution

In the late seventeenth century both England and France went through a phase of some industrial growth; but in France it was less vigorous and was very seriously checked by the wars and famines of 1689–1713, while in England several branches of industry continued to move ahead rapidly and were even stimulated by wartime conditions. After 1730 French industry was again expanding fast; English industrial growth accelerated in the early 1730s, was slowed during the long war of 1739–48, and burst forward rapidly in the interval of peace that followed. Over the first three-quarters of the eighteenth century, taken as a whole, industrial growth was at much the same pace in both countries; in the middle decades its acceleration was possibly stronger in France. The extent of growth is hard to establish with any precision, for it came largely through the expansion of a range of minor industries whose statistics cannot be very usefully aggregated. Though both woollen and linen industries continued to expand, they ceased to dominate the industrial scene so completely as they had done in preceding centuries.

Diversification away from the old textile industry was particularly marked in Britain, but even here the woollen industry was far from stagnant. The woollen and worsted industry of West Yorkshire was one of the most actively growing sectors of the economy. Its counterpart, however, was the decline of other producing areas: Devon, which had been the leading producer of worsteds in the first quarter of the century but then went downhill rapidly; the old Wiltshire-Gloucester industry, which by mid-century was left simply as a producer of the very finest fabrics; and finally East Anglia, which in the third quarter was sending yarn to Yorkshire to be made up into cloth that competed with its own Norwich stuffs. Generations of industrial employment had built up relatively high wage levels in the older producing areas, and the move to York-shire took advantage of lower wages there. But by mid-century the new industrialization of the north of England was pushing wages up rapidly, causing a search for ways to economize labour. Kay's flying shuttle, devised for the woollen industry in 1733, came into common use in the 1750s and 1760s, and the Wyatt and Paul spinning frame of 1738, which just failed to master the technical problems, was a woollen industry invention. Nevertheless, this industry of small masters, finding their buyers in the cloth halls of Halifax and Leeds rather than among the more conservative London merchants, exhibited a greater responsiveness to changing textile fashions than the great west country clothiers, and flourished for this reason. They first conquered a large home market for their produce, even breaking into the ring of government contracting, and then in the 1740s and 1750s began to adapt themselves to export markets. The export of English woollens, which was declining until well after mid-century, was recovered in the 1770s by the introduc-tion of new kinds of cloth – many of them imitations of German products – which recaptured markets in southern Europe that had been lost to France, and opened colonial markets that had not previously taken English woollens.

Alongside a woollen industry that had already reached maturity, other textile industries were built up. The English linen industry was small, but there was a strong wish in government and mercan-tile circles to reduce the import of foreign linens which was the only large element in English imports of manufactures. The Scottish industry making coarse linens was stimulated to improve its quality and expand by government subsidies after 1727; and the import of linen from Ireland – where a strong industry was estab-lished by Huguenot immigrants of the 1680s – was facilitated by the removal of the English tariff on it in 1697. The silk industry, assisted by prohibitive duties on French goods and by the immigra-tion of Huguenot craftsmen in the last quarter of the seventeenth century, advanced from producing ribbons to making every kind of silk fabric – even if, in the mid-eighteenth century, English silks had to be labelled as French-made to suit the fashionable buyer. This industry settled in London, where the luxury market was to be found. The cheaper ribbon-making side, however, migrated to Derbyshire and Cheshire in the second quarter of the century, attracted by a technical innovation – the Italian silk-throwing machine introduced in the Derby area by the Lombe brothers in 1717 – which supplied its raw material cheaply. Cotton, a very small industry, will be dealt with separately because of the special consequences of its later expansion.

The most striking advances, however, were in the metal industries, whose total output may have been approaching that of woollens in value by the 1770s. Two areas of heavy concentration, centred on Birmingham and Sheffield, produced nails, buttons, small arms, ornaments, locks, cutlery, tools and chains, but London had a variety of metal workshops, Tyneside made great quantities of ships' metal fittings, and the blacksmiths' work carried on in every small town and many villages throughout the country accounted for a large part of total output. The production of iron lagged behind the general growth of the industry, for many grades of Swedish and Russian iron were cheaper than home supply. The diffusion of Darby's process for smelting pig iron with coke instead of charcoal, however, enabled castings to be produced cheaply in England, and from mid-century this side of the industry was growing very fast as producers introduced cast iron to new uses. It was growing demand derived largely from the American colonies that pulled the metal industries forward during the first three-quarters of the eighteenth century; and an increasing output made it possible to secure considerable economies from division of labour, and this lowering of costs was able to stimulate demand further. In all the later processes requiring heating of the material, coal or coke rather than charcoal was now used; and indeed the general replacement of timber by coal as an industrial and (in the towns) as a domestic fuel brought a big expansion of coal production, from two and a half million tons in 1700 to six million tons in 1770.

Looking back from the extraordinary advances of the last two decades of the century, industrial growth in England was not very striking; but by any older standards it was very rapid, and the outward signs of it were already attracting comment, in the growth of big industrial towns at Manchester, Birmingham, Leeds, Sheffield and Huddersfield.

In France expansion continued in the woollen and particularly in the linen industry, and was accompanied by more intense regional specialization. The fast-growing Languedoc woollen industry captured Mediterranean and Spanish markets from the English and Dutch during the middle decades of the century. The woollen industry of the north-west was in retreat as the spreading demand for labour in linens and cottons displaced it, but there was a more intense woollen concentration in north-central France – Champagne, Berry, Touraine and Orleans. The fast-growing linen industry in the north-west was making great demands on labour supply, and was joined in Normandy by an advancing cotton manufacture. Over great areas of northern France, in fact, the supply of rural labour for industry, which had once seemed limitless, was now approaching conditions of scarcity. There are signs that in the 1770s the prosperity of these textile industries, and particularly of woollens, was beginning to slacken.

The pacemakers of industrial expansion, as in England, were the metallurgical industries. Iron-making was on a much larger scale than in England, with some 130–140,000 tons in 1780 (compared with England's sixty-two thousand) and expanded at a similar pace. The production of iron wares was not, however, supported by any substantial import of iron from the northern countries, and the total French output of these was therefore no greater than the English. Coal production was growing much faster than in England, but it was on an altogether smaller scale, its output in the 1770s not exceeding half a million tons a year. Iron-making and iron-working were scattered industries, found in many forested parts of eastern and south-eastern France, still generally using charcoal for fuel, and the whole of French industry continued to use wood rather than coal.

The growth of industry has to be explained in terms of its markets, the reasons why increasing quantities of its products could be sold. This is why it has been approached by first considering the prosperity of agriculture and the supply and price of food. Industrial growth was taking place during much of the eighteenth century largely because the supply of food increased faster than the numbers of people. This is not a matter simply of the short term – the years 1730–50 that have been so much discussed by English historians – but of the whole of the hundred years 1660–1760, in which food prices were usually well below peaks reached earlier in the seventeenth century. The English people were adequately fed with bread, while agriculture was nevertheless able to turn more of its resources to meat, dairy produce, fruit and vegetables for those who were prosperous. The solution of the worst problems of food supply in England in the second half of the seventeenth century made possible an earlier and more continuous industrial expansion which France could not easily overtake after 1730.

There were two sources of industrial demand associated with incomes from the land. In earlier ages the growth of rural population, pressing on the land with demand for more holdings and employment, had pushed up the incomes of rentiers and employers in agriculture, and enabled them to buy the produce of industries and of crafts. The same pressure reappeared in France in the second quarter of the eighteenth century, pushing up rents, and hence the disposable income of the rich, more steeply than they had been for nearly a hundred years. But this traditional source of industrial demand was now reinforced by the greater incomes that increased agricultural productivity brought to the peasantry, which enabled a substantial part of it to enter the market, not for luxuries, but for modest manufactures of soap, pottery, shoes, tools, cutlery and so on. These sources added to the demand of the middle-income groups, who were growing in numbers and also benefiting from cheap food, to provide a swelling volume of internal demand for the products of industry. This mass demand was a new thing in France; it was older in England but still expanding in the eighteenth century.

Industrial expansion was also influenced by overseas trade; in the first place by the substitution of home-manufactured goods for imports, and secondly by the expansion of export trade. The commercial war between France and England that began with the French tariffs of 1664 and the English embargo of 1678 gave a powerful impetus to industrial self-sufficiency in both countries. The French purpose of reducing the rising flood of English and Dutch woollens was quite well achieved, and part of the French woollen industry received a modest stimulus. But the woollen industry had long since become large enough to make the most of economies of scale, and could no longer reduce costs by spectacular improvements in organization brought about by modest expansion of particular sections. English imports from France, on the other hand, were a variety of minor products – fine linens and haberdashery, silks, soap, paper and glassware. The Huguenot immigration established these industries or improved the quality of production in those that already existed; and the exclusion of French goods enabled some new English industries to capture the home market completely and grow to some size during the decades around 1700.

The large export trades in manufactured goods from European countries had always been confined to textiles: English, Dutch, French and German woollens; French, Dutch and German lines; French and Italian silks. A number of narrow regions, scattered among those countries, had developed specialisms in particular kinds of textile production with such success that their products were able to overcome all the obstacles of transport costs and normal tariffs, and sell in large quantities abroad. Few other industries were able to develop such competitive advantages that they could sell their goods far from home, and none of them before the eighteenth century were of great importance. Indeed, the costs and difficulty of transport – particularly in France – had prevented most industries from reaching out to serve their own national markets completely.

The growth of colonies gave many industries opportunities for export expansion. We have seen that the population of British North America increased ten-fold between 1700 and 1774; by the latter date it contained well over nine-tenths of all British and French white colonial populations. All the colonies used some of their export earnings to pay for European manufactures. But the planters who produced English and French sugar, French coffee, and English tobacco and rice, spent a large part of their earnings in buying food, lumber and horses from *British* colonies in North America. The colonial market for French manufactures was simply the French West Indies; British industry had not merely the British West Indian market but a far larger North American market that built up its own purchasing power by selling provisions throughout the Caribbean, to French, Dutch and even Spanish as well as to English colonies there. A great part of the earning power of the colonies of all the powers in America was gathered into the hands of British North American merchants; and they spent it in England because the Navigation Acts did not permit them to buy directly from the continent, and largely on English goods because (apart from linens) there were few continental goods that were worth shipping through England. Their imports were of every variety except coarse woollens. The colonies were of some limited importance to particular French industries; they were of vast importance to a whole range of English industries, and particularly to newly rising ones. Half the nails produced in England were said in mid-century to go to the colonies, and a great variety of other goods found markets there which were hardly less important to them than the English market, and growing far more rapidly.

The colonies were responsible for most of the expansion of English overseas trade during the middle decades of the eighteenth century, providing tobacco, sugar, rice and coffee for re-export, and the main expanding markets for exported manufactures. But English trade with Europe was sluggish, and in consequence the overall expansion of English trade in this period was slower than that of France. It rose in real terms, between 1715 and 1783, by some 140 per cent, whilst French trade rose by 200 per cent. This is accounted for in part by the more rapid growth of the French trade in colonial produce, as France captured the northern European market in the greatest of all colonial commodities, sugar, driving out the English product from the 1720s, and pioneering the trade in coffee that grew rapidly to large proportions. But the export of French manufactures grew as well, not in colonial markets but in Europe; and on the whole in the traditional lines of woollens and linens rather than the products of newer industries. The superiority of the Languedoc woollen industry recaptured Mediterranean markets for France; and the government exploited the new political friendship with Spain to help French industry loosen the English and Dutch grip on the Spanish market and become the biggest supplier of Spain and Spanish America. Some branches of the woollen and linen industries depended greatly on overseas demand; but beyond these France, lacking a big colonial market, built her industrial expansion largely on the growth of purchasing power at home.

To some extent this industrial advance, both in France and in England, was self-reinforcing, for it enabled costs to be lowered. Though there were advances in techniques, the main sources of productive economies were organizational change and the breaking up of operations into specialized tasks as the market expanded. This was the point seized on by Adam Smith to introduce *The Wealth of Nations*. Such economies were least possible in the great old-established woollen and linen industries; but even these were able for a time to lower costs by moving into low-wage areas of Scotland, Ireland and the north of England. In this century, however, other industries carried on by individual craftsmen or in small workshops were able to expand to the level that made a new division of labour possible; as in pin-making, watch-making, ornament- and button-making, pottery and many others; while some industries with more simple products became large enough to develop putting-out systems, as in chain- and nail-making.

There were some innovations of real importance. In textiles, the stocking frame that had been invented as far back as 1598 came into wide use only from the latter part of the seventeenth century; silk-throwing machinery was built on Italian lines in 1717; and Kay's flying shuttle, invented in 1733, came into use after 1750. Here and there expanding demand can be clearly seen causing shortages or difficulties in production that required a search for new methods to overcome them. The best-known example, that of the cotton industry, will be discussed later. A more general advance of this kind was made with the substitution of coal or coke for timber or charcoal as fuel for industrial heating processes. This change went back to the salt-pans of Elizabethan times, and was still being extended right into the eighteenth century, assisted in its later stages by the development of the coking process to provide fuel for breweries in the decades before 1700. Its final victories were being achieved with the coke smelting of pig iron in 1709 (though this process was not widely known until after 1740) and the puddling of wrought iron in 1781. The growing demand for coal was, in its turn, a powerful stimulus to the development of the steam engine. The expansion of the demand for coal, requiring the search for it at deeper levels, led to the wider use of the primitive Savery and Newcomen steam engines for pumping during the early decades of the eighteenth century. The attempt to make this complicated machine more efficient, as it came to be a common feature of the industrial scene, was brought to success by James Watt in a series of inventions from 1769, whose industrial significance became apparent in the 1780s.

Industrial innovation was more vigorously promoted and more readily accepted in England than in eighteenth-century France. The reasons for this are of a general nature whose relative importance is difficult to assess; associated with the general character of the two societies, they cannot be readily linked with individual innovations. We can only say that in a society where innovations were more common, the chance of a particular innovation being sought for were greater than elsewhere.

One obstacle to innovation was state regulation of industry. On the whole the regulation of industry by gilds and by direct government inspection remained important longer in France than in England; indeed it was given new life under Colbert when it was rapidly in decline in England. It is true that most important French industries were in the countryside, and many of them were hardly reached by regulation there; and that mounting criticism of gilds and government interference appeared in the 1750s, weakening the whole system, and turning into a violent reaction against regulation that led in 1776 to the suppression of the gilds. Nevertheless, the long persistence of gild and other privileges, with monopoly and occasional subsidy as the counterpart of inspection and regulation, may be thought to have created attitudes of caution in making changes and of unwillingness to venture into fields where unbridled competition might be encountered, that were long lasting and still had influence on the conduct of producers even when regulation was being dismantled at the instance of the more enterprising of them.

A second important feature was the survival in England, under considerable restrictions, of religious sects outside the state religion. In France the Huguenots were fiercely suppressed in the 1680s, and a Catholic uniformity imposed with great severity. Thereafter, no dissent was permitted except to a few individuals – chiefly financiers – whose services were required by the state; and Frenchmen were treated alike either as good Catholics or, if they strayed from the faith, as criminals to be punished. In England, however, the Revolution settlement of 1689 expressly permitted freedom of worship outside the Church of England. It was a limited tolerance, however. The dissenter could not enter a university or any profession; or be a Member of Parliament or of any public corporation, or public servant, without engaging in some deception. The normal educational and professional outlets for young men of prosperous family were therefore closed to the son of the dissenter who had made his fortune, large or small, in industry or trade. He might, of course, buy a landed estate; but this was to enter his son into a Church and Tory squirearchy that was likely to be uncongenial. Thus a large group of people found the exit from mercantile pursuits into gentility was closed to them. This exodus of the successful and their sons, the withdrawal of capital and the abandonment of painfully built-up business connections, had long had a debilitating effect on the commercial life of many countries, by contrast with Holland where it was little known. Now an important part of the English industrial and commercial classes was cut off from this exodus, if perhaps unwillingly. Moreover, like other groups conscious of their separateness from the majority and suffering from disabilities, they drew together to help each other, preferring their co-religionists in business and supporting them in times of trouble, so that their possibility of business success was enhanced. Finally, well-to-do Presbyterians or Baptists were unwilling to send their sons to the grammar schools that were all controlled by the Church of England; in the early eighteenth century they were setting up schools of their own – the 'dissenting academies' – and in these instruction was not confined to Latin and Greek but went into such practical subjects as book-keeping, surveying and modern languages. Dissent was strongest in northern and midland England, where industry was growing most rapidly, and an extraordinarily high proportion of known inventors, innovators and successful entrepreneurs of the later eighteenth century have been shown to be dissenters. Their peculiar social position had no French counterpart; and France was economically the worse for this.

Finally and even more generally, England had a more open society. Social classes did not mix freely, but above the level of the poorest they did mix a little. There could be interchange of experience, news and ideas between people from different social milieux; and a willingness of the rich, even among the landowners, to invest small parts of their resources in the business enterprises of men of lower rank, whom acquaintance had brought them to trust. The English innovator of modest means could look beyond the family for support for his enterprise, and any success achieved could draw a wider circle to an interest in industrial matters.

None of this explains the coming of the Industrial Revolution. Wealth was being accumulated more rapidly than before in England and France; but the capital needs of industry were small by comparison with those of improving agriculture and communications. Agricultural improvement was beginning to release labour from work on the land; but in England the chief result was to increase underemployment and hardship in the south, where there was no expansion of industrial employment; while in France improvement could not go very far without requiring a dangerous tampering with the rural social structure. None of the important industries that have been discussed above grew in a spectacular way during the first three-quarters of the eighteenth century. The innovations in metallurgy made in this period were vital to the extension of the Industrial Revolution in the next century; they played no part in instigating it. Expansion of this modest kind could have continued indefinitely in both countries – if France had finally solved its subsistence problem as England had done – had it not been for the appearance of a particular innovation, brought in because of economic necessity but achieving its extraordinary results for reasons that were partly non-economic. This innovation was, of course, the transformation of cotton-spinning technology. Once this transformation had taken place, the spreading of its effects through the economy and society owed much to the advances in the general level of wealth and in the sophistication of industrial organization that have been discussed above; but it was not dependent on them for its origin.

The Industrial Revolution had its immediate beginning in the cotton industry, which in the middle of the eighteenth century was small in England and rather larger in France. In France it started around 1700, and for some decades was very small, confined to Rouen and its suburbs. About 1730 it began to expand its production and spread out in search of labour into the Normandy countryside, and in the next half-century it overran most of Normandy and pushed farther to the west. Its early expansion was limited by the prohibition in France on the sale of printed textiles (a measure aimed at imported oriental cottons) and it found most of its early market overseas, in Germany, Flanders, the West Indies and especially Spain. The relaxation of this restriction in 1759 gave the industry an enormous stimulus, and it leapt forward during the following two decades; the very decades, in fact, when in the more slowly growing English cotton industry the great cotton-spinning inventions were being made and applied. Production of French cotton goods doubled between 1732 and 1766 and thereafter it expanded even faster. In England, a tiny cotton industry was actually stimulated into growth by legislation of 1700 which banned the import of certain kinds of Indian cottons, for English-produced imitations were able to replace some of them. The industry's sales were normally in the home market, though when Indian export was disorganized by war for a few years in mid-century, English-made cotton goods were sold in Africa. Its growth accelerated only in the mid-1760s after the Seven Years War, and the really rapid expansion that appeared in the early 1770s was under the first influence of the great spinning inventions, Hargreaves' jenny and Arkwright's water frame, both of which came into commercial use in 1768. Throughout this period, and on into the 1780s, the output of the French cotton industry remained greater than the English; why, therefore, did the decisive inventions take place in England?

The most familiar argument is that necessity required it; that scarcity and the resulting high cost of labour urgently called for labour-saving inventions; that wages were rising fast, and that the merchant-organizer was having to distribute his cotton for spinning over increasingly wide areas to get the work done. This is true, but it has no special application to the cotton industry, or to the English cotton industry by comparison with the French. Tiny though the cotton industry was by comparison with the major textile industries, in both France and England it was carried on in areas where other textiles made great demands for labour. In England, the Yorkshire woollen industry had pushed across the Lancashire border and was busy in the Rochdale area, competing with cotton for labour; and in Nottinghamshire and Derbyshire, the other centres of the cotton industry, cotton-and worsted-stocking-making were expanding rapidly. A general argument has been put forward that the greater poverty of the French peasantry offered a far larger labour reserve in the countryside than was available in England; and that it was a distinctively English labour bottleneck, unparalleled in France, that called forth mechanical inventions. But the area of the French cotton industry was Normandy, and there labour shortage, affecting agriculture as well as industry, had become pronounced from the time that cotton emerged as a substantial competitor with linen-manufacture; the master cotton-spinners pressed constantly westward in search of more spinning labour. Inventions were badly needed in both countries to economize increasingly expensive labour. They would have been much more valuable in the big woollen or linen industries than in cotton, but the technical difficulties of machine spinning were most easily overcome in cotton. Once mastered there, the techniques were gradually adapted to other textiles. But the reason why the improvements came in England rather than in France cannot satisfactorily be assigned to relative labour shortage.

It could be argued that no explanation is needed. The events that were decisive were two in number; the invention of the spinning jenny by Hargreaves, and of the water frame by Arkwright. (The use of later inventions all followed from the impulse given by these two.) These two isolated events may have been fortuitous; the chance of personalities and their good fortune in seeking along the right lines. But the economic historian instinctively recoils from such explanations. The safest thing to say, perhaps, is that although the need for innovation was strong in France as in England, French society offered a less congenial climate to innovation than did English, and that the accident of these innovations nevertheless being made in France rather than in England did not occur. More significant was the striking difference in the eagerness with which the inventions were exploited in the two countries. The English inventions were quickly known in France, but their competitive impact was weakened by the very heavy protection against English goods that French industry enjoyed, until the Eden Treaty of 1786 ended the long commercial war between the two countries. A handful of jennies and water frames were introduced into France – and under French influence into Catalonia – in the 1780s, but the French Revolution of 1789 and the prolonged wars that followed go some way to account for the slowness of subsequent change in French industry. Yet, to return to an often-repeated theme, the agricultural base of the French economy once more revealed, in the 1770s and 1780s, its inability to sustain prolonged growth. In 1600–30, in 1660–90, in 1730–70 – time after time bursts of expansion came to an end in slackening demand as purses were emptied on ever-dearer food. If the indications in the last of these periods are uncertain, it is largely because landlord pressure was engrossing commons, enclosing land for the plough and so pushing production a little further forward; but this landlord reaction fuelled a peasant discontent that was to burst out savagely in 1789. Perhaps it was now impossible for France to undergo its industrial before its political revolution.

Finally, why did the inventions in cotton spinning, the traditional fireside occupation of women, set in motion a revolutionary transformation first of the British and ultimately of the world economy? The inventions were made because a need to economize labour appeared, and an atmosphere favourable to invention brought forth the inventors. But the reason for the stupendous effects of the inventions cannot be found simply by looking at their origins. Necessity is only the *mother* of invention; what can actually be invented to meet economic pressures is determined by the technical possibilities. There were labour-saving innovations in metallurgy and pottery-making that had no such dramatic effects. The inventor who saves 10 or 20 per cent on the cost of producing an article has done well and may die rich; such were the early weaving inventions. But the inventions of Hargreaves and Arkwright produced their unique results because they practically annihilated labour costs in cotton spinning, reducing them by 90 per cent and more. In doing so, they destroyed cotton spinning by hand as fast as machines could be built to replace it; there could be no long-drawn-out agony of hand spinners competing with machines by accepting lower and lower wages, as happened in weaving half a century later. They reduced the price of cotton goods so rapidly that they transformed the market situation; cheap cottons flooded England and were bought as fast as they could be produced. The new machines easily produced ten times as much yarn in 1790 as they had done in 1770, and twenty times as much in 1802; in doing so they called for ten and twenty times the supply of raw cotton, and of weaving and bleaching – called for them so urgently that they brought inventiveness to bear to economize labour with the cotton gin, the power loom and the Berthollet process. The success of machine spinning opened the way for a search to modify the process to suit the still more important woollen spinning, and in the 1780s and 1790s the woollen industry, too, was being re-made. Inventions of such shattering efficiency led to a string of fresh invention, in a way that a modest improvement like the flying shuttle had never done, because they dislocated a long chain of integrated processes and focused attention on the glittering rewards of improving each single link in the chain.

The cotton-spinning inventions also brought about revolutionary social change. The early spinning jennies could be manually operated, but the later, larger ones, and the water frame from its inception, required water power. The most economical source of power, the water wheel, was wasted if it was used to run a handful of machines; it could set to work scores or preferably hundreds of machines working side by side, connected with their prime mover by shafting and belting. This required the factory, where hundreds of machines were operated by hundreds of employees, working regular hours to conform with the needs of the machinery. There had been no true factories before, with the possible exception of the Lombe silk-throwing establishments. But within less than two decades the tens of thousands of hand spinners scattered in the villages and towns of the Lancashire and Cheshire plain and in the Trent valley had been superseded by factory workers in a few score great buildings tucked away in the Pennine valleys where fast-flowing streams were dammed for water wheels. The image that this cotton-spinning success presented to the world was the factory image; it was the success of the factory that caught the imagination of industry, and the factory and its disciplined life for wage-earners that changed the life of society.

It has been argued that the role of cotton in the Industrial Revolution has been overstated in the past; that an industry accounting for only 7 per cent of gross national income in 1800 cannot bear the responsibility for Industrial Revolution. Many chapters of this book have emphasized the point that no country could advance very far industrially if its agricultural base was weak. This remained true in the age of the English Industrial Revolution; if British agriculture had not found means to double its production between 1780 and 1830, Englishmen would have starved, with incalculable consequences to industry. Agricultural expansion was the indispensable support of the Industrial Revolution, and it did more, in absolute terms, to raise British national income than anything else. But on the side of industry, cotton's achievement was remarkable even in terms of the statistics. It shot from being a minor industry in 1770, of less importance than woollens, metalwares, leather and a good many others, and with only some 0·5 per cent of national output to its credit, to head them all in 1800 with its share of 7 per cent. In 1770 its share of exports was negligible; in 1802 its share surpassed that of woollens, the leader for more than three centuries. At the latter date it accounted for nearly a third of all income arising from manufacturing, mining and building. The social effects are concealed in the statistics by the very success in cheapening cotton goods; behind the rise in total value of cotton manufactures compared with that of woollens was an immensely greater increase in yardage, which, as it exploded on the market, was sold ever more cheaply.

The real importance of the changes in the cotton industry, however, goes beyond the statistics: qualitative rather than quantitative change was seminal, chiefly through the stimulus given to innovation in other industries, first in competing textiles and then in metallurgy and engineering to meet the needs of the cotton mills for machinery, power and transport. Above all it was the example of what power machinery in factories could do to the productivity of an industry and the profits of those who first introduced it that brought imitation. Perhaps no other industry was able to make such great gains in mechanization; but the gains made throughout industry were real enough and are the foundations on which modern society is based.

Maps

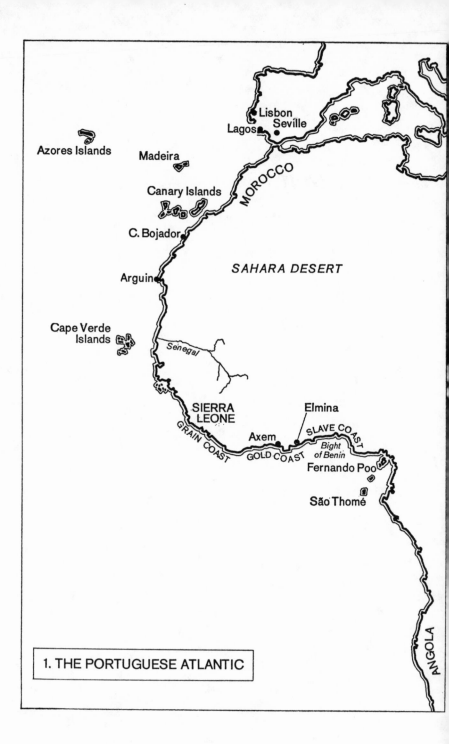

1. THE PORTUGUESE ATLANTIC

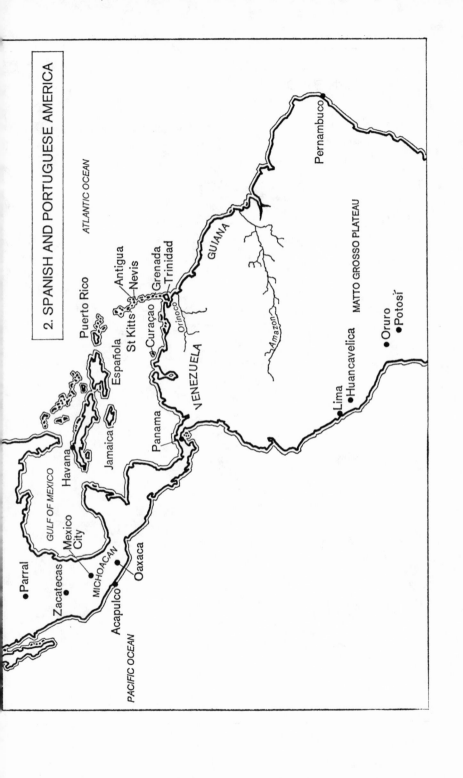

2. SPANISH AND PORTUGUESE AMERICA

ATLANTIC OCEAN

Pernambuco

Puerto Rico
Antigua
Nevis
St Kitts
Española
Grenada
Trinidad
Curaçao
GUIANA
Orinoco
Orinoco
VENEZUELA
Amazon
MATTO GROSSO PLATEAU
Huancavelica
Lima
Oruro
Potosí

Havana
Jamaica
Panama
GULF OF MEXICO
Mexico City
MICHOACAN
Oaxaca
Zacatecas
Parral
Acapulco
PACIFIC OCEAN

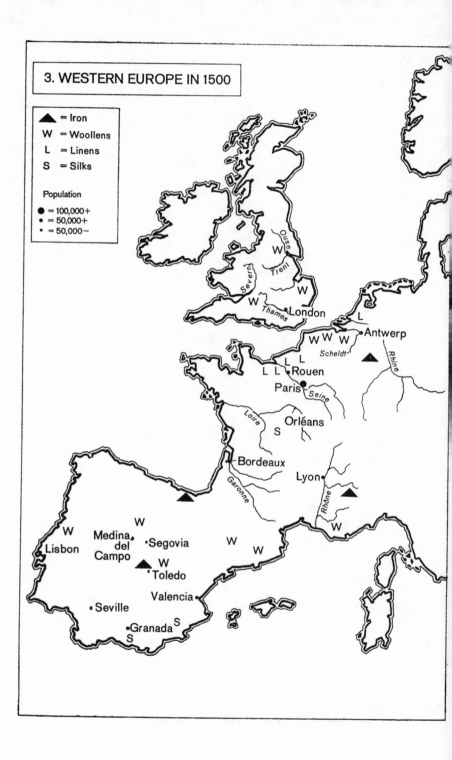

3. WESTERN EUROPE IN 1500

▲ = Iron
W = Woollens
L = Linens
S = Silks

Population
● = 100,000+
• = 50,000+
· = 50,000−

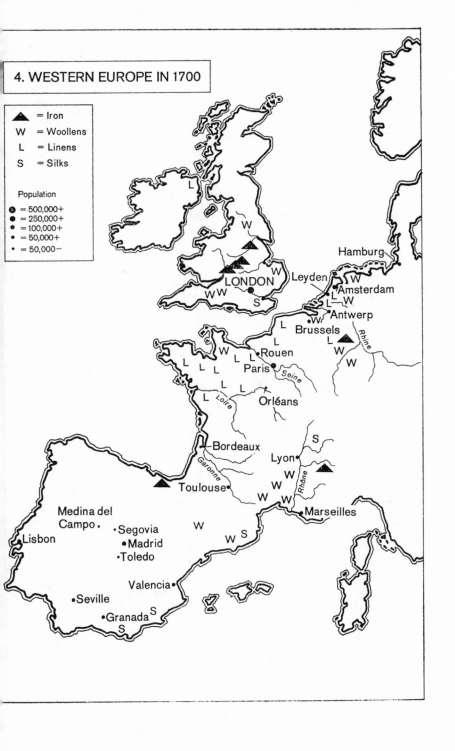

4. WESTERN EUROPE IN 1700

▲ = Iron
W = Woollens
L = Linens
S = Silks

Population
◕ = 500,000+
● = 250,000+
● = 100,000+
• = 50,000+
· = 50,000−

Hamburg
L
W
Leyden
Amsterdam
W
L W
LONDON
W W
Antwerp
S
W
Brussels
Rhine
L
W
Rouen
W
W L L
Paris
L L
Seine
L L
Orléans
L
Loire

Bordeaux
Lyon
S
Garonne
Rhône
W
Toulouse
W
W
W W
Marseilles

Medina del Campo
Segovia
W
Lisbon
Madrid
W S
Toledo
Valencia
Seville
Granada S
S

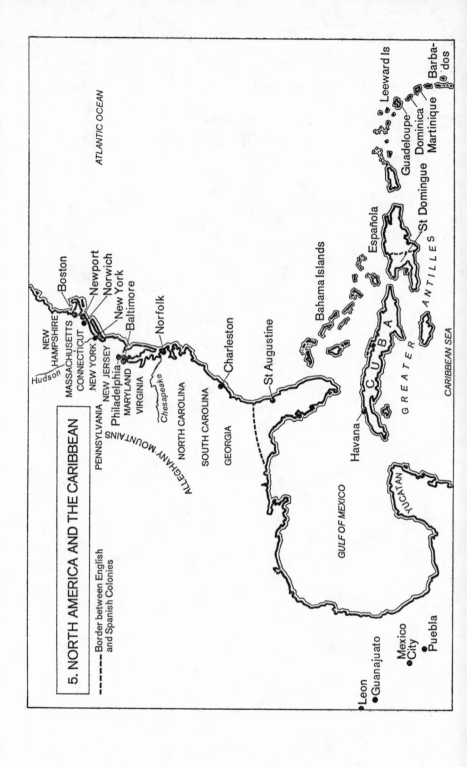

5. NORTH AMERICA AND THE CARIBBEAN

- - - - - Border between English and Spanish Colonies

ATLANTIC OCEAN

NEW HAMPSHIRE
MASSACHUSETTS
CONNECTICUT
Boston
Newport
Norwich
New York
Baltimore
NEW YORK
NEW JERSEY
Philadelphia
PENNSYLVANIA
MARYLAND
VIRGINIA
Norfolk
Chesapeake
Hudson
ALLEGHANY MOUNTAINS
NORTH CAROLINA
SOUTH CAROLINA
Charleston
GEORGIA
St Augustine

Bahama Islands

Española

St Domingue

Leeward Is
Guadeloupe
Dominica
Martinique
Barba-dos

GREATER ANTILLES

CUBA

Havana

CARIBBEAN SEA

GULF OF MEXICO

YUCATAN

Leon
Guanajuato
Mexico City
Puebla

Select Bibliography

The literature of the economic history of Britain, the Netherlands, France, Spain and Portugal is immense, and all I have attempted here is to list some works with which the interested reader may usefully supplement each chapter. On the whole I have listed books rather than articles, and works in English and French rather than in other languages, but occasionally I have had to go beyond these bounds to include important material. Extensive bibliographies will be found in the *Cambridge Economic History of Europe*, vols IV and VI (1967 and 1965) and in the many volumes of the fine French series, *Nouvelle Clio*, published in Paris under the general editorship of F. Boutrouche and P. Lemerle. Volumes in this series by Chaunu, Heers, Jeannin, Mandrou and Mauro are referred to in appropriate places below.

At the time of writing there is no modern, completed economic history of Europe or of western Europe on any large scale. In English the old work of H. Heaton, *Economic History of Europe* (London, 1936) still has much of value; S. B. Clough's *European Economic History* (New York, 1959) is less detailed, and E. Tuma's recent *European Economic History* (New York, 1971), though interesting in its approach, covers this period very thinly. J. Imbert, *Histoire Économique des Origines à 1789* (Paris, 1967) manages to pack a great deal into a short space. General works which are not specifically economic histories of the period, but which are closely concerned with subjects of this book, are F. Braudel's *Civilisation Matérielle et Capitalisme* (Paris, 1967; English translation, London, 1973), characteristically original in its approach and brilliant in its development of ideas; C. Verlinden, *Les Origines de la Civilisation Atlantique* (Neuchatel, 1966); and F. Mauro, *L'Expansion Européenne, 1600–1870* (Paris, 1964).

M

324

CHAPTER I: THE PORTUGUESE IN THE ATLANTIC

The background to fifteenth-century exploration is sketched, lucidly and elegantly, by J. H. Parry, *The Age of Reconnaissance* (London, 1963). The most thorough general survey is P. Chaunu, *L'Expansion Européenne du XIIIᵉ au XVᵉ Siècle* (Paris, 1969). M. Mollat and P. Adam have edited an important series of specialized essays on aspects of technique and finance in *Les Aspects Internationaux de la Découverte Océanique aux XVᵉ et XVIᵉ Siécles* (Paris, 1966). Q. de Fonseca, the authority on the development of the caravel, has a short work on the subject of this chapter, *Os Navios do Infante d. Henrique* (Coimbra, 1958). E. W. Bovill, *The Golden Trade of the Moors* (London, 1958) examines the trans-Sahara trade and the sources of the gold the Portuguese sought.

The most important specialized works on the economic history of Portugal and its Atlantic relations are V. M. Godinho, *A economía dos descobrimentos* (Lisbon, 1962) and his massive *L'Économie de l'Empire Portugais aux XVᵉ et XVIᵉ Siècles* (Paris, 1969). Godinho begins his work by sketching in the Portuguese background, as does C. de Lannoy in his still valuable *Histoire de l'Expansion Coloniale des Peuples Européens: Portugal* (Brussels, 1907). The basic general study of Portuguese exploration is J. Cortesão, *Os descrobrimentos Portugueses* (Lisbon, 1960); E. Prestage *The Portuguese Pioneers* (London, 1933) is a useful compilation of information. J. W. Blake, *Europeans in West Africa 1450–1560* (Hakluyt Society, London, 1941) is a collection of documents with a good introduction. The role of Prince Henry has been reassessed by P. E. Russell, *Prince Henry the Navigator* (London, 1960) and in the introduction to L. Bourdon's French translation of Azurara's *Chronique de Guinée* (Dakar, 1960). The early part of C. R. Boxer's excellent history of *The Portuguese Seaborne Empire* (London, 1969) deals with the period of the discoveries.

Duarte Pacheco Pereira *Esmeraldu de Situ Orbis,* referred to on p. 8, was published by the Hakluyt Society (London, 1937).

CHAPTER 2: WESTERN EUROPE: 1460–1560

The century between 1460 and 1560 has been much neglected by economic historians, the medievalists losing interest at its commencement, and the modernists taking up their pens from the mid-sixteenth century. It is hardly touched on in the *Cambridge Economic History of Europe,* except in F. Helleiner's stimulating section on population in Volume IV Cambridge, 1967). Nor is there a general survey in French, though

J. Heers, *L'Occident aux XIVe et XVe Siècles* (Paris, 1963) is a brilliant introduction to the period.

Much of the material listed in the bibliographies for chapters 6 and 7, below, is relevant to this period, and no attempt is made here at an extensive coverage of European economic history.

One of the great industries that emerged in the west at this time is examined by E. Coornaert, *La Draperie-sayetterie d'Hondschoote, XIVe – XVIIIe Siècles* (Paris, 1930) and 'Draperies rurales, draperies urbaines: l'évolution de l'industrie flamande au Moyen Age et au XVIe Siècle' (*Rev. Belge de Philologie et d'Histoire*, **28**, 1950); while H. Kellebenz examines the wider significance of rural industry in 'Industries rurales en Occident de la fin du Moyen Age au XVIIIe Siècle' (*Annales*, **18**, 1963). Two old but still valuable works on finance are R. Ehrenberg, *Das Zeitalter der Fugger,* (Jena, 1912); abridged English translation as *Capital and Finance in the Age of the Renaissance* (London, 1928); and M. Bresard, *Les Foires de Lyon* (Paris, 1914). Western Europe's relations with the Baltic are the subject of P. Dollinger's fine volume on *The German Hansa* (London, 1970), and M. Malowist 'Les Produits des pays de la Baltique dans le Commerce International au XVIe Siècle' (*Revue du Nord*, **42**, 1960) is an important discussion of relations between eastern and western Europe. The trade of western France is the subject of two books, M. Mollat, *Le Commerce Maritime Normand à la fin du Moyen Age* (Paris, 1930), and J. Touchard, *Le Commerce Maritime Breton à la fin du Moyen Age* (Paris, 1967).

There is a mass of modern work on Antwerp, but the best overall survey is to be found in two articles by J. A. Van Houtte, 'La Genèse du Grand Marché International d'Anvers à la fin du Moyen Age' (*Revue Belge de Philologie et d'Histoire*, **19**, 1940), and 'Anvers aux XVe et XVIe Siècles: Expansion et Apogée' (*Annales*, **16**, 1961). Among the more important detailed studies are E. Coornaert, *Les Français et le Commerce International d'Anvers* (Paris, 1961); J. de Smedt, *De Engelse Natie te Antwerpen in de 16e Eeuw* (Antwerp, 1954), and, for the Spanish and Portuguese connection in particular, J. A. Goris, *Étude sur les Colonies Marchandes Meridionales à Anvers 1488 à 1567* (Louvain, 1925). H. Van der Weee, *The Growth of the Antwerp Market and the European Economy* (Louvain, 1963) is a highly schematized survey giving particular attention to the fluctuations in Antwerp's fortunes.

CHAPTER 3: SPAIN IN AMERICA:
THE SIXTEENTH CENTURY

The most useful introductions are in J. H. Parry, *The Spanish Seaborne Empire* (London, 1966) and his contributions to volumes I to III of the *New Cambridge Modern History*, but B. W. Diffie's *Latin American Civilisation* (Harrisburg, Pa., 1947) contains much more economic detail, and C. H. Haring, *The Spanish Empire in America* (New York, 1947) has a mass of factual information. The most thoughtful modern work, however, is C. Gibson, *Spain in America* (New York, 1966), which takes a good deal of knowledge for granted and probes well below the surface of events. Many of the insights of A. G. Keller, *Colonization* (Boston, 1908) are still fresh and interesting. G. C. Vaillant, *The Aztecs of Mexico* (London, 1950) is an introduction to pre-Columbian society. H. and P. Chaunu's enormous work, *Seville et l'Atlantique* (Paris, 1955–60) is a mine of information on the geography, settlement and above all trade of the Indies. S. E. Morison, *Admiral of the Ocean Sea* (Boston, 1942) is outstandingly the best account of Columbus's work, and C. O. Sauer, *The Early Spanish Main* (Berkeley, 1960) is a splendid detailed discussion of the early decades in America, before the conquest of Mexico.

Much work has been done on early Mexican economic and social history, largely by Californian historians, but the remainder of Spanish America – even Peru – has been relatively neglected. The social relations between Spaniards and Indians and the settlement of rights over the soil are the subject of two fine works; F. Chevalier, *Land and Society in Colonial Mexico* (Berkeley, 1963), and L. B. Simpson, *The Encomienda in New Spain* (Berkeley, 1950), while L. Hanke examines some influences towards bettering the treatment of the Indians in *The Spanish Struggle for Justice in the Conquest of America* (Philadelphia, 1949). C. Gibson, *The Aztecs under Spanish Rule* (Oxford, 1964) is an exhaustive discussion of the social and economic organization in the valley of Mexico, before and after the Conquest. F. Benitez, *The Century after Cortes* (Chicago, 1965) presents a clear and detailed picture of the Spanish way of life in the New World. The fundamental works on Indian population are W. W. Borah and S. F. Cook, *The Aboriginal Population of Central Mexico on the Eve of the Spanish Conquest* (Berkeley, 1963), and *Indian Population of Central Mexico, 1531–1610* (Berkeley, 1960). A. W. Crosby 'Conquistador y Pestilencia' (*Hispanic American Hist. Rev.*, **47**, 1947) throws light on the process by which population was brought down. P. J. Bakewell, *Silver Mining and Society in Colonial Mexico* (Cambridge, 1971) is an outstanding work on the sixteenth century which goes on from silver mining into a wide-ranging discussion of the Mexican economy; and R. C. West, *The Mining Community in Northern New Spain: The Parral District* (Berkeley, 1949) examines the extension of mining to the far north in the early seventeenth century. Some special aspects of the Mexican economy are dealt with in W. Borah, *Silk Raising in Colonial Mexico* (Berkeley, 1943), R. L. Lee 'Cochineal Production and Trade in New Spain to 1600' (*The Americas,* 4, 1947), and W. L. Schurz, *The Manila Galleon* (New York, 1939) which is a careful examination of the trade of Mexico with the Philippines.

The beginnings of Peruvian mining are briefly examined in L. Hanke, *The Imperial City of Potosí* (The Hague, 1956), A. Jare, 'Dans le Pérou du XVIᵉ Siècle' (*Annales,* 22, 1967), and G. B. Cobb, 'Potosí, A South American Mining Frontier' (*Greater America, Essays in Honor of H. E. Bolton,* Berkeley, 1945). A. P. Whitaker, *The Huancavelica Mercury Mine* (Cambridge, Mass., 1941) discusses an essential material of the smelting process, and the influence of its supply difficulties on production. J. J. Parsons, *Antioqueño Colonisation in Western Colombia* (Berkeley, 1949) is a rare study of one of the minor Spanish colonies of the sixteenth century. G. Lohmann Villena, *Les Espinosa* (Paris, 1968) analyses the experience of a business house which played an important part in the early development of Panama and Peru.

CHAPTER 4: SIXTEENTH-CENTURY SPAIN

Chapters 1, 4 and 5 of J. Lynch, *Spain under the Habsburgs, I* (Oxford, 1965) provide a good summary of modern work on Spanish economic history, and J. H. Elliott, *Imperial Spain, 1469–1716* (London, 1963) has some valuable insights. F. Braudel, *La Méditerranée et le monde mediterranean a l'Epoque de Philippe II* (2nd and much revised edition, Paris, 1967) is a great general work which makes many penetrating observations on Spanish economy and society. J. Vicens Vives, *An Economic History of Spain* (Princeton, 1969) is a mine of information, and J. Gentil da Silva, *En Espagne,* attempts to bring statistics together to throw light on several historical problems. J. Van Klaveren, *Europaische Wirtschaftsgeschichte Spaniens im XVI und XVII Jahrhundert* (Stuttgart, 1960) is a brief general survey. R. Carande, *Carlos V y sus banqueros* (Madrid, 1943) is principally concerned with royal finances, but vol. I analyses the economic structure in the early sixteenth century.

A beginning has been made on the study of sixteenth-century agrarian history; two works which illuminate this and the structure of rural society are N. Salomon, *La Campagne de la Nouvelle Castille a la fin du XVIe* — *Siècle* (Paris, 1964) and B. Bennassar, *Valladolid au Siècle d'Or* (Paris, 1967), which examines the economy of the whole region around Valladolid. J. Klein, *The Mesta* (Cambridge, Mass., 1920) is a sound work which has been overused in interpreting Spanish economic development. A. Castillo, 'Population et Richesse en Castille durant la seconde moitié du XVIe Siècle' (*Annales*, 20, 1965) is an interesting discussion of incomes, based on tax returns. There is little specialized work on Spanish industry; R. S. Smith, *The Spanish Guild Merchant* (Durham, N. C., 1940) touches the periphery of the subject. H. Lapeyre's great work on Franco-Spanish trade, *Une Famille des Marchands; Les Ruiz* (Paris, 1955) illuminates a wide field of commercial and financial activity, as does, to a rather lesser extent, F. Ruiz Martin's long introduction to *Lettres Marchandes échangées entre Florence et Medina del Campo* (Paris, 1965). The Spanish-American trade is exhaustively examined by H. and P. Chaunu, *Seville et l'Atlantique* (Paris, 1955–60). Ruth Pike, *Enterprise and Adventure: the Genoese in Seville* (Ithaca, N.Y., 1966) is useful, but may give an exaggerated impression of the role of the Genoese in Spanish affairs. The basic work on the import of American silver to Spain, with a detailed exploration of all its economic implications, is E. J. Hamilton, *American Treasure and the Price Revolution in Spain* (Cambridge, Mass., 1934). In the course of four decades controversy has inevitably grown up around this work; a useful discussion of it in relation to Spain is J. Nadal, 'La Revolucion de los Precios espanoles en siglo XVI' (*Hispania*, 19, 1959).

R. Bishko, 'The Iberian Background of Latin American History' (*Hispanic American Hist. Rev.*, 56, 1956) is an excellent introduction to the literature at that time, and a brief but penetrating analysis of some themes drawn from it.

CHAPTER 5: WESTERN EUROPE AND THE ATLANTIC

There is an enormous literature on exploration and early colonization, from which I have listed only a few items specially relevant to the economic motivation and consequences, and the very earliest settlements. P. Chaunu, *Conquête et Exploitation des Nouveaux Mondes: XVIe Siècle* (Paris, 1969) is an excellent survey of the problems, with a large bibliography, and F. Mauro, *L'Expansion Européenne, 1600–1870* (Paris, 1964) touches on the subjects of this chapter. The most useful general works on early English and French colonizing enterprise, respectively, are C. M. Andrews, *The Colonial Period of American History* (New Haven, Conn., 1934–8) and C. A. Julien, *Les Débuts de l'Expansion et de la Colo-*

nisation Française (Paris, 1947). R. Mousnier, *Les Européens hors de l'Europe* (Paris, 1958) brings forward some stimulating ideas, and E. E. Rich's contribution to the *New Cambridge Modern History*, vol. I, is a useful compressed survey of the whole field.

Early English ventures in the Atlantic are examined by J. A. Williamson, *Hawkins of Plymouth* (London, 1949) and K. R. Andrews, *Elizabethan Privateering* (Cambridge, 1964); and G. B. Parks' fine work, *Richard Hakluyt and the English Voyages* (New York, 1928) evokes the intellectual atmosphere in which ideas of colonization developed. G. L. Jaray, *L'Empire Française en Amerique* (Paris, 1938) sketches the French background, and E. Sluiter 'Dutch Spanish Rivalry in the Caribbean Area' (*Hispanic American Hist. Rev.*, **49**, 1949) shows how favourable conditions for West Indian settlement were brought about.

A good brief introduction to the earliest colonies is E. E. Rich's chapter in *New Cambridge Modern History*, vol. IV. More specialized works on them are F. Rose-Troup, *The Massachusetts Bay Company and its Predecessors* (New York, 1930), G. M. Cell, *English Enterprise to Newfoundland, 1577–1660* (London, 1969) and H. A. Innis, *The Fur Trade in Canada* (Toronto, 1927) – this last a masterpiece in the identification of colonial economic problems. The earliest chapters of general economic histories of North America naturally cover this period; among them may be mentioned particularly C. P. Nettels, *The Roots of American Civilisation* (London, 1963); L. B. Wright, *The Colonial Civilisation of North America* (London, 1949); and H. G. J. Aitken and W. T. Easterbrook, *Canadian Economic History* (Toronto, 1963).

CHAPTER 6: THE SIXTEENTH AND SEVENTEENTH CENTURIES: POPULATION, PRICES AND INCOMES

R. Reinhard, A. Armengaud and J. Dupaquier, *Histoire Générale de la Population Mondiale* (Paris, 1968) is an excellent summary of the present state of knowledge, which considers each western country in some detail. R. Mols, *Introduction à la Demographie Historique des Villes d'Europe* (Louvain, 1956) discusses problems of evidence and methods. F. Helleiner's contribution to *Cambridge Economic History of Europe*, vol. IV (Cambridge, 1967) is shorter but clear and thoughtful. The work of T. H. Hollingsworth, *The Demography of the British Peerage* (London, 1964) raises questions as to the value of economic explanations of demographic change.

Modern discussion of long-term price movements begins with E. Hamilton's article, 'American Treasure and the Rise of Capitalism'

(*Economica*, **27**, 1929), and J. U. Nef's reply, 'Prices and Industrial Capitalism in France and England, 1540–1640' (*Econ Hist. Rev.*, **7**, 1937); and F. Simiand, *Recherches anciennes et nouvelles sur le mouvement général des prix de XVIᵉ au XIXᵉ siècle* (Paris, 1932). The most recent general survey is F. Braudel's and F. Spooner's contribution to *Cambridge Economic History of Europe*, vol. IV. Criticism of monetary explanations of the price revolution crystallized in E. H. Phelps-Brown and S. Hopkins, 'Wage Rates and Prices: Evidence for Population Pressure in the Sixteenth Century' (*Economica*, **24**, 1957) and 'Builders Wage Rates, Prices and Population' (*ibid*, **26**, 1959). A wider span of criticism is taken by P. Vilar, 'Problems of the Formation of Capitalism' (*Past & Present*, 1956) and M. Morineau, 'D'Amsterdam à Seville: de quelle realité l'histoire des prix est-elle le miroir?' (*Annales*, **23**, 1968). C. Verlinden, 'Mouvements des Prix et des Salaires en Belgique au XVIᵉ Siècle' (*Annales*, **10**, 1955) attributes them to such monetary influences as devaluation and the creation of paper substitutes rather than the influx of silver. For compilations of price data, see W. Beveridge, *Prices and Wages in England from the 12th to the 19th Century* (London, 1939); G. D'Avenel, *Histoire Economique de la Proprieté, des Salaires et de tous les Prix en général* (Paris, 1894–1926); E. Hamilton, *American Treasure and the Price Revolution in Spain, 1501–1650* (Cambridge, Mass., 1934); N. W. Posthumus, *Enquiry into the History of Prices in Holland* (Leiden, 1946–65); J. E. Thorold Rogers, *A History of Agriculture and Prices in England* (Oxford, 1866–1902); and C. Verlinden, *Dokumenten voor de Geschiednis van Prijzen en Lonen in Vlaanderen en Brabant, XV–XVIII Eeuw* (Bruges, 1959).

CHAPTER 7: AGRICULTURE IN THE SIXTEENTH AND
SEVENTEENTH CENTURIES

Agricultural history is generally written as part of national histories, and some references will be made in chapters on separate countries. However, B. H. Slicher van Bath, *The Agrarian History of Western Europe, 500–1850* (London, 1963) covers all countries with a collection of miscellaneous statistics and some useful commentary. On early agricultural improvement, his article on 'The Rise of Intensive Husbandry in the Low Countries' (E. H. Kossman and J. Bromley, eds, *Britain and the Netherlands*, vol. I, London, 1960) is important. Strong arguments for an early dating of agricultural improvement in England are presented by E. Kerridge, *The Agrarian Revolution* (London, 1967); more cautious approaches to English agricultural change are in J. Thirsk (ed.), *The Agrarian History of England and Wales*, vol. IV, (Cambridge, 1967) and

E. L. Jones 'English and European Agricultural Development' in R. M. Hartwell (ed.), *The Industrial Revolution* (Oxford, 1970). J. A. Faber discusses 'The Decline of the Baltic Grain Trade in the Second Half of the Seventeenth Century' in *Acta Historiae Neerlandica*, vol. I, (Leiden, 1966). Recent discussions of climatic history are G. Utterström, 'Climatic Fluctuations and Population Problems in Early Modern History' (*Scandinavian Econ. Hist. Rev.*, **3**, 1955), E. Le Roy Ladouire, 'Histoire et Climat' (*Annales*, **14**, 1959), and 'Climat et Recolte' (*ibid.*, **15**, 1960); H. H. Lamb, *The Changing Climate* (London, 1966) and H. Von Rudloff, *Die Schwankungen und Pendelungen des Klimas in Europa* (Braunschweig, 1967).

The thesis of the 'General Crisis of the Seventeenth Century' has its classical expositions in R. Mousnier, *Histoire Générale des Civilisations,* Vol. IV, *Les XVIe et XVIIe Siècles* (Paris, 1954) and E. Hobsbawm, 'The Crisis of the Seventeenth Century' (*Past and Present*, 1954). This concept of 'general crisis' underlies much modern French writing on economic history, and is notably given a new basis in H. and P. Chaunu's *Seville et l'Atlantique* (Paris, 1955–60), especially in the interpretative vol. VIII, and in H. Chaunu, 'Seville et la Belgique' (*Revue du Nord*, 1960). Attacks on some aspects of their arguments have been made by A. D. Lublinskaya, *French Absolutism: the Critical Phase, 1620–1629* (Cambridge, 1968) and I. Schoffer, 'Did Holland's Golden Age coincide with a Period of Crisis?' (*Acta Historiae Neerlandica,* I, Leiden, 1966). H. Kamen, *The Iron Century, 1550–1650* (London, 1971) is an interesting recent survey of the period, particularly useful for its insight into social pressures and class relationships.

CHAPTER 8: THE PEOPLING OF AMERICA

E. E. Rich's chapter in *Cambridge Economic History of Europe,* vol. IV (1967) is a useful general survey, though devoting much of its space to slavery. The general works on colonial history normally say something about migration. On colonial population, E. B. Greene and V. Harrington, *American Population before the Census of 1790* (New York, 1932) draws together a mass of information, but S. H. Sutherland, *Population Distribution in Colonial America* (New York, 1936) is more useful, providing a readable account of the course of population growth within different colonies, and of intercolonial movement. J. T. Bridenbaugh, *Vexed and Troubled Englishmen* (Oxford, 1968) examines the background of early English migration. The earliest chapters of M. L. Hansen, *The Atlantic Migration, 1607–1860* (Cambridge, Mass., 1940) cover the colonial period.

Specialist studies of indentured labour are A. E. Smith, *Colonists in Bondage* (Chapel Hill, N.C., 1947) and R. B. Morris, *Government and Labor in Early America* (New York, 1946); and for the French counterpart, G. Debien, *Les Engagées pour les Antilles* (Paris, 1952). G. Freyre, *The Masters and the Slaves* (New York, 1946), a general sociological survey of colonial Brazil, gives much attention to immigrants and their absorption. P. D. Curtin, *The Atlantic Slave Trade* (London, 1969) is a very thorough investigation of the size of this forced migration to the Americas; I have used his statistics for the table on p. 135. L. C. Vrijman, *Slavenhandlers en Slavenhandel* (Amsterdam, 1937) summarizes the history of the Dutch trade, and G. Martin's *Histoire de l'Esclavage dans les Colonies Françaises* (Paris, 1948) does the same for the French, though Martin's *Nantes au XVIIIᵉ Siècle: l'Ére des Negriers, 1714-44* (Paris, 1931) is a much better study of its more limited field. There is no corresponding work on the English slave trade, but the introductions to volumes of E. Donnan, *Documents Illustrative of the History of the Slave Trade to America* (Washington, 1931-5) will be found useful.

CHAPTER 9: SPAIN IN DECLINE

The works by Chaunu, Elliott, Lynch and Vicens Vives listed in chapter 4, remain useful. A. Dominguez Ortiz, *La Sociecad Espanola en el Siglo XVII* (Madrid, 1967) is much the best general survey of its period. Essays in the explanation of Spain's economic decline are E. Hamilton 'The Decline of Spain' (*Econ. Hist. Rev.*, 8, 1938); J. H. Elliott 'The Decline of Spain' (*Past and Present*, 1961); and, for the late seventeenth century, H. Kamen 'The Decline of Castile: the last Crisis' (*Econ. Hist. Rev.* 17, 1964). E. J. Hamilton's works, *War and Prices in Spain, 1651-1800* (Cambridge, Mass., 1947) and 'Money and Economic Recovery in Spain under the First Bourbons, 1701-46' (*Jnl. Mod. Hist.* 15, 1943) carry his explanation of Spanish economic fortunes into the eighteenth century. Among works of value on specific topics, M. Moret, *Aspects de la Societé Marchande de Seville au Début du XVIIᵉ Siècle*, gives its attention to trade with Europe as well as with America; and H. Kellenbenz, *Unternehmerkräfte im Hamburger Portugal-und-Spanien Handel 1590-1625* (Hamburg, 1954) shows the importance to Spain of its trading connections with northern Europe. J. Nadal and E. Giralt, *La Population Catalane de 1553 à 1717* (Paris, 1960) is a thorough exploitation of the evidence on this subject. G. Parker, *The Army of Flanders and the Spanish Road* (Cambridge, 1971) throws new light on the nature of the Spanish government's financial problems.

CHAPTER 10: LATIN AMERICA:
THE SEVENTEENTH AND EIGHTEENTH CENTURIES

The works by Chaunu, Diffie and Gibson, listed in chapter 3, remain useful for this period. W. W. Borah has an excellent brief survey of the seventeenth century in the *New Cambridge Modern History,* vol. IV (1970); his earlier work, *New Spain's Century of Depression* (Berkeley, 1951) is more detailed.

R. J. Morrissey, 'Colonial Agriculture in New Spain' (*Agricultural Hist.,* **31**, 1957) is a useful summary. An important general survey of the exploitation of previous metals is M. Bargallo, *La Minéria y la Metalurgica en la América* (Mexico City, 1955), which pays particular attention to technical advance. P. J. Bakewell's *Silver Mining and Society in Colonial Mexico* (Cambridge, 1971) contests the accepted presentations of a seventeenth-century depression in the Mexican economy; and D. A. Brading, *Miners and Merchants in Bourbon Mexico* (Cambridge, 1971) examines some aspects of the re-expansion of the mining industry in the eighteenth century. M. F. Lang considers the relationship of 'New Spain's Mining Depression and the Supply of Quicksilver from Peru' in *Hispanic American Hist. Rev.* (**68**, 1968). Apart from Chaunu, useful works on trade are W. Borah, *Early Colonial Trade Between Mexico and Peru* (Berkeley, 1944) and C. H. Haring, *Trade and Navigation between Spain and the Indies* (Cambridge, Mass., 1968), which is not wholly superseded by Chaunu's work.

For Brazil, B. W. Diffie, *Latin-American Civilisation* (Harrisburg, Pa., 1947) provides a good summary of early development. C. R. Boxer's works, *Salvador de Sá and the Struggle for Brazil and Angola, 1602–1686* (London, 1952), *The Dutch in Brazil* (Oxford, 1957) and *The Golden Age of Brazil, 1695–1750* (Oxford, 1962) all include detailed examination of internal economic development and economic rivalries. F. Mauro, *Le Portugal et l'Atlantique, 1570–1670* (Paris, 1960) is specially concerned with the Brazilian connection; and V. M. Godinho, 'Le Portugal: les Flottes de Sucre et les Flottes d'Or ,1670–1770' (*Annales,* **5**, 1950) concentrates on the critical change in the economic connection.

CHAPTER 11: THE RISE OF THE DUTCH
COMMERCIAL EMPIRE

Dutch economic history is thoroughly surveyed by specialists, in sections of *Algemene Geschiednis der Nederlanden,* vols. IV–VIII (Antwerp,

1949–55). The literature in languages other than Dutch is very scanty. A useful general study is C. R. Boxer, *The Dutch Seaborne Empire* (London, 1969). Early Dutch development is touched on in M. Postan's chapter in the Cambridge *Economic History of Europe*, vol. II (1952) and P. Dollinger, *The German Hansa* (London, 1970). V. Barbour, *Capitalism in Amsterdam in the Seventeenth Century* (Baltimore, 1950) contains much interesting material, and C. Wilson examines the 'Decline of the Netherlands' in *Econ. Hist. Rev.* (8, 1938). B. H. Slicher van Bath's 'Agriculture in the Low Countries, 1600–1800' (*Int. Congress of Historical Sciences,* Rome, 1955) supplements his work referred to in chapter 6; A. E. Christensen, *Dutch Trade to the Baltic about 1600* (The Hague, 1941) is an exhaustive survey of quantities of trade and methods of trading; and N. W. Posthumus, *Geschiednis van de Leidsche Lakenindustrie* (The Hague, 1933–9) is an excellent study of the branch of textile industry that came to prominence in the seventeenth century. J. C. Riermesma, *Religious Factors in Early Dutch Capitalism* (The Hague, 1967) analyses religious groupings and their relation to state policy and economic behaviour.

CHAPTER 12: ENGLAND: THE UNTROUBLED ISLAND

Three general surveys cover the sixteenth and seventeenth centuries: L. A. Clarkson, *The Pre-Industrial Economy in England, 1500–1750* (London, 1971); P. Ramsey, *Tudor Economic Problems* (London, 1963); and C. Wilson, *England's Apprenticeship 1600–1763* (London, 1965), which is altogether more detailed. P. Jeannin has surveyed the English experience from another standpoint in *L'Europe du Nord-Ouest et du Nord aux XVIIe et XVIIIe Siècles* (Paris, 1969). T. P. R. Laslett, *The World we have Lost* (London, 1965) is an original and useful examination of social trends, if at times it reads too much into limited evidence; and L. Stone, 'Social Mobility in England, 1500–1700' (*Past and Present*, 1966) is full of brilliant ideas that await investigation.

Agricultural history is exhaustively surveyed for its period by J. Thirsk (ed.), *The Agricultural History of England and Wales, Vol. IV, 1540–1640* (Cambridge, 1967), but E. Kerridge, *The Agricultural Revolution, 1570–1670* (London, 1967) presents an important new interpretation of the early history of agricultural improvement. P. Ramsey has edited a collection of essays on *The Price Revolution in Sixteenth Century England* (London, 1971).

Among a large number of histories of individual industries no single one covers the great woollen industry in its entirety; but the outstanding regional history, G. D. Ramsey's, *Wiltshire Woollen Industry in the Six-*

teenth and Seventeenth Centuries (Oxford, 1942) illuminates problems of
marketing and organization that were general. J. U. Nef's *The Rise of
the English Coal Industry* (London, 1932) is a solid study; and in *The Conquest of the Material World* (London, 1964) he has reprinted essays in
which he drew attention to rapid expansion among the minor industries
during the period 1540–1640. J. W. Gough, *The Rise of the Entrepreneur*
(London, 1969) summarizes the history of several industries.

G. D. Ramsay, *English Overseas Trade in the Centuries of Emergence*
(London, 1957) is an excellent general survey; several of the key essays
for modern interpretation are collected by W. E. Minchinton, *The
Growth of English Overseas Trade in the Seventeenth and Eighteenth Centuries*
(London, 1969), but the most important article deals with an earlier
period: it is F. J. Fisher's 'Commercial Trends and Policy in Sixteenth
Century England' (*Econ. Hist. Rev.*, 10, 1940). B. E. Supple, *Commercial
Crisis and Change, 1600–1640* (Cambridge, 1959) goes beyond a survey of
overseas trade to present an exceptionally lucid analysis of the relations
between commercial interest, economic thinking and economic policy,
and R. Davis, *The Rise of the English Shipping Industry in the Seventeenth
and Eighteenth Centuries* (London, 1962) relates overseas trade to problems
of transport. Works on banking and finance are listed in the bibliography
to chapter 14, but P. G. M. Dickson's fine study of the government
debt, *The Financial Revolution in England* (London, 1967) deserves mention
here.

E. M. Carus-Wilson (ed.), *Essays in Economic History*, vols. I and II
(London, 1954 and 1962) has collected many of the most useful articles
written in the past half-century.

CHAPTER 13: FRANCE: THE UNSTEADY GIANT

The new *Histoire Économique et Sociale de la France,* ed. F. Braudel and
E. Labrousse, provides in vol. II (Paris, 1970) a set of magisterial surveys
of the period 1660–1789 that makes further bibliography almost super-
fluous. However, another useful general volume is the special issue of the
journal *Dix-Septième Siècle* (70–1, 1966) devoted to economic history.
The great strength of French economic history is in its regional studies;
they are too numerous to be fully listed, but those particularly useful for
this period include P. Goubert's masterpiece, *Beauvais et le Beauvaisis de
1600 à 1730* (Paris, 1960); M. Venard, *Bourgeois et Paysans au XVIIe
Siècle; le Role des Bourgeois Parisiens dans la Vie Agricole au sud de Paris*
(Paris, 1957); E. Le Roy Ladurie, *Les Paysans de Languedoc* (Paris, 1966);
R. Baehrel, *Une Croissance: la Baisse Provence rurale (fin du XVIe Siècle –*

1789) (Paris, 1961); and A. Zink, *Azereix: la Vie d'une Communauté Rurale à la fin du XVII Siècle* (Paris, 1969). Little more need be said about agriculture, but J. Jacquart's contribution to *Dix-Septième Siècle (supra)* is useful and brief. J. C. Toutain has attempted to construct a statistical account of the growth of agricultural production in *Le Produit de l'Agriculture Française de 1700 à 1958* (Paris, 1958); it is severely criticized by E. Le Roy Ladurie, 'Les Comptes Fantastiques de Gregory King' (*Annales*, **23**, 1963).

Industrial history is much less satisfactorily covered. H. Lapeyre, *Une Famille des Marchands: Les Ruiz* (Paris, 1955) has a good account of the sixteenth-century linen industry; P. Deyon contributes a useful section on industry in *Dix-Septième Siècle (supra)*, and his *Amiens: Capitale Provinciale* (Paris, 1967) deals with an important cloth-making centre. W. C. Scoville, *The Persecution of the Huguenots and French Economic Development, 1680–1720* (Berkeley, 1960) examines several branches of industry, and P. Leon, *La Naissance de la Grande Industrie en Dauphiné* (Paris, 1953) is a good study of metallurgy. J. Delumeau has a summary of overseas trade in *Dix-Septième Siècle (supra)*; beyond this the reader should go to the histories of ports, such as R. Boutrouche, *Histoire de Bordeaux, 1453–1715* (Bordeaux, 1966); G. Rambert, *Histoire du Commerce de Marseille* (vols IV–VI, Marseille, 1954–7); and M. Trocmé and M. Delafosse, *Le Commerce Rochelais de la Fin du XVᵉ au Début du XVIIIᵉ Siècle* (Paris, 1952). C. W. Cole's *Colbert and a Century of French Mercantilism* (New York, 1939) examines the commercial policies of governments during the saventeenth century.

CHAPTER 14: CAPITAL, CREDIT AND FINANCIAL INSTITUTIONS

Sixteenth-century exchange and banking, and the role of exchange fairs, are examined in M. Vigne, *La Banque à Lyon* (Lyon, 1903) and D. Gioffré, *Gênes et les Foires de Change: de Lyon a Besançon* (Paris, 1960), while R. Ehrenberg elucidates the emerging role of Antwerp in *Capital and Finance in the Age of the Renaissance* (London, 1928). The working of the exchange system is illustrated in M. Lapeyre, *Une Famille des Marchands: les Ruiz* (Paris, 1955) and F. Ruiz Martin, *Lettres Marchandes echangées entre Florence et Medina del Campo* (Paris, 1965).

R. de Roover, *L'Évolution de la lettre de change* (Paris, 1953) is the standard work; J. M. Holden, *History of Negotiable Instruments in English Law* (London, 1955) explains how the favourable legal situation facilitated their proliferation in eighteenth-century England. H. Van der

Wee, 'Anvers et les Innovations de la Technique Financière aux XVIᵉ et XVIIᵉ Siècles' (*Annales*, **22**, 1967) shows some differences from de Roover's conclusions. A. P. Usher, 'The Primitive Bank of Deposit, 1200–1600' (*Econ. Hist. Rev.*, **4**, 1934) leads towards modern banking; J. G. Van Dillen, *History of the Principal Public Banks* (The Hague, 1934) has a chapter on each of them. Different aspects of banking development in England, the country where it progressed farthest by the eighteenth century, are examined by R. D. Richards, *The Early History of Banking in England* (London, 1929), D. M. Joslin, 'London Private Bankers, 1720–1785' (*Econ. Hist. Rev.*, **7**, 1954), and J. H. Clapham, *The Bank of England* (Cambridge, 1944). The institutions discussed in H. Lüthy, *La Banque Protestante en France* (Paris, 1959) were largely concerned with public finance, but there is a useful discussion of French banking in Braudel and Labrousse (see chapter 13). Institutions of public debt are further examined in R. Carande, *Carlos V y sus Banqueros* (Madrid, 1943–9); B. Schnapper, *Les Rentes au XVIᵉ Siècle: Histoire d'un Instrument du Credit* (Paris, 1958); and P. G. M. Dickson, *The Financial Revolution in England* (London, 1967).

A long historical controversy on the growing importance of bills of exchange in multilateral trade in the seventeenth century is summed up by J. M. Price, 'Multilateralism and/or Bilateralism' (*Econ. Hist. Rev.*, **14**, 1961), and S.-E. Åström, *From Cloth to Iron: The Anglo-Baltic Trade in the late Seventeenth Century* (Helsingfors, 1963). S. Homer's *History of Interest Rates* (New Brunswick, N.J., 1962) throws much light on relative scarcity of capital.

CHAPTER 15: THE TROPICAL COLONIES IN AMERICA

R. Pares, *Merchants and Planters* (Cambridge, 1960) is the best general discussion of the problems of the sugar planters, and his *A West India Fortune* (London, 1956) illustrates them from the long experience of a single family in Nevis. L. J. Ragatz, *The Fall of the Planter Class in the British Caribbean* (New York, 1928) examines, and perhaps overstates, their difficulties in the eighteenth century. N. Deerr's *History of Sugar* (London, 1950) is wide-ranging and makes possible comparisons between sugar-producing areas.

R. B. Sheridan has a valuable economic survey of all the West Indian colonies of the powers in *Chapters in Caribbean History* (London, 1970). On the particular colonies, useful works are F. W. Pitman, *The Development of the British West Indies, 1700–1763* (New Haven, 1917); L. Dermigny, 'St. Domingue aux 17ᵉ et 18ᵉ Siècles' (*Rev. Historique*, **204**, 1950)

338

(which summarizes scattered and inaccessible works of G. Debien);
L. P. May, *Histoire Economique de la Martinique, 1635–1763* (Paris, 1930);
C. R. Boxer. *The Dutch in Brazil, 1624–1654* (Oxford, 1957); and F.
Mauro, *Le Portugal et l'Atlantique au XVIIᵉ Siècle, 1570–1670* (Paris,
1960).

CHAPTER 16: THE BRITISH MAINLAND COLONIES

The economic history of colonial America, which attracted much attention in the early part of this century, has been relatively neglected in
recent years, and many gaps remain unfilled, while much good work is
confined to particular colonies, and is therefore of too narrow an interest
to be listed here. L. H. Gipson's monumental *The British Empire before
the American Revolution* (vols II and III, New York, 1960) includes
detailed description of the economic activity of the different colonies in
the middle of the eighteenth century. The most useful general history is
C. P. Nettels, *The Roots of American Civilisation* (London, 1963); S. C.
Bruchey, *The Roots of American Economic Growth, 1607–1861* (London,
1965) is slight but has some stimulating ideas. Useful regional studies are
P. A. Bruce, *Economic History of Virginia in the Seventeenth Century* (New
York, 1907), W. B. Weeden, *Economic and Social History of New England,
1620–1789* (New York, 1890); and D. E. Leach, *The Northern Colonial
Frontier* (New York, 1966).

L. C. Gray, *History of Agriculture in the Southern United States to 1860*
(New York, 1941) is comprehensive. M. Harris has a wide-ranging discussion of *The Origins of Land Tenure in the United States* (Ames, Iowa,
1953). The recent detailed analysis of the land history of a small community, P. J. Greven's *Four Generations: Population, Land and Family in
Colonial Andover, Mass.* (London, 1970) is extremely valuable and poses
new questions. Important discussions of colonial markets are J. M.
Price, 'Economic Growth of the Chesapeake and the European Market,
1697–1775' (*Jnl. Econ. Hist.*, **24**, 1964) on tobacco, and W. Sachs,
'Agricultural Conditions in the Colonies before the Revolution' (*Jnl.
Econ. Hist.*, **13**, 1953) on food supply to the towns. Two excellent volumes
on town growth and economic activity, by C. Bridenbaugh, are *Cities in
the Wilderness* (New York, 1960) and, especially, *Cities in Revolt, 1743–1776*
(New York, 1955). V. S. Clark's *History of Manufactures in the United
States of America* (Washington, 1929) covers the colonial period in vol. I.
There is no good general study of trade from the colonial end. R. Davis,
'English Foreign Trade 1700–1774' (*Econ. Hist. Rev.*, **15**, 1962) sketches
the structure of colonial trade and its impact on Britain. Much illumi-

nation can be obtained from the histories of individual business houses, such as J. B. Hedges, *The Browns of Providence Plantations* (Cambridge, Mass., 1952), P. L. White, *Beekmans of New York* (New York, 1956), and B. Fairchild, *Messrs. William Pepperell* (Ithaca, N.Y., 1954). The West Indian trading connection is discussed in R. Pares, *Yankees and Creoles* (London, 1956). The effect of British legislation on American trade and industry is the subject of O. M. Dickerson, *The Navigation Acts and the American Revolution* (Philadelphia, 1951), and recent controversy on the overall economic effects of the Navigation Acts is summarized in G. M. Walton, 'The New Economic History and the Burdens of the Navigation Acts' (*Econ. Hist. Rev.*, **24**. 1971).

CHAPTER 17: FRANCE AND ENGLAND IN THE
EIGHTEENTH CENTURY
CHAPTER 18: FRANCE AND ENGLAND: INDUSTRIAL
GROWTH AND INDUSTRIAL REVOLUTION

In England, the century before the Industrial Revolution has always attracted the interest of economic historians, and the literature is very extensive; in France, however, it has received less attention than the two preceding centuries. The best overall discussion, for France, is again F. Braudel and E. Labrousse (eds.), *Histoire Économique et Sociale de la France,* vol. II (Paris, 1970). R. Mandrou, *La France aux XVIIe et XVIIIe Siècles* (Paris, 1970) is also useful. Good general works for England are T. S. Ashton, *The Eighteenth Century* (London, 1955) and *Economic Fluctuations in England, 1700–1800* (Oxford, 1959); and C. Wilson, *England's Apprenticeship, 1600–1763* (London, 1965). This century has attracted some statistical studies, notably the earlier sections of P. Deane and W. A. Cole, *British Economic Growth 1688–1959* (Cambridge, 1967); J. Marczewski, 'Some Aspects of the Economic Growth of France, 1660–1958' (*Economic Development and Cultural Change,* 1961); and P. Léon, 'L'Industrialisation en France en tant que facteur de Croissance Économique du Début de XVIIIe Siècle a nos jours' (*Int. Conference of Economic History, Stockholm,* 1960). D. V. Glass and D. E. C. Eversley, *Population in History* (London, 1965) reprint a number of important essays on English and French demographic history.

Turning to specific sectors, English agricultural history is summarized by J. D. Chambers and G. E. Mingay, *The Agricultural Revolution in England, 1750–1880* (London, 1956), and E. L. Jones has collected a number of important recent articles in *Agriculture and Economic Growth in England, 1650–1815* (London, 1967). The background of change in the

N

cotton industry is examined in great detail by A. P. Wadsworth and J. de L. Mann, *The Cotton Trade and Industrial Lancashire, 1600–1780* (Manchester, 1931), while S. D. Chapman's more recent *The Early Factory Masters* (Newton Abbot, 1967) has demonstrated the importance of its north-midland origins. R. G. Wilson, *Gentlemen Merchants, 1700–1830* (Manchester, 1971) shows how the forms of relationship between merchants and producers in Yorkshire fostered the concentration of the woollen industry there during the eighteenth century. The best study of the metal industries is W. H. B. Court, *The Rise of the Midland Industries* (Oxford, 1938). R. Davis, 'English Foreign Trade, 1700–1774' (*Econ. Hist. Rev.*, **15**, 1962) analyses the statistics and discusses their implications.

E. Labrousse, *La crise de l'Économique Française à la fin de l'Ancien Régime et au Début de la Révolution* (Paris, 1944) is a superb analysis of the agricultural economy. For French industry, the works referred to in chapter 13 remain useful, and may be supplemented by P. Dardel, *Commerce, Industrie et Navigation à Rouen et au Havre, au XVIIIᵉ Siècle* (Rouen, 1966), B. Gille, *Les Origines de la Grande Métallurgie en France* (Paris, 1947), and T. J. Markovitch, 'L'Industrie Lainière Française au Début du XVIIIᵉ Siècle' (*Rev. d'Histoire Econ. et Sociale*, **46**, 1968). Volume IV of F. Lacour-Gayet (ed.), *Histoire du Commerce* (Paris, 1951) is a useful discussion.

There are innumerable works on the Industrial Revolution in England, most of which give a good deal of attention to the earlier background which is the subject of these chapters. Outstanding among them are P. Mantoux's classic *The Industrial Revolution of the Eighteenth Century* (London, 1928), D. Landes' penetrating analysis in his chapter of the *Cambridge Economic History of Europe*, vol. VI (1965), and P. Mathias, *The First Industrial Nation* (London, 1969), which is the best of the modern textbooks. A. E. Musson and E. Robinson, *Science and Technology in the Industrial Revolution* (Manchester, 1969) includes much interesting material. The final chapter owes much to F. Crouzet's fine study, 'Angleterre et France au XVIIIᵉ Siècle: Analyse Comparée de Deux Croissances Économiques' (*Annales*, **21**, 1966), which stimulated me to much thought, if in the end to some disagreement.

Index

Acapulco, 162
Aegean Sea, 9
Africa, 1–14 *passim*, 50, 65, 75, 96, 136–7, 148, 167, 169, 185, 206, 209, 242, 274, 311
Agrarian History of England and Wales, 1540–1640, 195
agriculture, 108–24 *passim*
Aix-en-Provence, 111
Albany, 272, 275
Alcabala, 68, 70–2
Algarve, 3, 10
Alleghany, 272, 278–9
Almadén, 51
Alva, 76–8
Amazon, 172–4
America, xiii, 11–12, 37, 39–43, 45–7, 50, 54, 60, 62–5, 67, 77, 80, 88, 90, 96, 100, 160, 165–7, 172, 180, 184–5, 191–2, 208, 235, 250–63 *passim*, 288; discovery of, xii, 12, 15, 73–5, 77, 87; colonization of, 81, 84–6, 125–42 *passim*; English, xi, 86, 125–42 *passim*, 172, 264–87 *passim*, 288; French, 125–42 *passim*; Latin, 37–55 *passim*, 157–75 *passim*; North, xi, xiii, 80, 82–3, 125–42 *passim*, 168, 172, 184, 243, 264–87 *passim*, 303, 306; Portuguese, 125; *see also* Brazil; South, xi, 37–55 *passim*, 38, 87,

135; Spanish, xi, xiv, 36, 37–55 *passim*, 57, 59, 62–5, 67–70, 72, 206, 226, 307; United States of, ix, xi; revolution, 251, 264, 266, 268, 273, 277–80, 282, 285–6; Declaration of Independence, 288
Amsterdam, 31, 34, 90; population, 94, 96, 118, 178–83, 186–90, 192–3, 206, 235, 243, 246–7, 256
Amsterdam, Bank of, 179, 185, 246–9
Anatolia, 9–10
Andalusia, 10, 18–19, 56–7, 59–60, 63–4, 67, 71, 148, 231
Andes, 38, 53, 55, 162, 170–1
Angola, 136–7, 185
Anjou, 220, 222, 225
Antigua, 133, 253
Antwerp, 21, 26–36, 64, 68, 76, 78–9; population, 94, 97, 105, 176–9, 183, 188, 190, 206–8, 224–5, 240, 243, 247
Arabia, 261
Aragon, 14, 56–7, 60, 62, 66, 124, 143, 155
Arequipa, 53
Arguim, 6, 8
Arica, 53
Arkwright's water-frame, 312–14
Armada, 155

Armentières, 30
Asia, 9, 26, 65, 75, 77, 79, 84–5,
    96–7, 185, 192, 206–8, 241
Asturias, 66, 153
Atahualpa, 41
Atlantic, 57, 63–4, 78, 80, 130, 162,
    168, 183, 185, 193, 207, 222,
    226–7, 270, 283–4, 294; economy,
    xiii, 37; and Portugal, 1–14
    passim; islands, 2–3, 7, 10, 29,
    136, 172, 272; and Western
    Europe, 73–87 *passim*; and Spain,
    90, 144, 148, 153–4
Austria, 138
Auxerre, 227
Avalon peninsula, 82
Aveiro, 28
Avila, 44
Axim, 185
Azores, 4–5, 9–10, 75
Aztecs, *see under* Mexico

Bahamas, 44
Bahia, 173, 175, 235, 256
Balkans, 9
Baltic, 18–19, 28, 30–3, 59, 79, 90,
    110, 116, 176, 184–6, 191–2, 216,
    235–6, 243; trade, xiv, 26, 118,
    177–8, 180, 182–3, 190, 207–8,
    222, 225–6
Baltimore, 267–8, 278, 283
Banque Royale, 248
Barbados, 84–5, 126–7, 132–3,
    136–7, 252–6, 258, 262–3, 284
Barcelona, 3, 33, 56–7, 69, 170
Basque, 18, 51, 63, 66, 153
Bayonne, 226
Beaune, 227
Beauvais, 221, 234
Benin, 8
Bergen-op-Zoom, 34
Berkshire, 203
Berry, 304
Berthollet process, 314
bibliography, xiv, 323–40
Bickford, Peter, 258
Bight of Benin, 136
Bight of Biafra, 7, 9
Bilbao, 56–7, 61

bills of exchange, 27, 242–9, 263,
    266, 276, 283–4
Birmingham, 205, 294, 303
Biscay, 62, 76, 225
Black Death, 3, 16, 54, 91, 93
Black Sea, 9–10
Bolivia, 55, 162
Bonny river, 8
book-keeping, 27
Bordeaux, 28, 225; blockade, 225,
    229
Boston, 271–6, 279, 282–3
boucaniers, 169
Bourbon, 156
Brabant, 31–2, 99, 176, 232
Brazil, xiii, 10, 12, 73–5, 80, 82, 95,
    109, 125, 132, 134–7, 139, 141–2,
    170–5, 184–5, 192, 207–8, 251–6,
    258–62
Bremen, 177, 181
Bridgewater Canal, 294
Brill, 178
Bristol, 75, 79, 130, 276–9
Britain, ix, 83, 193, 255, 258,
    260–2, 288–300 *passim*, 301–16
    passim; in America, 264–87
    passim; Molasses Act, 285;
    Currency Act, 279, 281, 286; *see
    also* England
Brittany, 29, 217, 220, 222, 225
Bruges, 26–8, 30–5, 64, 176, 178,
    242
Brussels, 94
bubonic plague, 95
buccaneers, 255
Buenos Ayres, 53, 158, 162, 170–1,
    256, 262
Burgos, 58, 64; Laws of, 166, 242–3
Burgundy, 213, 223, 294
Buriticá, 158
Byzantine Empire, 9

caballeros, 151
Cabot, John, 75
Cabral, 11
Cadiz, 13, 34, 57, 63–4, 235
Cairo, 9, 34
Calabria, 10
California, 42

Calvinism, 178-9, 187-9
Cambridge, 111
Cambridge, University of, ix
Campeche, 161
Canada, 83, 142, 270, 272, 275, 284
Canal des Deux Mers, 295
Canary Islands, 1, 4, 10, 13, 45, 64, 75, 251; discovery of, 2; conquest of, 43
Cantabrian, 57, 60-1, 67, 95, 124
Cape Bojador, 5-6
Cape Branco, 6
Cape Breton, 82
Cape Cod, 270
Cape Horn, 171
Cape of Good Hope, 11, 13, 242
Cape Verde Islands, 9
capital, 16, 20, 22, 107, 121, 183, 190, 193, 209, 220, 231-49 *passim*, 257, 261-2, 269, 279, 282, 309-10
capitalist, 20-1, 24, 26, 102, 161, 173, 187-8, 197, 219, 224, 231-4, 293, 296-7
Caracas Company, 238
caravel, 6
Caribbean Islands, xiii, 12, 37-8, 40, 55, 63, 73-4, 77, 80, 82, 87, 125-6, 135, 137, 142, 158, 166, 168-72, 184, 251-2, 254, 256, 273, 276, 283-5, 306
Carolina, 131, 133-6, 260, 268, 271, 274, 276-8, 281, 285
Cartagena, 162
cartography, 27
casa de contratación, 63, 75
Castile, 3, 7, 9, 13-14, 17-18, 20, 23, 27, 37, 39-43, 56-68, 72, 90, 95, 100, 117, 124, 143-4, 147-50, 152, 155-6, 171, 211, 212, 218, 225
Catalans, 2, 27
Catalonia, 56-7, 66, 95, 143, 148, 155-6, 225, 313
Cateau-Cambrésis, Treaty of, 88
Catholic, 65, 77, 80, 139, 179, 188-9, 209-10, 214, 309
Cayman Islands, 284
Champagne, 220, 222, 304
Charcas, 51

Charles I (England), 209-10
Charles II (England), 139, 210
Charles V (Spain), 35, 44, 48, 56, 64-9, 97-8, 147
Charleston, 268, 278, 282
Chesapeake Bay, 81, 86, 235, 264, 266
Cheshire, 200, 303, 315
Chester, 293
Chichimecs, 50-1
Chile, 38, 162, 171
China, 158, 161-2, 204
Christian, 1, 13, 40, 43, 57, 60, 65, 151
Church, 44, 48-9, 57, 68, 71, 125, 149, 164-5, 167-8, 188, 196, 278, 309
Church of England, 210, 309-10
climate, xii, xiii, 110-11, 122-4, 126, 139, 149-50, 215, 228, 291-2
Colbert, 212, 221-4, 226, 294, 309
Cologne, 28, 32, 183
Columbus, Christopher, xii, 11-14, 15, 37, 40-1, 54, 64, 73, 82, 125
colonization, 63, 73-87 *passim*, 126, 139-41, 175, 270
Columbia, 42, 50, 135, 158, 168, 170-1
Comuneros, 65
Congo, 136-7
Connecticut, 269, 273, 275
Constantinople, 2, 9-10
conversos, 60, 62
copyhold, 196, 198-9
Cordoba, 61-2, 170
corn, xiv, 3, 7, 17-20, 71, 111, 113-19, 122, 129, 152, 177, 182-3, 186, 190, 199-201, 215-19, 225, 227-9, 266, 282, 290-300
Cortes, Hernan, 37, 39-42, 44, 46, 54, 73
Cortes, the, 66, 69, 72, 98
cotton, 133, 170, 173, 175, 252-4, 256, 261-3, 303, 308, 311-16; cotton gin, 314
Council for Foreign Plantations (English), 132
Covilha, Pedro de, 11
Cracow, 32

credit trading, 27, 231–49 *passim*
Corbie, 67
Cuba, 37, 40, 42, 44, 135, 170, 252, 254–7, 260
Cunningham, William, ix
Curaçao, 169–70, 184–5
Cuzco, 39

Danish Exchange Bank, 248
Danzig, 19, 25, 177, 179, 181
Darby's process, 303
Dauphiné, 216, 220, 223, 233
Dee, 293
Delaware. 137, 275
Delft, 30, 178, 186–7
Denmark, 186
Derbyshire, 303, 312
Devon, 203–4, 301
diamonds, 174–5
Diaz, Bartholomew, 11–13
Dominica, 133, 251, 256, 261
Dorchester, 87
Dordrecht, 32, 34, 178, 187
Dublin Pale, 80
Dutch, 28–32, 34, 62, 67, 76–82, 86–7, 89–91, 96–7, 99, 105, 107, 113, 132, 143, 147, 153, 155, 159, 168–70, 173, 200–1, 221–3, 225–6, 229, 232, 235, 238–42, 248, 250, 252, 256, 263, 273, 284–5, 304–7; commercial empire, 176–93 *passim*; Anglo-Dutch war, 192; East India Company, 238, 242, 248; West India Company, 238; *see also* Holland, Netherlands

Eannes, Gil, 5–6
East Anglia, 203, 302
East India Company, United, 183–6, 207
Egypt, 9
Eldorado, 50
Elizabeth I, 72, 81, 205, 209, 211
Elmina, 7–8, 185
encomenderos, 44, 48, 53, 165–6
encomienda, 43–4, 47–9, 163–4
England, xi, xiii, 10, 13, 17, 19, 21–3, 27–31, 35–6, 39, 56, 62–3,
67–8, 72, 73–87 *passim*, 89–91, 144, 147–8, 150–1, 153–4, 168–70, 177–8, 180, 182–93, 194–211 *passim*, 212–13, 217, 222, 225, 227, 229–30, 231, 232–45, 247, 249, 250–3, 256–7, 259, 261–3, 288–300 *passim*, 301–16 *passim*; Industrial Revolution, ix, xii, 288–9, 301–16 *passim*; coal industry, 22; woollen industry, 26; relations with Spain, 77; population, 91–7, 289–91; corn prices, 99–100, 107; wages, 102–7; agriculture, 109–21, 123–4; Assize of Bread, 117; tax, 121; in America, 125–42 *passim*, 264–87 *passim*; Navigation Acts, 190–2, 263, 285–6, 306; Anglo-Dutch war, 192; open field system, 197, 201, 291; Parliament, 209–10, 238, 248, 268, 281; civil war, 201, 205, 210–11; waterways, 294; industrial growth, 301–16 *passim*; cotton industry, 303, 308, 311–16; embargo, 1678, 305; Eden Treaty, 1786, 313; *see also* Britain
England, Bank of, 242, 247–9
English African Company, 238
English Channel, 76, 80
English East India Company, 238, 242
Enkhuizen, 31, 178
Equador, 135
Esmeralda de Situ Orbis (Pacheco), 8
Espanola, 37, 40, 42–5, 82, 168–9; smallpox epidemic, 54, 255, 260
Essex, 200
estancia, 49, 164
Estremadura, 148
Europe, xi, xiii, 1–2, 7–9, 11, 13, 15–36 *passim*, 46, 50, 53–5, 60, 65–6, 69, 89, 98–100, 104–5, 110, 119, 122, 124, 127, 137–40, 145, 152–3, 156, 157–63, 167–8, 170–1, 173, 179, 182–5, 190, 194, 206–7, 214, 217, 222, 224, 226, 235, 240, 242, 244, 250–2, 255–7, 260–2,

Europe – *cont.*
269–70, 272, 276, 278, 282–7,
288–9, 306–7; relationship with
colonies, xi; history, xii;
economic hegemony, xiii;
Black Death, 93; population,
95–9; Eastern, 18; Northern, 3,
107, 181, 193, 255–6, 260;
Southern, 1, 124, 144, 207, 254,
268, 302; Western, xi, 15–36
passim, 70, 73–87 *passim*, 90,
100–1, 108–9, 111–13, 117, 123,
143–4, 148–50, 176, 179–80, 186,
191, 193, 195, 202, 234, 243, 248
Exeter, 79

Falmouth, 77
Ferdinand, of Aragon, 14, 43, 56,
58, 60, 62
Fernando Po, 9–10
feudalism, 45, 48, 155, 161, 167,
209
financial institutions, 231–49
passim
Finland, 123, 181–2
Flanders, 10, 17, 21, 30–1, 34, 66,
69, 105, 176, 178, 204, 222, 232,
311
Flemings, 203, 205
Flemish, 27, 30, 62–3, 68, 153, 221,
243
Florence, 3
Florida, 80, 81, 83, 85
foreign exchange, 27
France, ix, xi, xiii, 13, 17–19, 21–4,
26, 28–30, 35–6, 59–60, 67, 69,
73–8, 80–4, 87, 89–90, 98, 144,
146–8, 150–2, 155–6, 168–71, 178,
180, 182–93, 194–6, 204, 211,
212–30 *passim*, 231–4, 236,
238–49, 250–3, 255, 259–63,
270–3, 277–8, 284–7, 288–300
passim, 301–16 *passim*; Hundred
Years War, 17; population, 91–6,
289–90, 292, 294, 298–9;
Catholic revolt, 97; corn prices,
99–100; wages, 102–6; agriculture,
109–11, 113–22, 124; in America,
125–6, 128, 130, 134, 142; *see*

also America, French; colonies,
131–3, 135, 141; Frondist
revolt, 191, 214, 228; plague,
213, 227–8; famine, 213–14, 218,
229, 290; Peace of Paris, 286;
Revolution, 1789, 292, 313;
waterways, 294–5; roads, 294–5;
industrial growth, 301–16
passim; Industrial Revolution,
301–16 *passim*; Tariffs, 1664,
305
Frankfurt, 28, 32, 183
French East India Company, 242
French Guinea Company, 169
Friesland, 30
fur trade, 83–5, 126, 128–9, 207,
270–2, 275, 283

gabelle, 121
Gama, Vasco da, 11
Gambia, 136
Garonne basin, 295
General crisis of seventeenth
century, 108; *see also* agriculture
Genoa, 3, 9–12, 28, 33, 56–7, 63–4,
96–7, 147
Georgia, 268
German, ix, 17, 27, 29–35, 51, 90,
97, 107, 138–9, 181, 186, 188,
190–1, 193, 204–5, 212, 222–3,
240, 246–7, 302, 306, 311
Ghent, 94
Gilbert, Humphrey, 81, 84
Glanville, Lord, 278
Glasgow, 267, 279
Gloucestershire, 203, 302
Gobelins, 224
gold, 1, 4, 8–10, 40–1, 43–5, 50,
63, 67, 85, 96, 98, 128, 139, 158,
168, 171–2, 174–5, 242, 247, 250
Gold Coast, 7–8
Grain Coast, 8
Granada, 13, 41, 56–7, 60, 62, 251,
255, 261
Gravelines, 67
Grenoble, 234
*Growth of English Industry and
Commerce* (Cunningham), ix
Guadalquivir valley, 59

Guadeloupe, 131–3, 235, 253, 255, 258–9
Guanajuato, 171
Guiana, 253, 258, 260
Guinea, 10, 12, 75, 185
Gutenberg, 16

Haarlem, 178, 186–7
Habsburg, 30, 32, 35, 56–7, 65–7, 72, 89, 91, 144, 148, 156, 176, 178–9
hacienda, 164–5, 167–8
Hakluyt, Richard, 79, 140
Halifax, 302
Hamburg, 31, 90, 177, 179, 181, 192–3, 206, 235, 246–8
Hanse, 177–8, 181
Hanseatic League, 28–9, 32–3, 177–8, 182, 225
Hargreaves' jenny, 312–14
Havana, 153, 162, 168
Havre, 225
Hawkins, John, 76–7
Hawkins, William, 75
Henri IV, 213–14
Henry VIII, 76, 97, 200, 205, 209
Henry the Navigator, 5–6, 11
hidalgos, 150–1, 154
Histoire des Classes Ouvrières en France (Levasseur), ix
Holland, 21, 30, 36, 89–90, 109, 176, 178–9, 183, 185–93, 204, 208, 231–2, 238, 240, 246, 291, 309
Hoorn, 31
Hondschoote, 221
Huancavelica, 51, 159
Huddersfield, 303
Hudson Bay Company, 272
Hudson river valley, 86, 129, 134, 185, 269, 271, 285, 271
Huguenots, 76–7, 131, 139, 141, 204–5, 214, 229, 302, 306, 309
Hull, 79
Humber, 293
Hundred Years War, 17, 213
Hungary, 29
husbandry, 118–19, 122, 290; convertible, 112–13, 201, 228

Iberian peninsula, 13, 185, 208
Ice Age, Little, 124
Iceland, 75, 123
Incas, *see under* Peru
incomes, xiii, 15–16, 18, 70–1, 88–107 *passim*, 116, 119, 144, 149–50, 194, 198, 201, 217, 237, 279, 288–9, 292–3, 296, 298–300, 305, 315
indentured servitude, 130, 132–4, 138, 265–7, 275
India, 8, 11, 13, 39, 73, 184, 204, 207, 235, 311
Indian Ocean, 6, 11, 33–5, 74, 88, 90, 96, 172, 183–4, 192–3, 209
Indians (Latin America), 37–55 *passim*, 157, 159, 161, 163–8, 172, 174
Indians (North America), 83–5, 125–8, 137, 250–3, 264, 267, 269–72, 276, 285
Indies, *see* West Indies
Indonesian Islands, 184, 192, 207
Industrial Revolution, ix, xiii, 137, 232, 249; *see also under* England, France
Inquisition, *see under* Spain
Ireland, 80–1, 119, 132, 141, 200, 204–5, 263, 302, 307
Irish Sea, 80
Isabella of Castile, 14, 17, 39, 43, 56, 58, 60, 62
Isle of May, 284
Italian, 2, 12, 30, 35, 63, 147–8, 150, 155; silk-throwing machine, 303
Italy, 10, 17, 26–8, 41, 56, 60, 65–8, 79, 89–90, 94–5, 97, 107, 183, 186, 188, 193, 204, 207, 212, 220, 223–5, 240–4, 246, 306
Itinerary (Linschoten), 183

Jacobite, 210
Jamaica, 37, 40, 82, 133, 169–70, 252, 254–5, 257–8, 260, 262
James I, 210
James II, 201, 210
Japan, 13, 37
Java, 183, 252

Jews, 60, 139, 151, 173; conversos, 60

John II, King, 11, 13

juros, 68

Kampen, 32

Kay's flying shuttle, 302, 305

Kent, 203

King, Gregory, 217

Kings Lynn, 293

Konigsberg, 19, 177, 182

labour, 10, 18, 22, 24, 52, 64, 90, 105, 107, 112, 120, 125, 128, 132–4, 137, 142, 149, 151, 154, 159, 161, 163–7, 169, 173, 195–6, 202, 215, 220–2, 250, 253–4, 257–61, 264–5, 268–70, 290–1, 296, 302–4, 308, 311–12

laboureurs, 220

Labrousse, 195

Lagos, 6

Lancarote, 6

Lancashire, 312, 315

land, xiv, 231–2, 235–9, 264–8, 273, 275–9, 282, 291–2, 296, 298, 305

Languedoc, 216, 220, 222–4, 304, 307

La Rochelle, *see* Rochelle

lateen sail, 6, 29

lavrador, 260

Law, John, 248

Leeds, 302–3

Leeward Islands, 44, 132, 284

Leghorn, 79, 179

Leipzig Fairs, 192

Lemberg, 32

Lepanto, 67

Levant, 2, 9, 11, 32, 90, 183, 208, 226, 238, 242

Leyden, 30, 94, 178, 186–7, 221

Liège, 22, 27, 33, 205

Lille, 30, 94

Lima, 48, 53, 162

Lincoln, 200

Lisbon, 13, 34–5, 73, 79, 94, 96, 183, 235, 256

Liverpool, 267, 282

Livonia, 177

Loing Canal, 295

Loire, 111, 119, 215, 218, 294–5

Lombe brothers, 303

London, 26–8, 32–3, 64; merchants, 76–81, 83, 86–7, 90; population, 94, 96, 116, 119, 127, 130, 179, 187–8, 193, 200, 205–6, 208, 235, 243, 247–9, 263, 266–7, 273, 276, 281–4, 293, 302–3

long-distance trade, 26, 28

Lorraine, 223, 294

Louis XIV, 210, 214

Louisburg, 287

Low Countries, 16, 18–19, 30, 76, 89, 98–9, 105–6, 118, 180, 207, 244

Lübeck, 31, 33, 177

Lutheran, 189

Lyon, 27–8, 94, 220, 222–4, 234, 240, 294

Madeira, 4–5, 7, 9–10, 12, 75, 173, 251

Madrid, 56, 61, 94, 246

Magdalena river valley, 50

Maine, 21, 200, 225, 269–74

Malaga, 62

Manchester, 276, 303

Manila, 158, 162

Mans, 221

Maracaibo, 153

marine insurance, 27

Marseilles, 28, 224–7

Marstrand, 191

Martinique, 131, 133, 253, 255, 258–60

Maryland, 84–6, 127, 130, 134–5, 264–8, 277, 280–1, 285

Mary, Queen of England, 76

Massachusetts, 85, 126–7, 129, 138, 269, 272–5, 277, 280–2, 285

Massachusetts Bay Company, 84, 87, 129, 269, 271

Matto Grosso, 170

Mauritius, 252

Maya, 38

Medina del Campo, 27, 58–9, 68–9; Treaty of, 75

Medina de Rio Seco, 58

Mediterranean, 1–3, 7, 9–10, 12, 26–30, 35, 56–7, 73, 79, 90, 122, 124, 144, 148, 207, 214–16, 222, 225, 235–6, 256, 295, 304, 307
Mendoza, 170
Merchant Adventurers Company, 208–9
Mersey, 297
Mesta, 58
Mestizos, 55
Mexico, xiii, 62–3, 73–4, 77, 95, 125, 135, 142, 157–68, 170–5; Spanish conquest, 37–40, 42, 44, 46–55, 73
Mexico City, 42, 47–9, 161, 164–5
Michoacoan, 161
Middelberg, 32, 34, 186, 206, 246
Middle Ages, 21, 31, 56, 91–2, 113–14, 120, 123, 177, 200, 204, 208, 213, 222, 238, 240, 244
Middletown, 275
Midland, 293
Milan, Duchy of, 65–6
millones, 68, 70–1
Minas Geraes, 174
mita, 159
Mohammed II, 9
Mongol Empire, 9
Monserrat, 133, 253
Montreal, 83, 271–2
Moors, 1–3, 7–8, 10, 13, 63, 66, 150–1, 155, 225
Moriscos, 143, 149, 151, 154
Morlaix, 225
Morocco, 1, 3–4, 9–10, 13, 64, 75, 79, 208
Mulattos, 55
Munster, 80; Treaty of, 88–9
Murcia, 62
Muslims, 9, 65

Nantes, 28, 130, 222, 225–6, 229, 235
Naples, 66; revolt of 1647, 66
Napoleonic wars, 172
Navarre, 66
Netherlands, xi, xii, 17–19, 21, 26, 28, 30–2, 59, 65, 74–8, 88–94, 98, 101, 104–5, 144, 148, 150, 154–5,

176–93 *passim*, 194, 212–13, 217, 222, 225, 233, 236–8, 242, 244–5, 249, 253; division of, 34; revolt against Spain, 66–8, 97; agriculture, 109–17, 119, 124; *see also* Holland, Dutch
Nevis, 132–3, 253, 259
New Amsterdam, 185, 192
New Biscay, 50
New England, 86–7, 126, 128–31, 137, 188, 263, 269–77, 284–5
Newfoundland, 12, 73, 75, 82–3, 225–6, 270, 272, 284
New Galicia, 50
New Hampshire, 272–4
New Haven, 275, 283
New Jersey, 134, 137, 265, 275–7
'newlanders', 138
New Leon, 50
Newport, 273–4, 276, 283
New World, *see* America
New York, 131, 134, 137–8, 192, 272–7, 279, 282, 285
Nordlingen, 67
Norfolk, 267
Normandy, 21, 29, 119, 217, 220–2, 225, 304, 311–12
North Sea, 79, 144, 178, 186, 235
Norway, 31, 180–1, 190
Norwich, 203–4, 275–6, 302
Nottingham, 204
Nottinghamshire, 312
Nuñez, Blasco, 48
Nuremberg, 32

Oaxaca, 161
Ohio Valley, 264, 271–2
Oise, 295
Oran, 8
Order of Christ, 5
Orinoco basin, 38
Orleans, 227, 294, 304
Orleans Canal, 295
Oruro, 158
Oswego, 272
Ottoman Empire, 17; seapower, 28
Ovando, 43

Pacific, 84, 158, 226

Palermo, Bank of, 246
Palola, Island of, 1
Palos, 13
Panama isthmus, 37, 40, 42, 163
Paraguay, 170, 174
Parana river, 174
Paris, 33; population, 94, 116, 127, 187, 213–14, 218–20, 225, 229, 294–5
Parral, 51, 158, 171
Pasco, 158
pauperism, 101
Peasant Wars (1525), 35
Peckham, George, 81
Pennines, 293, 315
Pennsylvania, 129, 131, 134, 137–8, 263, 264–5, 267–9, 272–3, 275–8, 280, 285
Pernambuco, 252, 256
Persian Gulf, 184
Peru, xiii, 63, 73, 95, 142, 157–62, 164–6, 168, 170–1, 175, 178, 256; conquest by Spain, 37–55 *passim*, 96
Philadelphia, 271, 273–4, 276, 282
Philip II, 56, 65–9, 71, 76, 147, 150, 178, 210–11
Philippines, 178, 252
Phocaea, 10
Physiocrats, 292
Picardy, 21, 213, 220–2, 234
Pilcomayo river, 53
Pilgrim Fathers, 86–7, 270
Pinney, John, 259
Pisa, 64
Pizarro, Francisco, 37, 39, 41, 44
Plancius, 183
Plate, river, 53, 162, 168, 170–1, 173–4
Plymouth, 75–7
Poitou, 219, 227
Poland, 29, 32, 97, 107, 177
polder system (Dutch), 20
population, xiii, xiv, 15–17, 19, 54, 70, 88–107 *passim*, 108–11, 113–14, 116–18, 123–4, 126–7, 129–30, 133, 136, 140–1, 143, 147–50, 155, 157, 162–3, 171, 175, 179–80, 186, 194, 197, 200,

212–14, 216–17, 224, 226, 229, 232, 250, 269, 273, 275–6, 279, 281, 284, 289–92, 294, 298–9, 305
Porto Bello, 170
Porto Santo, 12
Portsmouth, 274
Portugal, xi, xiii, 18–19, 28–9, 33–5, 53, 73, 75, 79–80, 82, 95–7, 125, 132, 136–7, 139, 143, 147, 169–70, 172–5, 182–5, 250, 256, 259, 282; discovery of America, xii; in the Atlantic, 1–14 *passim*; and Africa, 1–14 *passim*; climate, 3; population, 3; fisheries, 3; trading and shipping, 1–14 *passim*; invasion of Morocco, 4; colonization of Madeira and Azores, 4; sea route to India, 11; Treaty of Alcacovas, 13; seizure of spice trade, 34–6; Treaty of Tordesillas, 37; revolt against Spain, 66; agriculture, 109, 116, 118–19, 122
Potosí, 47, 50, 52–3, 74, 158–60, 162
power loom, 314
prices, xiii, xiv, 18, 20, 71, 88–107 *passim*; price revolution, 98–107, 110–18, 150, 160, 163, 171, 194, 201, 209, 218, 227–8, 253–7, 265, 280, 282, 291–2, 295–300, 304
primogeniture, 196
Prince of Orange, 187
printing press, 16
privateering, 76–8, 80–1, 83, 140, 169, 183, 230
Protestant, 76–8, 80, 139, 141, 184, 205
Provence, 216, 231, 294
Providence, 274
Puebla, 161
Puerto Rico, 37, 40, 44, 170
Puritans, 87, 131, 139
Pyrenees, 95

Quakers, 129, 131
Quebec, 83
Quesada, 42

Raleigh, Walter, 81, 83

Ramos, 51
'redemptioners', 138
Red Sea, 9, 34, 184
Reformation, 34, 75
regional markets, 234–5
Reims, 220, 234
Renaissance humanism, 16
repartimiento, 48, 159, 166–7
Reval, 177
Rhine, 30, 32, 213
Rhineland, 138
Rhine Palatinate, 131, 138
Rhode Island, 273–5, 281, 285
Rhône–Saône basin, 294
Rhône valley, 28, 224, 229
Richelieu, 124, 214, 219
Riga, 177
Rio de Janeiro, 173, 175
Rochdale, 312
Rochelle, 28, 76, 130, 213, 225–6,
    229
Rocroi, 67
Rome, 10
Rostock, 177
Rotterdam, 178, 186–7
Rouen, 27, 64, 94, 222, 225; sieges
    of, 225, 311
Russia, 89, 97, 183, 208, 212, 242,
    303

Safi, 1
Sahara, 1–3, 5–6
St Domingue (Haiti), 133, 169–70,
    251–2, 254–5, 257–8, 260, 262,
    285
St Eustatia, 170, 184
St Kitts, 126–7, 133, 253, 269
St Lawrence, 80, 83, 126, 226,
    270–2, 274
St Malo, 222, 225–7, 229, 235
St Vincent, 133, 255
Salem, 274
San Juan de Ulua, 77
Sankey Navigation, 294
San Lucar, 75
San Luis Potosí, 51
San Salvador, 40
Santa Barbara, 51
Santa Maria, 12

Santo Domingo, 45
São Jorge de Mina, *see* Elmina
São Paulo, 173–4
São Thomé, 9–10, 136, 173, 251
Savery and Newcomen, 308
Saxony, 193
Scandinavia, 17
Scheldt, 30–2, 177, 179
Schmoller, Gustav, ix
Scotland, 30, 56, 119, 138–9, 141,
    200, 204, 245, 267, 302, 307
Segovia, 61, 153
Seine, 294–5
Senegal, 136–7
servicio, 68
Setubal, 28
Seven Cities of Cibola, 50
Seven Years War, 138, 311
Seville, 13, 23, 27, 31, 33, 41, 56–7,
    60–1, 63–4, 75–6, 90; population,
    94, 97, 235
Sheffield, 205, 234, 303
Sicily, 59
Sierra Leone, 8
Silesia, 193, 222
silver, xiii, 40, 42, 47, 50–3, 62, 64,
    67, 69–70, 73–4, 77, 85, 90, 95–8,
    100–1, 106, 139, 145–7, 157–62,
    170–2, 175, 176, 180, 183, 193,
    205, 242–3, 246–8, 250, 281,
    283
Simiand, F., 227
Skagerrack, 191
slave labour, 7, 44, 48, 125–6, 130,
    132–4, 142, 161, 163, 173, 254,
    259, 266–8
slaves, African, xiii, 11, 45–6, 51–3,
    61, 64, 132, 136, 158, 166–7,
    169–70, 173, 185, 235, 252–3,
    257–63, 264, 272, 274, 284
slave trade, 6, 45, 135, 137, 274
smallpox, 95
Smith, Adam, 288, 307
Smyrna, 10
socialism, 188
Somme, 295
Southampton, 75
South Sea Company, 169, 171,
    248

South Seas, 128

Spain, xi, xiii, 1, 13–14, 17–20, 23, 26, 28–30, 34–6, 73–87 *passim*, 89–90, 125, 135, 137, 141–2, 176, 178–9, 182–4, 187, 189, 193–4, 207, 211, 213–14, 217, 220–1, 224–6, 232, 234, 236, 238–40, 243–6, 255, 257–8, 262, 272–3, 282, 286, 304, 306–7, 311; decline of economy, ix, 107; discovery of America, xii, 12; Canary Islands, 2; American Empire, 36, 37–55 *passim*, 57, 59, 61, 157–175 *passim*; conquest of Mexico, 37; conquest of Peru, 37; conquests of Puerto Rico, Cuba and Jamaica, 37, 40; Spanish-Indian relations, 42; 'New Laws', 48, 166; Viceroyalty of New Spain, 48; sixteenth century, 56–72 *passim*; Inquisition, 60, 151, 173; Netherlands revolt, 66; Naples revolt, 66; Portugal and Catalonia revolts, 66; famine and plague, 1595–1602, 72; Treaty of Medina del Campo, 75; population, 93–8; corn prices, 99–101, 104; expulsion of Moriscos, 105; agriculture, 109–10, 112, 116–19, 122, 124; in decline, 143–56 *passim*; Royal Remittance Office, 246

Spice Islands, 184, 235

Staffordshire, 200

Steam engine, 308

Stockholm, 179

Stockholm, Bank of, 248

Stockholm Exchange Bank, 248

Suffolk, 200

sugar, 7, 10, 132–3, 135–6, 168, 170, 172–5, 183–4, 193, 205, 208, 235, 250–63 *passim*, 266, 268, 274, 276, 283–6, 306–7

Surinam, 133

Susquehanna, 275

Sweden, 109, 153, 181, 191, 205, 223, 303

Sweden, Bank of, 248

Tables, xiii; population, 126–7, 265; imports of slaves, 135; sugar production, 257; West Indies exports, 261

taille, 121

Tamerlane, 2

Tangier, 4

Tenochtitlan, 39, 42

Thames, 123, 200, 206, 293

Thirty Years War, 108, 190, 207, 214, 240

Ticonderoga, 287

Timbuktu, 1

tobacco, 85–7, 128, 130, 132–6, 168, 173–4, 183, 186, 205, 207–8, 235, 250, 252, 256, 260–3, 264–86, 306–7

Tobago, 255

Toledo, 61, 153

Tolfa, 10

Toluca, 161

Tordesillas, Treaty of, *see under* Portugal

Toulouse, 224

Touraine, 304

Tournai, 30

Tours, 220, 224

Toynbee, Arnold, ix

Trebizond, 10

Trent, 293, 315

Trinidad, 86, 274

Tristão Nuno, 6

Tucuman, 170

Tunis, 1, 8

Turkey, 2, 9–10, 65, 79, 89, 207, 225, 261

Tyneside, 303

typhus, 95

Ulster, 80, 128–9, 138–9

Valencia, 57, 66, 94–5, 143, 225

Valenciennes, 30

Valladolid, 56

Van Robais, 224

Venezuela, 135, 170, 260

Venice, 9, 28, 32, 34–5, 64, 73, 79, 96

Vera Cruz, 42

Villalon, 58
Virginia, 81, 84–7, 126–31, 133–6, 208, 231, 264–70, 274, 276–8, 280–1, 285
Virginia Company, 83–4, 128–9

Wales, 200, 212
Walloons, 203, 205
War, xii, 17, 34, 67, 110, 140, 144–8, 155, 183, 207, 210–11, 213–15, 218–22, 225–30, 252–4, 272, 274, 280, 285–7, 289, 301
War of Spanish Succession, 155
Watt, James, 308
Wealth of Nations, (Adam Smith), 288, 307
West Indies, 40–1, 43, 48, 63, 73, 85, 87, 125, 127, 129–31, 134, 136, 173, 184–5, 207–8, 226, 242–3, 250–2, 254, 256, 259, 261, 263–4, 268, 270, 272–5, 282–3, 285, 306, 311
Whitehaven, 267
White Sea, 118
Wilson, Charles, ix, x
Wiltshire, 203–4, 221, 232, 302
Winthrop, John, 263
Wyatt and Paul spinning frame, 302

Yeomen, 196
York, 25, 79
Yorkshire, 200, 203–4, 293, 301–2, 312
Yucatan peninsula, 38, 284

Zacatecas, 50–1, 74, 159
Zealand, 30, 32, 176, 178, 183, 187–9
Zuider Zee, 29, 31–2, 181